CISSP EXAM STUDY GUIDE

3 BOOKS IN 1

NIST FRAMEWORK, DIGITAL FORENSICS
& CYBERSECURITY GOVERNANCE

BOOK 1
CYBERSECURITY ENFORCEMENT AND MONITORING SOLUTIONS
ENHANCED WIRELESS, MOBILE AND CLOUD SECURITY DEPLOYMENT
BOOK 2
CISSP: CYBERSECURITY OPERATIONS AND INCIDENT RESPONSE
DIGITAL FORENSICS WITH EXPLOITATION FRAMEWORKS & VULNERABILITY SCANS
BOOK 3
CISSP: CYBERSECURITY GOVERNANCE AND RISK MANAGEMENT
POLICY CONCEPTS & DEPLOYMENT WITHIN ORGANIZATIONAL SECURITY

RICHIE MILLER

Disclaimer

Every effort was made to produce this book as truthful as possible, but no warranty is implied. The author shall have neither liability nor responsibility to any person or entity concerning any loss or damages ascending from the information contained in this book. The information in the following pages are broadly considered to be truthful and accurate of facts, and such any negligence, use or misuse of the information in question by the reader will render any resulting actions solely under their purview.

Table of Contents – Book 1

Table of Contents – Book 2

Table of Contents – Book 3

BOOK 1

CYBERSECURITY
ENFORCEMENT AND MONITORING SOLUTIONS

ENHANCED WIRELESS, MOBILE AND
CLOUD SECURITY DEPLOYMENT

RICHIE MILLER

Introduction

IT Security jobs are on the rise! Small, medium or large size companies are always on the look out to get on board bright individuals to provide their services for Business as Usual (BAU) tasks or deploying new as well as on-going company projects. Most of these jobs requiring you to be on site but since 2020, companies are willing to negotiate with you if you want to work from home (WFH). Yet, to pass the Job interview, you must have experience. Still, if you think about it, all current IT security professionals at some point had no experience whatsoever. The question is; how did they get the job with no experience? Well, the answer is simpler then you think. All you have to do is convince the Hiring Manager that you are keen to learn and adopt new technologies and you have willingness to continuously research on the latest upcoming methods and techniques revolving around IT security. Here is where this book comes into the picture. Why? Well, if you want to become an IT Security professional, this book is for you! If you are studying for CompTIA Security+ or CISSP, this book will help you pass your exam. Passing security exams isn't easy. In fact, due to the raising security beaches around the World, both above mentioned exams are becoming more and more difficult to pass. Whether you want to become an Infrastructure Engineer, IT Security Analyst or any other Cybersecurity Professional, this book (as well as the other books in this series) will certainly help you get there! But, what knowledge are you going to gain from this book? Well, let me share with you briefly the agenda of this book, so you can decide if the following topics are interesting enough to invest your time in! First, you are going to discover what are the most important secure protocols and how to implement them. Next you will learn about host or Application Security Solutions, endpoint protection, boot integrity; along with database security concepts, application security concepts, hardening various systems, whether it's an operating system or registry. After that, we'll cover disk encryption; hardware root of trust, TPM chip and the concepts of sandboxing. Next, we'll cover how to Implement Secure Network Designs using load balancers, network segmentation, virtual private networks, DNS, network access control or NAC, out-of-band management, and port security. Moving on, you will learn about access control lists or ACLs, route security, quality of service with implications of IPv6, port spanning, port mirroring, and port taps. We'll also talk about monitoring services, file integrity monitors and how to install and configure wireless security. We'll also cover cryptographic protocols, authentication protocols, methods, and installation considerations. Next, you will discover how to implement Secure Mobile Solutions, connection methods and receivers, mobile device management, enforcement monitoring, and several deployment models. After that, you will discover how to apply Cybersecurity Solutions to the cloud, using cloud security controls, high availability, and the subcomponents, including storage, network and compute. We'll also talk about various solutions, such as cloud access security broker, or CASB, Secure Web Gateways, along with cloud native controls. Next you will discover how to implement identity and account management controls. After that, we are going to cover authentication management, passwords, trusted platform models and hardware security methods. Lastly, you will discover how to implement public key infrastructure, along with the types of certificates, certificate formats, and certificate concepts. If you are ready to get on this journey, let's first cover what are the most important secure networking protocols that you should be aware of!

8

Chapter 1 Secure Networking Protocols

In the next few chapters we are going to cover secure protocols, but before we get into the details of what we'll cover, let's talk about why is this important. Well, secure protocols ensure communication is safe from hackers and also from prying eyes. It's critical to securing a company's data, intellectual property and competitive advantage. Ultimately a company's footprint, their reputation, their brand, your ability to maintain a job, their investor confidence, customer confidence, all of these things wrap up into one. Secure protocols help strengthen that security posture and make all of this possible or at least help to make all of this possible. We're talking about the secure protocols, not the non-secure ones. There are a lot of protocols that are insecure. I'm going to talk about the secure versions of those protocols and why we should use them along with the use cases. As we go through the protocols, I want you to think about each of these in your own environment and say, what are the use cases? Where can I use these protocols and make sure that I'm securing the environment as much as possible? Security should always be at the forefront of our thought process and looking for ways to secure and look for secure alternatives to the way we're doing things currently. Secure protocols, whenever given the option, we should always be looking to choose the highest security possible when establishing communication over an unsecure or an insecure medium, such as the internet. Such things as FTP, we want to look for FTP secure or HTTP web traffic. We should be looking for HTTPS or HTTP secure. Same thing with SSL and TLS, which is the underlying mechanism that a lot of this security or secure communication will take place. Secure POP or IMAP. Another way to think of that is web mail. Let's go ahead and dig in a little bit deeper here and talk about networking protocols. There are three main areas I want to make sure you're familiar with just you understand how things connect when they're talking to a network. We have IP or internet protocol, and that is connectionless. It's a connectionless protocol that's responsible for network addressing, and it provides routing of packets between networks. It allows us to give a more human-readable name or an address to a specific host or a specific resource on the internet or on our internal network that allows us to route and send traffic. It's just like a house number on the block in a neighborhood. Each of those pieces make up the address of that specific house just like an IP address. Some of the IP address will denote the network. Some of it will denote the host within that network or that subnetwork. Next we have TCP. When you put those together, we have TCP/IP. Transmission control protocol, that is a connection, or anti-protocol, and that establishes connections between endpoints and also provides guaranteed delivery of packets. What happens, it sends out a packet, and there's a wait time or a time to live on that specific packet. If the host that it's sending to or communicates with doesn't respond back and acknowledge and say, I have that packet, I've received it within a certain period of time, then that packet is assumed to be lost, and the host will resend again. That's why it's guaranteeing that delivery. Then we also have UDP or user datagram protocol, and that's a connectionless protocol. It's quick, but there's no guarantee of delivery or its best effort. These three things together make up the basis of how we communicate over an IP network or over the internet. Perhaps a bit of a refresher to you, but in case you're not familiar with this, let's just cover very briefly the three-way handshake that takes place during a TCP communication between two hosts. A three-way handshake establishes that

10

connection between two hosts. A client node sends a SYN packet, a SYN data packet, over an IP network to a server to determine if the server is open for a new connection. It's saying, are you available to talk? The target server must have open ports that can accept and initiate new connections. If in fact that's true, the server responds and returns a confirmation receipt, a SYN acknowledgement packet, a SYN/ACK. From there, the client node receives that SYN / ACK of the SYN acknowledgement back from the server, and it will respond with its own acknowledgement packet. It goes through that handshake process very quickly and establishes that communication. Now we know the basics at a high level of how that communication is initiated, let's talk about the secure protocols and the secure versions of some protocols you're probably already familiar with.

DNS SEC

First up is DNS Secure. DNS is the Domain Name System, and we're familiar with DNS is how we resolve web addresses to IP addresses. It allows us to browse the internet, type in a website, www.Google.com, DNS will resolve that through a series of servers that are out on the Internet, all the way down to the company servers, the company DNS servers within Google's domain, respond back with the host that is specific for the resource we're looking for, and then turn around and deliver that web page to the client. All of that happens very, very quickly. There is a secure version of DNS, and that is DNS Security Extension, or DNSSEC, that was designed to add security to the original DNS specification. DNS was not originally designed with security mechanisms in place. Remember, DNS was designed way back in the late 60's, and it was designed to make browsing or communication over a very large network very fast and very efficient. It's a hierarchical naming standard. Security was not a big thing back then. There may have been four or five hosts when things initially took off, so we don't necessarily know if the original designers envisioned, 4 billion, 5 billion hosts like we have today, but as things started to scale, it quickly became apparent we needed a way to secure some of this traffic. It was meant to be a massively scalable, hierarchical naming system that resolves URLs to IP addresses. All responses from a DNSSEC server, which is protected zones, are digitally signed and authenticating their origin. It doesn't provide confidentiality of the data, so it's not encrypted itself, but it does verify that the server is in fact a legitimate DNS server. It prevents such things as session hijacking and DNS cache poisoning, so a rogue DNS server can't be set up on the network and directing them to illegitimate resources. If we look at a DNSSEC example, let's say, for instance, we have a user, which is referred to as a resolver in DNS lingo, that resolver wants to connect to a web resource. Let's say for the example here we want to connect to www.Google.com, we want to browse Google's resources out on the Internet. The user would connect, type in Google.com into their web browser, it's going to contact the ISP's DNS server. Everyone that connects to the Internet has a DNS server configured, typically from their ISP. So from there the ISP would then refer that up to the root of the Internet, which is dot, the root servers out on the Internet. In a DNSSEC example, there are signed certificates that go through the chain of resolution. As we go through all these different DNS servers, every DNS server above has a signed certificate for the DNS server below. We can follow that chain of trust to make sure that nothing was intercepted or manipulated in that path. ISP contacts the root, the root says, hey, I don't know exactly where that is, but I do know the servers that are authoritative for the.com domain so I'll go check there. It responds back to ISP and it then goes out and contacts the.com or the top-level domain, asks the same question. There's a sign-in key and a digital signature of google.com, the DNS server a level below. So from there, same process, it goes back to the ISP, the ISP then goes out and contacts google.com, which is the second-level domain. It has the DNS key, and it's able to resolve that, and what's happening here is that we have this chain of trust so that everything goes back up to the root so it can be verified all the way through the chain and we know that no one has manipulated anywhere in that process, two main security issues, DNS hijacking and DNS cache poisoning. We know for a fact that everything is secure, there's a chain of trust, and nothing's been broken or compromised in that path. We can rest assured that that DNS server's response is legitimate. We can verify the authenticity of that response and know that we're connecting to a legitimate resource.

SSH

Some other secure protocols I want to talk about is SSH, or Secure Shell. Secure Shell is used for logging into remote hosts. That can be routers, switches, or servers, and it operates over TCP. Remember, we talked about TCP versus UDP. TCP is going to be a connection-oriented protocol. It's going to connect over TCP port 22. An IP address is one thing? We connect to an IP address, but there are also ports. We can put :22 at the end of that, and it would tell the host that we're connecting to we want to connect over port 22. A server, as an example, could wear a lot of different hats. It could be a DNS server. It could be an Active Directory server. It could be a video server, a mail server, you name it. All of those different services operate over different ports. By specifying what port we want to connect to, we're telling that server what service we want to communicate with. When we're talking about different use cases, Secure Shell allows us to remotely and securely log into our routers, our switches, and servers. We can open up a command prompt on a remote server and type commands just as if we're sitting at that server, but we can do that remotely. It saves us the time and energy and effort of having to go to each individual resource, sit down, either a console cable or just connect directly in person to that resource; we can do it remotely. It makes administration much, much easier.

S/MIME

Next, we have Secure MIME, or S/MIME. MIME is the Secure/Multipurpose Internet Mail Extensions. It's a public key encryption and signing of MIME data. We're sending emails, we're securing email delivery. There are some challenges; however, I want you to be aware of the protocol, but there are some actual challenges in implementation. When we're doing this, we want to send and receive, encrypted email between two hosts, a sender and receiver. Well, both parties have to have a public key/private key pair for them to communicate. That's either issued from an in-house certificate authority or from a public certificate authority. From a corporate standpoint though, that end-to-end encryption can defeat malware scanners. In practice, a company may not want to have that in place because then they can't go in and inspect the contents of that email, and they can't scan for malware because that data is encrypted. There are ways to put different types of SSL decryptors along the perimeter, and in some cases, it can strip that information off and decrypt it at the perimeter and then send it on to the recipient, but it's problematic at best, so something just to be aware of.

Secure Real-Time Transport Protocol (SRTP)

Next, we have Secure Real-time Transport Protocol, or SRTP. It's a secure version of RTP. SRTP is a security profile for RTP, or the Real-time Transport Protocol, and it adds confidentiality, message authentication, and also replay protection to that protocol. And as you may guess, is used to secure VoIP, or Voice over IP, traffic. It's great in that it has minimal effect on the actual IP quality, of that Voice over IP service. We can add security without decaying or degrading the end user experience, and that's key here. We want to make sure that when someone picks up the phone that communication doesn't sound jittery or broken up, so there's no reason to not have Secure RTP in place.

Lightweight Directory Access Protocol over SSL (LDAPS)

Next, we have LDAPS, or Lightweight Directory Access Protocol over SSL. LDAP, as we know, is the Active Directory mechanism we use to log into Active Directory services and find resources in a Windows network, and that operates over both TCP and UDP over port 636. What that does is secures traffic between the client and server over SSL and TLS, Secure Sockets Layer and Transport Layer Security. It does require all DCs to have an X.509 certificate installed. It may or may not be completely viable in your environment, or you may have a very distributed environment where you don't have everything sitting on one server. You may have a root certificate server and then issuing service below, so it just depends upon how your individual infrastructure is set up. But for purposes of our discussion, just understand what LDAP Secure is. It's a way of securing Lightweight Directory Access Protocol, or LDAP, and the ports that it goes over, 636, TCP, and UDP. Also, understand the transport mechanism and how it secures that traffic using SSL and TLS.

FTPS and SFTP

Next, we have FTPS, or FTP Secure, File Transport Protocol over SSL. And what this does, as you can imagine, is secure file transfers that use SSL for encryption, or that Secure Sockets Layer. Encryption can be turned off if other encryption is in use. So, for instance, if we have IPSec in place, we don't need to double dip here. We can turn SSL off and still have a secure communication, or secure transferring of files. And that's going to operate over TCP ports 989 and 990. Getting back to use cases, FTP is a very popular protocol people use to upload and download files all day long. If we're inside of a network or we're connecting from the outside, FTP typically, those credentials are sent in clear text, we don't want that. We want to use something that's secure. We're going to make sure we use FTPS, or SFTP. They achieve the same end goal. But in the back of your mind, we should always be looking for ways to add security to the way we do things. If we need to FTP, let's look for FTPS or SFTP. SFTP or Secure FTP, that sounds just like we just talked about. And the net result is the same, but it's a different way of doing it. It's SSH File Transfer Protocol. Before, we were doing FTP over SSL. We're using SSH. It provides for remote file transfer, access, and also management. It gives us a little more functionality, and what it does is utilize FTP over SSH. The FTP is tunneled through that SSH connection. TCP transport protocol, Transmission Control Protocol, connection oriented. We're going over TCP port 22.

SNMP v3

Next, we have SNMP version 3. Simple Network Management Protocol has been around for a while. There's versions 1 and 2, did not have security baked in. And since we're talking about secure protocols, we're looking for version 3. SNMPv3 allows for remote management and reporting of IP devices. All the different IP devices within our network, we can turn on SNMP, set up our community strings, and go out and have a management server, and then all of our clients, or the things we're communicating with, we can set up alerts. We can configure some devices. We can report on others to see if that device is up or down. If there's an alert, it can send a trap to that management server and allow us to report very quickly on the state of our environment, or the health of these different devices. Communication protocols can be intercepted and manipulated, it can potentially lend itself to a breach or release some type of denial of service or some other type of, degradation to our service. SNMPv3 will encrypt that data. Earlier versions didn't provide encryption, Wherever possible, if we can use SNMPv3, encrypt our data, encrypt our communication, we just take one more thing off the table that hackers were able to use or try to leverage to breach or otherwise to create performance for the end user. SNMP, whether it's version 1, 2, or 3, is going to utilize UDP port 161 by default.

SSL/TLS

Next, we have SSL and TLS. SSL and TLS is Secure Sockets Layer/Transport Layer Security. And just you're aware, SSL is the older implementation. TLS is newer based on SSL. What it does is adds confidentiality and data integrity by encapsulating other protocols. It's not a method of communicating in and of itself, but it's a way for us to add security to other protocols? We can encapsulate that data, and we can add confidentiality and data integrity by encapsulating other protocols. Confidentiality and data integrity are two prongs of the CIA triad, confidentiality, integrity, and availability. It initiates that stateful session with a handshake. As an aside in your environment, make sure all servers are patched for the Heartbleed Bug. That was an SSL/TLS vulnerability that hackers were using and leveraging out in the wild, Very important that all your servers are patched to avoid that vulnerability.

HTTPS

Next, we have HTTPS. HTTP is web traffic, so authentication of the visited website, as well as privacy and integrity of that data exchange. It allows us to connect securely to a web address or to a web resource, a web server, communicate with that web server, and that communication is encrypted. So our ISP doesn't see what we're doing. Hackers or someone else that's sniffing that traffic, they don't see what we're doing. It also provides that integrity and the authentication. We know that the person or the website that we're connecting with is in fact the website that we are looking to connect with. It's not a fake or a forgery. By the same token, the client could also authenticate to the server, although typically we're just worried about connecting or authenticating and verifying the integrity of the server that we're communicating with. It also protects against eavesdropping and man-in-the-middle attacks. If you see MITM, that abbreviation is for man in the middle, which means someone is injecting themselves into that communication. Remember the old example of Bob and Alice. The hacker injects themselves into that process. Bob thinks he's talking to Alice, but he's talking to the hacker. The hacker then relays that information to Alice, but he's manipulating that data along the way. Man-in-the-middle attacks can be remediated or protected against using encryption. Also bi-directional encryption of the communication between the client and server; we're encrypting communication, both ways, between the server to the client and also to the client to the server. Also just you're aware, it's TCP, TCP communication protocol over port 443.

Secure POP/IMAP

Next, we have secure POP and IMAP, so accessing webmail. When we talk about POP, or Post Office Protocol, or IMAP, we're talking about accessing webmail. We're doing that securely, again, using SSL and TLS. It's a way of encapsulating that data. Post Office Protocol, or POP, POP3 is the latest version. That's going to be TCP port 110 for normal traffic or 995 for SSL. Internet Message Access Protocol, or IMAP, that's going to be IMAP4 being the latest version, and that is TCP port 143 or 993 over SSL. We're talking about different ways we can secure our networks. If we require and mandate that we always use secure versions of POP and IMAP, we can cut down on eavesdropping. Mail, webmail specifically, is a big target for hackers because if they're able to access someone's email and scour through that, they can get a lot of information about who their friends are, the way they communicate, the words the verbiage, the language that they use. Then they can craft emails to other people and make it seem very convincing that it's coming from that person because they've gone through a bunch of emails. They know what they're interested in. They know what sites they visit, what resources, what they just bought. All of these things can put up a profile on a target or a victim, and then as that attacker crafts an email that's specifically geared towards that target, it seems very convincing. It's much more likely that that person will click on a link that's in that email or do some type of action or take some action on that email. And then as soon as they do that, boom, malware is installed on that system. It can go out and started downloading other pieces of software. It could potentially become a zombie in a larger botnet, or it could communicate back to some command-and-control server, allow a hacker to come in, gain a foothold on that system, start browsing through our network, find a way to jump over a pivot, jump over to another network, start accessing resources. As soon as they start to gain relevant privileges, install a back door and gained persistence, and then off to the races at that point. Let's see how much information we can possibly exfiltrate or steal from this network. Depending upon the type of hacker that they are, they may be very slow and steady, very stealthy, very surreptitious in their exploration of data, and they sit there for weeks or months or years where they could very quickly want to get in and get out or try to destroy data, and try to take the company down. It could be a very quick process, or it could be very long, and by the time we realize it, they're already in our backups and everything else. If we've got to restore, it's too late. All of these different things, securing our FTP traffic, securing our web traffic, Voice over IP traffic, and so on, all of these different things, as we secure them, we're doing what? We're building up a defense in depth. A layered defense. The more locks on the door, the longer it's going to take a hacker or someone who's trying to do harm to the company, it's going to take them longer and longer and longer to unlock all of those locks before they can get in. That gives us the opportunity to identify and notice that the breach is occurring or make it Difficult that we may not even notice, but it becomes such a laborious process that they just give up and go somewhere else where they may have an easier target.

Use Cases

We talk about different use cases. I don't want to dig in depth into each one of these and go off on tangents, but I just want to quickly bring these to your attention and have you think in the back of your mind, where can I tighten up security? Where can I add security or secure protocols in each of these different instances? More importantly than the individual protocol, understand why would you want to secure that type of traffic. Voice and video; we talk about time synchronization. Every computer or every host on that network needs to synchronize their time. It's important for directory services, for other applications that everything is in sync. Typically, in large environment, all of those devices will sync to an internal time synchronization server. Smaller environments are where individual users may go out and sync to a time server out on the internet? One of the military servers, that may or may not be the case, depending upon your specific environment, but it's important that those things are secure because, again, every piece of communication can potentially be hijacked, some type of man-in-the-middle attack or some type of data manipulation to corrupt data, denial-of-service attacks where you simply get in and try to infiltrate the network itself. All of these things should be triggering thoughts in the back of your mind, how can I secure these types of traffic? Email and web browsing. We talked about HTTPS. We talked about IMAP and POP secure and File Transfer Protocol. We talked about FTPS and also SFTP. If a hacker is able to sniff the network and monitor that traffic and they can browse our FTP servers or upload and download our content, they can, again, build a very detailed profile of what's important, perhaps steal intellectual property or things they're not supposed to have access to. But aside from the obvious, stealing data, they can build a profile and get very, very good very, very quickly of what's inside of our network, the applications, the services, the users, maybe the locations even. All of these things can be potentially gleaned from the files that they're able to download or even upload, viruses, malware. That defense-in-depth mindset will go a long way to securing the environment. The same thing with directory services - every time you log into a network, every time we browse for a specific resource, all of that communication is potentially going over unencrypted. We want to make sure we encrypt whenever possible. Remote access - we talked about Secure Shell. That should be a standard. It should be a given. There should not be a way to access hosts in an insecure fashion. Telnet, as an example. Get rid of it. Turn it off. Make sure it's disabled everywhere. Use SSH so that communication is then encrypted, whether you're protecting to router, switches, servers. Same thing with domain name resolution - DNS traffic over port 53. DNS traffic is a favorite for hackers to exfiltrate traffic because everybody has it. Everybody has DNS traffic internal. You also need to then go out to an external DNS server when you want to browse web resources. So firewalls will always have those ports open, and traffic can go very easily in and out of the network, or over port 53. Monitor for that. Monitor for excessive amounts. Baselining. Make sure that we understand what's normal. What are the normal packet sizes, what's normal data flow? That way, when there are very large spikes, it should be raising red flags. Wherever appropriate, secure zone transfers, making sure we don't have rogue DNS servers on our network. Security should be in place from the get-go. Talked about routing and switching, we talked about Secure Shell and ways to securely access all of these different devices within our network. But think about the additional ways you can secure routing and switching. We talked about port security, making sure we don't have rogue access points and rogue switches, Wi-Fi access points on the network. All of these things should be configured to check in or authenticate on the network. Then also, devices on our network that can scan for rogue access points to make sure that no one is just plugging into our network and trying to set up some evil twin or some rogue access point to either give out fake DNS information, fake DHCP information, man-in-the-middle attacks and more. Network address allocation, DHCP, same thing. We want to be monitoring to make sure that people are not trying to instantiate fake or malicious DHCP servers on our network. If we have DHCP security set up properly, those servers will check in, and if they realize there's already a DHCP server on that subnet, they'll shut down and not serve us requests. Then lastly, subscription services - that can mean a lot of different things depending upon what company and what industry you're in. Just think of all the things we've talked about so far and how you can secure whether it's a website, a service, or an application, how you can secure those individual piece parts. In summary we covered two main areas. We covered protocols and use cases. For protocols, we covered such things as DNS Secure, or DNSSEC, SSH, and S/MIME. We talked about SRTP, LDAPS, and FTPS, and also SNMPv3, SSL, and TLS. Also, HTTPS and secure POP and IMAP. These are all things that you're probably familiar with in their insecure versions, and we talked about the secure versions of these protocols to help strengthen that security posture and make the overall security footprint of your company stronger. Some use cases we talked about where voice and video, time synchronization, things like email and web and file transfer, along with directory services and remote access. Also, domain name resolution, routing and switching, network address allocation, and also, subscription services. Things that is useful and used every day within your organization, the ways you can avoid some common pitfalls, and also, again, strengthen those specific areas within your organization.

Chapter 2 Host or Application Security Solutions

In this chapter we'll be talking about Host or Application Security Solutions. We'll be talking about endpoint protection. We'll talk about boot integrity; along with database security concepts; application security concepts; hardening of various systems, whether it's operating system, registry; we'll talk about disk encryption; hardware root of trust and also the TPM chip; and then wrap up with the concepts around sandboxing.

Antivirus
When it comes to antivirus, they can detect viruses, malware, in some cases ransomware or crypto-malware, root kits. Well, AV software can be standalone. It can also be agent based or network based, and it can also be cloud based. In this specific instance, we're talking about host-based antivirus, which means it's going to run as an agent, typically, on that server or that PC or laptop. It can scan data on access, and it can also periodically scan the entire file system, much like their network counterparts or cloud-based counterparts. They can do things when you click on a file, when you go to save a file, or you can have it run every so often, maybe once a day or once every hour, and it will scan the entire system. Then if it finds something, whether it's a piece of malware, a virus, it will either quarantine that specific piece of code and then send some type of an alert, an email, or it can send it off to a NOC or a SOC, a security operations center, and it can also report back the details of that specific piece of code back to the company's headquarters, whether it's Microsoft or Trend Micro or McAfee. It can send that information back so that it can be aggregated and correlated across all customers in the

environment to see if that specific type of outbreak, whether it's malware, viruses, worms, if that's being seen in the wild.

Endpoint Detection and Response (EDR)

When it comes to securing systems on our network and within our environment, it's important that we have endpoint protection in some form or fashion, so applications and tool sets known as endpoint detection and response systems, or EDR systems, or sometimes they may even have threat detection in there as well. You might see endpoint detection and also threat detection and response, so it could be ETDR as well. Well, these things have a number of key features. Endpoint detection response key features are they monitor and collect activity on endpoints. It's not just an AV program, or an antivirus program. They can do additional things like monitor and collect activity, understanding when things are launched, how they're launched. They can then analyze that data to identify threats, patterns, or indicators of compromise, or IoCs, and then automatically respond to identify threats, to remove or mitigate them, and notify appropriate teams, security personnel. And then lastly, forensics and analysis tools to research threats and also search for suspicious activities. An endpoint detection program, or an EDR, may be a standalone application, or could plug into a larger system, like a SOAR system, S-O-A-R. We've talked about SOAR systems before, but just to reiterate, we have a SOAR platform that can do a number of things. It can gather information from event logs. It can gather things from our security incident and event management or monitoring tools, our SIEM systems, and then also EDR systems, endpoint detection response. All of those things can feed into a SOAR platform, which in turn can then do some automation for us, whether it be ticketing, IT ticketing, change control. It can open up tickets to remediate certain things that it finds. And then also controls, like alerting or whitelisting and blacklisting. If we whitelist an application, it means allow only this application, or only the ones we have whitelisted. Or if we blacklist an application, it means allow everything except for the ones that are on the blacklist. Whitelisting would be deny everything except what's on the list, and then blacklisting would be allow everything except for what's on the blacklist? Alerting, whitelisting, and then also third-party tools. That SOAR platform allows us to integrate a number of different things, including EDR systems and automate to a much greater degree.

Data Loss Prevention (DLP)
DLP, or data loss prevention, detects potential breaches and exfiltration of data. Especially in the age of PCI we want to make sure that we are capturing any attempts to exfiltrate data from our network. It does endpoint detection, things that are in use, network traffic, things are in transit, data in transit, and then also data storage, or data at rest. It allows us to understand, is someone storing credit card information? It might scan the network and look for things that have a series of nine digits separated by dashes. That might be a Social Security number. Or it may have 16 digits or whatever numbers represent a credit card. Things that might be personally identifiable information and things that are a no-no to store from a PCI standpoint, it will search for that and make sure that we're not storing data that we're not supposed to be storing in insecure locations. Then also, when things are attempted to be exfiltrated or stolen or removed from our network, it will capture those things as well. Additional methods we can use these DLP technologies to identify if someone's trying to remove data from our environment, we can do USB blocking, we can do cloud

based, and we can do email, we can check all of these things as well. Is someone inserting a USB drive into a computer and trying to pull data off the network? Are they doing it from a cloud instance? Are they trying to upload things to some type of cloud storage or cloud application? And then, of course, email, self-explanatory, is someone trying to email something that they should not be emailing? The types of data to secure, we have data in transit, data that's being sent over a network, whether it's wired or wireless. A VPN connection will encrypt the data while in transit, wired or wireless. That could be a good thing or a bad thing. It's good because we're not sending data that could be compromised, so it saves us from being sniffed on the network. But if we're trying to detect what's being sent, it blocks that from our view. You have to take that into consideration. VPNs and encryption can work in our favor or they can work against us. Next we have data at rest, data sitting on a hard drive or removable media, Local to the computer or remotely on SAN or NAS storage, so that's data that's sitting there. And then we have data in use, data that's not "at rest," and only on one particular node or a network. It's being used in some fashion. It could be a memory resident piece of information, swap/temp space. We want to make sure we're protecting against all three of these categories to make sure data's not being exfiltrated or stored improperly on our network.

Next-generation Firewall (NGFW)
When it comes to firewalls, we have a general understanding of what a firewall is and what it does. But one thing you may or may not be familiar with is the concept of a next-generation firewall, or an NGFW. A next-generation firewall, they go beyond traditional firewalls and what we know a traditional firewall to do, such as stateful packet inspection or VPN services. Well, next-generation firewalls

also offer advanced services like deep packet inspection, so it goes much deeper into the packet than a traditional firewall. Also, it can offer application firewalls. We can block things based on application based on the application itself, not just an IP address or a packet type? We start to move up the OSI stack. Also, things like intrusion detection and also intrusion prevention. We can do things like TLS and SSL inspection where we can decrypt packets, inspect what's inside that packet, and then send it on its way. And also, things like bandwidth management. Next-generation firewalls can combine the functionality of several different appliances or several different platforms into one device or one piece of equipment. As an example, a few next-generation firewall vendors and this is not in any specific order, and it's not an endorsement of any one product over another. I'm just giving you an idea of some of the vendors out there if you want to do a little more research on your own. We have vendors like Fortinet or Forcepoint. Also, Palo Alto Networks, SonicWall, Barracuda. Cisco also makes some next-generation firewall. Check Point advanced threat protection. Checkpoint was one of the very first VPN and firewall manufacturers out there. Also, Sophos, Juniper Networks, and the list goes on and on? These are not an exhaustive list, it's not an endorsement of one over the other. Just to give you an idea of what's out there if you want to do a little more research on your own.

HIDS/HIPS

HIDS and HIPS, host-based intrusion detection systems or intrusion prevention systems. They're similar in function to the network versions, the network intrusion detection or prevention systems; however, they run on a specific host. They don't cover an entire network. They cover a specific host. Like their network versions, they can detect anomalous behavior, and they can alert on that specific behavior. The difference is, this is a host-based, so it's running on a specific host, one system, not an entire network or a subnet or a specific part of a company. It's on a single host. When we're talking about host-based intrusion prevention systems, again, similar functionality to the network versions. They can take similar action or similar functionality to the detection systems, but they can then take action, shut down a port, run a script, do some type of workflow, in addition to alerting administrators. Very similar functionality we can run these things on a grand scale in a network environment, or we can run them specifically on individual hosts.

Host-based Firewall

When it comes to firewalls, we talked about a few different types. And in this case, we're talking about a host-based firewall. Firewalls, as we know, will typically block traffic based upon port, protocol, IP address, or perhaps application. Most server-based OSes and client-based operating systems will contain some type of virtual private networking, some type of host-based firewalls, some type of antivirus checking. You have some of these host-based tools built in to most operating systems. Then, of course, you can download free versions. You can download commercial versions. You can install enterprise-wide versions, all of which have different use cases and may fit in different environments for different reasons. But they all function generally the same way. They're going to manage and alert on some type of crossing the threshold, some type of trigger. Whether that is a port, a protocol, IP address, you can allow certain things that pass through, and you can restrict others. On host-based systems, we'll typically do that by restricting applications. You can go into that server's built-in firewall and say let these 4 or 5 or 10 or however many applications through and block everything else. Applications can be whitelisted or blacklisted. When you whitelist an application, you're saying here's the 5 or 10 or 15 applications that I'm going to allow to run. Conversely, if you say application blacklisting, you can say go ahead and run everything except for these 5 or 10 that I explicitly deny. Its two different approaches. One allows everything except what you say not to. The other one says block everything except for the 5 or 10 that I explicitly allow.

Boot Loader Protections and Secure Boot
Talking about boot loader protections, and what is a boot loader protection? Well, it's made up of a couple things here. We have secure boot; we have a measured launch; IMA, or Integrity Measurement Architecture; and then, of course, our BIOS, or UEFI, and we'll talk about each of these in more detail. Secure boot is a feature of UEFI, that allows only signed boot software to load. UEFI is Universal Extensible Firmware Interface. It's a new type of BIOS. You can think of that as the BIOS in newer systems. It allows or enables a very secure booting mechanism. If code is not signed properly, then it will halt the boot process. If we go through the steps here, firmware boot components, it's going to be digitally signed, and it's going to be digitally signed by the maker of that laptop or that piece of hardware, typically, all. It can only run certain OSs or certain boot files. It can locked down so it can only run a specific type of operating system. That firmware boot component is digitally signed, as I said it, comprised of a boot manager, again, digitally signed. It'll pass on to winload functionality, again, checks certificates, goes to the Windows kernel startup, and that will interface with the AV software initialization, and, again, checking certificates to make sure everything along the way is signed properly. That passes it

back to the kernel startup, goes into additional OS initialization, passes over to boot-critical driver installation, loads our drivers, necessary to boot the system, passes it back, and then, of course, we see the windows login screen. Anywhere along that process, if those digital certificates are not on the up and up, if they've been tampered with or they're just missing, then the boot process would halt. That prevents things like root kits and pieces of malware, spyware that try to load onto the system before the actual operating system, before the antivirus software loads. If something tries to tamper in that boot sector or some type of pre-boot startup malware, this will fix that. This will prevent that from happening because it's going to alter the digital certificate. In a nutshell, when that PC starts, the firmware's going to check the signature of each piece of boot software, including firmware and drivers. If the signature's are good, the PC will boot. If not, it's going to halt that process. Not all systems have this, and you can add additional certificates in. If we have an operating system, for example, that is not included in that initial list of digital certificates, it is possible to add that in after the fact and give additional options, as far as booting that piece of equipment.

Measured Launch

Boot components have been measured, and what that means is they've been identified cryptographically. We have a hash against those things. The cryptography hashes are checked at boot to validate each component. It's part of what's called the Intel Trusted Execution Technology, or Intel TXT. And what it also does is provide a detailed log of everything that happens before the load of that actual antimalware software. If we have to go back and try to understand what happened, something got installed on our system, some piece of malware got introduced, we can go back and check this log and see exactly where that happened. As you can imagine, it will aid in our troubleshooting and overall analysis.

Integrity Measurement Architecture (IMA)

And then next we have IMA, or Integrity Measurement Architecture. IMA is an open source alternative that creates a measured runtime environment. It creates a list of components that need to load for that operating system or for that PC to boot up. It anchors that list to what's called a TPM chip, the Trusted Platform Module. It anchors it to that chip to prevent tampering. That way, if anything changes, any type of malware tries to install and it will alter those files if they don't match, then it prevents that boot.

BIOS/UEFI

Next, we have the BIOS or UEFI, universal extensible firmware, it's an alternative to the traditional BIOS. It offers a few advantages. We can boot from disks larger than 2 TB. It's also CPU independent architecture, CPU independent drivers, so we can work whether it's on Mac, Linux, Windows system, it's not dependent upon the operating system. It's also a flexible pre-OS environment offering options of Boot menu, network boot. It gives us that secure boot environment if we need it and gives us just more options than a traditional BIOS would allow.

Hashing

Hashing is a mathematical algorithm that's applied to a file before and after transmission. If anything within that file changes, the hash will be completely different. We have a couple options, we could use MD5, SHA1, or SHA2, and that's your choice depending upon which algorithm you want to use, they will each produce a different result. In the real world, if we hashed an entire file or an entire disk, if anything has changed on that disk or in that file, depending on the example, it will result with a different hash file. Whether we're trying to send something to someone, we could take a hash first and then let them hash again when they get on the other side and see if the numbers match, if they match, we know nothing has changed, it hasn't been manipulated. Or from our forensics point of view as an example, we can take a hash of an entire hard drive, and then anytime we want to prove the veracity of that image, we can just run a hash against that again, and as long as those numbers match, we know that nothing has changed on that hard disk.

Salt
Password or passphrase salting is random data that is used as an additional input into a one-way function or hash. It defends against dictionary tax and/or rainbow table attacks. What we're doing is adding additional information to our password so that it creates an additional level of randomization, makes it harder to guess, makes it harder to bruteforce. This adds additional complexity and also makes it much more difficult to try to guess.

Secure Coding Techniques
The goal of this chapter is not to make you a very highly skilled coder. We're not deep diving into the actual nuts and bolts of coding here, but the general concepts the general mindset behind coding so that as an IT security professional you can have those conversations with the DevOps folks and with the coders and make sure that these concepts are being followed. When it comes to secure coding techniques and proper error handling. We need to make sure the errors don't crash the system, allow for elevated privileges, or

expose unintended information. In having these discussions, again, with programmers and coders, understand, ask the questions, show me how error handling works. Show me what happens if unintended input is entered. What happens if the system crashes? What does it give back to the end user? Proper input validation is another. We want to make sure that we sanitize the data to mitigate such things as cross-site scripting and cross-site forgery requests. If someone goes into a web portal, we want to make sure that data is sanitized so they can't put in some rogue piece of information and get unintended results back. Also, normalization on the database back end. We want to ensure database integrity and optimization of data. You may ask yourself, what does this have to do with security? Well, normalizing the database ensures that there are no insertion or deletion anomalies. Downstream impacts might be if something gets deleted improperly or if something gets added improperly and our database and our tables are out of sync, it could return unintended consequences, or could have unintended consequences, and return unintended data, so normalization is key. Also stored procedures. We want to utilize vetted, secure procedures, verses writing new code on the fly. Whenever possible, reuse code if appropriate, or use stored procedures that have been vetted and are known to be secure. Next, we have code signing. We want to ensure that validated and trusted code is used. We want to mitigate risk from unsigned code being allowed to run. Because, again, if we allow things that have not been vetted, have not been signed, we don't know where that's coming from, we don't trust it. If we allow those things to run, we introduce risk, potential for malware, potential for spyware, ransomware, you name it, unintended results. Hackers can use these things to try to crash the system, inject code into the application. Unsigned code is a no-no.

Encrypting the data, that's going to mitigate the risk of compromise should the actual computer go missing, lost or stolen, or the drives housing the data become lost or stolen. Then we have obfuscation or camouflage. This goes hand in hand with encryption. Masking the data, encryption is an example, to avoid detection by static code analysis. That typically involves such things as a decoder and the encoded payload. You can look at these things in one of two ways. Encryption is going to keep the data out of prying eyes, but it also keeps someone from potentially reverse engineering what we're doing. If we're encrypting our code or obfuscating otherwise, camouflaging that code, they can't do static code analysis against that program and spot potential errors. It goes both ways. Those two things can either work for you or against you, depending upon which side of the fence you're sitting on. Then we have code reuse and dead code. Code reuse is simply code that can be reused, as the name implies, for some future use, future project. The challenge becomes, when people try to write code that they can reuse later, they start to bring in things that may not be necessary for the project they're working on but trying to think of future uses or future bugs they might encounter or future issues they may come up with. They try to write code that is going to counteract those things, when in reality they're probably not going to capture all those things anyway. But by focusing on what's in front of you, you stand a much better chance of writing a very clean, secure piece of code.

Server side versus client side
Take into account where validation, input sanitation, where those things occur, and the way those controls can be bypassed. Server side versus client side depends upon where those things, where those validations and those sanitizations

take place. They're easier to bypass on the client side than it is on the server side, typically. Where we have the option, servicer side is typically better., not always, there's always exceptions to every rule, but just some things to think about, so the conversations to have with the coders when you're discussing how the applications work and how they function. Next is memory management. That's going to ensure that code calls and manages memory properly to avoid heap and buffer overrun errors. These things could cause the system to crash, they could cause system instability and data exposure. Things to ask your developers, making sure you're both on the same page, making sure they've thought through these things, which they may or may not have. It's always good to validate. Don't just assume that because someone works on code that they know how to do it securely. There are obvious conversations that need to be had. Then we have third-party libraries and SDKs, or software development kits. Ensure that you understand any third-party, any third-party's security requirements, their vetting processes, where their data is stored, interaction with other apps or data. Again, don't just assume that they have the same level of security that you do. Always vet that and remember that security's only as strong as the weakest link. Make sure that there is some type of service-level agreement or an understanding between companies, how they vet their process, how they take security as a consideration. Is their security up to the level of yours? Because it doesn't matter how strong your security is; if theirs is weak, then an attacker's able to come in through the side door through their weaker security and then pivot and then come through into your application or your network. That poses a challenge, and of course a breach can occur. Then, lastly we have data exposure. What types of data are exposed? If unexpected inputs are put into the system and cause the system to crash or cause some unintended result, or what errors are returned if incorrect data is entered. In other words, if someone puts in some type of string, they try a cross-site scripting or cross-site forgery request or they go through some type of fuzzing exercise or they just try every single combination of characters and letters to see what happens, to see if the system crashes. If and when it does crash, what types of information are returned? Does it tell you the operating system, the kernel version, all those things an attacker could potentially use to fingerprint the system, or if the website, as an example, asks for a username and a password, and they put in the wrong username, does it tell them, hey, this username's not valid. Well, that lets them know, hey, that one's, strike that from the list. That one's not valid. Let's try the next one. And it allows them to brute force that. Versus if it simply says, hey, if this was correct you'll get an email back or an email was sent or some type of a more ambiguous error message it doesn't give them any insight into what's valid or not valid. It's all a matter of conversations that you should have with, the coders and developers to make sure that everyone is on the same page. They will then understand how security factors in, and you will get a better understanding of how the applications interact with each other.

Chapter 3 Coding, Fuzzing & Quality Testing

We have static code analyzers; we have dynamic analysis; other words, fuzzing; we have stress testing; sandboxing; and model verification. Secure coding concepts, some things to keep in mind. Application development is often a balancing act between time to market and security. There are the developers and the general IT folks, and then there's the security folks. But we're all working on the same team, and we're all trying to do the same things, so it's important that we all work together. Building for security, that's going to add to development time. That's the general consensus, or the general understanding. But here's the key part. If you don't have time to find the vulnerabilities, guess who will? The bad guys. It's very, very important, it's crucial, in fact, that we spend the time, we do security up front, we incorporate security from the get go, not as an afterthought, not as a bolt-on. It should be done from the beginning. And the old adage is, if you don't have time to do it the first time, what makes you think you're going to have time to go back and do it a second time? If you can't do it once, how are you going to have time to do it twice? Some additional things with secure coding, error and exception handling. We need to look at what does the application do when it encounters an error? Does it continue running? Does it restart a process or a chapter? Or does it completely crash? And what type of data is exposed when it crashes? Does it give that attacker the ability to elevate privileges and get in and then do all the things that they typically would do, install persistence and go on from there, or does it give away information that tells about the type of operating system that it's on, the kernel level, some information that the attacker can use to then further dig into that system? Also input validation. It's important that we validate and sanitize what is entered at the client side or the server side, depending upon, again, your coding mechanisms and your preference. But either way, that needs to be processed and sanitized before it's passed and executed upon. That's going to allow us to mitigate attacks, cross-site scripting attacks and also SQL injection attacks, two big ones that can be avoided or mitigated if we sanitize that input properly. Metasploit, Exploit-Me, there's browser add-ons, Netsparker, there are a number of different tools out there that can allow an IT security professional to do these types of tests ahead of time. You can either throw them up to the wind and just use your best guess and hope that this stuff works and nobody tries to get in and nobody's able to get past your defenses. Or you can be proactive and use these tools and think like an attacker, think like a hacker, and start running tests against your own systems. If you don't have the expertise, bring in a pen testing team. But it's important that we test these things, we try to break things along the way so that we get to it before the attackers do.

Static Code Analysis

Static code analysis is also known as source code analysis. It's part of a code review process for something that's referred to as white-box testing, so it allows you to see under the covers. It's also part of the implementation phase of the Security Development Lifecycle or the SDL. So it finds vulnerabilities in non-running code. It's static code analysis. We're looking for those vulnerabilities, either through taint analysis or data flow analysis. Data flow analysis is used to collect runtime or dynamic information about data and software while it's in a static state. Taint analysis, on the other hand, attempts to identify variables that have been tainted by user-controllable input and then traces that to possible vulnerable functions also known as a sink. If a tainted variable gets past to a sink without first being sanitized, it gets flagged as a vulnerability. We're looking for vulnerabilities, we're looking for input sanitization, looking for places where a user has the ability to control that input. If they can put in something, this is where SQL injection and cross-site scripting attacks come into play. If they're able to use some type of technique either as fuzzing or just straight up SQL injection, they can try every single possible combination of codes, letters, characters, and if that is successful, and that code does not get sanitized, they can crash the system or have unintended results. This data flow analysis and this taint analysis allows us to go in and identify these things ahead of time. It's part of the defensive posture that we need to take as IT security professionals, does every IT security professional know all of these different things? No, of course not. There are areas of specialization, but it's important for you to have a general concept and a general understanding, number one, to know, is this an area I want to go into, number two, even if it isn't, you need to have those conversations with the people that are responsible for this, and if you don't know about it, it's hard to have that conversation. As an IT security professional, it's important to have a good understanding of everything, not a deep dive, but a good understanding, so you know who to talk to, who to coordinate with, whether they're developers, pen testers, coders, your DevOps folks, or IT security folks, your infrastructure folks, all the different lines of business, you can reach out to all these different areas, coordinate efforts, and make sure everyone is on the same page and everyone is working towards the same goal.

Fuzzing

Fuzzing is intentionally trying to crash a program or an application by providing invalid, unexpected or random data. Fuzzing is a set of tools. It's not a specific application, it's a suite of applications. It can be one or a dozen or more. Each hacker, each attacker, each forensics person, they all have their own toolsets that they like to work with. It's used by application designers and testers internally, as well as hackers on the outside, but if we're going to use it internally, it helps us to find bugs and defects, also security holes in our applications. It allows us to identify things we didn't account for. Hackers, they'll use fuzzing techniques as well. They'll look for zero-day vulnerabilities, and a lot of hackers will go out there and they'll gather up these zero-days and they'll sell them on the dark net, they'll hoard them, sell them to companies, sell them to security companies or perhaps rogue states or nation states. There are three-letter agencies within the U.S. government that buy these zero-day vulnerabilities from various hackers, so they'll hoard them as well. And then these hackers will also sell them to the bad guys. It's a very effective toolset, it can yield some great results, it can be used for good or bad, but it's important for us to use those same techniques to identify things internally. Whether we're trying to crash applications or websites, we want to make sure we get to our vulnerabilities before the bad guys do. There are a few fuzzing applications out there. One that makes it easy for you, there's a Linux distribution called Kali Linux. They have a suite of fuzzing tools built in, al. Also, CERT has one called BFF, or the Basic Fuzzing Framework, that you can download from the web link, and that allows you to bring in a full suite of fuzzing applications. Whether you go Linux distribution or you download a framework ahead of time, it allows you to install and use the same types of tools that these hackers use. I urge you to become proficient in what these things do, or at least

41

develop on your team someone who is proficient in this so that you can then coordinate their efforts.

Here we have Kali Linux, which I downloaded from their website, and I'll bring up their actual web page within the actual VM that I'm running here. This is a virtual machine, so it's a little bit slower than it normally would be, but if you were to go out to Kali's website, which is kali.org, this is a reincarnation of BackTrack, which is a pen testing tool and a Linux distribution that's geared towards security. If you're familiar with BackTrack, this is the newer version of that toolset, so Kali Linux. And from there you would go to Downloads. If you're running VMware, this is a great way to get up and running quickly. You click on that and it will bring you over to this web page from Offensive Security, and then from there you can download custom ARM images and also VMware images. You would just pick one for your specific VMware flavor of choice, and from there, once you install it, which is what I have running here, you're up and running with Kali Linux and you can explore all the things that it has to offer. Under Applications down under Kali Linux, this is where all the good stuff, this is where all the magic happens. It's out of the scope of this book to go into any of these in any depth, but I wanted to make you aware of where they're located and how to get your hands on a copy of Kali Linux

You can explore on your own. From the fuzzing testing tools that I was referring to, that would be under Vulnerability Analysis and then down under Fuzzing Tools.

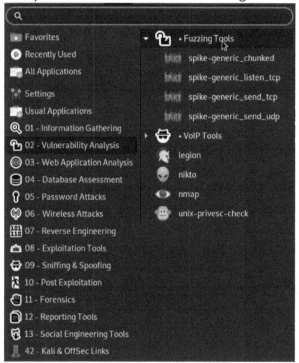

You see there's a number of ones available. There's also Database Assessment tools, Reverse Engineering, Stress Testing, Exploitation Tools, so there's a lot of stuff here, If you're interested in digging in, I highly recommend that you download this application, or this distribution of Linux, and then start exploring the applications that are inside here, so I just want to make you aware of where these things were located.

Additional Secure Coding Concepts

Stress testing is placing load on the system or the application. We want to see where the performance and the usability breaks down, where that application either crashes or simply can't perform anymore. We can test via automated processes with like LoadRunner or Iometer or use some type of appliance like a load dynamics device, some piece of hardware, and we can stress test whether it's an array, whether it's an application, a server. We can see where things fall apart. We can turn up the number of users, the number of connections, the number of processes that's being processed at once. We do that to simulate where is that going to break down in the real world. If we have 5 users, it's great. If we have 500, it's a little iffy. If we have 5000, it falls apart. Well, we need to know that ahead of time, before we put into production. We put an ad on TV and all of a sudden we have 10,000 users trying to hit our website at the same time or hit our application at the same time, and it falls apart. It's not good for our reputation or for consumer confidence. Not to mention, if it doesn't fail gracefully, it could expose information and be a security risk. Next, we have sandboxing. Sandboxing is isolating the application from other systems so that we can test without impact to other applications to production. We've talked about a few ways to sandbox. We can isolate the networks logically or physically, we can use VMware or some other type of hypervisor and virtualize that environment. It allows us to just as segment that off from the rest. And then we have model verification. This is testing to verify that the product or the application that's produced aligns with the proposed model. Does it do what we said it's going to do? Does it behave in the way that we thought it's going to behave? Because it's possible to build something that's going to behave or interact with other systems that's totally different from what you thought it was going to do. Model verification is critical to make sure all the boxes are checked and make sure that we understand all the downstream impacts and how this specific application or this specific system interacts with everything else that's in production.

Peripherals Security

Peripheral security is something we typically think of, a mouse or a keyboard, what's the harm? Well, wireless keyboards, wireless mice, all of those things can be sniffed potentially. The average environment, maybe not a big deal, but depending upon how critical your infrastructure is or how crucial your job function or the industry you're in, all of those things are attack vectors, so they need to be considered, Wireless keyboards, wireless mice, displays, we've talked about emanations from displays before, such things as TEMPEST-proof rooms, Faraday cages. Also, Wi-Fi-enabled MicroSD cards, we have a camera digital device, a lot of those things days have Wi-Fi-enabled SD cards, you can upload pictures and data from that SD card directly. Well, all of those things are potentially open for compromise. Hackers are getting into everything, embedded systems, Internet of Things, even cars on the highway. It's important to always understand that every single thing in our environment is a potential attack surface, we need to remove things we don't need, and then the things that are left, we need to make sure we monitor, update, and patch. Same thing goes with printers and MFDs, the multi-function devices, external storage devices, and digital cameras. All of these things contain data that, if not either removed or strictly controlled, the access is strictly controlled, data can be pulled off of those devices if they're accessed or if they're compromised. When we talk about updating, just the overall peripheral security, a few things we should be doing, some common-sense things, and that is update and patch. We need to make sure we keep all of our systems and all the peripherals patched and updated. Just because it's an embedded system, or an appliance, doesn't mean it shouldn't be monitored, patched, and updated. Then we need to make sure we physically secure devices. Treat peripherals like any other asset. They could contain sensitive data, so don't let things walk out the door. Make sure you have an eye on things in a way to monitor, whether it's barcodes or sensors or what have you, make sure we can keep an eye on all of our assets. And then, require credentials to access, Printers or copiers, and don't just let anyone access your resources. Make sure they have to badge in or put in some type of access code so that way you can monitor who is using those resources. Last but not least, we should definitely require encryption of removable devices, external storage, or Wi-Fi connectivity, whenever possible. All of these things combine to help to strengthen our security posture and mitigate risks as much as possible.

Hardening the Environment
When we're talking about hardening the environment, I'm talking about open ports and services, locking things down that we don't need, and making sure that it is secure as it can possibly be, and still be useful. There is a fine line, you can lock things down much to the point where it's not useful anymore or people have to write down passwords, usernames and have sticky notes everywhere. It is possible to overdo it, but in this instance, let's talk about what we can do proactively to harden the environment. When you build your systems, your servers, desktops, even mobile devices, develop the mindset to do an analysis of the environment, of that application, of that device and see there are a lot of things there that we don't need. We can turn those things off. It's never going to do X, Y, Z, so we don't need to have that service listening, we don't need to have that service active because as we remove or disable services, shut down

ports, we're doing what? We're shrinking the attack service. So open ports and services is one and there are things within the registry, and the registry in a Windows system at least, is sort of like the DNA of the system, it has all the fine-grained controls, it allows you to shut certain things off and make things harder to access or just disable services. Disk encryption we've talked about before as well. We need to make sure we're covering our bases. And if, in fact, a piece of equipment gets stolen, removed out of a car, out of the data center, out of a storage closet, and if the disk is encrypted, it's going to be much more difficult for that bad actor to access the information on that disk. And then OS hardening, just like we talked about with open ports and services, we want to remove unnecessary services at the OS level as well, shut down things that aren't necessary, remote desktop protocol, as an example, there are many more, but that's just one. If we don't need it, then shut it off. That removes that ability or shrinks that attack service. Next is patch management. We need to make sure that we do that religiously, and that goes for third-party updates and also auto update. Auto update may or may not be something you want to do in your environment and larger environments. We want to do things on a cadence. We want to be able to download those updates offline, test them in a very small group, do some regression testing, make sure they don't break anything, and then roll them out systematically to the environment at large. That way it gives you the opportunity to phase things in, and that way you don't just automatically update something and have a break. It's not to say you can't automate the process, but you just don't want to automate patching without testing it first.

Common Ports

When we talk about ports and services, there are things called common ports. It's beyond the scope of this book to go into all of the reports. There are over 65,500 ports. The first 1,024 are defined by RFC or request for comments, and they're known as the well-known ports. They're defined by typical applications. But these are some of the ones that you should be familiar with, port 20 and 21 for FTP as an example, port 23 for Telnet. Here's an example of one you may or may not need. If you don't need to Telnet your service or into your server or your desktop, then disable that service. It just shrinks that attack surface. If you go down the list and look at things like, as an example, Internet Relay Chat, port 194. Well, this isn't 1985. People don't use IRC anymore. If you need in your environment, great. Keep it up. But if you don't, block those things at the firewall. Block those things at the individual host as well. By doing so, we're removing or at least shrinking the attack surface. Is it foolproof? No. But why give attackers or bad actors more fuel for their fire, more ammunition. Shrink it as much as possible; help to make things more secure.

Registry Hardening

When we talk about registry hardening, registry being the DNA of the operating system, at least on the Windows side. An example of some registry hardening settings, configure permissions, deny anonymous access as an example. Deny remote registry access as an example. If you need that in your environment, then by all means don't do that, but this where it comes down to an analysis of each individual environment. Everyone's going to have different needs. Everyone's going to have different working parameters or guidelines or guardrails that they have to operate within. Make sure that you configure your permissions appropriately. But make them as restrictive as possible and still being useful. Also, I would disable access to registry editing tools at the host level as well. That way, someone can't go in at the host and start editing the registry. That goes for disabling the command prompt and also PowerShell access if it's not needed. There might be instances where you do need that, and if so, then by all means keep it enabled. But by doing that, by making people local users on the machines, taking away access to certain things that allow them to bypass some of the controls you're putting in place, it makes the system more secure. It reduces your troubleshooting and shrinks the attack surface. And then Whitelist and blacklist applications. The difference between whitelisting and blacklisting. Whitelisting is we have a list of acceptable applications. Everything else is no go. If you only have three applications on that list, then they're the only three things that we can run. Conversely, if you have a blacklist, we can run everything except the ones that are on the blacklist. It's just two different approaches to achieve the same net effect.

Self-encrypting Drives (SED)
Self-encrypting drives, also known as SED drives. These things are very much like a typical disk drive, except they have additional functionality. They can self encrypt and they maintain that information on the disk itself, so you don't need to maintain third-party encryption keys. Encryption keys are self-contained in the drive's firmware, and they're maintained separately from the CPU, which, again, reduces the attack vector. That's the name of the game here. We want to shrink the attack vector as much as possible. There's something else that I want to make you aware of, and that is the Opal Specification, and that deals with self-encrypting drives. It was created by the Trusted Computing Group, or TCG, and it's a security subsystem class that specifies how

data is encrypted on the drive. If we look at this in a little more detail, this is a very high-level overview of how it works. But you have your host interface in which you input plain text, you have your plain text that you want to encrypt onto the storage device. We have what's called a KDF, or a key derivation function. That's how we're going to create the key-encrypting key, the KEK. That key-encrypting key, usually a password, an authentication PIN here or a password, is then used to create what's called the MEK, or the media encryption key. We're taking a key, a master key, if you will. It then unlocks the media encryption keys and allows that data to be unencrypted or encrypted, depending on which way it's going in, whether you're writing it or reading it from disk. You don't need to necessarily understand the nitty-gritty of how it works, but just understand at a high level that self-encrypting drives are secure. They're a little more secure in the fact that we don't have to maintain third-party encryption keys. They're also more efficient in that we don't have to worry about the CPU or burdening the CPU with additional cycles to have the software or a software layer encrypt and decrypt the data. It's handled at the actual drive level, and those keys are stored in the firmware. That makes it very secure. It gives you very good throughput and takes that latency out of the process of the software layer, having to do the encryption and decryption, which puts additional cycles onto the CPU. By removing all of that, we make the encryption process more streamlined.

Hardware Root of Trust

Next, we have a concept referred to as the hardware root of trust. What does this mean? Well, you can see that it goes up the stack from the hardware to firmware, Hypervisor, operating system, up to the application, and what that means is that root of trust begins with systems that are inherently trusted, just like we have PKI and we have certificate authorities and root certificate authorities, that same level of trust needs to be there. If something is compromised at the very low level at the base hardware, if the BIOS of a system are compromised, then how can we trust anything that sits above that? If the BIOS itself is not inherently trusted or inherently secure, then we can trust as we go up that stack and test that the other things in that stack can be secure as well. A few concepts regarding that hardware root of trust, it needs to be secure by design, it also needs to perform security-critical functions like the TPM chip, as we mentioned, as an example, or boot firmware is another example. There are two NIST guidelines I'd like to call your attention to, NIST SP800-147, which is BIOS protection guidelines, and then NIST SP600-155 which is BIOS integrity measurement guidelines. Those two guidelines I encourage you to download and look through. They'll give you some additional information around the general concept and how that applies within your organization.

Hardware Based Encryption

Next up, and a few things that you should be aware of here, TPM being one of them, the Trusted Platform Module and TPM is a hardware chip that's embedded on a computer's motherboard. Typically, you're going to see these in laptops. They're used to store cryptographic keys used for encryption. The TPM chapter is built onto a motherboard. The takeaway here is it cannot be added later. If your desktop or your laptop or whatever the device is does not have a TPM chip, you cannot add it later. It's built into the motherboard itself. Conversely, we have HSM, or the hardware security Module. It functions in much the same way as a TPM; however, this can be external, or it could be plugged into a server or a laptop. It is something that can be added later. Imagine that we have a network device, a network-based hardware security chapter, and this is used for storing and generating keys for encryption. Whether you have a PKI on your network or you're looking for some type of encryption technology, this can do that at the network level. There's also cards that can be plugged in to a specific server. HSM, the takeaway would be it's similar to TPM. The hardware security chapter is very similar to the Trusted Platform Chapter; however, HSMs are removable or they're external. They can be added later. That's the takeaway. TPMs are built in, HSMs are not. Both are used, however, for encryption keys, encrypting rather, and using RSA keys. Next, we have USB encryption. For the most part, when we say removable media, we're talking about USB or thumb drives. It's the same type of thing. Encrypting the contents of our USB drives, it prevents that data from being accessed if stolen, or if someone maliciously tries to copy data onto a USB drive and hand it off to someone else, that data's encrypted. The receiving party can't do much with it unless they have those decryption keys. Then we have hardware-based encryption around hard drives. Encrypting the entire contents of a hard drive, that provides that data at rest encryption, and it guards against data leakage if lost or stolen. Again, someone smashes the window or breaks into a place of business and steals computers, steals laptops, that data is inaccessible. It's also used in conjunction with the TPM or HSM chapters. These things help generate the encryption keys in a very secure environment. That way, if it gets lost or stolen, there's not much you can do with it. As an example, we have BitLocker. This would give us an entire or full disk encryption. We can turn on, go into our control panel, and turn on BitLocker at the drive level, where we have multiple drives, and ensure that those things are encrypted and, of course, inaccessible if they were to be either stolen or fall into the wrong hands.

Sandboxing

Sandboxing can be used in a couple of different contexts. In this specific context, it's isolating code, upgrades, and testing from the production environment. In other words, we're operating in a closed or a walled garden, so we can test changes, and we can do things without affecting production. We can do such things as test code changes, we can roll back changes very quickly, we can also regression test against various applications, or execute and even observe malware. We can purposely allow malware to do its thing, but it's in a sandboxed environment, we're observing it, trying to reverse engineer it, or at least see what it's doing, what's the payload? Sandboxing in an environment allows us to put those walls up and operate safely. When we're talking about sandboxing applications, it isolates the application from other user data, resources, you can think of it as virtual environments within your device, a mobile device, laptop or desktop. It can prevent malware and viruses from interacting with the application or with other applications, and each application has its own environment on the host. That prevents an application crash from affecting other applications running on the host. It's not anything that's revolutionary, but it is a tried-and-true practice that allows us to operate securely without affecting other applications. And we can do it sandbox from a network perspective, we can do it from an application perspective, we can do it to test code and roll back changes, or we can create live environments that each application can live in on a specific device, separating those applications from each other. In this chapter, we covered endpoint protection; we talked about boot integrity; and database security; along with application security, hardening, and the importance of doing that around ports and services, the registry, OS; we talked about disk encryption; we talked about the hardware root of trust, along with a Trusted Platform Module; and then we also talked about sandboxing in a few different contexts.

Chapter 4 How to Implement Secure Network Designs

In this chapter, we'll be talking about Implementing Secure Network Designs and we'll be covering such things as load balancing, we'll be talking about network segmentation, we'll talk about virtual private networks, DNS or domain name service, we'll also talk about network access control or NAC, also out-of-band management, and then wrap up with port security. A load balancer, as the name implies, balances the load between devices. A load balancer can be put in place in a number of areas. It could be a server. There could be other devices as well. It can be hardware. It can be software. It just depends upon price point, functionality, how extreme the load balancing needs to be. If it's a small environment, a server may be fine. If it's a large environment, very high volume, then you're going to need a dedicated appliance. If we have a number of users, there's the external network, and then there's a load balancer in place, and it can be one or more. It doesn't necessarily have to be a single device. It could be multiple load balancers. In this instance, let's just say we have web servers, and it's going to balance the load and determine, which is the best performing server at that specific point in time, and I'm going to send the load to that server. It may go in a round-robin fashion. It may use some algorithm to determine, but depending upon the load balancer itself, it's going to determine in some fashion, which is the best server or the best device to send that load to. It allows you to spread it out across. And as a load starts to pick up, as websites become more busy, it can spread it out so that no one server gets completely overwhelmed. A few terms I want to make sure you're familiar with regard to load balancers. As far as scheduling is concerned, we have two terms, affinity and round-robin. Affinity means if we have multiple servers, that a load balancer can serve traffic too. Well, if it has affinity in place, then the server that initially serviced the request for a host, it will use that same server for the entirety of that session. It's not going to just completely just go to the next available one. It locks into that server, and as long as that session is active, that post will communicate over that load balancer into that server, so the host to server will take the same path through the load balancer. In a round-robin fashion, we may have multiple load balancers. We may have multiple servers to get through to the back-end database or the back-end application. While in a round-robin fashion, it will pick the next available or the next best one in line, It won't necessarily wait or lock into a specific server and hold communication throughout the entirety of that session. It will go to the next available one. When we're talking about active-passive dealing with load balancers, that refers to the fact that we may have multiple load balancers. Even load balances have load balancers. The load balancer itself is operating in an HA or a highly-available fashion. The active-passive nature means one load balancer is handling or servicing all that traffic. There's another load balancer that's acting in a passive state, and it's monitoring what the first load balancer's doing. It's keeping track, but it's not doing anything. It's not actively servicing requests. Its job is to jump in in case the primary load balancer were to go offline or have some type of failure. In an active-active capacity, we have both load balancers servicing the load or it might have multiple, three or four, however many are in this configuration. But for this example, let's say we have two load balancers. Well, if they're acting in an active-active fashion, they're both servicing the load, spreading it evenly. The downside of that is in an active-active situation, both load balancers end up servicing requests near their maximum capacity. If one load balancer were to go down and there's no other load balancer to take over, then we'll start slowing down and customers will notice a degradation in service. In an active-passive fashion, one load balancer is servicing everything. If it starts to go down, the other one kicks in and takes over, so there's no noticeable difference, no noticeable degradation to end users. And then the last one I want to cover is virtual IPs. A virtual IP, or a VIP, is an IP that sits in front of all of the actual IPs that the load balancers use, so that way the end user doesn't necessarily need to know the IP addresses of the individual load balancers. All they need to know is the one, and it will cycle through and make sure that it goes to the proper load balancers behind the scenes. That way you don't have to change things. If you add additional load balancers or you switch things up behind the scenes, end users, all they need to know is they have to connect to that virtual IP address.

Security Segmentation Models

Let's now talk about segregation, segmentation and isolation. We have a few security or segmentation models I want to call to your attention. First is physical. We can physically separate or segment nodes or hosts on a network. We can also do that logically with something called VLAN, or virtual LANs, virtual local area networks. We can also do it with virtualization, so an isolation model or a segmentation model. Then we also have air gapped, meaning there is no connectivity to the internet or to the network at large. So, what do I mean by that? Well, with physical or logical, we have devices that are all on the same segment, the same Ethernet segment or the same LAN, the same local area network. And in this example, you can assume that they're all connected to the same switch, so that is a physical connectivity to the network. Well, we can also logically

57

separate those networks. We can take that same layout, but we can use something called virtual LANs, or virtual local area networks, and group them accordingly. We can have a VLAN10, we can have a VLAN20, and in this case, a VLAN30. What that does is separate those devices out. What it does is create separate broadcast domains, separate security domains, and it reduces the chatter. Let's look at another example. Imagine that we have a multi-floor building. We have wiring on each floor that goes back to a home run, and it goes down between floors. We have devices on the first floor and a switch, we have devices on the second floor and a switch, and then devices on the third floor and a switch. It's not the only way to wire, not the only way to do it, but in this example, we have each floor going to a wiring closet. In that wiring closet, a switch, and then those switches are connected via home runs. They're all physically located in different locations. Well, we can also group those together just like we did in the previous example. They don't have to be sitting next to each other. We can group them again logically, VLAN10, VLAN20, and then VLAN30. In other words, if we had groups of computers that may be on different floors, let's say we have finance people that sit on all three floors or HR or our graphics department we can group them within our switches. We make sure that all the switches have the same VLAN associations, and that way they're grouped logically together. Those VLANs can group hosts that are in different locations, into logical groupings. That creates smaller collision domains and it reduces chatter. As an example, if you have a very large cafeteria, everyone's talking. It's very hard to understand because everyone's talking. Everyone's clashing into each other. They're colliding the conversations. If I took all of those people in that cafeteria and separated them out into five different rooms or in this example three different rooms, well, I have one third of the amount of people in each room, so the chatter is going to be less, so the collisions are less. It helps increase efficiency. Then also it can be used to create security boundaries to segment traffic so that one host doesn't necessarily see broadcasts and doesn't see traffic designated for hosts in another VLAN.

Virtualization

Virtualization is a method of segmenting or isolating, so we can keep a host in a sandboxed and isolated environment, meaning it's separate from the host that it's sitting on. We can also allow for snapshots. We can quickly revert changes, we can use virtualization to isolate or segment. We can do all of our testing. We can test changes, we can even test viruses or malware to see what it does without affecting the rest of the network and without affecting the host that it sits on. It also separates the guests from the host, the guest from the hypervisor. If we have Hyper-V, or VMware, or KVM, or virtual box, or whatever the case might be or whatever our virtualization technology is, this allows us to keep those individual guests separate from the host. Other devices may be virtualized as well. We can virtualize other infrastructure, such as routers, switches, load balancers, firewalls, and we'll talk more about that when we get into SDN, but the nice part is those things can be instantiated or spun up on demand, so as a load increases, we could spin up additional load balancers or, if we have applications that need specific firewalls, instead of having to go through the normal change process and buying equipment and racking and stacking and all the things that are associated with physical infrastructure, we can do it virtually, very quickly, spin that device up, use it while we need it, and then we can tear it down just as quickly.

Air Gaps

An air gap is a method of isolating a computer or a network from the internet or from other external networks, or other networks aside from the one you're on. So, it doesn't necessarily have to be just from the internet, it could be from other networks within your company. If you have a very highly secure environment that you need to make sure that there's no chance of malware or viruses being introduced, then you would set up an air gapped network. As with anything, there is no 100% guarantee, as we've seen in the past with things like Stuxnet and some other very highly visible and highly cited instances where malware has jumped into air gapped environments, nothing is 100% certain. But it's used for critical infrastructure, SCADA systems, as an example, and I refer back to Stuxnet where the SCADA systems were still compromised, highly secure classified networks. There are some advanced techniques, however, to jump air gapped networks, like I said, that's been demonstrated, emanations, there's technology and it's been completely demonstrated where they can view the emanations coming off of a computer, whether it is the sound of the hard drive whirring, or even the heat being generated by the hard drive spinning up. If you're close enough to that device, you can pick those things up from the device and discern what's going on, you can read data from that device. Pretty advanced stuff and it's not something the average hacker can do, but just understand that an air gap is a very good way of isolating the network, but it's not 100% foolproof. In fact, the US government and other agencies around the world have specific guidelines to create additional security. The US uses something referred to as TEMPEST, which protects that room, it has to be a certain thickness of walls and has to have additional coding and protections, Faraday cages, and things that just prevent emanations and monitoring from nearby locations. Emanations, FM frequencies, even some hard drives that have a small LED light on the front that shows activity of that drive, you don't see that too much anymore, but it is possible that if you have a line of sight visibility to that light going on and off as the hard drive writes, you could read, almost like Morse is code, what's going on with that hard drive and read data from that device. Pretty scary, but the average hacker is not going to be employing that. More than likely, you can rest assured that your home network is safe.

East-west Traffic

East-West traffic is data moving between devices within a data center. More and more traffic is being generated days East-West, just as a side note, with less and less traffic going North-South, meaning entering or exiting the data center. Again, depending upon your data center in your company, you may refer to North-South traffic as traffic leaving the top of rack and going to another area within the data center. Sometimes terminology can be co-mingled depending upon the company, the data center, but generally speaking, East-West is within the data center, North-South is exiting or entering the data center. Traditional firewalls and monitoring look normally or traditionally at North-South traffic. Our firewalls are on our perimeter, and we want to guard against what's coming into our networks and what's leaving the networks. That lack of visibility can add to an attacker's ability to move laterally around in a network undetected. Once they get into the network, once they penetrate our defenses, there's normally not as much tooling and not as much visibility into the movement within the data center, the thought being that once you're inside the network, it's a trusted environment. We'll talk more about zero trust in just a moment, but understand that that lack of visibility can allow an attacker to move around virtually undetected, at least for a period of time. How do we combat that is we implement network monitoring to identify that East-West threat or the East-West traffic. An IDS, or an IPS, or a network IDS, or network IPS system combined with tools like Suricata or Zeek, again two open-source recommendations, not the only things out there and not an endorsement, just giving you some ideas of things to look at, but Suricata and Zeek can identify malicious activity and can integrate with other systems as well, again these intrusion detection and prevention systems, and they can be leveraged to identify that malicious activity and take steps to mitigate it.

Zero Trust
Keeping with that theme, let's talk about zero trust, which I mentioned just a moment ago. Zero trust in today's world, castle moat philosophy where everything behind the firewalls was thought to be safe is no longer valid. That is not the recommended way to do things anymore. We need to take a more granular approach. Internal and external traffic should be monitored nothing implicitly trusted, whether it's internal or external. Micro-segmentation and granular access, providing only the levels of permission required. In other words, we don't just assume if you're inside the network, you're good, go ahead, don't necessarily worry about it. As we talked about, that allows an attacker to go around and move around, laterally jump networks, peruse the parking lot, and see which car they want to steal. We don't want that. That micro-segmentation, granular access, locking things down to only give people the level of permissions required, which sounds familiar. We do that anyway, typically with ACLs on resources like file shares, but we also want to make sure that we do it at the resource

level, the servers, the storage arrays, data protection, so on. A couple of tools we can leverage would be MFA, or multi-factor authentication, IAM, identity access management, and then we can leverage orchestration and analytics along with encryption. All of these more modern toolsets and these technologies, combined with detection and prevention tools, can lock down the environment enough so that it's not an easy target for an attacker or a bad actor, but we still need to make it usable, for our internal users. It's a fine line, but just understand the old way of doing things is not applicable or should not be applicable in today's environment.

VPN

The next thing I want to talk about is a VPN, or a virtual private network. A VPN is going to be something you should probably be familiar with. But if not, I'll give you a very good understanding here and the general concepts of what a VPN does. A VPN creates a virtual private network across a public network. You could be sitting in a coffee shop, for instance, very securely tunnel from that coffee shop to your corporate environment and access corporate resources without worrying that someone is potentially sniffing the traffic, accessing or picking up a sense of information like usernames, passwords. There are a couple of components of a VPN that we need to be aware of. Tunneling protocols such as L2TP, or Layer 2 Tunneling Protocol, and also PPTP, Point-To-Point Tunneling Protocol, and then IPSec, or IP security. What do these things mean? Well, there are separate components that make up the VPN because there are two components that we need to talk about. There's the tunnel, and then there's the encrypted data that passes through the tunnel. When we're establishing a VPN connection, the first thing we do is establish the tunnel, and then you establish the secure connection or the encrypted connection between the two endpoints. Security comes from the tunneling protocol and the encryption combined, and that's very important to understand. You can't have security unless you have both of those things in play. You need to establish the tunnel and then establish the security with encryption that passes data through that tunnel. Just because you have a tunnel established, if you don't have the encrypted communication taking place over that tunnel, then it's not going to do you much good as far as security is concerned. Many VPNs use something referred to as two-factor authentication. RSA is a very good example of that. They're one of the bigger vendors recently acquired by EMC. And RSA can provide hardware and software tokens, and what happens is every 30 seconds, or so, the number on that token or that Django, as it's called, will change. That number is in sync with the VPN concentrator or the VPN server back at the corporate headquarters, back at the endpoint. There's an authentication mechanism that keeps both of these in sync. Every 30 seconds that number changes on both the endpoint and also on the token. When you go to establish your connection, it's going to ask you for that username and perhaps your PIN or a password if you're going to use something like an RSA token. It will ask you for that. You have two things, what you have and what you know. You know your username and the token is what you have. That's going to change every 30 seconds, making it much more secure. Even if someone steals your laptop and they know your username, they still won't be able to gain access or get into a VPN connection and get back to the corporate headquarters because they don't have what? They don't have that PIN or that token that changes every 30 seconds. They're going to have to physically take that RSA token as well. Then even if they have the RSA token, they'll still need to know your PIN because once you put your PIN in, then, of course, the token will pop up. It's an extra layer of added security. With VPNs, many companies provide VPN access to their remote employees, so it allows corporate access to resources from an offsite or remote location. Depending on how things are set up, it can be given complete access to the network. Once you VPN in, once you make that connection, you could have complete access to the corporate network, or access can be restricted to only certain parts of the network. Depending upon how that VPN administrator sets things up, a person dialing in or VPN-ing into the network can have access maybe to only a certain subnet or a certain set of files and folders, a certain server. Here's an example of two different types of VPN connections. We have a VPN connection between two corporate networks, and it's a VPN connection in a tunnel, and you have a VPN router on both networks? Pretty much in these instances, a lot of times, it's set up as a constant connection, and then we have a VPN connection from a remote user. In this instance, that user is sitting out on the internet, again some public network. It could be a home office or remote office, some coffee shop somewhere. In other words, it's somewhere outside of the corporate environment proper. That person connects to their ISP. Now they have internet connectivity. When they initiate that VPN connection, it connects them to the corporate environment. They establish the VPN connection, the tunnel, and then the communication is secured over the public internet. They don't have to worry about someone being able to sniff their traffic.

Split Tunnel
In a split tunnel situation, we have an outside or an external user who is external to the company network or the

corporate network. Imagine that we have our 10.x network that's our internal corporate network. The user who is sitting external, maybe their home, at a coffee shop, some remote location. While they want to access those corporate resources, but as a company, it doesn't make sense to have that user go into our corporate network and then back out again to access external resources. So by using a split tunnel, we make sure that that external user accesses our corporate resources over the VPN so they have secure access to company resources, but then, when they want to reach external resources, they do Directly without going through the corporate network.

IPSec and Transport Encryption
Next, we have something referred to as IPSec, or the internet security protocol, and this allows us to encrypt communication over the internet over that insecure or unsecured network. There is two components here we have an authentication header, an AH, that provides authentication and integrity that does not encrypt the data, it just allows you to prove that you're communicating with who you think you're communicating with and that the data has not been manipulated or somehow tweaked while in transit, someone then pulled off the wire, manipulated it, and put it back on, so it proves authentication and integrity. We have the original IP header, the TCP section, and the payload. This is a data packet. What we're doing is adding an authentication header. No encryption as the AH only offers integrity, so it proves authentication and integrity. If we want to encrypt that data, then we're going to need something referred to as the encapsulating secure payload, or ESP. That provides also confidentiality, along with optional integrity checking, so it adds a header, a trailer, and an integrity check value, or an ICV, so that works as such. So

now we have that data packet, the original header, we're going to add in an ESP header, the encapsulating secure payload, TCP is the transport protocol, the actual payload, which is the data that we're sending, it's going to an ESP trailer and ESP authentication, so that's going to give us a fully secure data pack as it traverses over that unsecure medium, and that's encrypted, which provides data confidentiality.

VPN Concentrator

We've talked about VPN several times before, but in this specific instance, we're talking about a VPN concentrator, and that has the ability to create large numbers of VPN tunnels. It's not just a single tunnel, a single point to point. A concentrator can do numerous tunnels, typically used for site-to-site architectures. In this example here, we have a site-to-site VPN, and we have two networks? We have a secure network on one side, a secure network on the other side, and in that tunnel, we have multiple VPN connections going through that tunnel, because we have VPN routers that are concentrators on either side of that tunnel. Conversely, we have a remote access VPN where we have a single person, maybe a remote teleworker or a very small office where we have one person or a single tunnel going from that remote location into the corporate internet. You'll still have a VPN concentrator on the one side, but then you have an ISP being used from the guest or the host or the small office on the other side, and they'll be going through that VPN tunnel. It's a concentrator, because even though that specific location may only have one tunnel going through, you may have multiple remote locations. So it has the ability to create multiple tunnels at once.

Chapter 5 Network Access Control, Port Security & Loop Protection

NAC or Network Access Control or Network Admission Control, depending upon, where you read or what context it's being used in, it refers to a set of policies that define a minimal set of requirements each device must have before being allowed on the network. We want to make sure that if someone pulls out their laptop and tries to connect to our network, it's going to check and say, hey, do you have this level of firmware, do you have this level of virus or anti-virus patching, do you have, all these different required security patches maybe for the OS, and if you don't, well, we're not going to let you on the network, so it does a check before it allows that access. This becomes more and more important as BYO devices become prevalent within the environment, people bring their own laptops or their own mobile phones. A couple applications that can help with that, I'm just giving you some examples, Good Messaging, Mobile Iron, and Airwatch are three mobile device management tools, or MDMs, that allow us to make sure that those devices are in compliance before they're allowed to connect to the network. Devices can be denied access, or they can be placed in what's called a secure zone until those minimum requirements are met. It may give them a cordoned-off area and says, you can connect to our network in this little safe space, and from there you can download the required patches or the required security fixes, applications, and until you do that, you can't go anywhere else. It gives them a chance to remediate the issue. Once those things are done, it will check again, and if they meet compliance, then they're allowed onto the network. Network Access Control can also be implemented in one of three ways. We have what's called a permanent agent, and that's persistent, that's persistently installed on the host device, and runs continuously. From an enterprise perspective, this is the best option, because we know for a fact that it's installed on that device we can tell what's going on all the time. From the end user perspective, they may or may not want that, especially if it's a BYO device. They may say, I don't want someone snooping on my device or potentially, pulling data off that I don't know about. Well, that's a choice you have to make within your own environment, but permanent agents are typically preferred at an enterprise level. And then we have a dissolvable agent. This is one that runs in a portal. A user will connect, it will download the agent, and it's going to run once. It will then disappear. If they need to use it again, it can be either re-downloaded or it can be fired back up again, but it doesn't run continuously in the background. Then we have agentless, which can come in a few different forms. In this instance, it's embedded within Active Directory, and that NAC code verifies that the host complies with access policies, typically when they join a domain, when they log on or when they log off. Normally it will trigger and will run or scan that device when one of those three things happen.

In-band vs. Out-of-band Management
Network devices can be managed and access both in-band and also out-of-band, depending upon preference, architectural decisions or limitations. In-band means traffic can be examined in real time, so it means we're accessing via the production network typically. Access is provided over common protocols, Telnet or SSH. And if we have an opportunity or a choice between Telnet and SSH, we should always choose SSH. Telnet is not encrypted, so therefore not secure, whereas SSH is an encrypted connection. Also with in-band, we're closer to the point of entry into the network,

typically. Also less to manage and reconfigure when inserting into the network. We don't have to do a lot of rerouting or trying to move traffic around to access those devices out-of-band. Conversely, out-of-band, more reactive in nature versus real time, so we're not monitoring that traffic in real time. It has to go up to some external or out-of-band management device or some type of analytic device to monitor that traffic - not in real time. It also requires additional design or redesign to enter into or insert into the network and requires additional upstream provider components to provide similar security. The in-band is going to be less intrusive, less to manage and less to reconfigure. You get the idea. If we have the option between both, in-band's going to be less work; however, if the primary network goes down, our access goes down. So out-of-band gives us another way to access those devices. If we can't access the device via our primary or production network, we still have that access out-of-band, which gives us remote functionality. We don't have to drive to the data center or drive to wherever that location or that device is located, saving us time and effort. Then the last on our list is that endpoint compliance is not as granular, meaning client traffic is sent to a common VLAN. As an example, when clients enter our network and they want to be quarantined or checked for compliance, they're going to be sent to a common VLAN versus monitored in quarantine real time and separated from other clients entering the network. For a little more detail on in-band access control, here we have a client that is accessing an access switch. That access switch contains such things as a Policy Enforcement Point, or a PEP, an authenticator, and a Policy Decision Point. This is for granted access, network access control, to our local area network. When we're doing in-band, that functionality is typically incorporated into the switch or some other device that's placed inline on our production network. To access the switch to go through this decision making process, the Policy Enforcement Point, the authenticator, and the Decision Point, it decides, does that client meet our specifications? Are they allowed to access the LAN? If that were an out-of-band process, then it would have to go out to some external device outside of our typical network, traffic would have to be rerouted, a client may get a different IP address while they're being authenticated, and then rerouted back onto the corporate LAN once they're authenticated. It adds some additional overhead and some architectural designs, just something to keep in mind. It's in our best interest if we had the opportunity to have both in-band and out-of-band management and access. If for some reason our primary network or our production network goes down, we still have access to those devices. Another example of out-of-band access will be an out-of-band NIC, so a separate interface for management networks, whether that is a management VLAN or a separate physical network. It's used for lights out management. That way, we can monitor and audit or log. We can also use the patch, install operating systems or troubleshoot a host that is offline and won't boot. Typically, we can remote into a desktop or a server using RDP or some type of remote connection software. But if that actual device won't boot or is not operational, and therefore the remote desktop software or the remote control software is not functioning, we're dead in the water. If we have an out-of-band NIC that has a lights out functionality or lights out feature, we can still access as if we're sitting at that PC or at that server. That gives us the opportunity to manage, patch, reboot, even when the server at the OS level is down. It saves us a trip to the data center.

Port Security and 802.1x

The next concept I want to talk about is about port security in 802.1x - securing physical access to the network. What do I mean by that? Well, we want to control the ability of someone to just walk into our environment, whether it be at a kiosk or retail store or a library or a school, or even within our corporate environment, we don't want necessarily someone to be able to walk up, pull out their laptop, pull out a Cat 5 cable, plug it into the wall and get access to our network. One way we can do that is through something called port security. This is particularly applicable to things like kiosks, and schools, and libraries, but not necessarily throughout an entire environment as it becomes a little bit unwieldy at that point, but for specialized situations that we want to control specific access to specific ports, port security is definitely a good fit. What we can do is configure a switch so that it only learns one MAC address per port We can keep attackers from sending multiple fake addresses, someone can't pull out their laptop, plug in and then just start bombarding our network with fake MAC addresses, because, if you recall, when we have our devices and it connects to a switch, that very first time it does, it goes out and tries to get an IP address via DHCP, or it may have one hard-coded. It's going to try also to ARP for some resources. It might go to DNS, it might go to whatever the case might be, trying to resolve a URL. Whatever action is taking place, it's going to put datagrams or data packets onto the network. As soon as it does that, the MAC address of that device is attached to that datagram, and then it gets recorded within that switch, whatever switchport it's connecting to. The switch, which is a Layer 2 device, will learn or memorize the MAC address and associate it with that port, and so the switch will learn over time all of the devices that are connected to it, what MAC addresses are associated with which ports, so that way when information comes in, it knows what port to send that information out of. It's a very directed process. Broadcasts will go out of all ports, but if there is traffic between PC 1 and PC 2, as an example, PC 1 is connected to Port 1, PC 2 is connected to, say, Port 10 in this example, it will only go in Port 1 and only out of Port 10, so that way it keeps things more secure. However, we have malicious individuals or malicious activity that can take place, where someone could flood a specific port and overrun the MAC table on that switch and bring it down. By setting port security and allowing only certain MAC addresses, or in this case one MAC address per port, we negate that ability for someone to do that type of activity. We can also use that in conjunction with something called 802.1x to strengthen security at the wall jack, with school settings as an example, or a kiosk. We have something called 802.1x authentication, which is EAPOL, or Extensible Authentication Access Protocol over LAN, or local area network. That Extensible Authentication Access Protocol gives us the ability to say, when somebody connects to our wall jack, we're not going to allow them to communicate until they authenticate with the network. In this example, they're going to authenticate with something referred to as a RADIUS server, it's an authentication server. In this schema it's a multi-part process. The client in this case is referred to as a supplicant. The client is going to initiate a request, they're going to plug into a wall jack, let's say, as an example, they take out their laptop, and they plug it into the jack. They're going to say, can I communicate, can I get an IP address. The switch is going to say, no way, not until you authenticate. It will only allow EAPOL traffic to pass through that port. It will send it off to the authentication server, all of these things have to be configured in place so that this process takes place properly, but once it's set up, that port will not be activated until the authentication process is complete. The supplicant will send information over to the switch. The switch will then forward it on to the authentication server. Once that authentication server validates, once the credentials are validated and verified, in other words, the client is authenticated, the authentication server sends that information back and says, yes, you can communicate. The port is wide open, and of course the supplicant, or the client in this case, can communicate on the network.

Loop Protection and Flood Guards

When we're discussing ensuring availability on our network, another concept that you need to be familiar with is loop protection and flood guards. We talked about securing physical access to the network. We want to make sure that the network is available for someone to securely access. By ensuring availability via flood guards and loop protection, we have a couple concepts we need to talk about. Loop protection is a Layer 3 context. Remember, Layer 3 deals with IP routing and with the network. It's the network layer of the OSI model, and routers live with this layer. Layer 3 deals with, routing IP packets across the network. As those IP packets travel, every time they cross over a router or every time they hop, they decrement with something called a TTL, or a Time to Live. Every time they cross over a router, that TTL will decrement by one. An IP packet, has a finite lifespan to live on the network. If it lives too long, then the packet gets dropped. In other words, if it doesn't reach its destination in a certain amount of time or a certain number of hops, it gets dropped. And that's specifically designed to prevent packets from just endlessly looping around the network. As an example, we have a couple networks separated by some routers, and in a normal fashion, the packet will just traverse those routers. Every time it crosses over, it decrements by one. The TTL will decrement. The routers know how to get from point A to point B. The packet goes from one network to the other. In a misconfigured situation, however, we have that packet, it would traverse the network, and it would just loop endlessly. If it were to do that and just loop forever, we would have a flood, and it would bring the network down. If the routers aren't configured properly, and they don't exactly know where to send the packet, router A thinks it should go here, router B thinks it should go somewhere else, it's going to get in a looping scenario. And if we didn't have that TTL in place, the Time to Live, every time it crosses over one of those routers it decrements, if that weren't in place, that packet would loop endlessly forever. And then as the next packet were to come onto the network, there'd be no room left. There'd be no bandwidth. As you can imagine, very quickly, that network would get overrun. By having that TTL in place, we negate that scenario from occurring.

Chapter 6 Spanning Tree, DHCP Snooping & MAC Filtering

In the layer 2 space, we don't have the TTL benefit. We don't have the ability to decrement. Layer 2 of the OSI model deals with things like switches and bridges. In layer 2, we have something referred to as a Spanning Tree Protocol, or STP. This accomplishes the same thing as a loop protection. It just does it in a different fashion. Spanning Tree Protocol is typically unable to prevent layer 2 loops, so switches can also prevent ports from flooding the network by clamping down once broadcasts hit a certain percentage. As an example, we have two switches. We have information that needs to pass from point A to point B. But if we have switches, which are multi-port bridges, and information comes in one port, goes out another, if the switch doesn't know exactly which port to send it out of, you can get in a looping situation. If switch A sent out Fa0/1 to switch B Fa0/1, and then switch B sent Fa02 out to switch A's Fa0/2, you can just see, we get in this looping fashion. What we have is the concept of an election. That election takes place between things called a root bridge, a designated bridge, and a root port. The root bridge is the center of the network. The designated bridges or the designated bridge are forwarders. They're going to send data to the root bridge, and then the root port is the port that sends data toward the root bridge. And if we didn't have the ability to shut down the non-necessary ports, we would just get loops all over the place. It doesn't mean those other paths aren't available. It just means they're not active. If we have a failover situation where that path becomes inactive or fails, the switches would then failover and activate those ports. It might take a few seconds, maybe 15 to 20 seconds potentially, depending upon the size of the network. But, a certain amount of time for all those things to synchronize and go through this process until all the other paths come up. But the network would, as you can imagine, it would heal itself. It gives us the ability to clamp down and not have these looping situations, but it doesn't take those other ports out of play. It just puts them in a non-active state. If it identifies that something needs to be brought up, maybe another port is down, it will bring those ports back up. It might take a little bit to converge so that everyone knows about the path so that all the switches know how the network is laid out. But once those ports come back up, the network will heal itself. At any one point in time, we only want one path from point A to point B., incidentally, root bridges are designated by the lowest MAC address, typically. As you can imagine, the lowest MAC address is going to be more than likely the oldest device on your network. You don't want to necessarily let the automatic process take place and allow that root bridge to be elected automatically because it's more than likely going to be the oldest device, and you might have, the least capability on that device. By manually selecting the root bridge, you can pick perhaps a more beefy switch or a newer piece of equipment so that we can ensure just a higher level of stability within the network.

DHCP Snooping

DHCP snooping sounds like that might be something an attacker or a bad actor might do, but DHCP snooping is a layer 2 security technology that monitors for rogue DHCP servers. What we're talking about is an actor will be on the opposite end of this specific technology. They would try to install or implement a DHCP server, a rogue DHCP server that hands out IP addresses, binding that MAC address to an IP address and giving them the ability to potentially compromise that system. Switches can be configured to prevent malicious or malformed DHCP packets. You can in essence turn that on so that if it detects malformed packets or malicious packets or it's coming from a server that's not a trusted or already configured or preconfigured DHCP server, then it would drop that packet. When a violation is detected, the event will be logged and alerts should be generated for further follow up or action, security personnel should be alerted and they should follow that up to see hey, what's going on on the network? Why is there a rogue DHCP server? Why is there someone that we don't know about trying to hand out DHCP packets?

MAC Filtering

MAC filtering, or Media Access Control filtering predefines which Media Access Control addresses can connect to a router or an access point. MAC addresses reside at layer 2 of the OSI model, and it's a 48-bit hex number that's burned into the NIC, or the network interface card. That won't prevent a skilled hacker from spoofing an allowed MAC address. A hacker with even a modest amount of skills and the toolsets can monitor or sniff the wire, understand what MAC addresses are valid, and then spoof the MAC address to allow themselves onto the network. With regard to MAC filtering, here we have a copy of Wireshark, and we're capturing packets on the network. From there, we can expand that out and dig down and see the MAC addresses of hosts communicating on the network. MAC addresses are very easy to spoof. Tools like Kali Linux, which we talked about briefly, and Wireshark can allow an attacker to scan a network and discover valid MAC addresses. Using things like aireplay-ng or aircrack-ng, we can send what's called deassociation packets to the client and then connect in that clients place. These tools exist. It's not something that you have to be particularly skilled for. If you have the distribution of Linux, Kali Linux, in this case, a lot of these tools are already built in, or you can go out to the web and download these tools. These things can be done manually or even faster via scripts. It can take literally a matter of seconds to sniff the wire, grab a valid MAC address, send a deassociation packet, reconnect as that client, and then you're on the network. The takeaway being, don't develop that false sense of security and think, hey, I have MAC filtering in place. Only authorized clients can connect. Well, as we see, that's very easy to bypass. Always remember the mantra of defense in depth. We have to place multiple locks on the door so that if they are able to bypass one is to have another and then another and another to get through. Hopefully with enough locks on the door that we can make enough noise that we can hear them trying to come in or they'll say this is too difficult and then move on to somewhere else. In summary, we talked about load balancing, we talked about network segmentation, virtual private networks. We talked about DNS, along with network access control, or NAC. Also talked about out-of-band management and also port security.

Chapter 7 Access Control Lists & Route Security

In this chapter we'll start off with network appliances. We'll talk about access control lists, or ACLs, along with route security. We'll talk about quality of service along with implications of IPv6, port spanning and port mirroring, along with port taps. We'll also talk about monitoring services and then file integrity monitors. First, let's talk about the concept of a jump server. A jump server is a server that's used to connect to devices in remote networks, typically used to perform admin tasks in a network with limited connectivity. What do I mean by that? Well, there might be issues with firewalls, with bandwidth, you may have a remote office or an area of your existing network, or your local network that you can't get to very easily. You may have firewalls in place that will block a lot of the tools that you may need to do work in that subnet, but normally, you can remote into a server, you can open up the ports to allow remote connectivity, an RDP session, or a Citrix session, or open up some type of VDI desktop, in that specific subnet, and then you can do all your things local in that subnet. So, the only thing it's passing through the firewall is your remote connectivity traffic. Everything else is taking place as if you were sitting in that subnet. The jump server allows you to perform those tasks without having to worry about punching holes in the firewall, and then additionally, from an admin's perspective, a lot of times when you have like vendors come in, or you're doing some type of work, patching or upgrading, you don't want to necessarily tie up the admin's workstation or laptop doing those remote tasks, especially when it comes to maintenance work or patching. By utilizing a jump server, you can have a vendor or someone you're working with also remote into that server, and they can work off that local server rather than the admin's workstation, or the admin's laptop. It serves a dual purpose and allows connectivity, but it also allows you to perform tasks without tying up your workstation. Some security risks will exist potentially if it's not configured and maintained, if it's bridging networks? If you have a jump server that's sitting between two networks, which is typically not good, a dual-homed machine, typically that's going to be a no-no, but if the jump server is maintained correctly, if it's patched properly, if it's maintained just like any other server on your network, then you should be in pretty good shape, but just understand that security risks do exist. If it's a remote office, and it's something that you forget about, and you don't patch, and you don't maintain regularly, well, that's going to pose potentially a security risk, so keep those things in mind.

Proxies

Let's talk about proxies and the difference between a forward and a reverse proxy. As far as forward proxies are concerned, which is what we're typically used to, a forward proxy normally have a number of clients that are trying to access some type of internet resource. What they're going to do is forward the requests to the proxy. The proxy then goes to the internet out to the external resources. What it does is potentially speed up access or the appearance of speeding up access for clients internal to the network and everyone attaching to the proxy. If someone else is already contacted that resource previously and that content has not yet expired on the proxy, well then the client will retrieve most if not all of that information from the proxy rather than going out to the actual resource. Some content is dynamic. Some things need to be refreshed constantly. Not everything will be retrieved from the proxy potentially. Again, it depends upon the resource being accessed. But it does a few things.

It speeds up or potentially speeds up the access, but it can also act as a network address translation or a NAT device and hide the actual IP addresses or the internal IP addresses of the clients inside the network from external resources. So from any one of the websites that they see on the web servers, what they see is a request coming from the proxy server. They never see the actual internal clients requesting that access. They'll see the public-facing IP address of the proxy server, but not the internal IP addresses of the resources on that internal network. Conversely, there's something referred to as a reverse proxy, otherwise known sometimes as a load balancer. We have external resources, clients from the outside, wanting to connect to some internal resource, whether that be a web server or a database server. We have all the external clients coming in from the internet. We're going to hit the reverse proxy or load balancer. This could be one server. It could be a pool of servers. What it does is then take that request and then forward it on to the appropriate resource. It could be four servers. It could be 40. It could be 400. It just depends upon the size of the network and the resources. The reverse proxy or the load balancer will then take those incoming requests and distribute that request onto the available resources, and it will do so in a very programmatic fashion. Some load balancers or reverse proxies are more advanced than others. Some do it in more of a round-robin fashion where it just distributes the load across one server, then the next, then the next. Others have advanced algorithms where they'll be able to tell dynamically which server is least busy and will forward the request to that resource. Next, we have something referred to as a transparent proxy. A transparent proxy is an intermediary system that typically sits between a user and a content provider. It can be multi-purpose as well. It can do caching. It can do filtering, which is content filtering or application filtering, websites or services. It can allow or deny based upon type of content or a specific type of website or a service. And it can also provide gateway functionality, which is rule based, typically requiring registration or user acceptance. A lot of times in public spaces, coffee shops, you'll see these captive portals, that are, in effect, a gateway, a transparent proxy, that requires a user to register in some fashion, maybe a username, or at least accept some type of end user agreement to provide access. The transparent proxy gets its name from the fact that an end user doesn't have to configure anything. Typically, with a proxy, a user will configure something within their browse or to point to a proxy server. With a transparent proxy, there is no configuration needed. As soon as that user attaches to the network, whether it be Wi-Fi, the requests are automatically intercepted by that transparent proxy, and then some type of application filtering or content filtering is applied, or the user's prompted to register or accept some type of end user agreement before they access the network.

Web Security Gateways
Security gateways or a proxy server with advanced features, such things as virus scanning, it could prevent connections to inappropriate sites like peer-to-peer networks or file sharing sites, data loss prevention, which is a big thing nowdays, so if it determines or it can sense, does this communication contain nine digits maybe with two dashes, maybe a social security number, or does it contain 16 digits for a credit card number or, so it can identify different types of traffic and block that from escaping the network. Or you can block connections to inappropriate sites, peer-to-peer, file sharing, dropbox, box.net. A lot of users, even in the corporate environment, will use these types of services like Dropbox to

share files back and forth, primarily because it's easy, but the downside of that is, there is no governance around that? A lot of companies want to restrict access to those types of sites so they can much more tightly control what types of data is leaving their network. You can also block things like ActiveX controls, Java applets, third-party cookies, malicious websites have a lot less chance of infecting or doing damage in a corporate environment if those attack vectors are mitigated. Activex control, Java applets, a lot of times malware or misbehaving sites utilize or leverage those specific technologies to inflict harm on users. It can also enable granular access to websites so that you can access the website, but maybe not all of the website? In other words, you could access LinkedIn, for instance, but not allow someone to do a job search or you could allow people to access Facebook, but prohibit them from posting content or playing games.

Chapter 8 Intrusion Detection and Prevention

The next thing is going to be intrusion detection and prevention. This is another security concept. We have an IDS and an IPS, NIDS and NIPS. Network intrusion detection system or prevention systems vary a little bit in how they operate. There is a lot of commonality, but then as far as the lack of action that they take, this differentiates the two. They can be used to log alert or take action when suspicious activity occurs on the network. Depending upon how they are configured, they can either simply detect that there is activity taking place and I'll go ahead and log it, or they could take action and say, as soon as this happens, do A, B, and C. They may reset a TCP connection, they may block a port, they may kick off some type of a forensic data capturing activity We have active systems that can take action to prevent an attack, or we have passive systems that simply record and perhaps utilize that data for later analysis. In terms of the difference between IDS and IPS, the network part aside, just generally speaking, we have intrusion detection systems and intrusion prevention systems. IDS has been around for quite a while, fairly common, and it's easy or relatively easy to set up, but as you may gather from what we've talked about already, it simply logs, alerts, and events, so it detects the intrusion, it doesn't necessarily do anything with it, it may alert an administrator or something, but it's not going to kick off any preventative measures. So it allows for a reactive response and further research into malicious or suspicious activity. An IPS, or an intrusion prevention system, is a newer platform, it's been around for the last few years, but it enables prevention. Such as perhaps blocking an IP address, blocking a port, resetting TCP connections, their TCP/IP connections, those types of things. It takes some type of preventive measure to shut down that communication or shut down that action so that malicious activity is halted in its tracks. The downside with an intrusion prevention system is you could have a false positive that could ultimately block legitimate traffic. Worst case scenario, let's just say, for example, you have an IPS set up, and if it detects malicious activity, go ahead and block port 80 for 5 minutes. Well, you could have legitimate traffic that comes in, maybe just a heavier than normal workload that comes in that IPS would falsely identify that as malicious traffic when it's not, shuts down the internet traffic over port 80 shuts that down for 5 minutes, well, you've just created a Denial of Service against yourself. Those things have to be set up with care, as that they do have the potential for false positives, but it also gives you the ability to prevent things, when in fact, you do have malicious activity taking place. The different components of intrusion prevention and detection systems; I'm going to go through a list but this is more just for your informational purposes than anything, but we have a couple components that you need to be aware of. We have alerts. an alert is a message generated from something called an analyzer and the analyzer indicates anything that it may deem as interesting traffic or an interesting event has occurred, so that alert might be an email, that alert might be a pop up on a screen. In some form or fashion, it's going to alert us that something has occurred. The analyzer processes data collected from one or more sensors. The sensor collects data or triggers data and then it looks for suspicious activity and the analyzer is going to take that data and look for what it deems to be suspicious or malicious activity, it could be deterministic, or it could be rule-based. We could just say, hey, if it meets this signature, than it's probably malicious, go ahead and fire off some type of alert or some type of action. The data source itself is the raw data that's being analyzed. That could be log files, it could be audit logs, system logs, network traffic itself, it just depends. It depends on the system and it depends upon how it's configured. Then we have something called an event. An event is an indication, that something suspicious has occurred, it could be malicious, it could be suspicious, it could be a false positive, but in some fashion, the system has determined that this needs further investigation, so that can trigger an alert or notification. Or if it's confirmed and it is malicious activity, then that event would become an incident. Next we have a component called a manager, and the manager is the intrusion detection system console, that's the piece of software that comes up on your screen and that's what you use to manage the system. Next is a notification, which is the process by which the operator, which is someone who is working the system here, they are alerted to an event or an incident. The operator, as I said as a user, it could be an admin, someone that's responsible for that intrusion detection system. They're actively working the system. They don't necessarily need to be sitting there. They could be alerted remotely, email, but there is someone that's responsible for the operation of that system. And then the sensor is a primary data collection point for that intrusion detection system, or the IDS. A sensor could be a device driver, it could be baked into a piece of firmware on a system, or it could be a separate physical device that's attached to a network that collects data, so it could be a separate device collecting data and then processing that in real time.

IDS/IPS Component Workflow
If we look at the components of an IDS system and how they all fit together, it may make a little more sense. We have a data source, we have a couple sensors, we have the

analyzer, the active response and then a manager, and then the administrator and the operator. There are security policies that will tie all of this together. The security policies dictate what action is taken. The administrator and the operator may also analyze some of this data for trending and reporting purposes. And an active response could trigger some type of action, whether it be shutting down a port or whether it be resetting connections. The data source has some type of activity, the sensors will pick up on that, and it will generate an event. That event goes to the analyzer to be analyzed, is this something that I need to be worrying about, and if it is, it generates an alert to the manager or the management console. That console sends a notification to the operator or the administrator, depending upon, who's who, that can be used for trending or reporting purposes only. We just want to know about it, we're not going to do anything at this point. Or it could send off an active response and say, wait a minute, we need to do something here, that's when it triggers the shutting down of a port or resetting of a connection.

Four Approaches to IDS

There are four approaches that I want you to know about as far as IDS systems are concerned. We have behavior-based detection. That's variations of behavior, increased traffic, policy violations, something that's just out of the norm. We have signature-based IDS systems, and that's going to use attack signatures and audit trails. In other words, look for traffic that looks like it might be IP spoofing or might be cross-site injection, or it might be somebody hammering, doing a port scan on our external firewalls. It could be a thousand different things, but there are going to be signatures that it's going to be looking for. They're not necessarily as robust has some of the other systems because if the signature doesn't exist or if it's a brand new, let's say, for instance, a zero-day exploit or a zero-day threat, meaning there is no signature defined yet, then those things are vulnerable to be bypassed. We have anomaly detection IDS systems, and, again, similar to behavior based in that it learns what's normal, then it looks for deviations from that baseline. In this instance, over time it's going to learn, 30% workload is normal for this specific segment. All of a sudden, if it's 60 or 70% above workload, all of a sudden we've got a ton of IP connections coming in, well, that's not normal. Go ahead and kick off some type of trigger or some type of an alert. It just depends upon what's normal for that specific environment. What's normal for one may not be normal for another. Then we have heuristic IDS, and that's going to utilize algorithms to analyze data traffic as it passes through. It's not signature based in that it has a certain set of parameters that it looks for. It has some type of internal algorithm that's going to depend upon the system so it will vary from place to place or from system to system, but it's going to use that algorithm to analyze the traffic as it passes through the system in real time and then make a determination at that point.

Network-based IDS
When you have network-based IDS systems, you can place those in a couple different places within the network. You can place them in front of your firewall, you could place them behind your firewall, or you could do both. For example, if I have an IDS system placed in front of the firewall. People from the internet are trying to get into my network, whether it's web servers or there's some type of a public-facing component that they can access. Rather than have them hit the firewall first, and then if they pass the muster, and they pass through the firewall, then if I hit the

IDS system and I start analyzing traffic, well that's great, I have a reduction in the amount of stuff I have to analyze, but I don't get a good indication or a good idea of potentially who's banging against the firewall, who's potentially trying to initiate some type of an attack. Conversely, if I do what I have here in the picture and I have the IDS system placed in front of the firewall, well, I'm going to get a lot more traffic to analyze, but I'm also going to get a better indication of attacks against that firewall. If you want to look at the best of both worlds, you would place an IDS system in front of your firewall and behind. That way you get a good indication of everything that's banging against the firewall. Some gets in, some doesn't. Once it passes through the firewall, then you have a secondary IDS system that can dig deeper and look for variations in policy or anomalies, depending upon the type of system. that's going to write out to some type of an event data database, and there's lots of different ones out there, and then typically, that's going to pass those types of things, once it has a trigger for an alert or notification, up to the network operations center, or a NOC, depending upon the size of the environment, you may or may not have a NOC in place, or you may use a third party for that purpose. But then the NOC is going to either take some type of remediation immediately, they may have some steps, they have some NOC analysts that will say, hey, if this happens, do ABC. Or they may page out a person who's on call, if it's after hours, or engage a specific team to come in and take some action. It simply just depends upon the size of the company.

Security Device Placement
When we're talking about security device placement, we have things like sensors, collectors, correlation engines, filters, proxies, firewalls, VPN concentrators, SSL

accelerators, distributed denial-of-service mitigators, aggregation switches, and taps and port mirrors. I'm just calling all of these things out you're aware of what they are and understand that any of these things, for the most part, can be placed in various places within the network. They could be placed internally. They could be placed on the perimeter. They could be placed in a DMZ on a firewall in either location or in multiple locations. In the case of sensors, as an example, you may have sensors all throughout the network on many devices, both internal and external, and they may all feedback to your intrusion detection or prevention system to let you know if somebody is trying to get into the network in some fashion or people are logging in when they're not supposed to, doing something that they're not authorized to do so. Collectors are along the same lines. Sensors and collectors, correlation engines, they all take that information and they correlate across multiple devices to show you a common timeline to help identify trends. Filters, proxies and firewalls, are typically going to go on the perimeters. They will filter content, they'll filter access requests. Proxies, as we know, will aggregate requests internally. And then that way, the person requesting a website or some resource internally if someone else just recently requested the same thing doesn't have to go out to the internet to that device. I can pull it from the proxy. Firewalls, we know what a firewall does. It blocks based on port or protocol or some type of application and only allows things through that we want to allow through. VPN concentrators, we talked about. SSL accelerators or load balancers can again be placed in front of say a web server, could be placed in front of an application server, and they can be spun up dynamically if we're using something like SDN so that we can add additional resources when we need them. Same thing with DDoS mitigators - it can detect automatically when we're having a denial-of-service attack and it can shut down ports or take some type of response to mitigate that threat. Aggregation switches will aggregate data from smaller switches, you'll have a small network and an aggregation switch that will combine a number of small networks. They could be placed anywhere throughout the network, depending upon how your network is architected, whether it's a mesh, a full mesh, a core edge. Then we have taps and port mirrors. And what it does is place that switch or that port in what's called promiscuous mode. That way you can mirror the traffic on another port, and typically that's done from mirroring or auditing or forensic investigations you can mirror all the traffic on a specific port and then analyze that without affecting the traffic on the port itself.

Chapter 9 Firewalls & Unified Threat Management

What's the actual purpose of firewalls? Well, a firewall is, generally speaking, designed to isolate one network from another. It can be hardware or it can be software based. It can be either. It can be a standalone device, or it can be an integrated device integrated into some other equipment, in other words, routers or switches. Whether you're a small office or a home office, you may have a small Netgear or Linksys or even a Cisco router, that combines a lot of functionality together. You can have a firewall. It can do NAT, or Network Address Translation, and, of course, routing functionality as well, perhaps even switching. It just depends on the size of the network, how specific you want to get. There are different devices that can perform very specific functions, or there are integrated devices that can perform a lot of different functions together. If we have a diagram of outside users outside of the firewall, and you see the firewall denoted by a brick wall. And, incidentally, the term firewall historically came from buildings that were built very close to one another, and in order to prevent fire from jumping from one building to another when they were very close together, think like row homes, for instance, they would build these brick walls in between these different buildings to prevent that fire from jumping from one to the other. That brick wall would act as a firewall, to prevent fire from jumping from one building to the other. The same concept is carried over here. And that's why you typically see a firewall being illustrated as a brick wall. As you can then imagine, firewalls are typically used to block or limit outside traffic from entering a network. Whether it's corporate, medium-sized office, small office, or a home office, they all serve pretty much the same types of functions. However, firewalls can also be placed internally, inside of a network to segment one area from another. For instance, you may have a large corporate environment that has different areas that you don't necessarily want them to communicate, or they shouldn't communicate, from one to the other very easily. You can punch holes in the firewall to allowed traffic. But, generally speaking, these things are cordoned off from one another. For instance, if you have a PCI Secure zone, like say you have a very large enterprise that has some typical day-to-day workers, and you may have an R&D department, you may have an accounting department, a finance department, PCI Secure means it contains credit card information and some type of personally identifiable information. You want to have that information cordoned off from the rest of the network. The finance folks don't necessarily talk to the R&D or maybe the graphics department, just to prevent internal browsing of those resources. A firewall can be put into place between those segments on your internal network as well. It's important to understand, and just to recap very quickly hardware vs. software, firewalls can either be hardware or software based. They can be standalone devices or integrated into other devices, like routers and switches. Even if it is a hardware-based solution, it's still going to contain software, you can't just run it on hardware by itself. There has to be some software running behind the scenes. You can drop it onto a server and have that server function providing firewall functionality. Or it can be a separate, standalone piece of hardware. However, that hardware is still going to contain software or firmware. What are some types of firewalls? Well, we have packet filtering firewalls, and packet filtering firewalls allow or block traffic based upon a specific port, HTTP traffic as an example, web traffic that typically comes in over port 80. FTP, or File Transport Protocol, that's generated on port 21 typically. You can configure the firewall to allow web traffic but don't allow FTP traffic or allow DNS but don't allow NetBIOS or time lookups or whatever the case might be. You can break it down by port by port by port and get very specific, get very granular. Doing it based just on port, there's not a lot of intelligence there. It just simply looks at the port, and then it will either allow or block the traffic at that point. Next, we have proxy firewalls. a proxy firewall is going to be dual homed, which means it's going to have two network interfaces, typically one on each network or on separate networks. It's going to segment internal users from the outside world, and it can mask the IP address using something called NAT, or Network Address Translation. That gives an added layer of security because the outside world won't know who is communicating. All they'll see is the address of the proxy firewall. And a proxy can also cache requests to improve perceived speed. If you have multiple users as an example that are accessing the same website, well, the first person to access that website or that URL will go out and pull it down from the web or from whatever resource it's getting it from. Subsequent requests, as long as that information is still sitting in the cache on that proxy server, so the next user goes out to that same web resource? Instead of going out to the web out to whatever resource they're getting it from, they'll get it directly from the proxy server, from the cache. It gives the perception that things are faster and that your network is all of a sudden more responsive. The next type of firewall is something referred to as a stateful packet inspection firewall, or SPI. An SPI firewall examines the packets and keeps the packet table of every communication channel. So, in other words, it has more intelligence than a simple packet filtering firewall, and it does a deeper dive, examines what's inside. SPI tracks the entire conversation, so it gives you an increased level of

-

security because it only allows packets from known active connections. In other words, if someone's trying to spoof or jump into the middle of a connection or a conversation, an SPI firewall understands that. They say, hey, wait a minute. I don't know who this is from. I haven't seen this before. This is in the middle of a conversation. There's no initiation. There's no back and forth to establish that connection. This just came out of here, so I'm going to drop that. It drops the packet. It gives you that added layer of security. It's better than simple packet filtering, which only looks at the current packet. However, it's possible to attack by overloading that State Table. As you go through all of these different types of routers and switches and pretty much any type of infrastructure or equipment in our network, just understand that nothing is foolproof. There's always going to be a way, there are always going to be hackers that are trying to somehow penetrate that device, crash it, and get elevated privileges. Nothing's foolproof. That's while we're all employed and how we all eventually make the big bucks. The battle goes on and on and on. Check Point Software introduced the concept of a stateful inspection or stateful packet inspection firewall in the use of its FireWall-1 software, which was introduced in 1994. So, it's been around for quite a while.

Web Application Firewalls
A web application firewall differs from a network firewall in that it operates at the application layer of the OSI model. Web application firewalls, or WAF, operates at application layer 7 of the OSI model. That's, the application layer, and it's designed with very specific or granular rules for web servers. And these types of firewalls can analyze traffic to prevent typical web server type attacks, such as, SQL injection attacks, cross-site scripting attacks or forged HTTP

requests. Any time you see a website that has a form that you can fill in, very skilled hackers, can craft either a cross-site scripting or SQL injection attacks, and they'll write SQL code that they'll use as the code in the form. It may ask you for your name, as an example, on a web form. Well, instead of putting in your name, the hacker will try to put in some type of long SQL code, some SQL query, and if it's formed correctly, it can crash that server. If the server's not protected against that, if it doesn't sanitize that input properly, then it can initiate some type of SQL query on the back end and perhaps crash that web server or crash the website, return some type of information, or even give some type of increased elevated privileges to the server. That's why these types of firewalls are in place, to understand these things as they come in in real time, analyze what's happening, and shut it down before it has a chance to do any harm., some well-known web application firewall vendors, just for your own knowledge, are things like Cisco, Citrix, Barracuda Networks, F5, and eEye. There are probably 30 or 40 more well-known vendors, but these are just a few to give you an example. If you wanted to dig a little bit further, these are just some of the major players in that space. As an example of a firewall, there's one from Check Point and they run the gamut from small firewall appliances, and it gets bigger and bigger as we go on. We have an entire chassis system with blades installed. They can range from very small software-based implementations, to small hardware-based implementations, and on up. Depending upon the size of the company and the enterprise, they can go from a few hundred dollars up to tens of thousands of dollars and more.

Unified Threat Management (UTM)
We've talked about VPNs, and firewalls, and intrusion detection and prevention systems, and all of these different

things as individual pieces of software or individual applications, but there's also something referred to as a UTM, or Unified Threat Management suite. That's a multipurpose suite of tools, and it does things such as firewalls, network intrusion detection or prevention systems, gateway anti-virus and anti-spam. It can provide VPN functionality, content filtering, load balancing, and also DLP or data loss prevention. These newer types of tools can pretty much do everything and take the place of all of these individual components. The advantage being you have a single pane of glass that you can look at all of these things, and you can correlate events across all these different applications much easier as well. It makes troubleshooting and also incident or event investigation much easier. If you haven't taken a look at these yet, I highly recommend that you look at some of the UTM software that's available and see if it fits within your environment. It could save you some time and effort in deployment, troubleshooting, patching, and also incident or event management.

Content Filters

A content filter can be hardware or software, and its purpose is to limit or restrict access to certain types of content. Inappropriate material, it could be malware, viruses, could be worms or trojans, and also things like spam or spyware. Misconfigured devices can overblock or allow content that should, in fact, be filtered. Additionally, these things can also violate censorship laws and regulations, depending upon your location or what you're filtering. Content filters are, in fact, valid. I'm not saying they shouldn't be there, just that an extra level of due diligence should be placed on them to make sure that they're configured properly, that they're blocking what they should be blocking, We don't develop that false sense of security.

Something else to keep in mind is that these things can be built into firewalls, UTM devices, or they could be standalone software. They don't necessarily have to be a specific separate device. They can be built into things like firewalls and Unified Threat Management, or UTM, devices.

Implicit Deny and ACLs
It's a firewall access control list, or an ACL, and it specifies what type of traffic is allowed. If it's not on the list, it denied access. Much like if you go into a club, or a restaurant, or some VIP event, and you walk up to the front door and the bouncer standing there all intimidating and you read off your name and say, hi, I'm so and so and he looks on his list and says, nope, you're not on the list. You're not getting in. Well, as frustrating as that might be, that's the same concept here. You walk up and your name is on the list, yeah, good for you. You can go in the front door, but if you're not explicitly allowed, then you're implicitly denied.

Route Security
Routers connect networks together and external routing protocols like BGP, or border gateway protocol, are inherently insecure. They were created years ago back when security wasn't a major concern. The main emphasis, at that point, was connectivity and getting everyone connected together, security and all the different types of threats that we face today weren't top of mind or even a consideration back then. What I'm talking about here with BGP specifically, it consists of autonomous systems, or AS groups, groups of systems that are managed by the same administrative system, Misconfigurations and deliberate route hijacks can result in outages. It's possible for someone to misconfigure their system and advertise routes that shouldn't be there and create outages. Typically, it's not necessarily a direct

attack, although it can be, but oftentimes the outages that have been experienced in the past have been a result of misconfiguration on the systems. It's beyond the scope of this book to dig deeply into this, but I do want to call your attention to the NIST publication, NIST SP1800-14, which proposes securing BGP and they talk about things like route origin, validation, and also resource public key infrastructure, or RPKI. What it does in a nutshell is put some security guardrails, on the BGP protocol and only allow secure or preauthorized systems to communicate with each other and not allow rogue systems or misconfigured systems to advertise out on the internet so we can prevent some of the things that we've seen in the past. Unfortunately, this has not been widely adopted yet, but the proposal is out there, so I would encourage you to read more deeply if you want some more information on that specific topic.

Quality of Service (QoS)
QoS, or quality of service is a set of technologies to ensure critical applications or services have a certain level of performance. We're talking about packets that are marked to identify service types. You may have audio, video. You may have critical applications like in a medical facility or finance applications or things that just need a guaranteed level of bandwidth. It will reserve bandwidth for those applications, and then everyone else gets what's left. So routers prioritize packets, and they'll create virtual queues to ensure bandwidth. They put the most important applications to the front of the line. You can almost think of it like as a fast pass, if you would. If you've ever been to Disney World or some of these amusement parks, you have the concept of a fast pass you don't have to wait in the line or wait in the queue. This is a very similar type of scenario where we will mark the packets that we want to push to the front of the

line. The things we're talking about with quality of service, things like bandwidth and latency, the amount of bandwidth or how big is the pipe that they can go through. Latency being how much delay is there. Packet loss usually resolving around the fact that the network is too congested and the packets time out, so we lose those packets. Then something referred to as jitter, which refers typically to audio and video, where we have packets that arrive out of sequence or out of order, and it can make audio calls sound scrambled or digitized or it can create skipping in streaming applications. By ensuring quality of service, we make sure those applications that need that level of performance get what they need. Then as more and more IoT devices, or Internet of Things devices, come online, having bandwidth for real-time monitoring, as an example, becomes more and more important. Things that need real-time performance, real-time monitoring, so we need to make quick action or quick decisions based upon that information, QoS comes in handy because it allows us to guarantee a certain level of performance for those applications and for those devices.

Implications of IPv6

Now let's talk about the implications of IPv6, or Internet Protocol version 6. So, IPv4 addresses, which have been around since the dawn of the internet, the mid-60s, late-60s, IP version 4 is a 32-bit addressing scheme. With that, roughly 4 billion IP addresses when it first came out, we thought, that's going to be more than we'll ever need, not a big deal. Well, as it turns out, as more and more devices have come online, we're running out of IP addresses. So, NAT, or network address translation helps to a degree. We could put a bunch of internal IPs behind one external IP. But as new devices come online, IoT devices, that problem will only continue to expand. And in some parts of the world, we've already run out of IPv4 addresses. IPv6 is natively enabled on most devices nowadays, so the issue is, the implication is, it's often overlooked and can mean open door if it's not secured properly. Sometimes if it's not configured properly, if it's not something you think about, you may say, well, I have IPv4 rules in place, I have things locked down, I'm good. But if IPv6 is enabled on the devices and it's not secured, it's just as is out of the box, well, that could have some security implications potentially. Security policies often aren't uniformly applied, from IPv4 to IPv6. Meaning the things that we have locked down with version 4, we don't necessarily have the same level of parity, or the same level of lockdown, when it comes to v6. That false sense of security in the IPv4 is locked down, it's filtered, but again, IPv6 could be wide open to attack. Another thing is with IPv6 being relatively new, although it's been around for a while, it's relatively new as far as actual adoption is concerned, that lack of experience with countermeasures against IPv6 hacks and attacks, so subject matter expertise is not as widespread, and hacking tools are taking advantage of IPv6 vulnerabilities. It's becoming more and more of a problem if we don't start to lock down these devices and make sure that things are turned off if we don't need it, or if we are using it, that it's secured properly. Hackers are taking advantage of this because the majority of the hacking tools that are out there are being upgraded, they're being patched, and, new versions coming out, just like regular traditional software or commercial software, they're upgrading their stuff as well. As new technologies come online, those tools are updated as well to take advantage of vulnerabilities in that new technology.

Port Mirroring, Port Spanning, and Port Taps

Now let's talk about the concept of port mirroring, so also known as port spanning or SPAN, or Switched Port Analyzer. What it does is a switch sends a copy of all network packets seen on a port, or it could be an entire VLAN, to another port to be analyzed. In other words, if you recall how a switch works, where it maintains a MAC table, a MAC table or MAC addresses of all the hosts attached to that switch, and it knows what hosts live on what port. It only sends traffic out of the port that that host is connected to, so it helps to reduce traffic. When we're doing port spanning or a Switched Port Analyzer, we can copy all of the data off of a port, or the entire switch or an entire VLAN, and send that to another port and it can be analyzed, so intrusion detection systems, trouble shooting, we could use it for forensics, we could use it for user monitoring. Those things are in play to allow us to identify and monitor or dig into the packets on a specific port or a specific VLAN. As an example, if we have a switch, there are four ports on the switch, and then we have four computers attached to that switch. This is a traditional connectivity scenario. We have all of these different devices connecting to a switch. When we're talking about port mirroring, well, we have the same devices. Let's say, in this case we have three devices connected, and they're connected to that device via ports 1, 2, and 3, well, then we're also going to have a monitoring device on port 4, and that will utilize port mirroring. In the first scenario, the computer attached to port 1 wants to communicate with the computer on port 3. Well, since the MAC table exists on that switch, it knows where those two hosts live, and it only sends traffic out of the port that that host lives on, so that way it's reducing traffic and it helps make things more secure. But in the second scenario, you'll notice that all the PCs, or all the hosts connected to the switch, like they're communicating, well, all of that traffic gets sent out of port 4 to the port mirroring device, and it allows that port mirroring device to capture those packets, analyze those packets, and do whatever it needs to with that information. A similar concept would be port taps. In this instance we have East/West traffic, we talked about that before, traffic occurring inside the data center. All of the devices attached to the switch, if it needs to communicate to another network within our data center, it would send that to the router and then off to its destination. Well, a similar concept to port mirroring is something referred to as a port tap. In this situation we would insert a tap inline between those two devices, and that tap would then go out to out-of-band security or monitoring tools, so it would be placed inline and then capture all the packets and do it in real time. It's quicker and it's more efficient than doing port mirroring, where you don't have the potential of duplicating packets, doing it inline. However, it may or may not be applicable for your environment. This can work for Ethernet networks and then also Fibre Channel networks, but when we do these types of activities, they can be disruptive, so these things have to be planned out ahead of time to make sure that we don't disrupt connectivity between applications, between hosts and servers, but just two concepts to keep in mind that we can use to monitor traffic on a network.

File Integrity Check

A file integrity check protects against tampering by ensuring a file has not been modified. You can look at a few different things or a few pieces of metadata to understand if that file's been tampered with. You can look at credentials. You can look at privileges and security settings. You can also look at the content, the actual content of the file itself, attributes in size or hash values. If any of these things don't match, that's going to be indicative of some type of tampering, an indicator of compromise, perhaps the first steps in a larger breach. This might give you some advanced warning that someone's coming in, and they're starting to manipulate our files. We need to jump on this quickly, see if we can lock this down, perhaps follow what's going on, maybe even let that person do whatever it is they're doing for a short period of time while you monitor them you can then get a better understanding of who it is, where they're coming from. What happens is it's going to compare a current good state. It's going to take a baseline of that system, the file system, individual files. Typically it's going to run a hash against those files. If anything changes within that file, that hash value will be different. It's going to compare a current state against a known good state. If they don't match, then that's indicative of some type of compromise or tampering. As an example, Windows has something built in called the System File Checker, you can run that by running SFC. SFC will scan the integrity of all protected system files, and in this case it will replace ones that it finds either corrupt or changed or modified in some way with the correct Microsoft versions. You can do SCANNOW, VERIFYONLY. You can have it scan and then automatically repair what it finds, if it finds anything. Or you can say, go ahead and scan, but just verify only and report back to me. Don't repair anything yet. In the example down below, you have sfc /SCANNOW, or you can say VERIFYFILE, and you can point to a specific file You can check just one file at a time, not necessarily your entire file system. Or you can say, VERIFYONLY, and if you find anything, report back. That way you can take some further action if necessary. I summary we covered network appliances. We talked about access control lists, or ACLs. We talked about route security along with quality of service. We also covered the implications of IPv6, port spanning, port mirroring, and port taps, along with monitoring services and file integrity monitors.

Chapter 10 How to Install and Configure Wireless Security

In this chapter, we'll be talking about installing and configuring wireless security settings. We'll be talking about four main areas. We'll talk about cryptographic protocols, authentication protocols, also methods, and then installation considerations. Let's first cover some wireless definitions. WEP, or Wired Equivalency Protocol, was originally designed to provide security equal to a wired network. If you're familiar with WEP at you understand that it doesn't provide security at all anymore. It can be cracked within minutes or sometimes within seconds if you have the tools. Vulnerabilities have emerged, and this has since been deprecated. It's not recommended for a secure environment whatsoever. If you have no other choice and you have older legacy equipment in your environment that needs to communicate, in other words, make it backwards compatible, then you may have to have WEP. It's better than nothing, but not in the grand scheme of things. Anyone with an off-the-shelf-set of hacker tools or penetration testing tools, can crack WEP encryption relatively easily. The alternative to that, or the newer standards, would be Wi-Fi Protected Access, which is WPA or WPA2. WPA itself was based upon WEP, and it was used as a stop gap. WPA has also been cracked relatively quickly. WPA2, which is the newer standard, it fully implements 802.11i protocol, and that provides for additional security enhancements. We'll talk about why these things are so insecure, why we had some of these vulnerabilities to begin with. Then, for definitions sake, I want you to understand that Wireless Application Protocol, or WAP, not to be confused with wireless access point, which is also referred to with a WAP acronym, Wireless Application Protocol, that deals with mobile devices and providing mobile devices with internet connectivity. It's a suite of protocols similar to TCP/IP. But, it deals with mobile connectivity. It uses Wireless Transport Layer Security, or WTLS, similar to regular TLS that we would have seen in the TCP/IP suite when we're dealing with encryption or HTTPS, as TLS or SSL, as we spoke about in the previous chapter, and it provides for authentication, encryption, and data integrity.

WEP/WPA/WPA2

To define this a little bit further, with WEP, WPA, and WPA2, the standard WEP, used what was referred to as an RC4 stream, and it was a 24-bit encryption. The length of that encryption key is what led to its insecurity or its vulnerabilities. That IV, or the initialization vector, it's vulnerable to an IV attack, meaning that 24-bit encryption was not long enough. So, packet injection can crack WEP in literally several seconds. And what it boils down to is that initialization vector, 24-bits long is just too short. Every so often it has to repeat. There are only so many different combinations of initialization vectors that it can send. As communication takes place over any length of time, if someone's sitting there sniffing the wire for a period of time, they'll see that initialization vector. That's a hard one to say. They'll see that repeated every so often, so they'll be able to pull that off the wire because that IV, or the initialization vector, is static, and it's reused, and it's part of the RC4 encryption key. You already have a piece of the information once you understand what the initialization vector is, and it's also set in clear text. You have three or four pieces of the puzzle to begin with, and if you use standard penetration testing tools, those tools allow you to crack that encryption key very, very easily. It's not recommended for any type of secure environment. It should be avoided unless, backwards compatibility is needed.

WPA and WPA2 Security

As you move on to WPA and WPA2, WPA, or Wi-Fi-protected access that partially implements the 802.11i standard. It was a stopgap. It uses something called Temporal Key Integrity Protocol, or TKIP for Short and what it does is it takes a 128-bit wrapper, and it wraps that WEP encryption. That 24-bit encryption that we've already talked about as being too small, and it's reusable every so often, or it is reused every so often, it's too small. Well, with WPA, it wraps that entire encryption packet within 128-bit larger encryption packet. It generates a second key based upon the MAC address of the sender and the serial number of the packet. It mixes this key with the Initialization Vector, it mixes it with the IV, and it creates a per-packet key. It's more secure than WEP, but it's still using RC4 encryption, and it's backwards compatible with WEP. We know it is not considered a secure protocol because, again, it's been cracked very easily, again, using off-the-shelf tools. If we move to the next one, WPA2, that fully implements to 802.11i standard. That uses something called CCMP for enhanced security, or the CC-MAC protocol. It's Counter Mode Cipher Block Chaining Message Authentication Code Protocol. CCMP, it's 128-bit AES encryption algorithm. It's not backwards compatible with WEP, but it is much more secure. Having said that, is it completely secure? Is it completely foolproof? Well, the answer is No. That has also been cracked. Given enough time and if you have enough of a skilled hacker on the other end of sniffing that traffic, it is crackable. Wireless security examples. Well, WPA and WPA2 can use something called a Pre-shared Key, or PSK, or Enterprise Authentication. Pre-Shared Keys, if you have a home office or a small office home office, or a SoHo network, or a small business, you may be already familiar with Pre-Shared Keys. It means you have some password on the client. You have a password on your Wi-Fi router or your access point. As long as those two things match, then you can connect to the network. Enterprise uses something called RADIUS, which is an authentication server, and digital certificates. You have to have that certificate, and you have to have an account on that RADIUS server or some way to authenticate to that RADIUS server, so it provides for an even greater level of authentication. If we have a laptop that may again connect to a wireless access point. That wireless access point, if we're using Pre-Shared Key, all I need is that secret or that Pre-Shared Key on the laptop and on the wireless access point, and as long as they match, we connect and off we go. If we're using RADIUS, you'll see the laptop will connect to the wireless access point, or in a larger environment, you may have multiple wireless access points, in which case you would use a wireless LAN controller, and that way you can set up your information and your configuration once and push that out to all the wireless access points within your network. You can do that in one shot, so it just makes the management easier. But, you would connect to the wireless access point, which would forward your connection request over to the RADIUS server. The RADIUS server would check to see, is this person able to connect or authenticated to connect? Because if I can back up one, if we use a Pre-Shared Key, as long as we have the secret on both the laptop and the wireless access point, it connects. We don't know who it is that's connecting. If we're using authentication or Enterprise Authentication, then we have to authenticate with that RADIUS server. It's going to authenticate the user, as well as the laptop. This gives us a greater level of security.

WPA3

Before we get too much further along, let's talk about WPA3, which is the newest version of WPA and for all intents and purposes will replace WPA2. WPA2 is still very much in play, but WPA3 is making its way into the marketplace and into all the newer gear that's being released. WPA3 adds AES-GCMP, which is Galois/Counter Mode and also security jumps up from 128-bit SAE, and we'll talk about that in just a moment, to 192, which is optional for personal use. In actuality, it's 256-bit encryption, but the way things flush out when it's all said and done, it ends up being 192. SAE stands for Simultaneous Authentication of Equals, otherwise known as Dragonfly key exchange with forward secrecy feature, meaning If someone captures this traffic and then tries to brute force it maybe six months, a year, and whatever down the road, they're not going to be able to do anything with it. That forward secrecy prevents brute force attacks and prevents someone from trying to decode that data at some future date. Key features, brute force protection. Also individualized encryption for each user using unauthenticated Diffie-Hellman Pairwise Master Key. In a nutshell, it's referred to as a PAKE, or a Password Authenticated Key Exchange. That provides mutual authentication and negotiates a fresh session key each time someone connects. That forward secrecy, is a prevention of offline dictionary attacks. If we look at this in more detail, it was released in 2018, and WPA3 is the successor to WPA2, and it offers several security enhancements. So 256-bit in actuality, but the overall effect for Wi-Fi is effectively 192-bit. Simultaneous Authentication of Equals, or SAE, You hear that term come up over and over again. Add that acronym with an abbreviation to your toolbag as well, also known as the Dragonfly key exchange with forward secrecy feature, as we've talked about. And then perhaps one of the biggest advancements is Opportunistic Wireless Encryption, or OWE, which protects unsecured networks such as libraries or coffee shops, airports or hotels. This will replace unencrypted open networks. So OWE will provide individualized data encryption to users connecting to public open networks to protect against eavesdropping. Each user gets their own distinct encrypted session without them having to do anything. On open networks, an attacker connected to that network, could read or even modify other users traffic. HTTPS to an extent can provide protection against some of this stuff on an open network, but OWE uses an unauthenticated Diffie-Hellman key exchange during that association, resulting in what's called a Pairwise Master Key, or a PMK. And they use that to derive, then the session keys, and that's unique to each user. Each user that connects gets that unique session key. There's no provisioning required, and the encryption process is entirely transparent to users. The users would see and join the Wi-Fi network as they would any typical open network as they've done in the past, but they don't have to do anything additional to get that encrypted connection. So OWE is a big improvement over current open wireless networks. Then just keep in mind, we use SHA-2 for each input. And then Wi-Fi Easy Connect is another big advancement that uses Device Provisioning Protocol Secure, or DPP Secure, and that will replace WPS, or Wi-Fi Protected Setup, so it makes things much easier. Using your smartphone, you would scan a QR code on that device and then automatically pair any new devices that would connect it to the network, so it makes provisioning much, much easier. Then lastly, WPA3 is not susceptible to the KRACK attack like WPA2 was. WPA2 was susceptible to something called the KRACK attack, which came out in roughly 2017, and it rendered WPA2 vulnerable. WPA3 is not vulnerable to that same attack due to the way they use Simultaneous Authentication of Equals, or the SAE key exchange.

Wireless Security Examples

Let's take a look at a real-world example of how a hacker could gain access in an environment. Let's say, for instance, we have our two wireless access points that we have. Well, if someone wanted to come in, they could set up what's called a rogue access point. They could issue a Denial of Service against our existing wireless access point, take it offline or make it so that it can't respond to requests. They could put a wireless access point using something called open authentication, which means there is no password required. The laptop, whoever's sitting at that laptop, they would connect to that wireless access point, otherwise known as an evil twin. That's a term you should be familiar with or you should remember. But an evil twin is there to fool someone connecting to the network. They think they're connecting to the wireless access point. Even though they have credentials to connect to the legitimate wireless access point, that's going to be DDoSed so they can't connect. They're going to connect to the evil twin. It's using open authentication, which means they don't need a username and password to connect. They're connected. And if we are in control of that wireless access point, of that evil twin, we can set it so that it pops up some type of authentication message. The user sitting at the laptop would think, something must have happened; it's prompting me for my credentials. They'll go ahead and put in their username and password, or they'll do that several times. We just keep putting up fake messages until we capture enough information that we can be pretty confident that we have what we need off of that user. Then we can just disconnect and off we go. In that case, we could very easily compromise that communication. We could capture everything, or we could have it connected to the network and let them pass through and connect. We could just sit there and monitor everything that they do as that communication passes through the wireless access point. Just be advised that those types of things are, in fact, possible. You could be sitting at a coffee shop, and someone could do something similar to that. It doesn't necessarily have to be in a business environment. It could be anywhere that you would connect using a wireless access point.

Wireless Security and Pen Testing Tools
There is a number of off-the-shelf penetration testing, or pen test, tools that can quickly compromise insecure wireless protocols. We're talking about WEP and even WPA and WPA2. There are some tools, Kali Linux is one, or it used to be called BackTrack. There's some off-the-shelf scripts that can do packet injections and things that allow them to very quickly break those types of encryption protocols., what would happen is, it allows you to do network sniffing, Even if a specific wireless access point is not broadcasting, it's SSID. Even it's not broadcasting it can still sniff the wire because those things are being transmitted in the clear. Even though your laptop may not pick it up and say, hey, there's a wireless network available, it's still being broadcast, and if you have the tools, you can gather that information. It'll allow you to locate all the wireless networks and show what types of encryption they're using, what types of protocols, if they're open or secure, whether it's WEP WPA. And once you find one, you can then capture the packets on that network to capture the SSID. From there, you can send out what's called a deauthentication packet, or you can knock those clients off the network. By deauthenticating them, then they're going to reconnect pretty much away. As

they're reconnecting, you're going to capture those packets, and you'll be able to capture the actual login. It's encrypted, but you'll be able to capture the packets and you can identify that as login attempts because it's what's called a four-way handshake as they reconnect. And once you have that information, then you can brute force your way in or dictionary attack or hash attack to discover that password. If it's something simple, you can get through that relatively quickly. If you're using more secure passwords or a stronger password with like uppercase, lowercase, special characters that wouldn't necessarily be in a dictionary, then it could take longer. It could take days, hours, weeks, months, just depends upon the strength of your password. Having said that, there are other tools available that can bypass even having to crack the password. Most routers, especially the home office and SOHO routers, have what's called WPS. It allows you to do a push button on either side and automatically configure the client and the server, or the client and the wireless access point, rather. There are insecurities or some vulnerability within WPS, the PIN that it generates, that it can go out and attack that at the wireless access point and crack the WPA or WPA2 password. There are some tools available that do not take an extreme amount of knowledge to utilize. You need to be aware of these things. You need to make your networks as secure as possible.

EAP, PEAP, and LEAP

The next sets of concepts I want to cover are EAP, or Extensible Authentication Access Protocol, and then two variations of that, PEAP and LEAP. EAP, or Extensible Authentication Access Protocol, is a set of authentication frameworks for wireless networks. What you need to understand is that there are five different types of Extensible

Authentication Access Protocol that are in existence, two that we need to know for the exam that are adopted by the WPA and the WPA2 standard. We have EAP with TLS. We have EAP with Pre-Shared Key, and we have EAP with an MD5 hash. Those three have been deprecated. The two that we need to be aware of are LEAP and PEAP. Let's cover that in a little more detail. LEAP stands for Lightweight Extensible Authentication Protocol, and this one is not in use, but we need to be aware of what it is. It's a proprietary protocol developed by Cisco, and it was a stopgap to WEP insecurities, and it lacked Windows support. It was not in use or used by the Windows environment. It was strictly for Cisco environments. That itself is why it doesn't have the wide acceptance or it's been deprecated. It's easy to configure, no digital certificates, which is great. But it's also bad because it's easy to configure and there are no digital certificates. You have a lot of insecurities there. Clear text transmissions. And, it has since been deprecated. The one that we need to be focused on is PEAP, or Protected Extensible Authentication Protocol, and that was jointly developed by Cisco, RSA, and then Microsoft. Cisco develops the networking protocols. RSA deals with security. And then Microsoft with the operating systems. This joint effort ensured that it is in use or wide adoption throughout the IT and the tech community. It has Windows support, and it uses digital certificates on the authentication server. It gives you that extra layer of security by authenticating saying, I'm not going to just connect to any rogue access point, like we mentioned previously with that evil twin. If we're using PEAP, that will prevent that from happening. We have to authenticate to what we're connecting to, to the wireless access point and then ultimately to the server. It's going to establish an encrypted channel between the client and the server via a TLS tunnel. It gives us that extra layer of protection.

802.11x Wireless Protocols

Let's now talk about IEEE 802.11x wireless protocols. What we're talking about here is wireless communication and 802.11 standards operate either over 2.4GHz or the 5GHz radio frequencies. Over time, we've gotten an increase in speed for the most part, and we've gone from 1 Mbps or 2 Mbps up to 14 Gbps, theoretically. 802.11 was the original standard, and that was 1 Mbps or 2 Mbps, and that operated over the 2.4GHz frequency. Next was 802.11a, and that was a big jump. That was 54 Mbps over the 5GHz frequency. Then the next iteration of that was 802.11b, and that dropped down to 11 Mbps and operated over the 2.4GHz range. But wait a minute, that's a step backwards. Why are we doing that? Well the big difference between the two is the fact that 5 GHz has a much shorter range than 2.4 GHz. So for those devices that needed very high speed or high throughput, you could in fact use 802.11a, but the range was much shorter than it was with 802.11b. That's the big difference is the range. 802.11g, however, was a big jump up, and that gave us pretty much parity with 802.11a as far as throughput, 54 Mbps. But it had the advantage of operating over 2.4 GHz with an expanded range. Then we jumped to 802.11n up to 600 Mbps, again a huge jump, 2.4 or 5 GHz. Then, up until recently, 802.11ac was the latest and greatest with throughput up to 1.3 Gbps. That operated only over the 5GHz network. And we have 802.11ax, also known as Wi-Fi 6, and that can theoretically go up to 14 Gbps, although, in reality, probably a lot less than that, at least for. But as devices get better and the frequency range expands, we'll see speeds approaching that 14,000 Mbps or 14 Gbps. it operates over 2.4GHz or 5GHz range. You may also see something referred to as 802.11i. That's often referred to as WPA2, and that provides for additional security enhancements focused on authentication. But it does not refer to speed or frequency like the other things we just mentioned.

RADIUS Federation

A concept I want to make sure we're clear on is RADIUS Federation. We've discussed what RADIUS is, remote access dial-in user service, and federation is simply connecting systems or combining systems. A RADIUS federation connects a common system of authentication and credentials database. It uses RADIUS servers to connect these systems wirelessly. Additionally, because it's a federated system, it can be used by multiple applications or platforms.

Wi-Fi Protected Setup (WPS)

WPS is designed to make it easy for devices to join Wi-Fi networks with minimal effort. Devices without screens or keyboards are ideal for this. Some printers, as an example, they can easily join a Wi-Fi network by pushing a button on both devices, one on the actual printer, in this case, and then the access point on the other. Or some devices without that push button functionality will have a hardcoded pin, usually on a sticker somewhere on that device. Even though WPA2 encryption is used, assuming the actual wireless access point is using WPA2, it's very secure. As of the time of this writing, it has not been cracked. It's considered very, very secure. However, the WPS pin can be easily cracked. That pin is eight characters long, but only seven of those characters are used. The eighth character is a checksum. The first three and then the last four are in two separate groups. It ends up being fairly easy to brute force crack given the power of today's PCs.

Captive Portal

When we're dealing with public or open Wi-Fi networks, the concept of a captive portal comes into play. You may have been in a coffee shop or some location, a hotel, where you've attempted to log on to that Wi-Fi network and then you get some pop-up that says, before your able to access the network, you need to either agree to our acceptable terms of use, or you need to put in your username and password. It might be your last name and your room number or whatever if it's a hotel. Once you put in those credentials, then it allows you access to the network. That captive portal in quarantine or put you into a walled garden and say, you can't get any further until you authenticate. Once you do, then it allows you through, and you can have full access to the internet. Well, those types of things are vulnerable to different types of attacks, again depending upon the implementation. But one example would be packet sniffing. If a hacker sits on the network and is sniffing the packets, once you authenticate, again, it just depends upon the sophistication of the captive portal and of the network itself or the tool that's being used. But if it's simply just looking for authentication by, like say, username and password, well, it knows your IP address, and it knows you're MAC address. Once you provide those credentials, it says you're authenticated, off you go. Well if someone is sniffing the network and they get your IP address and the MAC address, they could then, in turn, spoof both of those pieces and make it look like it's you. As soon as they hop on the network with that IP address and the MAC address, well the captive portal thinks that they're already authenticated, and it allows them to go through as well. That's one method. Or they could put up a fake captive portal. Again, if you're in some type of coffee shop, there may not even be typically a captive portal in place. But you, as the unsuspecting user, would not necessarily know that if you see a pop-up and says hey, you need to put in your username and password, 9 times out of 10, people don't think twice about it. They just go out and start putting those things in. Well those things could, in fact, again, be captured by someone sitting there just being malicious and capturing this information to get usernames, passwords, or whatever other things are trying to gain from a credentials point of view.

Installation Considerations

When it comes to installing Wi-Fi on our networks, some installation considerations to take into account. We can do things such as site surveys, which are a walkthrough of a facility to visually confirm locations, potential hotspots, impediments, maybe brick walls or some other things that could impede the flow of our signal. We can visually inspect those things to make sure that we have those accounted for. We can also generate things called heat maps, and that is typically done with software and some type of analyzer to visually show where signal is weak or non-existent you can add additional hotspots or access points. That's used in conjunction with Wi-Fi analyzers, that is, again, hardware and software that allows a tech to walk a site and identify areas of weak signal and what channels are best. It will show what devices are attached to what channels, which are better than others, and will allow you to switch channels potentially to find the best one for that specific device and improve the overall quality of the signal for a specific device.

Access Points/Wi-Fi Security

Let's now talk about some concepts around securing your network from things like access points, Wi-Fi security. So rule number one is to disable SSID broadcast. That's not a foolproof method. It doesn't mean someone still can't find you. But why give out extra information if you don't have to? Disable the SSID broadcast. It's the Service Set Identifier, the Wi-Fi network name, in other words. Also, it doesn't provide security. This SSID can still be sniffed. However, let's not give away too much information. Next, use something referred to as MAC filtering. We talked about a MAC address before, with MAC filtering, we pre-select what MAC addresses can connect to the Wi-Fi network. It still doesn't make it completely foolproof because people can do MAC spoofing just like they do IP spoofing. If they can sniff the network or if they explicitly know the MAC address ahead of time, it's possible to spoof that MAC address and then still connect to the network. Also, common sense administration. Always change the default admin username and password. I know it sounds ridiculous, but in all honesty, if you do a quick bit of research, you'll find that common usernames and passwords, literally password or password123 are out there, and they're very common, so people don't take the time to secure their networks. Also, we want to make sure we use the strongest encryption and authentication available. In other words, don't use WEP when we have WPA or WPA2 available. Keep things up to date and use the strongest encryption and authentication possible. Also, keep access points up to date with patches and firmware. There are a lot of home networks, small office networks, mid-sized companies, they install a router or Wi-Fi access point, and then they forget about it. They don't go back and touch it again. Make sure those default usernames and passwords are changed. Make sure they're locked down. Make sure you use the strongest encryption possible. But just like any other computer, any other device, make sure we keep things patched and updated. Next, we want to make sure we have antenna placement and signal strength flushed out. Antenna placement is critical for proper coverage, so it should be placed near the center of the area to be covered, and antennas can be internal or external. There is not one type that's better than the other. It depends upon the manufacturer, and it also depends upon the type of router. However, there are always new models coming out, and you can also add additional access points within a Wi-Fi network to extend coverage. Next, we have antenna placement and signal strength. Antennas can be omnidirectional or unidirectional. Omnidirectional provides coverage in a 360-degree fashion, whereas directional antennas focus the signal primarily in one direction, usually over longer distances. If you have an area where you want blanket coverage everywhere, then an omnidirectional antenna is your best bet. If you have somewhere where you want to broadcast coverage or direct coverage to one area but not to the sides or not behind you, as an example, then a directional antenna is your best bet. Something else to consider is antenna signal strength. Antennas are rated in terms of gain value or dBi numbers. A wireless antenna with a 10 dBi would be 10x stronger than a 0 dBi. Some routers, some wireless routers provide control over that. You can turn the power levels up or down, depending upon the environment. Some out-of-the-box routers may not have that functionality, but you can download hacked firmware that can give you that additional functionality. It's there, but it's not exposed via the common, out-of-the-box user interface. We can combine with site surveys to identify optimal placements. You can take devices and walk the site, and determine where the signal strength is going to be best. Additionally, you can also identify where there's going to be dead spots. You may need to position your antenna so that you account for those dead spots, or you may add additional access points to the network.

Band Selection/Width

When we're talking about Wi-Fi connected access, there are two main bands that you connect with. You have 2.4 GHz and also 5 GHz. 2.4 GHz was the earlier band. It's 100 MGz wide, and it spans from 2.4 GHz to 2.5 GHz. Just 14 channels and used by many devices outside of just Wi-Fi collectivity, such as microwaves, baby monitors, Bluetooth, wireless video cameras. In reality, only channels 1, 6, and 11 are separated from each other with enough space or enough frequency in between to not overlap. That's an important consideration to keep in mind when you're doing channel selection, especially if you have multiple access points within the same building, or if you have neighboring Wi-Fi access points, perhaps from other companies or neighbors, and you want to make sure you're not overlapping and getting a diminished signal, not having frequencies overlap. In order to do that, you would pick channels 1, 6, or 11 to ensure that you have some distance between you and the next set of channels that you'd want to use. On the 5 GHz range, we have 25 10-MGz channels, and the bonding of channels is possible within the 5 GHz range. So 802.11n bonds 2 20-MGz channels, and also 802.11 ac bonds 4 20-MGz channels. 802.11n, would give you 40 MGz of bandwidth, 802.11ac can bond 4 20-MGz channels for a total of 80 MGz of bandwidth. If we look at this in a little more detail, the 2.4-GHz channel frequencies, channels 1, 6, and 11 are far enough apart, there's a 3-MGz space in between those channels, so they don't overlap. If you're looking for the spread that has the most channels without overlapping, these are the 3 that you should pick, 1, 6, and 11.

Fat vs. Thin Access Points and Stand-alone vs. Controller-based

Fat or thick access points have everything needed to manage wireless clients, so all the intelligence and all the management features are in fact built in to the actual client. Multiple access points need to be managed individually, so that's the downside. The upside is it's easy to install. It's great for small offices or small environments. We have everything we need. We don't need additional hardware. However, if we have multiple points as our environment starts to grow and we have more than one access point, they need to be managed individually. A thin access point is just the radio and the antenna and can be managed via a central switch. As you may have guessed, multiple thin access points can be managed and configured centrally. We have the benefit of being able to do everything at once from a centralized location. If we have a large environment or one that has many access points, that very quickly becomes an advantage. When we're talking about stand-alone versus controller-based, it's very similar to fat vs. thin. Stand-alone access points provide everything required to service clients. They do, however, have limited encryption, typically no load balancing, and no enterprise class functionality. Not to say that some don't, but typically we have less functionality, less features, less encryption than we do with controller-based. To compare and contrast the two, it's very similar when we're talking about stand-alone versus controller-based, it's very similar to fat vs. thin with regard to features and functionality and ease of management. One, it's very easy to set up, it's very self-contained, but it doesn't scale very well. Stand-alone access points are usually found in smaller environments. Typically much less expensive, a little bit easier to configure on one-by-one basis. But as we start to scale, that becomes a little bit unmanageable. For stand-alone controllers, well suited to smaller environments, contain everything needed to manage clients updates and patches, however, need to be done individually. That's where it starts to become unruly. If we have multiple access points, we don't want to have to go around and do that to every single one, especially if we have dozens or potentially hundreds depending upon the size of our environment, especially if we're in between multiple buildings and we have some type of geodispersement. Also no load balancing and limited redundancy. Also, we have limited IDS or intrusion detection functionality. Conversely, with controller-based, we have enterprise-level features and also scalability. Access points are configured and managed centrally. Again, as that starts to scale, that becomes a big deal. Updates and patches are distributed from a central location. It's much easier to manage at scale. Load balancing and redundancy also between access points. As we move throughout an environment, it has the ability to load balance or to find the best or the closest access point, the one that can service the client the best. Also, we have more full-featured IDS functionality. Something to keep in mind, the fat client or the thick client and also the stand-alone controllers very well suited to small environments or medium-sized environments that work well. However, as we start to scale, we want to able to manage things from a central location. In summary, we various cryptographic protocols and the underlying information for each. We talked about a number of authentication protocols, including the relatively new WPA3 and its associated authentication protocols and some of the benefits of WPA3. And we talked about the various methods and then installation considerations, including site surveys, heat maps, Wi-Fi analyzers, antenna placement.

Chapter 11 How to Implement Secure Mobile Solutions

In this chapter we'll be covering Implementing Secure Mobile Solutions. We'll be talking about connection methods and receivers, along with mobile device management, also enforcement and monitoring, and then deployment models. At a high level, we want to talk about connection methods. We want to talk about mobile device management concepts, also talk about enforcement and monitoring, and then also deployment models. There's a lot of information in each of these categories, and it's important to understand that we have a good concept or a good understanding of how these things tie into our overall security posture. Mobile connectivity is a big deal. Everyone is mobileadays, we have remote workers, teleworkers, so it's important that we understand how this fits into the big picture. Let's go ahead and dig in and talk about connection methods. There's a lot of ways that we can connect to our corporate networks. We can connect via cellular, Wi-Fi, SATCOM, not as common as some of the other ones, but for military installations, SATCOM is a big deal. Also Bluetooth, NFC or near field communication. We also have ANT or ANT+, which connects health devices and gym equipment. Also Infrared and then USB. There's connection concerns and security concerns with all of these different methods of communication. If we take a look at each of these individually, there are some unique challenges that we face. To start off with cellular, cellular or mobile phones in general have numerous potential security risks, not the least of which, if we have a cell phone that we're carrying around in our pocket that connects to our corporate resources. If we have no password or no pin on that device, if we leave it somewhere, if it's lost, stolen, or somehow compromised, anyone could pick up that device and have access to corporate emails, corporate resources, or more depending upon what is on that device. It's important that we make sure all of our devices have passwords or pins, and we'll talk more about that later as far as mobile device management so we can force that. If someone's using a device to connect to our corporate resources, we can make sure that they do, in fact, have a password or a pin. Also, unpatched operating systems or applications. If people download applications to their phone, or even if we push applications out in a corporate setting, if we don't update those applications or update the operating system on the phone, it's just like any other operating system or any other application. The phone is no different or a cellular device or mobile device is no different than a PC, laptop, server. They need to be patched and updated periodically. Next, you have jailbreaking or rooting. It's very popularadays, especially with iPhones, to jailbreak that device or gain root access to that device so they can install their own applications. They can bypass the App Store, download things or increased functionality or turn on features that may not be readily accessible from the stock or the factory OS. Jailbreaking is a definite security concern for IT professionals or security professionals because those phones are no longer managed or manageable. Those phones are able to bypass our security settings, and they can install whatever they want. When you bypass the app stores, especially in the iOS space, those things are very well vetted. They have security guidelines and best practices they must follow to even be admitted into these App Store. When you bypass that and you go to your own app stores, these off-on-the-side jail broken app stores, people will create their own apps and add functionality that is not vetted as thoroughly as it would be in the App Store. You run potential security risks by having that in the environment. Then, we have unauthorized applications.

They can either jailbreak the phone from the Apple Store perspective of the App Store perspective, whether it's Apple or Android, or they could install unauthorized applications from a company perspective, meaning the company says you can install applications A, B, C, and D, but the person goes in and installs their own applications. That could potentially bypass the security because IT security, again, doesn't know what ports they go over, what things they access, or what mechanisms they have in place that could potentially be a security risk. As an IT professional, we should mandate or have a list of what applications can and cannot be used on those corporate resources. Then last but not least in this category, everyone's favorite topic is malware. Malware is everywhere, laptops, PCs, desktops, servers, so on. It also exists in the mobile phone space or the cellular space. If you have a mobile phone, iOS is not as susceptible, but it still exists. Android much more so because it's more of an open environment. People can create apps not necessarily through a rigorous vetting process like they have in the Apple Store. But malware exists on both sides. Don't develop a false sense of security and say oh, I have an Apple device. I'm completely immune. There is malware. There are potential security risks with every device. Some methods to secure our mobile devices and our cellular communication in general would be authentication or two-factor authentication. We want to make sure that we authenticate. We put in a username and password. We want to make sure we have a pin or some type of biometrics, thumbprint or fingerprint of some sort, or a two-factor authentication. If we're going to go connect to a specific service, a lot of those services will offer a two-factor authentication. Typically that means they will send an SMS or a text to that phone, you'll need to have the password. Then you'll also need to verify that you're on the phone that was registered with that service. They'll send a password to that device via text. You'll put that text password back in, and that's the two factor. That way someone has to have your phone in addition to being able to try to access that specific resource. There are some other ones out there like context-aware authentication, which we'll talk about in a bit that offers a little easier experience, less friction involved. You don't have to have the device and go through an extra couple of steps by getting that pin or that text from the website or the resource to put back in again. We'll talk about those in just a minute as well. But then we want to also make sure that we verify and authenticate downloaded applications. We need to make sure that if we download something from the App Store or from the internet or from wherever that we have a mechanism in place to verify and authenticate that that application is authorized by the company, is not manipulated or somehow tainted or tampered with prior to delivery. Also, make sure we put in anti-malware software just like we have on a PC or laptop. We want to make sure we have anti-malware and antivirus software on those mobile devices. That way we capture the malware before it gets a chance to take a foothold within our system. Also, we have firewalls. It's a good idea to have a firewall in place if you're in an environment where the risks necessitate that. Everything we talk about within IT security in general, there's a risk/reward. There's a what's the chances of it happening? What's the actual damage if it occurs? What's the likelihood of it occurring? The annual loss expectancy and the single loss event. A lot of things go into play when we're talking about risk analysis. Does the amount of effort that's going to have to be put in place outweigh or justify the actual action? In other words, to put it another way, if we have to spend a thousand hours or say a million dollars for some type of security solution, but the actual thing that's preventing might only cost us 10 hours and maybe $1000 to remediate, well then it's not worth it. We have to have that risk return mentality. Then it goes without saying, we need to have the ability to do a remote disable and/or remote wiping. Most phones have that ability already built in for the individual users, and then there's a corporate or an enterprise mechanism that allows that as well. If that device is lost, stolen, compromised in some way, we can number 1 locate it. We can look on a map and geolocate that device. Or, at the very least, remote disable that device so they can't use it or remote wipe it. All the data is completely removed from that device. And then last but not least, we need to make sure we have encryption in place. That way, if for some chance, the remote disable or the remote wipe doesn't work or is inaccessible, well then we can make sure, at the very least, that the data is encrypted on that device. Someone would need to use a biometric mechanism like a fingerprint or username/password to get into the phone. They couldn't use a third-party tool to extract that data.

Securing Wi-Fi

When it comes to securing Wi-Fi, a couple main things that we should be aware of, and you're probably familiar with some of this, but just to reiterate, we need to make sure that we are disabling the SSID. None of these are foolproof, none of them are going to stop an experienced attacker from doing what they're doing. But disabling the Security Set Identifier, or the SSID, more skilled hackers from finding the network, but it will prevent clients who are just casually browsing from discovering your network. You're going to eliminate some of the casual ones that could eventually end up becoming problems. You're not going to eliminate the experienced hackers, however. Next is MAC filtering. MAC filtering predefines which Media Access Control, or MAC addresses, can connect to that router or that access point. it will not prevent a skilled hacker from spoofing that MAC address, but it does keep the casual browsers, the casual, lower-level hackers, or miscreants, or, whatever you want to call them, from attaching to your network, because you're going to say only these MAC addresses are allowed. If they're skilled, they will be able to spoof that MAC address and then connect anyway. And then, Require Security Connectivity Protocols, we want to make sure we're using the most secure protocol available. No WEP, no WPA. If it all possible, require WPA2-PSK with AES, or Advanced Encryption Standard. That uses a pre-shared key with AES. That's currently considered the most secure standard, there are some other ones you can do at enterprise level, but they have to contact a RADIUS server, or they have to have a certificate, but for the average user, especially for a home environment or a small office, a medium-sized environment, WPA2 with a pre-shared key using AES, make sure you don't use TKIP, use AES, that's considered most secure.

Near Field Communication (NFC)
Most commonly, we're seeing near field communications in use for things like contactless payment systems, the iPhones, Android devices, Apple Pay. All those types of things have the NFC infrastructure in place, but it does pose some security concerns, things like eavesdropping, data corruption or manipulation, or interception. Just like with any communication, there's always that potential for a man-in-the-middle attack or someone to intercept that communication. With near field communication or NFC, they're hampered because of the fact that it's a very close-range technology. They have to be very close to you to be able to do any of those types of things anyway. However, that's not to say that someone can't sit next to or stand next

to some type of payment checkout system and gather information, try to manipulate that data or intercept the communication. Don't just assume just because, I only have to be maybe a foot away that I'm safe. No, someone could be standing nearby or they could have some type of device placed nearby that could intercept that communication. Some ways we can prevent some of that is by establishing secure channels. If those secure channels are established and that communication is encrypted, then we thwart a lot of those efforts. Even if they do intercept that communication, they're not going to able to do anything with it because, that communication is encrypted.

Additional Areas of Concern
Some additional areas of concern are common attack vectors like intercepting data, man-in-the-middle attack, and data corruption. These things can apply to any type of communication interaction between two devices. Some additional areas of concern are common attack vectors that are common to any communication mechanism. Like intercepting data, man-in-the-middle attacks or data corruption. These things apply to things like satellite communications, Bluetooth, we're going to talk about Bluejacking and Bluesnarfing in another chapter, ANT or ANT+, which is the connection between health and gym equipment, heart rate monitors, and then infrared devices. We need to disable unnecessary or unneeded services and ensure that devices are patched, updated, and encrypt communication where possible. With things like satellite communication, there are some vulnerabilities. Some of them are embedded and maybe not easily upgraded, but it's important that we understand that every type of communication has its own unique challenges, and there are common exploits, or at least in concept, among all these

different types of communication mechanisms. SATCOM used by government installations, military installations, very important that we keep those things patched and updated. Make sure that we understand that vulnerabilities do exist. Just because it's a military grade, whatever, it doesn't mean it's impervious or immune to viruses, malware, and the targets or the information they're trying to get at. They would be considered typically high value targets. Bluetooth, if you don't need it for anything, turn it off because they are susceptible to things like Bluejacking and Bluesnarfing. But, as new devices come on board, smartwatches that have that connectivity, while there may be an opportunity for hackers to exploit that, currently not as much of a problem. Infrared, a lot of laptops, especially the older ones, have infrared built in. Some of the desktops have infrared built in. If you don't need that, which typically you will not, then turn that off because even though it's a line of sight communication mechanism, it is exploitable. It is vulnerable. You can use infrared ports to gain information or gain access to a system. Turn those things off. We want to harden our systems by disabling unnecessary things. Because the more things that are there, the more things that are exploitable. If we don't even know that they're turned on or we don't know that they're in play, then we're not going to monitor them, and they're going to fall out of compliance over time and then introduce additional vulnerabilities into our environment. Disable unnecessary services, harden our systems where possible.

MicroSD HSM
A MicroSD HSM offers the same features as PCIe-based HSM chapter that we find in servers. It can be used to encrypt communication, to encrypt storage, for key generation or for digital signatures. It can also provide, depending upon the

type of card, it can also do true random number generation, provide TRNG functionality, and then also cryptocurrency use cases, we can use it as a cold wallet of sorts and encrypt those transactions. A MicroSD HSM can be used for all of these purposes, can be mobile, and be moved from device to device, and give the same levels of encryption and security that we find on servers and bring that to the mobile environment, assuming your device can handle a MicroSD card.

Mobile Device Management (MDM, MAM, and UEM)
Next let's talk about mobile device management, and three things here, we have MDM, or mobile device management being software that enables the provisioning of mobile devices, application of policy, remote wiping, and some security policies that we can push down via certificate to these mobile devices and provision them, whether it be a corporate owned device or a BYO device. Next, we have mobile application management, or MAM, and this is more granular control over mobile devices, especially BYOD Devices where policy enforcement can be set at the app level along with application containerization, meaning we can apply policy to a specific application, but not affect the rest of the applications on a user's device. We can even control what can be copied between applications on a device or if things could be uploaded to the cloud based upon policies pushed down from mobile application management software. Then we have unified endpoint management, or UEM, and this is an evolution of MDM EMM, which is enterprise mobility management, and also, MAM, or mobile application management. UEM combines the features of these different types of technologies along with being able to manage desktops, laptops, Internet of Things devices, pulling all of these different feature sets under one umbrella.

SEAndroid

Next, we have security enhanced Android, or SEAndroid, and this is an SELinux, or a security enhanced Linux kernel security chapter and its purpose is to provide a mechanism for supporting access, control security policies among other things, and when I say that, I mean things like mandatory access control where we mandate that things must happen in a certain fashion, it's not discretionary, it's mandatory, and it was originally developed by the NSA and released to open source in December of 2000, so it's been around for a while, and it's been part of the Android code base for quite a while as well. The takeaway here is it restricts actions that installed software can take with the end goal being to enhance security on that device. We all know the Android app store has some vulnerability issues, but guess what, Does the iOS app store, so there are vulnerabilities on both sides of the fence, so it's a bit of a religious argument as to which side or which camp you're in, but understand that both sides of the fence, whether it's iOS or Android, both try very hard to make things as secure as possible, and SE Android, or security enhanced Android, is one of the mechanisms put in place to help achieve that goal.

Device Security

Mobile devices pose a number of challenges? We've talked about some of those. What if that device is lost or stolen? What if it is compromised while on public Wi-Fi, or how about asset tracking? Do even know where all of our mobile devices are? Do we even have a mechanism to know if they've been lost or stolen, or perhaps going into areas where they shouldn't be going into? Do we know our mobile devices? Do they have applications that they're supposed to have or ones they're not supposed to have? And what mechanisms do we have in place to manage that and prevent that from happening? There are some ways that we can enforce that. Corporate policies need to be enforced. Let's start with policy-based enforcement, strong passwords, we're going to require that via policy. It's not just a recommendation, we're going to require it. We'll push it out with our mobile device management software, group policy if we're talking about Active Directory environment, we want to ensure that we're pushing out that strong password and/or a pin requirement. We want to make sure that we require lock screens and screensavers so that that phone is not used within whatever 30 seconds, a minute, minute and a half. Then that lock screen kicks in, or if it's a desktop or laptop, and then a screensaver kicks in. That way, if they walk away, we can be assured that that resource is secured. Then, disabling unnecessary services. This goes, of course, for iPhones and Android devices, mobile devices, in general, but it also goes for laptops and desktops. We want to make sure that we disable things we don't need. Then application and software control. We want to make sure that we have policies in place and mechanisms in place to make sure that only approved applications are installed and then software control so that the ones that are installed get updated and patched on a routine basis. Everyone knows there is nothing worse than reaching into your pocket, expecting to find your phone, and then all of a sudden, I've lost my phone, or you think you lost your phone You start searching everywhere, you start opening drawers, looking in your desk, and so on, all over the place, your heart stops, everything comes to a screeching halt and then you reach into your other pocket and realize, oh, thank goodness it's in my other pocket. And all of a sudden, everything is with the world again. All of our lives are wrapped up in our phones today, everything from personal information, banking information, personal photos to corporate access, corporate resources, and corporate emails. We want to make sure that we have these things locked down and secure, and we have the ability to remote wipe them or disable them if they're, in fact, lost. For device security, we want to make sure we have a few things in place. We want to have full device encryption, we want to make sure that the contents of that device are not able to be retrieved by an unauthorized person or persons, so full device encryption, even if they remove that hard drive or they connect that phone to some specialized device, we don't want them to have access to that data. Next, we have remote wiping. If in fact, that phone is lost or stolen, we want to have the ability to push a button and remotely wipe that device. Even if it's off the network, the command is issued, and then once that device attaches to the network, the remote wiping would take place. Next, we want to make sure we have GPS enabled or some type of location services, whether it's find my iPhone, or find my Mac, or some Android equivalent, we want to make sure that GPS is enabled We can see where that asset is geographically. We can geofence and say it's not allowed to leave this area, or if it goes into this area, please alert us, that way we can have secure areas that people should not be going into or we can pre-define areas they shouldn't leave and then be alerted, it goes both ways. And then we have mobile device management. In general, we need to have some software and some infrastructure in place to manage those mobile devices, and there are a few different ways to do this. We can either manage the entire device or we can cordon off a piece of that device, so if someone wants to use their own personal phone or their personal device, we can install MDM software on that device and cordon off a piece of that device for corporate use. That way, it's encrypted and it has remote wipe capabilities, and we don't affect the rest of that person's personal information of personal phone, but regardless of how you do it, mobile device management software is critical because we have people using mobile phones and mobile devices more frequently than they're using computers nowadays or laptops. Mobile devices are very much a part of our corporate infrastructure just as much, if not more, than PCs, so they need to be secured appropriately.

Application Security and Key Credential Management
When we're talking about application security, we want to make sure that we have such things as authentication, we need to make sure that applications are only allowed if they're authenticated, they are vetted either through some type of external process like an app store, or an internal process through our company. Some corporate process that says you're only allowed to install these 4, 5, 10 whatever applications, anything else is denied. Next, we also want to make sure we have geo-tagging. We want to have the ability to say this person is either in an area they're supposed to be or they're not, and if that phone travels in and out of an area or is lost or stolen, we can be alerted very quickly. Next will be biometrics, application security, we should have some method of requiring some type of biometric login for very secure applications. The iPhone has one built-in, Android devices are similar, where they have a fingerprint reader. Yes, you have a fingerprint reader to get in to the actual phone itself, but then certain applications require an additional level of authentication before the application will open. We can enforce that as well. Even if someone left their phone unattended and someone were to come by and pick that phone up while it was unlocked, they still couldn't get into those applications where we deem them to be highly

secure, because they'll need that additional authentication like biometrics. Next, push notification services. If we have a large environment, it's going to be very unwieldy and certainly not scalable to have someone go around and talk to one person at a time and say, by the way, update your software; hey, by the way, update your software, and on and on and on, not scalable. In a small office, sure, we can stand up in the front of the room and say, everyone, update your iPhone or update your software. In an environment with multiple offices, thousands of employees, not scalable. Push notification allows us to push out to everyone in one shot, hey, update that piece of software, update that application, we can push notifications out across the board. We've talked about encryption. We want to make sure that our devices are in fact encrypted, and a lot of these things are built into the newer devices, so they become less and less of a of a management issue. The iPhone, Androids can be encrypted. IPhone by default is fully encrypted. That way, if the device is lost or stolen, it's a lot less likely that that information will be compromised, and also key or credential management. Let's take a look at that a little more deeply. With key or credential management, we want to manage the device content, access, and authentication. That is critical to providing a secure environment. The company needs the ability to manage the devices and control access. Digital certificates are often used to authenticate. It pushes down a certificate, so if you want to connect to the corporate resources, there is a certificate that's going to push down a profile to your phone, and it's going to mandate certain things. Maybe the screen saver will kick in or the device will lock after a certain number of minutes, or you can only access these specific types of applications, or you'll need this to connect and authenticate to our Wi-Fi; whatever the case might be. That way you have the ability to control with some granularity how people access and connect to your corporate resources.

Authentication

Then we're talking about authentication, securely connect to corporate resources. Again, we talked about PKI, that public key infrastructure helps to manage how people connect, and if they don't have the certificate, they don't have the authentication, they don't connect to our resources. Also, enforce password policies. We can make sure that people don't use the same password over and over again. We can make sure they change passwords every X number of days, let's say every 45 days. We can also enforce password history and also complexity requirements so that they can't use the same password, maybe say five passwords deep. That way they can't just reuse two passwords back and forth over and over again. We can also say their password has to have some type of complexity. In other words, it has to be maybe capital letters and lowercase, alphanumeric, or special characters or it may have to be a minimum length or a maximum length, so all of these things can help make our environment more secure. Then also, VPN or two-factor authentication. If they want to connect to corporate resources remotely if they're out in the field, coffee shop, they need to VPN in, and that way is over an encrypted secure channel. Even if that communication is, in fact, intercepted, it won't be readable to the hacker or to the person doing the interception. The VPN encrypts that communication. Then also, two-factor, RSA, as an example. Rather than just putting in a username and a password to connect to a VPN, you might have also a two-factor, which means they have to have an RSA token or some type of digital token that says every 30 seconds or every minute, this is going to change so that way the person trying to connect to that VPN, and ultimately to our corporate resources, needs to know their username and password, but also has to be in possession of that token or that two-factor device, whatever that might be. As an example, Google authenticator allows you to manage that two-factor authentication and for a number of services, Gmail, Dropbox, lots of different things can use Google authenticator to manage those keys, and of course, there are other companies, like I mentioned, RSA and a few others that can do the same thing.

Chapter 12 Geo-tagging & Context-Aware Authentication

Geo-tagging is important for a number of reasons. Pictures and documents can be tagged with the GPS coordinates of where it was made. A lot of people don't realize that when they upload pictures to social media, as an example, or they send that picture to others, there is a mechanism in place, it's called the EXIF data, E-X-I-F, if that data is not removed from that photo before it's uploaded, then that data is sitting there, and that person can use an EXIF tool to extract that information from that photograph. It's a potential security risk, as it allows someone to pinpoint that location. You can see here under the details, if you look down towards the bottom, it shows the GPS coordinates of where that picture was taken. The details being latitude and longitude, and also even the altitude of where that's at. Someone can punch in those coordinates and see exactly where that picture was taken. If it's a selfie with your girlfriend or boyfriend or whatever, probably not a big deal. But if it's a military installation and you're taking a picture of some type of battlefield location or government location, or something that has some type of security around it, and you don't realize this and you upload it to whatever, Instagram, social media, send it to someone else, and that other person uploads it to some social media, and that picture gets passed around versus text or instant message, or some other mechanism, that EXIF data is there. That is potentially a big security risk. There's software that can be used to remove EXIF data before things get uploaded, that comes down to corporate policy. You can have a policy in place that says, any photo that needs to be uploaded to any social media should have that information removed. That way it can't be pulled off for any reason.

Context-aware Authentication

Next, you have context-aware authentication. This is a type of two-factor authentication or 2FA, that provides for a more "frictionless" experience. It uses pre-defined rules to determine authentication, or if a more stringent challenge should be used. What do I mean by that? We can set it up to be based on things like device fingerprinting, geo-location, geo-fencing, or geo-velocity. What that means is when you register that device, it's going to look at the device itself. Where are you located? Are you East Coast, West Coast in the US? Outside of US? Where are you on the globe? Also, device fingerprinting. Let's say for instance it's a laptop. Well it can look at your browser, it can look at what fonts are installed, the browser version, drivers, screen size; all these different things that are unique, and when you combine all of those things together, it makes your device very unique against all others, because nobody has exactly the same thing; software, fonts, applications, security settings, screen size, color, depth. All those things go together to make a fingerprint, so that could be one thing. Also geo-location, like I mentioned, where are you located? Geo-fencing. Are you going to leave or enter a certain location? Or geo-velocity, meaning who checked in at say 2:00 in the afternoon on the East Coast, and then you're accessing the same website from 3:00 on the West Coast; that geo-velocity means, it's not feasible that person could've traveled across the country in an hour, or three or four hours. It's not feasible, so it would deny access. What happens is you can automatically allow things to occur if those things met, it's the same IP address or the same device fingerprint, or the same geo-location; you can allow them to just get in with the username and password. Or you can say if they fail any one of these pre-defined rules, then I want to challenge them additionally. Then you might ask for a pin, a two-factor authentication, an SMS text be issued or something. That way, it's frictionless up to the point where it can't verify via this context or authentication mechanism, I'm going to challenge you with some other thing, and then if they pass that, they're given access. If access fails any of the pre-defined rules, then the user can either be denied access out and say, nope, you don't gain access, or, we can be prompted for that more stringent authentication.

Enforcement and Monitoring
When it comes to enforcement and monitoring, there are number of things we need to be aware of, and I'm just going to touch on these briefly just you're aware that they exist and you have to make sure you keep eyes on these things. And that's things like third-party app stores. You have to make sure that our devices are not jailbroken or we restrict access to third-party app stores. We only want the people going to either the app store from Apple or Android, Google. Or we may have an internal company app store and only allow the applications we want them to have, and we would deny access to every other app store or every other download possibility. Next, also rooting in jailbreaking. We need to understand that people will try to root and jailbreak phones. When they do that, they're going to bypass security mechanisms. We need to make sure we have things in place to detect when those devices try to connect to our network and deny access. Also side-loading, custom firmware, carrier unlocking, or firmware over-the-air updates. All of these things should be prevented by corporate policy so that people can't bypass our security. We should make sure we have things in place. If we're going to have a corporately managed mobile policy and mobile infrastructure, we need to also make sure we have the corporately managed

enforcement mechanisms so they if any of these things happen, people try to do their own firmware updates outside of what the corporate policy allows, they try to do carrier unlocking, any of those things should be denied and alerted so that we can go back and investigate further. Why is this person trying to do this? Also, we have camera usage. Some areas don't allow camera use on the phones, so they'll have them either disabled or they require phones without cameras, which is becoming more and more difficult nowadays. Pretty much every phone has a camera, but we can disable that so that people can't take pictures inside of our secure locations. Also, we have SMS or MMS. You want to make sure you understand how those things are being used, understand the security implications. People can text pictures, they can text PDF documents, they can text screenshots of data. It's up to each individual company, do you want to allow or disallow SMS and MMS. Also we have external media. We want to have policies in place to either allow or somehow restrict that external media usage, flash drives, USB drives, thumb drives. Do we want to allow people to be able to plug in and copy data or not? And then we have USB OTG or on the go. This is where USB devices, typically you have a PC and then say a disk drive, a master/slave configuration. Well USB on the go allows both devices to change roles. You can have two devices that typically wouldn't connect with each other be able to connect, and one takes the master, one takes the slave role, and transfer data between the two. There's potential to take a USB drive and plug it into a non-PC device or vice versa and transfer data back and forth. Do we allow that, or do we not allow that? And then recording microphones, that can be a big one. People could potentially go in and turn on a microphone on a laptop or turn on a webcam or so forth and record information without the person knowing. Actors will do that all the time, not to mention people intentionally doing it. You could have someone sitting in a meeting and turn on, record on their laptop, record the contents of that meeting. You may or may not want to allow that depending upon your environment. If in fact that's an issue for your environment, then you can disable that via policy. And we have also GPS tagging. We want to make sure that people are aware, and some of this is with training, that people are aware that GPS tagging exists with photos, with documents, so that they understand what is applicable. They understand what's advisable to send and not send and also the security implications when they do these types of things. And then also policies in place for things like Wi-Fi direct or ad hoc. We want to remove any rogue devices from our network. We want to scan for that and have infrastructure in place that detects when rogue devices are connected. We can even have it set up so that it scans for the manufacturer address. The first half of the MAC address defines the actual manufacturer. We can have policies in place that goes out and scans the network so that if someone were to plug in a Linksys or an ASUS or NETGEAR router, we can scan for those things. In other words, everything in our environment is, say, Cisco, we could scan for any non-Cisco routers or access points connecting. And if that happens, immediately shut that part down, send out an alert, and then have security investigate further. And then we have tethering. Do we allow devices to tether or not to tether? In other words, can someone take a laptop that doesn't have a cellular device inside and tether that to their phone? But that could be potential security risk because someone can then copy the data or send the data from their laptop over a carrier device that's not being monitored through our corporate infrastructure. There are potential security risks involved with that. It's a company choice whether we want to allow that or not. WE also have payment methods. Payment methods are one that has some potential for abuse, If we have the ability to do that in our environment, we need to make sure we secure those resources especially well because that's a big target for hackers and thieves.

BYOD Concerns and Deployment Models
Next we have BYOD concerns, BYOD or bring your own device. That's great for employees because it allows personal choice. You can have whatever device you want and use that in our corporate environment. It's a security challenge, however, for employers because they need to understand the nuances of many different platforms, patch management, lifecycle management. If we have two or three phones that we manage, it is very easy to understand what needs to be managed, the lifecycle of each of those devices, how to patch them, how to keep them updated. If we have 30 different devices, especially if we don't have that exact device in house, then there's nuances to that device that we're not aware of. It's important that we understand how those things function, how they need to be patched. BYOD challenges occur with monitoring, patch management, security leaks, access to data. It saves the company money. They don't have to invest in all of those mobile phones and mobile devices. But there's a trade-off. It comes down to personal choice. As a company, you need to decide which method is best for you. And then we have COPE, corporate owned, personally enabled. This bridges the gap by providing corporate-owned resources that employees can use for personal tasks. Some companies will give you a corporate device and say you cab only use this for corporate work, for corporate endeavors. More and more companies are saying we'll give you a device, we'll give you a phone. You can use it for whatever you want, but understand that we're going to

monitor it. We're going to take ownership of it. We have the ability to remotely wipe it whenever we want if you feel that's lost, stolen, compromised. We own that device. There's trade-offs. It bridges the gap, but doesn't necessarily reduce costs because you still have to buy all the devices. But it also keeps people from bringing in their personal devices, so it gives you the ability to manage a little more tightly, but still allow them to use the device for personal tasks. And then we have CYOD, which stands for choose your own device. Again, a variation on the same concept. You have, say, five different devices that you can choose from. It gives them some choice, but the company owns that device, and it's still used and managed and falls under that corporate policy. And then we have two other deployment models. One is corporate owned, and that's the traditional. The company owns the equipment, and they dictate and monitor everything about that piece of equipment, what applications are installed, how it's used, how it's accessed, and, of course, they monitor everything. It also incurs the biggest cost to the company because they have to buy everything. Then we have also VDI or virtual desktop infrastructure. This is where a company provides a thin client to a user where the actual desktop resides on a centralized server. The device or the thin client that the person uses, it can even be a remote desktop session on a full-blown laptop. It doesn't necessarily have to be just a thin client. But the end user uses some mechanism, thin client or RDP connection, to a VDI server, and their actual desktop is then brought up on that VDI server. The nice part about that is all the desktops are essentially managed. They can be patched very quickly. They can be updated and also monitored or shut down or new instances spawned very quickly. That works great in instances where you have a lot of remote workers, perhaps contractors, offshore resources. You can give them a VDI instance very quickly, and then you can either maintain persistent desktops or non-persistent, non-persistent being every time they log on, they get a brand new desktop just like it's the first time they've used it. It will have the applications that they need, but it's a fresh install. Or you could have a persistent desktop meaning when they save things on their desktop, they save the configuration, the look and feel, that stays. That way when they log off and they log on the next day, all of those things, all of these changes they made the modifications will stay. That's better for developers and people that have a lot of customizations that they need. Otherwise, if you have, like, say, teleworkers or telemarketers or people that just do very repetitive tasks that they don't have any specialization or customization needed, then that non-persistent desktop works just as well.

Additional BYOD Concerns
Some other BYOD concerns, just something to think about, is data ownership. When you have people bring their own devices, who owns the data on that device? Again, all of these things should be called out in policy. People should sign off on this. They should read through your policies and sign off when they agree to connect their personal device to the corporate network. There should be some language and definitions around data ownership. Then next we have support ownership. Who's going to support the device if something goes wrong? Patch management. Who's going to push patches out? Is it the user, is up to them to do it, or is the company going to push patches out to make sure that it maintains a certain level to connect to that corporate resource? Same thing with antivirus management. Also, forensics. Do they have access to the entire device, to only a piece of the device, or do they have access at all? Again, it

should be called out within your corporate policy. When it comes to privacy, does the user have any expectation of privacy? If it's a corporately owned device, they don't. But if It's a personally owned device, and they're attaching to corporate resources, there needs to be a clear definition of what is considered private data and not. That's where mobile device management software comes into play. You can cordon off or restrict or containerize a piece of that phone for corporate use, and everything else stays outside of corporate purview, in theory. And then we have onboarding or offboarding. What policies, what training does someone have to go through when they join a company, and then also, when they leave a company? Next, adherence to corporate policies. They have to read a policy that says, you're going to adhere to our policies. It seems a little redundant, but you as a company need to make sure your policies are in place and then also make sure the person has read those policies and agrees to them. Otherwise, they shouldn't have access to that corporate resource. And that leads into user acceptance. You need to make sure they read the policies and then accept. Also, infrastructure considerations. What infrastructure is required to support these BYOD devices? If I allow someone to bring whatever model and version of a device they want and connect to our resources, connect to our corporate environment, should I, as the company, also have a copy or a duplicate of that device? If it's a Galaxy, whatever, S8 as an example, do I need to have an S8 on hand so I can support, understand patch management and lifecycle management of that device. That's, again, cost considerations. And then legal concerns, the legal considerations around acceptable use, which we have here, things they can and can't do, places they can and can't visit, who owns the data, support, and all these things fall under that acceptable use policy. Then last but not least, on-board cameras and on-board videos. In most environments it's not a big deal, but if you're a government installation, a highly secure environment, a factory or a plant, maybe it has highly explosive chemicals, or is potentially a valuable target for hackers or terrorists or, cyber criminals, organized crime, then as a company, you may say, I don't want anyone taking any video or any pictures inside of our environment, maybe inside of a data centre. All of those things need to be spelled out in our acceptable use policies, signed off, reviewed by legal, and signed off by the individual before you gain access to the network. In summary, we covered four main topics at a high level. We talked about connection methods. We talked about mobile device management concepts. Also talked about enforcement and monitoring. And then we talked about deployment models, keeping yourself and your workforce secure while on the move or at a remote location.

Chapter 13 How to Apply Cybersecurity Solutions to the Cloud

In this chapter, we'll be talking about Applying Cybersecurity Solutions to the Cloud. We'll be talking about cloud security controls, talking about high availability, and the subcomponents, including storage, network, and compute. We'll talk about various solutions, like a cloud access security broker, or CASB. And we'll also talk about Secure Web Gateways, among other things, along with cloud native controls. As we start talking about cloud and cloud security solutions, we need to define what's the main reason or one of the main attraction points to going to the cloud. Security is one component, but also high availability. Let's talk about high availability across zones. What we'll see here is that we have availability zones or failure zones. We have a primary site which will be on-prem in this example, and then a failover sight that lives in the Azure cloud. We have duplicate resources, if you will. So high availability ensures that a resource (and whether that's an application, a service) remains available even when some of the subcomponents fail, whether it be network, storage, compute. We need to architect to make sure that if any of those things fail that we have failover capability to able to move that over to alternate infrastructure. Most cloud providers can enable HA across various pieces of infrastructure when initially creating or after installation. You don't necessarily have to pick that choice away; it can be instantiated after the fact in most cases. Applications need to be architected properly, however, to take advantage of these failover capabilities. It's not magic, we don't just pull a legacy application from an on-prem or something that's old or oldish, it could be a year old, but that's ancient in IT times, things move so fast. A legacy application, you can't just necessarily take it from on-prem, drop it in the cloud, and magically it's HA. It has to be architected to take advantage of failover capabilities, and wherever possible, have the data abstracted above the infrastructure layer, that persistence lives at the application, not necessarily the failover between the subcomponents - storage, compute. If we architect it properly, we could pull a server in and out, and the end user should not even notice. In this case we have resources that are grouped into what's called availability zones, which can be in the same data center, that's not optimal, but it's possible, we could have like four corner redundancy, as we call it. But what we talk about when we're saying availability zones is to have them in separate locations. That way, if one area goes down, even if a datacenter goes down, we can failover to that alternate facility very quickly, and keep things up and running.

Resource Policies
Resource policies enforce organizational standards and compliance. It can also control access to resources and allow access and control what actions may be performed. Not just allowing access to a facility or to a location or to a specific application, but then at a very granular level, say what specific actions can be performed. Also, what types of resources are allowed? Examples are what size VMs could be created. As an example, you might have a self-service portal or a service catalog for your end users where they can spin up resources. While you can set policy to say you have T-shirt sizes, you can have a small, medium and a large - the different sizes and what that means, it will be different for each organization. There is not one size fits all. But by implementing these resource policies, you can deploy and manage your resources in a very standardized way, the one-off applications, the one-off server, or infrastructure, or

switch that's not like everything else and it needs to be cared for, managed differently than every other piece of infrastructure. The more we have standardization, the more we have things identical, then the less we have to troubleshoot. If something goes bump in the night, we can pull that out, put a new piece of infrastructure in. You know exactly how it's configured because they're all the same, and it can reduce our troubleshooting time quite drastically.

Secrets Management

When we're talking about the cloud and we're talking about DevOps, secrets can be thought of passwords, keys, APIs, tokens used for applications. The tools and methods for managing digital authentication credentials, secrets. It's just another word for digital authentication credentials. Some things to keep in mind with proper secrets management. Let's take a look at that. Proper and secure storage is critical. Cloud providers offer native secrets management tools. AWS has something referred to as Secrets Manager, Google Cloud Platform has KMS, or Key Management Service, and Azure has something called the Key Vault. There's also third-party secrets management platforms, such as CyberArk, and also HashiCorp has one called Vault. It's critical to have those things properly secured and not stored with your code. It's possible that unauthorized people could have access to those credentials. A few best practices are using resource policies and secrets management to enforce standards and also compliance. Best practices would be to authenticate all access requests that use non-human credentials, APIs. Also, enforce the principle of least privilege. We've always advocated for that in an on-prem environment. It's even more critical when we start talking about cloud and cloud resources. We need to make sure that we have the least privilege necessary People can access and do what they need to do, but not Much that that access can have unintended consequences. Also, enforce role-based access control, or RBAC, and then regularly rotate those secrets and credentials. The ones that I mentioned from Azure, from Google, and from AWS, they have auto rotation capabilities, so it's not something that you necessarily manually have to do; it can be done programmatically. Then also, automate the management of those secrets, and then apply consistent policies. Whether it's on-prem, whether it's on the cloud, or whether it's between multiple clouds, you might be a multi-cloud environment, make sure those policies are consistent across the board, and then track access and also maintain a comprehensive audit trail. It's very important to able to audit and then also go back if something happens to be able to go back and see what exactly happened and why. Remove secrets from code, from configuration files, and from other unprotected areas to make sure that that stuff is not there. So following those best practices will go a long way to making sure that's secure and keeping it from unintended access when in the cloud.

Storage in the Cloud
When it comes to storage, whether it's on-prem or in the cloud, there's three main options, and this pertains to the cloud, as well as on-prem. We have block storage, which can be thought of as local disk? It's either SAN Fibre Channel, or iSCSI. So from a host point of view, that storage appears as a local disk. And then we have file, which is network attached storage, and that's going to give you either CIFS, or SMB, or NFS. Whether it's a Windows box or a Linux box, typically you'll have CIFS or NFS or SMB and NFS. Then we have object, which is relatively new. That's synonymous with S3, although that's not the only object protocol. But S3 is the main one that everyone knows about and most people

design, too, so that stores data as objects. It has objects, the metadata about that object, and a GUID. Those three things are stored together in buckets. When it comes to storage and making sure that things are secured properly, a couple things to keep in mind. We want to make sure that we define and then also audit who has permissions to the storage, and, the actual infrastructure as well, not just the file shares or the exports, the actual physical hardware of the infrastructure, or the virtual hardware, but the underlying infrastructure, not just what's exposed to the end user, along with the files and folders, objects. Then encryption. We want to make sure that the data that needs to be encrypted is encrypted, whether that's encrypted at rest, whether it's hardware or software-based; hardware-based will typically give the best performance, software-based usually will have overhead. Then key management. If we need encryption, it's important to understand what impact, if any, that encryption will have on the performance of the disk. Because in some instances, depending upon the piece of infrastructure, encryption can place an extra load on that data. And then also key management. Are they self-encrypting drives? You have a third-party key management platform? All of these things need to be taken into consideration when designing and architecting your encryption strategy. And then replication. Will the data need to be replicated, either on-site between arrays within the data center or within a location, or off-site? Are you replicating to a remote location, are replicating to the cloud? All of these things have funding implications. Then retention policies will also have an impact on the amount of storage required, the funding required. Then we have data sovereignty. If we replicate that data out of a specific location, perhaps a specific geographic location, are there data sovereignty implications? It's important that we understand those things. Then also, when we replicate, are we replicating to a read-only copy, making it perhaps an immutable copy to guard against ransomware? Or is it going to be a fully read-write copy, more of like in an HA environment? And then, we have high availability. High availability costs, location, additional requirements, such as network and compute, the architecture of the application may need the change, so all of these things should be taken into consideration when you're designing your storage, architecting your needs, and just understanding general implications around funding, the amount of infrastructure you need.

Virtual Networks

When we're talking about moving our infrastructure to the cloud or instantiating to begin with, maybe we're starting net new in the cloud, the networks that we'll set up are going to be virtual networks. Virtual networks are created much like physical networks, it's the same concept, the same layout. It's designed to segment traffic and secure communication. Virtual infrastructure is created for various roles. We can have things like load balancers, NAT devices, network address translation devices, traffic managers, Quality of Service, or QoS, managers, also firewalls and secure zones. All of the things that we would see in a physical world or physical infrastructure, there are virtual counterparts, and those things are typically set up in a self-service fashion when we're talking about cloud infrastructure or cloud resources. As an example, imagine if we have a virtual network, this is an example of a virtual network in an AWS instance, or an Amazon Web Services instance. A Virtual Private Cloud, or a VPC, is set up, and as an example, we have a internet gateway, we have a NAT gateway, we talked about that before, a bastion host, which is otherwise known as a jump server. That gives us something to remote into to then access infrastructure behind the firewall. Also the concept of availability zones, we have availability zone 1, 2, and 3, and these are set up to provide us with failover capabilities, whether it's HA or just failover in general, so that if one instance goes down, or one piece of infrastructure goes down, we can failover to another availability zone. That gives us resiliency and makes sure that our applications continue to run even if individual components fail. Availability zones, and then you also see we have public and private subnets, public subnets meaning things that are accessible to the public, private subnets meaning things that are behind a firewall or behind some type of gateway, and then the concept of segmentation, we're segmenting our network, public and private. We're also doing segmentation to give us additional failover capabilities, to reduce chatter, to segment, perhaps, different types of infrastructure or different groups, maybe one group should not talk to or should be cordoned off from another group for security reasons ? You have a number of different components here that we're talking about, but all of these things are set up virtually. They're all set up via a self-service portal when you instantiate within, whether it's AWS, or Azure, or Google, or any of the cloud providers, they have these self-service capabilities that allow you to click a few buttons, and then turn on this infrastructure. It's very convenient. You can provision infrastructure and resources very quickly, and duplicate what you could do, or what would take weeks or perhaps months in a physical world, if you have to go through acquisitions, and RFPs, and then go through your supply chain, and go through all the different hoops that you would typically have to go through to have infrastructure provisioned, you can do in a matter of minutes in the virtual world.

API Inspection and Integration

APIs being, application programming interfaces. A Gartner report recently said that by 2023, over 50% of business to business, or B2B, transactions will be performed via real-time APIs. What that means to us as security professionals is that securing those APIs is going to become more and more important, critically important as things go on, because more and more businesses will be conducted, not necessarily through a GUI front end, not necessarily through any type of human interaction, but through APIs, so if those things are compromised or not secured properly, that could lead to some pretty catastrophic results. Just to give you some examples of how things can be secured, so here we have a user that will send a request, they're going to click on something, but behind the scenes, it's going to be connecting through to an API. So the raw request goes through and then we have things set up that will parse through that request and make sure that it's valid. As it parses through that request, it then takes the key and value representation and runs it through a filter in real time to identify all the things that are being passed through the API. Before it reaches its destination, it's going to go through a parser that then goes through it line by line and says, this is valid, this is valid, this is valid, and you'll see as it goes through it may identify something that's malicious or not constructed properly, and it will deny that. This type of security mechanism you can almost think of as a firewall for an API. It allows things to pass through that are valid, but it will parse through each individual piece of this, and if it finds something that's not legit, or malicious, it will block that request.

Growth of Enterprise Cloud Application

We have user-led, business-led, and IT-led. The reality of it is, again, according to some recent reports, is that roughly 30% of enterprise apps are user-led, about 68% are business-led, meaning roughly about 98% of the cloud applications are led by either business or by users. Only about 2% or maybe a little bit less than 2% are led by IT. What that means is if IT is not in the loop, we have a lot of shadow IT possibilities, a lot of things that can go around IT, so it's important that IT get in the middle of this so they can become the broker to make sure that things are secured properly because if it's business-led or user-led, what's their goal? They want the application, they want the usability, they want the functionality of that application, they're not necessarily thinking about the security implications, so it's important that IT get out in front of this and not be a gating factor because if IT or if security makes things too difficult, what happens? Users just find a way to go around it, we have to make sure that we get in front of it, but we're also an enabler of that technology, not as a service? If we constantly say no, that won't work, you can't do this, you can't do that, can't do this, they'll just stop asking and they'll find ways to get around us. They'll pull out their credit card and they'll just buy the app or they'll provision it via some Software as a Service or a cloud app and we never even know about it. It's important that all these things tie together and that IT gets in front of these things.

Cyber Kill Chain in the Cloud

Cyber kill chain was developed by Lockheed Martin back in 2011. It's based on the military concept of a kill chain. If you understand how things work like the steps that an attacker would need to get from beginning to end and you understand the different points within that process, then you can develop defenses. Like any chain, if you break a link, then the chain falls apart. What we're doing here is looking for ways to break the links in that chain. Starting off, we have recon. When we're doing recon, it's probing for a weakness, harvesting login credentials or info that can be used for a phishing attack, as an example, and when we're talking about the cloud, publicly available information on company staff, executives, LinkedIn, Facebook, social media networks give out a lot of information. The reconnaissance process allows them to garner a lot of information about their subject. And then we talk about weaponization, step two in the cyber kill chain. Weaponization is creating the deliverable, a deliverable payload, using an exploit in a back door. Based upon publicly accessible information, a lot of times it's easy to create or easy to craft a message, whether it's malware, spyware, ransomware, we could put that in a malicious piece of email, a phishing attack and craft it so that it's very, very specific to the user, we're weaponizing and delivering that payload. Next is delivery. Sending the payload to the victim, a malicious email was quite often the attack vector, but often vulnerable users are discovered via social engineering and publicly available information. Also, Cloud services start to make this more and more efficient because the URLs, certificates are familiar to the user. If they have their weaponized payload delivered via a cloud hosting platform, that URL is familiar to the user, they don't necessarily look at it and question it, they just see I know what that is, and they click on it and then it gets delivered. Next, we have the exploit, so that's executing code on the remote system. Cloud services make this more effective or easier to exploit because popular cloud services are typically whitelisted, so they're allowed to get through the firewalls a lot of times. Instance awareness would help mitigate this step because the platforms and the tools we have that are instance aware can differentiate let's say, a corporate Gmail, or a corporate cloud services account, and a personal cloud services account, so you can allow some things through and not others, rather than just whitelisting everything. Next, would be installation. Installation is installing malware on the target asset. Again, with many cloud providers being whitelisted, this allows attackers to typically evade detection. Instance awareness, again, I'm mitigating control. If we can identify what's corporate and what's personal, we can block the personal accounts, so anything that an attacker would use as an example would be deemed personal or not corporate so it will be blocked, but it would still allow internal users to access these cloud services because it would be identified as a corporate resource. Next, you have command and control and this CNC is creating a channel and persistence where the attacker can control the system remotely. The cloud is great, but it has the potential to make things a little bit easier for the attackers as well, so cloud services make this challenging due to them being trusted in many environments and many popular applications can assist in masking that communication channel. They can use those communication platforms that are typically allowed in an organization, they can use them to deliver their payload and a command and control back and forth. Then we have the action in the cloud, persistence becomes more problematic because the attackers can move laterally across cloud services, they can escalate privileges, potentially encrypt data, or take services offline, they can also steal data or exfiltrate, and then instantiate new instances of cloud resources for things like crypto mining or crypto jacking, a distributed Denial of Service, botnets. It's important that we understand the steps in the kill chain, and then we develop defenses and then break the link in that chain somewhere along, the earlier the better, before it gets to step seven. They're getting what they came for.

Compute in the Cloud

When it comes to compute in the cloud, we have the concept of security groups, so controls like IAM, or Identity Access Management, things like secrets management, which we talked about, ACLs, or access control lists, and the concept of least privilege all become even more important with cloud resources. And why is that? Well, in the cloud, we have a much bigger attack surface. Cloud-based resources and cloud providers are, of course, big targets for hackers. And also, we have the concept of multi-tenancy. We have multiple clients that exist in the cloud, and that gives attackers a much wider berth to go after. You may not even be the target of a specific hack or a specific intrusion or breach, but if you're on the same infrastructure or shared infrastructure with other applications that are managed by groups or organizations that are the target of a breach, then you could potentially be impacted as well. So keeping all of these different pieces of the puzzle secure, as you can imagine, become even more and more important. Then we have the concept of a dynamic resource allocation. With the cloud, one of the big benefits and one of the attractive value props, or value propositions, is the ability to spin up resources on demand, but that also brings security, automation, and cost implications if not managed properly. In other words, if we spin things up and then forget about them and they just run, and run, and run, well, it does the bill. That gets higher and higher as well. Also, automation. If we spin things up and don't necessarily check it, and it just runs, and runs, and runs, and perhaps creates instances or creates load, or test, or whatever the automation is set to do, again, every time we run any process, we use any CPU, any cycles, any ingress or egress of data, all of those things incur costs. We need to make sure that someone's looking at those things, audits them periodically, and generally make sure that things are architected correctly and that we're not using too much resources because one of the whole benefits of the cloud is that we don't need to buy all the infrastructure up front. We need just as much as we need for that specific purpose, and then we can scale as required. The corollary to that being we tear the things down when we don't need them anymore so those costs don't continue to increase. Then we have instance awareness, understanding the differences between personal, corporate, and partner instances of cloud services, and then apply security policies accordingly. Instance awareness is a technology that's incorporated in some secure web gateways, next gen secure web gateways. It's an understanding of the difference between a personal account and a corporate account. A user at a company could have a personal and a corporate version of a cloud service. Typically, those things get whitelisted because you need access from the corporate side. However, if that user has a corresponding personal account, that would get through as well. That gives the opportunity or the potential for them to save things to their personal account, bring things in from their personal account. With an instance-aware technology, you can differentiate and block certain things that you don't want to get through. And then we have the concept of virtual private cloud, or VPC. A VPC endpoint, the same thing we talked about before. All of these different things, IAM, secrets management, ACLs, concept of least privilege, all of these things become more and more important for all the reasons we talked about previously. VPCs, or virtual private clouds, they're very, very convenient, they give us our own little mini data center, in the cloud. All of the things that we would take into consideration when designing a real data center, we need to make sure we do so in the cloud as well, and even more so because I said we have a multi-tenant environment where we have other companies and organizations that are sharing infrastructure with us, so security becomes important across the board. You're not controlling just your piece of the puzzle. Then container security, very much the same concept as dynamic resource allocation. We can spin things up on demand, but in doing so, we bring about security and automation and cost implications. If things are not managed properly, then we have the potential for costs to spin out of control or at least become larger than we anticipated.

Cloud Access Security Broker (CASB)

A Cloud Access Security Broker, or a CASB, it's a security policy enforcement tool or mechanism. It can be either on-premise or it can be in the cloud, and it's placed between the company or the consumer and the cloud provider. It ensures policies are enforced when accessing cloud-based assets, and allows us to make sure that we have a consistent set of policies between what we have onsite and what we have in the cloud. Having those things consistent gives us an added layer of security because we can ensure that things are going to be treated the same way, whether they're onsite or in the cloud. Authentication/single sign-on, as an example, credential mapping, device profiling, and also logging. All of those things should be consistent between both environments. That way we don't have discrepancies between the environments and perhaps miss something, thinking that we've configured it, but we only configured it on one side and not the other.

Application Security

Some other security considerations, application security - when we're designing these things, who can access the application? That sounds like a no brainer, but we have to make sure that we're not giving access to those who don't need it. Also, what dependencies exist and are those dependencies secured? Because it doesn't do us very much good to put a very expensive lock on the front door, but leave the back door wide open or a side window open, you get the idea. We have to make sure that all the interdependencies between applications are secured so we don't have a weak link in that chain. APIs, endpoints, single sign-on, we need to make sure all of these things are secured properly. Also, what technologies are used to defend against attacks, is it a cloud access security broker, is it a next gen secure web gateway, which we'll talk about in a moment, instance aware tools. We need to make sure that we're applying them consistently and that they're configured properly. Some of these tools have lots of bells and whistles and lots of knobs to turn, and if they're not configured, it gives us a false sense of security. It's very important that we apply consistent policies across the environment, but that we also understand what each of those policies do.

Next-gen Secure Web Gateway (NG-SWG)
Next-generation secure web gateways or next-gen SWGs. What this does is combine the features of multiple cybersecurity tools, such things as a cloud access security broker; DLP, or data loss prevention tools; activity controls, We can control at a very granular level who can do what and what specific activities they can and can't do; also instance-aware, we talked about being able to differentiate between corporate or personal or vendor or partner accounts and services, and then block or allow accordingly; and then some other things, like traditional secure web

gateway functionality, API checking, policy enforcement, compliance enforcement, all those good things. All of those things combined make up a next-gen secure web gateway just understand what that tool is and the various features that it provides.

Firewall Considerations in a Cloud Environment

Next, let's talk about some firewall considerations in a cloud environment. Traditional firewalls performed IP filtering and packet inspection. They were able to identify threats at the perimeter, but they don't differentiate between corporate versions and personal versions of services. This is where instance-aware things come into play. Traditional firewalls did not address that. And then we have cloud-based apps, like Software as a Service, and APIs introduce new challenges. Again, many more points that are publicly accessible, which means many more points that are, of course, targets for attack. Cloud access security brokers, also multi-cloud nuances. If you use each individual provider's firewall services, well, there's nuances between, so the configurations may not necessarily be consistent between environments. Also, multi-tenancy, that brings up different challenges as well simply because you have a lot of different groups that are utilizing the same infrastructure. Also, support, reskilling staff, change management, governance. All of these things come into play and, of course, should be a consideration when looking at firewall providers should you allow the cloud provider to also do on-prem firewall protection. All of these things should be thought about and considered when choosing firewall options, providers. There's a lot of nuances, there's no or wrong answer, and there's no one answer that's going to fit everybody. So, this is an area that will depend upon your specific organization. And then we also have DDOS, or distributed denial-of-service mitigation. Being able to detect in real time or close to real time and then scale as needed to be able to respond to different OSI layer attacks and then reroute traffic as necessary to reduce impact or drop it into a black hole? Then virtual firewalls, Firewall as a Service. These things enable granular segmentation? We talked about segmenting different areas, or micro-segmentation even, as needed around specific servers, applications, and services. You can segment at the subnet level, or you could scale down and get very granular and segment or firewall off at the actual application layer.

TCP/IP and OSI Models
The OSI model is a reference model designed to illustrate and standardize communication protocols, methods and devices. There's seven layers to the OSI model: application, presentation, session, transport, network, data-link, and physical. There's an OSI model, and then there's a TCP/IP model which breaks that into four layers instead of seven.

Application Layer, Protocol Layer, and Volumetric Attacks
If we have an attacker that's going to go ahead and create a botnet. They're going to infect a bunch of PCs out on the internet. And what they do with that botnet is send a bunch of HTTP GET requests to a web server, or to a target server. And in doing so, we're doing it at volume here with a bunch of hosts all sending these GET requests, and each time they do that, it spins up resources at the target. The attack is aimed at the OSI layer 7, for web servers. In a nutshell, the HTTP flood overwhelms the target system with requests that ends up exhausting resources on that target, and it takes it out of service. It makes it unable to service legitimate requests. Next, we have protocol attacks, and here we have the attacker with a bot, and what they're doing is aiming this

at layer 3 and layer 4 of the OSI model, specifically targeting firewalls and load balancers. An attacker overwhelms the target with requests. In other words, they send the requests, the victim responds, but they never get the final confirmation from the attacker, so that just leaves it open. It never closes that connection, and it just exhausts resources. They send a bunch of SYN packets to the victim. The victim responds, but they never get the final confirmation. As that continues on and on, those requests build up. The victim or the target system just eventually runs out of resources. Next, we have volumetric attacks. Here we have an attacker, again, with his trusty bot and we have a bunch of DNS resolvers out on the internet. That attacker will use the bot or the botnet to send a bunch of requests over to DNS resolvers, but I have a fake or a spoofed IP address. The IP address will be that of the victim. That way, when a DNS server responds with the response, or the answer, to that request, they're sending it to the victim instead of to the bot. That goes over and over and over again. As the attacker spoofs DNS queries with the IP address of the victim, the DNS responses get sent to the target and eventually overwhelm, or consume, all of the target's bandwidth. They can't answer their own requests, they can't originate requests, and they get taken offline. They have no bandwidth left to do legitimate activities.

Cost

Costs are always a factor no matter what organization you're a part of, and at first glance, it usually appears that the cloud is cheaper than on-prem, and in many instances, it is, but like with everything within IT, there is a big old depends, in air quotes. If you spin up a bunch of resources, but you don't use them, its uptime, you have things up, you're not using them, you're still paying for them. If you do that same activity on an on-prem situation, you're not paying for that other than just the power, but you're not paying for all of the different sub pieces of that that you would be paying for in the cloud. Also, elastic expansion is great, but if you don't tear those things back down when you don't need them, costs continue to increase. Also, data ingress and egress depending upon the application, how much data goes in and out, you can be charged for all of that. Depending upon the application, depending upon what resources you have on-premise already, it could be cheaper, it just depends on the situation, how often you need it or how busy it is. Also CapEx versus OpEx, that's an organizational preference. Some organizations are very CapEx friendly, some are very CapEx adverse. In other words, some would like to spend capital so they can depreciate the asset, all those like to do it as an OpEx, or an operational expense, so again it just depends upon your organization. There is no or wrong answer there.

Cloud Native Controls vs. Third-party Solutions
There are some nuances, and there are some pros and cons. With cloud-native controls, we have integration with the cloud provider. They are their native controls, so they work well across the board. To that point, security features are typically integrated with the other services that cloud provider offers. One potential downside, maybe, maybe not, is that the cloud provider, since it's their own tools, you and your team will need specific skills. A general set of skills typically don't apply because they're very specific to that cloud provider, and they may change from provider to provider, and also a bit of vendor lock in when you're looking at migrating or perhaps using multi-cloud environments. Then not necessarily always designed to be the most cost efficient. Not saying that they are, not saying that they're

not, but they don't necessarily guide you along the way. There are services you can get, like well-architected solutions and things like that to make sure that you are doing things in the most efficient way possible, but if you're doing it on your own, it's more of a self-service environment, you're not always going to necessarily design the most cost-efficient architecture, understanding when to take things up and down. With third-party solutions, you can manage similarly across clouds, so the same toolsets can be used no matter which cloud you're in, for the most part. Optimizations exist to reduce costs wherever possible, because they're not tied to a specific provider, so they try to make things as financially optimized as possible. And then additional security features around API access, privileges, secrets managements, you may have toolsets or features or functionality that don't exist with a cloud-native solution. It may or may not, depending upon the solutions that you choose. Then integration with other non-native applications, services, and automation. Third-party toolsets quite often are designed to work with a very wide range of tools of other third-party tools that aren't necessarily cloud native, so it gives you some options and potentially features that you wouldn't get in a cloud-native control or a cloud-native service. That doesn't apply all the time, of course. The cloud solutions are getting more and more full-featured every day. The big three come out with new services almost daily, so that becomes less and less of a distinction. And then tools typically work in a multi-cloud environment. If you're going to do all your work and you're never going to leave AWS or a Google Cloud platform or Azure, then great. If you're going to stay there forever, then that's not necessarily a concern. But if you do want to have a multi-cloud environment, maybe Cloud HA, the tools that you choose then become more critical. In this chapter, we covered a lot of great information dealing with cloud and cloud security, talking about cloud security controls, such things as high availability. Also, storage, network, and compute, the big three when it comes to the meat of any application or service. Also talked about various solutions like cloud access, security brokers, Secure Web Gateways, incidence aware. Then we talked about the pros and cons and the nuances between cloud-native controls and third-party toolsets.

Chapter 14 How to Implement Identity and Account Management Controls

In this chapter, we'll be covering implementing identity and account management controls. We have three main areas in this chapter. We have identity, we have account types, and then account policies. When it comes to identity, a few things to talk about. We have identity providers, or IdPs, and an identity provider stores and manages a user's identity. Something that which could be a username, or a password, or perhaps a PIN. Something that you have, which would be a badge or a smartphone. Then something that you are, a fingerprint, a retina scan, or some other type of biometric characteristic. This is used to authenticate users, otherwise known as principals, or other devices. It could be a laptop, a tablet, some other type of device. And then using two or more attributes to identify a user would be, as we know, multi-factor authentication. Depending upon the system that you're using, it may be that you only provide one of those three, or it could be multiples if it's a multi-factor authentication system. authentication factors, something that a password or some type of secret, something that you have, could be a smart card, could be a two-factor token, a PIN, or something that you are, like we talked about, a fingerprint, retina scan, some biometric characteristic. Then multi-factor authentication, two or more pieces of information used to authenticate, a PIN, a password, or a fingerprint. Also something to keep in mind is it must be from different categories. A password and a PIN, for instance, would only be one factor because both fall under something that you know. So for it to be multi-factor authentication, it should be from two different categories.

IdP Example

Here we have an IDP example, and we have Alice and she wants to access a ticketing application. Let's say it's a ticketing application for her work, and it is perhaps cloud based or uses an IDP or an identity provider. So she's going to attempt to access that application. It's going to realize that she's not currently signed on. What it does is it then goes out to an SSO provider or a single sign-on provider, and it will issue a request and say hey, can you let me in? Well, the single sign-on provider also realizes hey, she's not logged in. I can't authenticate her yet. It's going to prompt her to log into that application. It will then send her an SMS code, a username a password along with an SMS code, so it's going to be a two-factor authentication. Once Alice provides that information, it sends it back to the SSO provider who then will query an IDP. It'll issue what's called a SAML request to the IDP. A SAML request is a security assertion markup language, and it's a standardized way to tell external applications and services that a user is who they say they are. It doesn't authorize, but it authenticates. It sends that SAML request to the IDP. The IDP within authenticate, send that SAML response back to the SSO provider or the single sign-on provider who, in turn, then sends that SAML assertion back to the ticketing application and saying yes, Alice is who she says she is. Go ahead and let her log in to the application. When we're talking about attributes, an attribute is a piece of information about a user. It could be a username, an email address, a physical address. It could also be things like a company association, a role, a specific title, or contact info. There's many other things as well. These are just some examples of attributes, but these are what's contained potentially inside of an IDP record.

Certificates, Tokens, and SSH Keys

Digital certificates are electronic credentials that are issued to people, computers, and other electronic devices. Typically, people, or laptops, desktops, smart phones. They're used to authenticate and provide non-repudiation or to enable secure communications. It can also be applied in certain circumstances to IoT devices. Next, we have tokens. A token can have various uses, typically to authenticate an ID token, or to grant access to an API or some type of web application, which would in this case be called an access token. That's the two main types, ID tokens and access tokens, and we've talked about tokens in more depth in other chapters, so no need to dig in too deep here. And then we have SSH keys. They're used to securely authenticate when connecting to servers over SSH using a public key/private key certificate. As an example, if we are logged into Kali Linux, we have a terminal session opened, and from there you issue the command ssh-keygen, and that will generate a key that you can use to then connect securely to a remote system over SSH. If I open up that key file that was just generated, we see here's our private key, and then we can also take the corresponding public key, upload it to that server, and then use that to then securely communicate or connect with that session. Using tools like PuTTY or some other way to connect to a remote system, we can import that public key and then use it to securely connect and encrypt that communication to that remote server.

Certificate Issues

Certificate issues can result in people having access to a resource that they shouldn't have. If our certificates aren't correct, someone is able to have access to a rogue certificate or get one issued that they shouldn't have issued and they can have access potentially to resources they shouldn't have.

Mechanisms need to be in place to quickly recall or replace a compromised certificate or a compromised certificate authority. We also need the ability to rotate keys and certificates and also keep track of how resources are secure. Keeping everything in a giant spreadsheet is not going to cut it, for a small environment, maybe, but at any type of scale, that's not going to be manageable. If that spreadsheet gets lost, if the keys get lost, if things aren't backed up, we could potentially lose access to those backups, or those resources, or whatever the case might be that we're talking about. We need to make sure we can secure that properly and also refer back to it when necessary. Many organizations don't have the infrastructure to quickly invalidate a compromised certificate. If a certificate authority within their network gets compromised, all the certificates that are issued by that certificate authority should also be recalled. If there is no infrastructure and no mechanism to do that, then you're potentially putting all those assets at risk. As an example, if you're not familiar with the certificate hierarchy, we start off with a root CA, a root certificate authority. Typically, we'll install that on our network. If we're going to self-serve our certificates, be our own CA, we would install that on our network, and then once everything is set up and configured, take that offline so that way it can't be compromised, we're taking the ability to have that root CA breached. We have a root CA that's offline, once it's configured, it will issue certificates to subordinate CAs. We'll also take those offline. this is for a large enterprise, we have disparate networks, we have maybe offices in different locations maybe in East Coast or West Coast, or maybe a global organization, the root CA that sits at the top of everything would issue certificates or subordinate CA certificates and all of those will be taken offline so that they're not compromised. From there, they would issue certificates to down-level CAs, the issuing CAs, those who remain online. That way when clients enroll in the network, they can contact that issuing CA and get a certificate for whatever it is they need a certificate for, accessing a resource, logging into the network, so on. Those things will stay online, but that way, if one of those issuing CAs is compromised, it's only for that small subset, it's not for the entire environment. If the subordinate CA or the root CA were compromised, then it's a much bigger deal, we want to make sure we break this up compartmentalize so we derisk the environment as much as possible. We also make it easier for our clients to get certificates. If someone on the West Coast is logging in, they don't want to necessarily have to contact the root CA, which may be in another part of the world. If we break this up in a hierarchy much like DNS or any other type of hierarchical system, we're attaching to a resource that's closest to where we are.

Smart Cards

Smart cards gives us access control, and it's also a security device. It contains a small chip, or an amount of memory on that card, and that card can contain information about us. It can be metadata about who we are, it could contain medical records, it could contain access, as far as like what doors we can access within a building, also, different levels of authorization or authentication for network resources. So, user permissions or access information. It's also typically combined with multi-factor authentication, such as a PIN or a password. One is something that you have, the other is something that you know. For it to be true two-factor authentication, it has to be from separate categories. We can set it up so that incorrectly entering a PIN or password X number of times can even shut that card down and render it invalid. That way, if it's stolen and someone's trying to just randomly brute force their way in, that will shut things down and not allow that to happen.

User Accounts

Under account types we have user accounts, the basic building block of our environment. User accounts are unique and are used for each person accessing a resource. It's a unique identifier that's assigned to each account. As let's say for instance in a Windows environment, we could have two users, there could be two users with the same exact name. But when I create the first account and the second account, they're going to have a unique ID or security identifier. In a Windows environment that's referred to as a SID. If I delete that account and then add it back again, well, the new account is a different SID. Even though the user account name might be the same, the security ID or the SID is going to be different. Every user should have their own account and be given the least amount of privileges required to do their work. It's known as a concept of least privilege. We don't want to give them more than they need, because that gives them the opportunity to then start exploring, perhaps delete things they shouldn't have access to, access things they shouldn't have access to, install malware, spyware or ransomware.

Account Management

Under account management, there are three main tenants that we want to be aware of. When dealing with shared and generic accounts and credentials, each user should have their own account, but even more importantly, each user should have their own non-admin account. Shared accounts are also too difficult to troubleshoot or audit in the event of a breach. Shared accounts are a no-no. Every user should have their own account, that account should be a non-admin account. That way, if that account is compromised, the person doing the compromising doesn't have that elevated privileges. But because typically, when ransomware, malware, or spyware is installed, it's installed in the context of the user account that installed it. If they're an admin, guess what? That malware or that spyware has admin privileges potentially. Next, when dealing with guest accounts. Guest accounts should be used sparingly if it all. Typically, best practices is to say, disable them. But, if for some reason we need to use them, use them sparingly. In kiosks or other public access locations, they may be acceptable or they may be required. The operating system should be reimaged frequently and locked down as much as possible in these environments. Typically in a kiosk environment, you may want to reimage that machine every day so that if someone goes out and installs software, malware, spyware, each day, well that just gets reimaged and you reduce and mitigate the likelihood that those things will permeate through the system. Next, when dealing with service accounts, service accounts should only be used for, not surprisingly enough, services, not for users, and they should also be unique for each service. That way you can quickly identify what service account is accessing which service or is representing which service. Troubleshooting, audits, and revoking permissions becomes much easier when we understand what that service account impacts. If we use one service account and we give that to everything, 5 applications, 10 applications, and then we need to disable that for some reason, well, we've just disabled potentially 5 or 10, 15, 20 apps, however many we have assigned to that. It makes it very, very difficult to troubleshoot.

Password Complexity

Passwords should be complex enough to be hard to guess, that's a no brainer; however, they shouldn't be so long or so complex that our users need to write them down. That's the key differentiator here, and I think there's a fine line between usability and security. We want to make them secure enough so they can't be brute forced or easily guessed, but not Much that we have to have them written down to remember them. Passphrases often are easier to remember. Instead of having an eight character password, you might have a complete sentence or maybe a couple words in a sentence, but if it's something that's easy for that person to remember, a sentence, it's long enough to become very difficult to guess, but still easy enough for them to remember without having to write things down. Just something to keep in mind that might work in your environment. Also, we can enforce the minimum length. We have to have a password be at least six characters or at least eight characters, or whatever is appropriate for your environment. With policy, we can enforce those types of restrictions. We can also say you have to have a special character, whether it is an asterisk or an exclamation point, parentheses and so on. By having special characters, again, we're making things more difficult to guess. Also, upper/lowercase. We might mandate that the password contain at least one uppercase letter just to make things more difficult for someone to try to guess or brute force.

Password History

All of these things are used in conjunction with one another to limit or mitigate the risk of someone trying to brute force or guess someone's password. Password history, that's going to dictate how many passwords are remembered by the OS before a user is allowed to reuse a password if they ever are.

The minimum amount of time before a user can change passwords is also very helpful. And if we use these two things in conjunction with one another, we have a very secure policy. And how that works is that okay you have to go through, let's say, 5 or 10 passwords before you can reuse that password again. Let's just say I like the password. P@sswOrd1. Well, when it comes time to change, what do users typically do? it's P@sswOrd2. Comes time to change again, P@sswOrd3. And they'll cycle through until they get back to what they like, which might be P@sswOrd1. If we have a 10-password reuse cycle, they have to go through 10 passwords before they can get back to P@sswOrd1. Well, sometimes if we don't have this minimum amount of time in place, users are a little wise, and they'll sit there and they'll change your password over and over and over and over again. They'll cycle through those 10 different passwords so they can get back to P@sswOrd1, which is the one they like and that's the one they remember. That's a no-no. That defeats the whole password history and the changing your password option. By putting the minimum amount of time that a user must maintain that password before they can change it, we mitigate that risk. If we make it say you have to have that password for two days before you can change it again. They change it to pass from P@sswOrd1 to P@sswOrd2. They try to change it to P@sswOrd3 away, no good. It's going to say no, you have to wait 2 days before you can change to P@sswOrd3. That might be frustrating to them a little bit, but from the company's perspective, much more secure. It prevents that getting around the password history requirement.

Password Reuse

We can define via policy whether the user can even ever use the same password again. If you say no, once you use the password, you can never use it again, you might have a mutiny on your hands, that could be problematic for some users, but a password history of 15, 20 might be even a little bit excessive, but it certainly is doable and much more workable than saying once you use it once, you can never use it again. I wouldn't necessarily recommend that policy, but we can do all of those things of policy and enforce that across the enterprise. It can be used in conjunction with the password history. We can say it'd have to go through X number of passwords before they can, in fact, reuse that password. Next is password length. We want to make sure we define a minimum number of characters and why do we do that? Well, we don't want it to make easy to guess. We don't want the password to be one or two or A or B, we want them to have a minimum number of characters. Most secure passwords are six to eight characters in length, it can be used in conjunction with complexity requirements to ensure that users have to use uppercase, lowercase, or some type of special character, asterisk, exclamation point, and so on.

Time of Day Restrictions
Another one that may or may not be appropriate for your environment, or every environment, is different, but is time of day restrictions. What this does, it will limit a user's access to files, folders, servers, or the entire network, depending upon the time of day. What it does is it keeps users who have no need to access corporate resources after hours, or from a certain set of hours, from accessing, poking around, and potentially getting access to sensitive company information. It keeps them from having additional opportunities to exfiltrate data. By limiting a user's access to just before and just after normal working hours, you limit that exposure risk by roughly 16 hours a day. That may or

may not be appropriate for your environment. As we know, in IT, there are typically people on standby around the clock, depending upon the type of industry in your environment. It may not be applicable, but if so, if it makes sense, then consider time of day restrictions. That way you can ensure those users who have no need to be in your network don't have access.

User Access Best Practices
When it comes to user access best practices, three things I want to talk about account maintenance. We need to automatically disable temporary accounts after a period of time, periodically audit to ensure group memberships are appropriate as well. What do I mean by that? Well, when contractors come on board, typically, it's going to be for a finite period of time, whether that's a month, 3 months, 6 months. While the day that account is created, we should have an auto expire after some period of time, let's just say 6 months. If we need to extend that, we could have an automated process in place where the manager gets an email says, hey, this account is about to expire, do want to extend it. Reply yes or no, and if yes, then that automated process will extend that account for another 6 months or they may log into a portal and just click on that user account and say extend, but by doing that every 6 months or whatever that period of time is, it ensures that we don't forget about it and ensures that that user account, that contractor account that was created, 5 years ago isn't still active because if it's an account that no one is accessing, then if a hacker continuously tries to get into that account and locks it out every so often why no one is going to notice because no one is trying to use the account. It's very good, best practice in fact, for us to automatically disable those temporary accounts after a period of time. Also ensure

group membership doesn't change without our knowledge. Next, we have group-based access control, again important that we assign permissions to groups and not individual users. Well, why is that? Because when we start to assign to individual users, it becomes a nightmare to try to troubleshoot. If a user is a member of five different groups and we know what all those different groups' permissions are, but they still can't access a resource or they're still having some type of trouble, well, then come to find out they have a different level of access assigned to their individual user account, it can conflict potentially with what's assigned at the group level. As an example, if they have deny assigned, they could be a member of five different groups that have full control to a resource, but if they have individually been assigned no access, well that's going to trump everything else. The effective permission is no access, so always assign permissions at the group level. Then location-based policies. As users move from place to place, we need to ensure permissions and access adjust accordingly. Because, we don't want to assign more access and more privileges than the user needs? Always keep that concept in mind of least privilege. If you can always remember that, it's going to go a long way to ensuring users don't have more than they need and it will help mitigate that risk overall.

Permissions Auditing and Review

When it comes to permissions, auditing and reviewing, permissions are not a set it and forget it thing. I had that in quotes. It's not something we should do once and then never look at again. Periodic audits are going to ensure permissions are intact and also still appropriate. What do I mean by that? Well, as a person changes jobs, from time to time, and are given more responsibility, less responsibility, they may change roles, go to different departments, their permissions are going to change as well. As they go to a new role and they get new permissions, new access to different things, we need to make sure we're removing the old ones, the access to the old things. That way they don't start to accumulate things over time. They've been at a company for 20 years, all of a sudden they have access to everything because they've been gathering along the way. It's important to make sure that we have policies in place, automated, if possible, so as they change roles, their group membership will automatically dictate what they do or do not have access to. By periodically reviewing and auditing as well, it's going to give us the opportunity to ensure that additional s haven't been granted or changed without permission. At some point in time, someone gave someone s they shouldn't have had access to, or they may have gotten something temporarily and it was never taken away. By periodically auditing these things, we can ensure people have just what they need to do their work and no more, getting back to that concept of least privilege.

Recertification

Credentials and required clearances need to be audited and periodically recertified, whether that's every 6 months, once a year, once a quarter, floor certified individuals coming into your data center, technicians working on pieces of equipment or having access to resources hardware, software, or data. Levels of access and also the locations being accessed should be periodically audited and they should be recertified because as a company grows over time or they deal with different contractors, different vendors, the vendors themselves will shift personnel around from time to time, well, if that person that was accessing our data center 6 months ago has moved on to another position, or perhaps even another company, we need to make sure we revoke that person's access because if it's left there, guess what, that's an account that potentially is not being monitored, something that a hacker can then use and bang against if he gets locked out every so often, no one cares because no one is trying to use it so no one sees that it's locked out, and then when the lockout resets itself, the hacker can try again and he has the opportunity to potentially bruteforce those accounts, Disable the accounts and revoke access as soon as that is no longer needed. Also, when we deal with equipment or infrastructure, when infrastructure is refreshed where application is updated, we should recertify them again, make sure that the connections, the security protocols, the firewall changes that are in place are still applicable. Do we need more or do we need less? If something changes, an application changes, and it used to use 10 different ports and the updated version of that only uses 1 port, well, there is an opportunity to reduce or mitigate our risk by removing those 9 ports, by closing those 9 holes in our firewall. Periodically, auditing and recertifying infrastructure and applications is definitely a good practice.

Group Policy
Within a Windows environment, we can use group policy to enforce password rules. We can use it to enforce such things as complexity, meaning a user has to enter a password that is, meets certain criteria whether it's a minimum number of characters, it could be uppercase/lowercase, it could have special characters like an exclamation point or parentheses. We can also say, when does that password expire? Is it every X number of 30 days, 45 days, 6 months? If we have

contractors, we can set up an automated process that says, every six months that account will expire unless it's automated to extend. Certain environments might say, contractor comes in, you automatically get six months of access, or shorter if you need it, but six months max. Then if the actual company needs to extend that, maybe the person who hired that contractor might get an automated email that says, password is about to expire. Do you want to extend that? And in a lot of instances, the actual employee or the hiring manager might just simply say approve or just send back an email, that'll kick that workflow off and extend that contractor's account for another six months. But it's a good practice so that things don't extend out further than they need to. We can also enforce group membership via group policy, say who belongs to what groups, and we can also make sure that users don't try to sneak themselves into privileged groups like administrators. It can automatically run and say, these users need to be in this group, let's say the admin's group or domain admin group; or whatever we define as a special group or a privileged group, and if so and so sneaks in the back door, well every 30 minutes or so that's going to rerun through that policy and say, wait a minute, you don't belong in here, and pull him out. That makes sure that we increase our security footprint as much as possible or strengthen that position I should say, so that people don't slip in and try to go in unnoticed. We can also set things like remote access time of day, and then the length of a connection. In other words, let's just say people can remotely access our systems, but if it's after 6 PM, so that shrinks our exposure window by 12 hours. For a 24/7 shop, that's probably not the best policy. And we can also say once you log in, you can only stay connected for an hour, two hours, six hours. By limiting how long they can stay connected, again, we reduce the amount of damage someone could do if they're in here trying to do something harmful to the company.

Expiration

The next thing is password or account expiration. Temporary accounts should have an expiration date set when they are created. The reason I say that is because as an administrator, if we are in a relatively large or very large environment, we're not going to remember to disable that account we created 3 weeks ago, or a month ago, or 6 months ago, just too many of them to manage. If we do that in an automated fashion, and say, every user account that we create, if it's a temporary or a contractor account, as an example, we're going to give them 30 days, or maybe 3 months, or 6 months of access. At that point, it automatically disables unless we extend. There are a number of systems out there, and again it's going to depend on your environment, but there are a number of things that we can due to plug into your directory management or your account management system that will say, 15 days, or maybe, 3 weeks before that account is set to expire, we'll start emailing the account creator, or the hiring manager, and say, this is getting ready to expire, if you want to extend this, just reply back to this email, or log into this website, or send an email to the, the AD, or the directory service administrator, somethings are more automated than others, but by doing that, we automatically guarantee or build in the fact that user accounts, temporary accounts, contractor accounts are not going to extend beyond their useful life That way, after a couple of years, we have 30, 40, 50, 100 temporary accounts that people are long gone, but those accounts are still active, those things become security risks, they are things that are not monitored. It's an attack surface for a hacker, and they have an account that they can bang against and try to brute force or do whatever with it

187

that no one's monitoring, those are all risks that, as security professionals, we need to mitigate. It ensures that administrators don't forget to disable and expire accounts, we covered that. We leave accounts intact, just disabled, that's the differentiator. We don't want to necessarily delete that account, we want to just disable it. It can always be enabled later because if we delete that account, we also delete the security ID, or the SID, associated with that account. If there are encrypted files or things that we need that are specific to that exact account, if we delete it, even if we, even if we recreate with the same username, that SID is different. In effect, from the computer's perspective or from the OS' perspective, it's a different account. So, we can also, extend that account through some type of automated method, so there's no way or wrong way to do that, but just the main take away is we want to automatically or pre-configure that expiration to take place at X amount of days after that account is created.

Recovery

Can users recover their own passwords? Some environments, that's applicable, some it's not. It just depends upon your environment. However, if you have a password recovery process, let's make sure that security questions aren't easily discovered. We want to make sure that they don't put in like their kids names, pets names or favorite vacation spots, so these types of things are more of a training issue than an automated issue, but we need to make sure that users are very well versed in this because as a skilled social engineer and if I realize that most people are going to use their dog's name or their children's name, their favorite car, vacation spot, sports figure, there are a handful of things that most people will use as a password if given the choice. If I sit down and have a conversation with someone, I strike up a conversation at the water cooler or in the break room and say, hey, where you guys going for vacation this week or it's an awesome a picture of your kids I saw on your on your on your desk, what are their names, or I love your dog, what's his name? When you spend five minutes and just have a conversation with someone, you can get very valuable pieces of information that you can then use to try to guess bruteforce people's passwords, so those types of things should be educated into users in the back of their mind, don't use these things as passwords, or if you're going to do that or if they do it, make sure they replace those characters with special characters and enforce a uppercase lowercase policy. And then policy will define if users need to call the help desk or if they have self-service options, maybe some type of call-in or IVR System, or a web portal they can visit, or they may have to just wait 15, 20 minutes, 30 minutes for that account to unlock itself.

Impossible Travel/Risky Login

Impossible travel or risky login is a security feature many cloud-based applications have, and you may even have it internal to your organization, but in this instance, it will utilize AI and ML, or artificial intelligence and machine learning, to determine what's normal and also what's risky. Logins from IP addresses or locations within a timeframe that is shorter than the expected travel time, as an example, that requires an initial learning period typically like a week or so to understand what's normal and what's not normal, but it allows you to programmatically understand what should be a normal log in. For instance, if someone logs in from the East Coast and then 20 minutes later, they log in from the West Coast well, unless they've developed some type of time portal, and if they did, I don't know why they'd use it the log in from one coast to the other, I'd probably use it for some other purpose, but let's say they did, well then, of course, that would be normal, but assuming they don't have a time travel portal or can't travel faster than the speed of light, then that would be an unusual login., of course, they could use a VPN and log in from different locations, but that would also be part of the learning process. During that learning period, we may learn that user A logs in from a VPN periodically depending upon what they're doing, so that may eventually not get flagged as unusual, but for the most part, that would be flagged as a risky or an impossible travel login. And as an example, if we look at Azure cloud security portal ready for this specific instance, we see there are some alerts generated impossible travel activity for a specific user or a specific service? We flag that and then issue alerts to the administrator and say, hey, there is something suspicious going on, this user logged in what we're flagging as impossible travel or risky log in, here is the information, here are the details, and then the administrator could then take further action, if necessary. There are a number of ways to do this, we could do it manually or programmatically through this cloud app security, as an example, but it's not the only way to do it, but just understand the concept of an impossible travel or a risky log in. We're trying to flag activity for users that would just not be able to do what it is they're doing. It could be indicative of someone trying to hacking account, if someone logged in from the East Coast and then a half hour later or 10 minutes later, they logged in from another country, they couldn't possibly travel that far, well it could be, it could be normal activity via VPN, or it could be someone hacking that account from another country that's trying to get in to that account, so it definitely warrants some additional investigation.

Lockout

A policy should be put in place that automatically locks a user's account after "X" number of times that they incorrectly log into the system or try to log into the system. Typically it's 3-5. You can adjust that up or down, depending upon your environment. But, once an account is locked out, it will typically stay locked out for 20-30 minutes or maybe upwards of an hour. But the key thing here is we want to make that lockout duration long enough to thwart brute force attacks. A 30 minute period is usually good. That way a user can't just continuously run a script or sit there at a keyboard and trying to bang away one after the other after the other, trying to get information or trying to guess a user's password. It will lock out after three attempts or five attempts. Then they have to wait a half an hour.

Disablement

That brings me to disablement, and I talked about this briefly before, but we should disable unused accounts instead of deleting them. And we have already covered the fact that a user account has a security ID, or a SID, under the hood? We look at the user account as lowest X, or lowest one, or lowest two, or whatever, but under the hood, it's some long string of characters alphanumeric numbers that is the security ID. That's what the computer recognizes as that account. If we delete them, they can have a different SID, even if we recreate them with the same username. If that user encrypted documents or did some things that are specific to that user account and then we delete them, we're going to have a much harder time trying to recover that information. Instead of deleting, let's just disable. Once we do that, we can always re-enable it later. In this chapter, we covered three main areas. We talked about identity and all the things associated with a user account, IDPs, attributes, multi-factor authentication. We also talked about various account types and we talked about account policies like lockouts, disablements, impossible travel, risky logins, and various ways to make sure that our accounts are secure as possible.

Chapter 15 How to Implement Authentication and Authorization Solutions

In this chapter, we'll be covering implementing authentication and authorization solutions. We have three main areas again. We have authentication management, talking about passwords, trusted platform chapters, hardware security methods. Some of these terms should be familiar to you. Also authentication methods, talking about protocols and platforms that we use to authenticate users in the environment. And then access control schemes, talking about security settings and methods. When we're talking about authentication management, there's some concepts that you should be familiar with; password keys. We're talking about public key or private key, or it could even be a master key to key vaults. You should be familiar with both PKI infrastructure, public key/private key, and also using them whenever possible, whether it's for SSH connections to servers, whether it is certificate management for various connectivity for communication, transfer of files, or connecting to remote servers, and our master keys to key vaults. And when I say a key vault, I mean a password vault. A secure platform that enables you to store passwords for either automated retrieval or manual retrieval. You can place passwords in this vault to allow users to access them so they don't have to keep them somewhere where hackers or attackers could get access to them easily. A password vault would be a secure area on the network, typically a platform like CyberArk or KeePass as an example. Some are more enterprise ready than others. But you can place your passwords in there and either use them just as a dumping ground, where you have to go in and manually retrieve them, or some of the more full-feature platforms are API enabled Your applications and programs can programmatically access those vaults, the API, and use the passwords within there without having to extract or type those things in manually. Some can also rotate passwords on a predefined schedule, again, removing some of that manual user intervention from the process. Then we've talked before about the Trusted Platform Chapter, or TPM chip, which is a secure area usually embedded on a device, whether it be a laptop, a server, perhaps even a smartphone, they have secure areas within those devices as well, so that's where we can store cryptographic keys to keep them out of prying eyes. Then we have hardware security chapters, or HSMs, and this is similar in form and function to a TPM chip; however, this is on a card that can be inserted into a server and also be used to securely store cryptographic keys. Then we have knowledge-based authentication, otherwise known as a secret question. It's a component of MFA, or multi-factor authentication. In this case, a user's asked a secret question, perhaps what's your favorite dog's name, or where'd you go to high school, or what was your first place that you held a job? These things are good to an extent. Keep in mind if you do use knowledge-based authentication and you have common questions like this, a lot of things out there on social platforms are geared towards getting the answers to these questions. You'll notice on some of the social media platforms they have quizzes and little games you can get into where they'll ask you your high school mascot or test your knowledge about the first place you worked. Well, those things could conceivably be used to gather information that could then be paired with user identities down the road. If they're able to get this information and then pair this up with usernames or passwords that is either stolen from that person or that application directly or combined with other breaches, that can give a lot of information that can answer some of these secret questions. If you have the ability to set up secret questions within your organization, make them such that they're not easily guessable or something that a social engineer would be able to pull from someone just by asking a few innocuous, or at least seemingly innocuous, questions.

Extensible Authentication Protocol (EAP)
EAP, or Extensible Authentication Protocol was defined by RFC 3748 and then replaced by RFC 5247. It's an authentication framework, as opposed to a specific authentication mechanism, but EAP is widely in use across a number of different formats, roughly 40 different formats currently, and some of which you may be familiar with, such things as LEAP, EAP-TLS, or EAP-IKEv2. The takeaway being that an Extensible Authentication Protocol, extensible, meaning it can be added to, you can plug things into it. It gives us a framework that other things can use, whether it's TLS or other authentication mechanisms, perhaps that haven't even been invented yet, but it gives that framework that these things can then plug into very easily.

Challenge Handshake Authentication Protocol (CHAP)
Next, we have something referred to as CHAP, and CHAP stands for challenge handshake authentication protocol. CHAP was originally used to authenticate PPP clients, or point to point protocol clients, to a server, clients dialing in or accessing a remote server. It's a one-way hash based on a shared secret, in this case, a user's password is compared at both the client and the server. Plain text is never sent over the wire, and as an example, we have a client that wants to log into a server. When that client connects to that resource, the server will turn back and say enter your password. The client does not enter or send the password in clear text over

195

the wire. What it does is it runs a challenge handshake authentication protocol, or CHAP, it hashes the user's password, and then passes the hash over the wire. The server on the other side knows that user's password has it in its database, it's going to run that same hashing algorithm against the password. If the hashes match, then the client is given access to that resource.

Password Authentication Protocol (PAP)

Next, we have something referred to as PAP, or Password Authentication Protocol. This has been deprecated. It's a username and password that's sent in plain text. With a username and password being sent in clear text, it's easy to see why that's no longer used. Again, as an example, we have the client and the server. The client's going to send their full username and password in clear text. Anyone with any type of packet sniffer can pull that information off the wire. What's happening is the user sends their username and their password in clear text, the server's going to check that against its database and then grant or deny access. But as we know, as security professionals, that's a bad idea. Sending things in clear text, very easy to pull that information off the wire using Wireshark or some other type of protocol analyzer or network sniffer. We don't use this specific authentication protocol anymore.

Port Security and 802.1x Authentication

The next concept I want to talk about is port security and 802.1x, securing physical access to the network. We want to control the ability of someone to just walk into our environment, whether it be a kiosk at a retail store, or a library, or a school, or even within our corporate environment, we don't want to necessarily have someone being able to walk up, pull out their laptop, pull out a CAT5 cable, plug it into the wall, and gain access to our network. One way we can do that is through something called port security. This is particularly applicable to things like kiosks, schools, libraries, not necessarily throughout an entire environment, it becomes a little bit unwieldy at that point, but for specialized situations where we want to control specific access to specific ports, port security is definitely a good fit there. What we can do is configure a switch so that it only learns one MAC address per port. We can keep attackers from sending multiple fake addresses. So, in other words, someone can't pull out their laptop, plug in, and then just start bombarding our network with fake MAC addresses. Because if you recall, when we have our devices and it connects to a switch, that very first time it does that, it goes out and tries to get an IP address via DHCP, or it may have one hard-coded, it's going to try to ARP for some resources, it might go to DNS, it might go to whatever the case might be, try to resolve a URL, whatever action is taking place, it's going to put datagrams onto the network. As soon as it does that, the MAC address of that device is attached to that datagram. It's a layer 2 piece of information. The switch, which is a layer 2 device, will learn, or memorize, that MAC address and associate it with that port. And so the switch will learn over time all of the devices that are connected to it, what MAC addresses are associated with which ports, so that way, when information comes in, it knows what port to send that information out of. It's a very directed process. Broadcasts will go out all ports, but if it's traffic between PC1 and PC2, PC1 is connected to the port 1, PC2 is connected to the port 10, as an example, it will only go in port 1 and out port 10. So that keeps things more secure. However, as I was mentioning, we have malicious individuals or malicious activity that can take place where someone could flood a specific port and overrun the MAC table on that switch and bring it down. By sending port security and only allowing certain MAC addresses or one MAC address per port, we negate that ability for someone to do that type of activity. We can also use that in conjunction with something called 802.1x to strengthen security at the wall jack. As I mentioned before with, school setting as an example, or a kiosk, we have something called 802.1x authentication. What that is, is EAPOL, or Extensible Authentication Access Protocol, over LAN, over a local area network. That Extensible Authentication Access Protocol gives us the ability to say, when somebody connects to our wall jack, we're not going to allow them to communicate until they authenticate with the network. They're going to authenticate with something called a RADIUS server. It's an authentication server. In this schema, it's a multi-part process, the client, which is in the terms of this authentication process, is called a supplicant, the client is going to initiate a request that they're going to plug into the wall jack, they're going to say, hey, can I communicate? The switch is going to say no, not until you authenticate. It will only allow EAPOL traffic to pass through that port, it will send it off to the authentication server, all of these things have to be configured in place so that this process takes place, but once it's set up, the port will not be activated until that authentication process is complete. The supplicant will send information to the switch, the switch will then forward it onto the authentication server. Once the credentials are validated and verified, in other words, the client is authenticated, and then the authentication server sends that information back and says, yes, you can communicate, the port is wide open, and of course, the supplicant or the client can communicate on the network.

RADIUS

We have something we refer to as RADIUS, and that stands for Remote Authentication and Dial-in User Service. It started out as Remote Authentication and Dial-In User Service, but people are coming in from cable, from fiber, from other mechanisms, so it's not just referring to dial in, but the concept is the same. It provides AAA capabilities. When I say AAA, I mean three things. It provides authentication, and authentication identifies the user and allows or denies access. We're going to identify that user and either allow them or deny them access. We can also challenge for additional credentials, a two-factor authentication, such as a PIN or a rotating code. They may have a key fob or a dongle. Then next, it's going to provide for authorization, and that deals with providing things like the length of time allowed on the network, access control lists, or ACLs, for various resources, and then on top of that, we're going to provide accounting. Accounting is used for tracking the start and stop time of each session, and it can be used for billing, or perhaps showback, to show how long the user was connected to that service. If we look at an example, we have Alice and she's referred to as a supplicant. We're talking about a RADIUS example where we have a supplicant, we have an authenticator, and then an authentication server, or AS. And you'll also see an AD or LDAP server off in the distance here. That is the actual mechanism that's going to pull up the user account and make sure that they're in the system. Alice perhaps wants to access a resource. She wants to connect to a wireless access point in this example. Well, rather than have each individual wireless access point have her username and credentials, there may be dozens within her environment, they simply are configured to point to a RADIUS server. That way, Alice goes to log in, the supplement to the authenticator. The authenticator is simply going to pass through that request to the RADIUS server. The RADIUS server is what provides the authentication. The RADIUS server's going to contact AD or LDAP, depending on how it's configured, and say, does Alice exist, and what are her credentials? Is she allowed access or not? And if so, we'll reply back positively, replies back to the wireless access point, and she's allowed access. We can further go on, and if we wanted to layer on 802.1X authentication, we can also make sure that Alice's machine can log into that wireless access point as well. We can not just necessarily filter by MAC address or by IP address, we can also filter by account credentials as well. There has to be a valid account on the network before authentication is granted to that wireless access point.

Single Sign-on (SSO)
Next up is single sign-on and single sign-on is a method of allowing users to access all resources that they're going to need, within an environment with a single username and a password. It negates having to remember multiple usernames and passwords. We talked about previously, whether it be a Kerberos realm or Active Directory or some other authentication mechanism or directory service, by having that in place, a user can sign on once to a directory server or an Active Directory server and some type of directory service and then access everything within that environment. Of course, they have to have access granted to them? They can't just login and automatically access everything. Each individual resource is still controlled by ACLs, but they don't need to remember username and passwords for each resource, so it makes it much more secure, mitigates risk by keeping users from having to write down credentials. If you have to remember, 50 different passwords or 100 different passwords for your work

environment, it's going to be very difficult to keep those straight in your head, you're going to have to start writing those things down. Once they're written down, make the task much easier for a hacker to come in and retrieve that information, not to mention the fact that come password changing day, it's a lot easier to change your password once and have it propagate everywhere or have access everywhere rather than having to remember to change your password on 50 different resources or 100 different resources, whatever your environment entails by having to do that each and every time become a very tedious process.

SAML

SAML stands for the Security Association Markup Language, and what this is authenticating through a third-party to gain access to some resource. That resource being accessed isn't responsible for the authentication. You may see this a lot when you're browsing websites out on the Internet, you may go to a website and it asks you to log in, but you're not going to login on that site specifically, you might log in with your Google ID, or an email address, or some type of open ID, or your Facebook account, or your Twitter account. These different things can act as a trusted third-party that will pass through to the site you're trying to access. The authentication requests are passed to that trusted third-party server, the user authenticates to the third-party server, they're issued a token, that token is passed to the target resource. We have a client, we have a resource server that we're trying to get to, and then we have some AS server, the authentication service so that's going to be SAML, in this case. If we look at an example, we have a client, the resource server, and the AS server. The user wants to access a URL, they want to go out to a resource. Well, what's going to happen is that resource server will post to the AS, with an authorization request to the SAML server. If that user is not already logged in, then they're going to be asked to log in, they're going to log into that AS server, or the SAML server, because there is a good chance you may already be logged into one of these third-party services, and you may be logged into Twitter or Facebook or whatever ahead of time. When that happens, you're redirected to the resource that you're trying to get to with the SAML token and you're logged into that resource server represented with the web page or the resource that you're trying to get to. There are some SAML alternatives. The federated ID concept has several methods that are currently in use. SAML is not the only one. SAML is one that we mentioned, but then we have also OpenID and also OAuth, so they all provide similar features and functionality. However, many of the most popular websites function as the trusted third-party, they use either OAuth or open ID. If you log into a website using your Facebook credentials or your Google ID or your Twitter account, you're using one of those too, probably not SAML, but the concept is the same. I just want to make sure you understand the concept and how it's passed from that trusted third-party onto the site that you're accessing.

TACACS

TACACS stands for terminal access controller access-control system. TACACS was originally developed in 1984 for controlling access to MILNET - the military network. TACACS is not in use anymore, it's been replaced by newer versions, but I just want to give you an idea of where things have come from and where we're at currently. TACACS has been replaced by something called XTACACS, Extended terminal access controller access-control system. This was a proprietary set of extensions to TACACS developed by Cisco in 1990. It added those three additional features that we talked about previously authentication, authorization, and accounting. RADIUS had it, TACACS, at that point, did not. However, the takeaway here is that XTACACS is not backwards compatible with TACACS. We added three things, authentication, authorization, and accounting, and then no backwards compatibility with TACACS.

TACACS+

Next we have TACACS+. This is the most common implementation of TACACS, which is why I wanted to focus in this area, just give you an idea of where we've come from with the other two previous versions. TACACS+ is the most common implementation, it's going to run on TCP over port 49. It also encrypts the entire communication, so that's something new for TACACS+. Previously, it only encrypted the very beginning piece. We encrypt the entire communication, much more secure. It's not vulnerable to the security issues associated with radius. Some key differentiations and I'm going to compare and contrast those two here in just a moment, but remember that, not vulnerable to security issues because it encrypts the entire communication, and it also separates authentication and authorization to allow more granular control. We can split those out to separate servers, so we don't necessarily have to have everything running on one server. As with the previous version, it's not backward compatible with its predecessors. If we look at RADIUS versus TACACs+, there are a couple things we should be aware of. With RADIUS, it combines authentication and authorization, it encrypts only the password, requires each network device to contain authorization configuration, there is no command logging, minimal vendor support for authorization, UDP, which is connectionless, and, of course, the UDP port set operates upon 1645 and 46, 1812 and 13. It's designed for subscriber

AAA, not necessarily for administrator or administration. TACACS+, on the other hand, separates all three elements of AAA making it more flexible, it's also going encrypt the username and the password. That's very important to understand. It also allows for centralized management of authorization and configuration, so that's going to give us a lot more flexibility and allow it to scale on a much larger sense. It has full command login as well and it's also supported by most major vendors. It's TCP oriented, which is connection oriented? UDP is connectionless, TCP is connection oriented, it operates off of TCP port 49, and it's designed for administrator AAA.

oAUTH

OAuth is an open standard for authorization. It's commonly used as a way for internet users to log into third-party websites using their accounts at some of the big providers - Google, Facebook, Microsoft and Twitter. But, it allows them to do without exposing their individual password. They can log in or use the login credentials from those bigger services, that's a trusted third-party, and then when you access whatever resource it is you're going to access, they query Google or they query Facebook, and make sure that you are who you say you are and you have the proper authorization. It allows access tokens to be issued to that third-party client by an authorization server with the approval of the resource owner. It's all tied in. As an example, you have a user that wants to access some client applications. They're going to request a service, they're redirected back to the authorization server, and then there's an authorization between user and authorization server, that authorization is granted. They're redirected with that authorization code. It then requests a token with that authorization code, which goes back to the client application. It goes all the way out to the actual resource server, which comes back to the client application, response is sent back to the user, the user requests the service, request for the data with the access token is sent to the resource server, and then it's sent back to the client application and then back to the user. All of this happens behind the scenes, so all you do is click on a resource, you sign in with your Google or Facebook or whatever, Twitter account, that authorization takes place. All of this happens behind the scenes, you don't even see any of this, and all you know is you log into that resource. So, just understand that there are some things taking place under the covers, and that you need to know the basics of the process. However, you don't have control over how Google or Twitter or Facebook mandates their process. Just understand that they're a trusted third-party, and that authentication is used to authenticate to other external resources.

OpenID and Shibboleth

OpenID is a standard, it's an open standard that provides SSO capabilities. The cooperating sites that participate in this OpenID framework, they're called relying parties or RP. A user chooses an OpenID provider, and there are a number, and they use that account to log into any website that accepts OpenID authentication. I'm sure you've seen this before where you go to a website, and it may give you the option of creating an account or logging in with your email address. Or you can log in with your Facebook credentials, Google account, Twitter. It gives you that ability to log in with a trusted third-party ID. And then we have something referred to as Shibboleth, and that's based on SAML, we talked about previously. It provides a free and open source federated single sign-on and attribute exchange framework. It's similar to OpenID in concept. Shibboleth also provides extended privacy functionality, which allows a user and their home site to control the attributes released to each application. You have some finegrain control over what is shared. When you log on it may be configured to just send perhaps your username and email address, or it could send additional attributes as well, whatever is configured within that framework, to share between entities.

Kerberos
Kerberos is, in Greek mythology, a three-headed dog that guarded the gates of Hades, and its applicable here because there's three components when a user or a client wants to access some type of service. It's a network authentication service that was originally developed by MIT, and is used for mutual authentication between client and server. This gives us that dual authentication I talked about before where the client authenticates to the server, the server also authenticates to the client. Some key terminology before we get into the details here. We have something referred to as a KDC, or a key distribution center; we have an authentication service, or the AS; we have a ticket-granting ticket; we have a ticket-granting service; a principal; and an authenticator. If we look at this in a little more detail, I'm just going to cover this at more or less a high level. You don't need to dig down into the nitty-gritty details for the exam, but just for your own information, there are a couple of things that go on here in the background. The client wants to connect to a service. The client needs to authenticate, we're using KDC, or a key distribution center, which in a Windows environment is going to be the domain controller. That's going to contain the authentication service, and also the ticket-granting service to give those TGTs. The client will send that request to the KDC, or the authentication service, the authentication service will generate what's called a

session key. It's going to encrypt that session key with the user's password and it encrypts the session key and this user's username, which is also referred to as a Kerberos principal. It's going to create what's called a service ticket and send that back to the client. There's two pieces to that. The client can decrypt the first part, because it has its password. The password, incidentally, is not ever sent over the wire. It's a hash on the client side and it's a hash on the domain controller, so that is used to encrypt, and then it's sent back. The client can decrypt that first part. It cannot decrypt the second part because it doesn't have that, only the service does, but the client will encrypt that second piece along with a timestamp, which is referred to as an authenticator, and it sends that service ticket over to the service or the server that it needs to connect to. The server can then decrypt because, again, it has that information that only it can decrypt, so that's where this mutual authentication is going back and forth. Only the client can do what it can do because it's the only one with the password. Only that server can do what it can do, because it's the only one with the password. If anyone were to capture that in between, it's not going to do much good, because, again, we have things timestamped as well, so that prevents replay attacks. Once all this is done and the service looks up and says, I trust the KDC, the client trusts the KDC, the KDC says, yes, the client is valid, go ahead and grant that service, they connect. Going forward, each time that needs to happen again, rather than having to go through this process for every single connection, you get what's called a ticket-granting ticket. That takes that first part out of the loop, so the next time it needs to make a connection, the client goes to the KDC, to the authentication service, requests that TGT, send that over to the service, and that's encrypted by the session key that was originally set up with that AS. It only has an 8-hour lifespan, Every so often that's going to need to be regenerated. But the point of that is, the very first time it needs to connect to a service it's going to go through the process, encrypt, get those two pieces sent to it, it's going to be able to decrypt one. It'll re-encrypt the second piece along with the timestamp, send it over to the service, the service can decrypt. Next time around, it uses a ticket-granting ticket to shortcut that process so it doesn't have to re-authenticate. It's already valid with a session key that's valid, again, for 8-10 hours, so that way it can just pass directly over to the service and make a connection.

Attribute Based Access Control (ABAC)
Attribute-based access control, or ABAC, it's dynamic, so it's considered more or less the "next-gen" authorization mechanism, and its policies comprised of attributes that can be about anything or anyone. We can get very granular, and it's not confined to a set of predefined rules or a specific type of role. It allows for set-valued and also atomic-valued granularity, and that can be combined for complex Boolean rule sets. Let's take a look at what comprises attribute-based access control. We have three things at the architecture level. We have a Policy Enforcement Point, or a PEP, and that protects the resources being accessed. The PEP generates authorization requests and sends it to what's referred to as the PDP, so that is the Policy Decision Point. The PDP evaluates incoming requests against configuration policies. The PDP permits or denies and may request additional information, metadata in other words, from something referred to as a Policy Information Point, or a PIP. The PIP is a bridge between the PDP, the Policy Decision Point, and external sources of information such as LDAP, specific databases. You can get very granular as to say who can do what. If a person is a specific type of role, perhaps, if they

have a certain type of clearance, perhaps, if they're trying to do a specific type of action. If we look at that in more detail, these specific attributes, we have subject attributes, so that could be anything about the user requesting access. It could be their age, security clearance or their job title. All of these are specific things that you can use to key off of when granting or denying access to a specific resource. Next, we have action attributes. That refers to the action, or actions, being attempted, whether it's read, write, delete, approve, deny. And then we have resource and object attributes, and that describes the object being accessed, the type, the department, the classification, the sensitivity. Much more granular when we start combining all of these things together, who they are, where they're coming from, their age, their clearance, their title, combined with who the user is, what action they're trying to do, what object they're trying to access. Then we have contextual or environment attributes, and this can be things like time, location, or other dynamic aspects. When you combine all of these things together, as you can imagine, you can get a very complex if/then Boolean type of logic around decision making. What it does is it gives us that granular, dynamic ability to provision. We don't have to do things ahead of time. We can let it happened on the fly, depending upon who that user is, where they are, what their title is. As they move throughout the day, move throughout locations, as they change titles, that specific, read, write, delete, approve, deny, all of those things will change, as the attribute about that person changes.

Rule-based/Role-based Access Control (RBAC)
Next, we have rule-based access control, and RBAC is used in two separate context. In this specific one, we're talking of a predefined or a preconfigured security policy and that's

going to define and decide access. We could say explicitly deny all of those, except in an allow list, or we could say deny only those who specifically appear in a denial list. It's very much a list-based control mechanism, it's more flexible than MAC or mandatory access control, but less flexible than discretionary access control. That list is configured ahead of time. Then we have another role-based access control, or RBAC, context and that is a role-based access control and that access is based, on the user's role. Group membership determines what a user can and can't do, so that's pretty much how most enterprise operating systems and most enterprise environments are functioning. So once a user changes roles, then their access will change accordingly. As an example, a user might be moving from human resources to finance. So if we have a few folks that are in human resources. If they move over to finance, well they're going to lose access to that human resource document and all those files and folders. However, they're going to gain access to the payroll files. Just by virtue of moving from one group to another, they're going to lose access to their old stuff, but they're going to gain access to their new stuff. It's easy to manage, an administrator doesn't have to go in and specifically give s to each individual person, he can pre-configure those rules and those access s to a group, that way, when people come in and out of that group, they're automatically granted those permissions.

Access Control Methods
There are four main methods of access control that I want you to be aware of for the exam. We have mandatory access control. Or MACs, and that is very inflexible and it's very rigid, but it's also the most secure. Things are written in stone, there is no flexibility, no one can pass your information on to somebody else, it's very, very inflexible.

Next, we have discretionary access control lists, and they are a little more dynamic, they're flexible, they're also the least secure so things can change on the fly. Then we have role-based access control, or RBAC. Role-based access control is access based on a role or a group membership. This is what pertains typically in a Kerberos environment, Linux environment, Apple, and also within Microsoft's Active Directory. You place users into groups, you give access to those groups. If you pull a user out of a group, then that access gives away. Then last we have rule-based access control, again, using RBAC, so that's access based on a predefined list. That is saying, if you're on the list you're in, if you're not, you're not. We can either have explicit permit or explicit deny lists depending upon how we have things set up.

Mandatory Access Control (MAC)
Mandatory access control, or MAC, is a predefined set of capabilities and access to information, who can share what and also to whom. As an example, we have a finance folder here we can control who has access to what files and folders, but we can also control, this is written into the program, or it's controlled by a centralized security administrator that says, this person has access to these files and folders, but they cannot share those files and folders with someone else. Even if they create a file, they can't share it, it's very inflexible, and it's very rigid. But it's also the most secure model. But it must be carefully thought out and planned ahead of time because, that lack of flexibility makes it very rigid. If it's not planned properly, it can be a nightmare because people cannot do their work, so it has to be very carefully thought out before it's implemented. But once it is implemented, it's also very easy to spot breaches or

deviations because everything is very clearly defined, so if there's any deviation from that, it's very easy to spot.

Discretionary Access Control (DAC)

Discretionary access control, or DAC, that allows users to dynamically share information with others. This is what most environments are comprised of. It's less secure, and it's harder to control information leakage, however, it is how things get done. If I create a file or a folder, I should be able to share that with someone else, that's the general thinking. I may not necessarily be able to share someone else's documents, but if I'm in control of my own stuff, I should be able to say this person can view it, or copy, delete, or this person cannot, I should have control over that. In a mandatory access control environment, there is no flexibility. In a discretionary access, we have that flexibility, but again, less secure, but there is the opportunity for information leakage.

Conditional Access

This is a policy-based access framework based upon if/then type logic to determine the level of access or actions required. We're talking typically around cloud-based services, cloud-based applications, in this case, a software application as a service, or a SaaS application. If it's a certain user or part of a certain user group, or perhaps maybe if it's a certain type of device, or a certain network, or a certain network location, or even a certain application, well, if it's any one of those things, then we could apply policy and say, then either block access, or we could say, then require multi-factor authentication. Let's say, for instance, if a user is part of a specific group, and they're using a specific device, and they're trying to access a specific application, then require multi-factor authentication, or we could say block that, or we could say we're going to require a password change the next time they log in. All of these things can be done programmatically from the portal or from the configuration tool set, but the takeaway being conditional access is based around an if/then type of methodology. If a user or a device meets these certain set of criteria, and then apply some type of action.

Privileged Accounts
Privileged accounts should only be used sparingly as well. We should use non-admin accounts, non-privileged accounts, for most normal day to day activities. Non-admin accounts reduce the likelihood that something can get installed in our systems and in our environment that we don't want, and if they do happen to get installed, it does with a reduced set of privileges. We should only have these privileged accounts to perform admin-level functions, even admins should have a non-admin account and then an admin account. They would use their lower level account when they want to do day to day activities, and then when they want to do something that is administrative, they would execute that account under that admin account, whether it's an administrator account or pseudo account, it depends upon the operating system, but use those things sparingly. Users, should use non-admin accounts for their daily tasks and their daily activities. Invoke privileged accounts when necessary to perform specific tasks. Separation of those accounts makes things much less likely to be abused.

Filesystem Permissions
When it comes to filesystem permissions improper permission settings on files, folders or even symbolic links, can give attackers unintended access. That means web servers, the files and folders that sit on the web server if

they're accessible and they're not properly secured, it could have unintended consequences. We're also talking about database servers, file servers, pretty much any type of file system within our network, if they're not secured properly, it can have unintended consequences and it could be giving away critical information. So, Windows servers typically have read, write, and execute as their permissions. Linux servers can get more granular. But just understand that auditing should be enabled on critical, or restricted files and folders to make sure that these things are secured properly, and also that they stay that way. Because it's possible, for things over time to get changed or shifted either intentionally or unintentionally, and then if we're not aware of those changes taking effect, it could have, unintended consequences, leaking personal information or confidential information, things we don't want others to see, and certainly things we don't want attackers or bad actors to have access to. In this chapter, we covered authentication management, passwords, TPM chips, HSM chapters. We talked about authentication methods, various protocols and platforms that enable authentication across our enterprise. We also talked about access control schemes, security settings, methods.

Chapter 16 How to Implement Public Key Infrastructure

In this chapter, we'll be covering implementing public key infrastructure. We'll talk about public key infrastructure along with the types of certificates, certificate formats, and then certificate concepts. What are a certificate authority and a digital certificate? But just understand that it boils down to PKI, a public key infrastructure, and that facilitates a secure communication between sender and recipient. That communication can be sent over a secure network, something internal, perhaps within a company, or it can be used to communicate over an insecure network, i.e. the internet. By using that public key/private key combination, we can encrypt, as we talked about previously, we can encrypt bulk encryption keys or symmetrical keys we can use a combination of the asymmetrical encryption functions, public key/private key, along with symmetrical functions, which gives us the ability to bulk encrypt, stream large amounts of data quickly, and the combination of the two allow us to securely communicate over that insecure medium.

Certificate Authority
A certificate authority can be internal to our organization or it can be external. As an example, we have one that's external, it's going to live out on the internet, and it will be used as a trusted third party for both Bob and the financial institution, in this case, a bank. They want to communicate. Bob wants to initiate some transaction. So, the certificate authorities that are out on the internet can be Thawte, they can be Verisign. There are a number of major certificate authorities that provide credentials pretty much for the majority of the internet and most of the companies on the

internet. The CA is trusted by both Bob and the bank. When Bob connects to the bank the first time, he's presented with that bank's public key if he wants to establish a secure communication channel. He has the public key that's given to him by the bank. He will use that public key to encrypt session keys that he sends back to the bank. The financial institution is the only one that can decrypt that communication because they have the private key. Bob can be sure that the bank is the only one that can decrypt. Bob can also, if need be, verify the credentials that were presented to him with that certificate authority and make sure that they're still valid. Just like if a police officer pulls you over and checks your credentials, check your license, he's going to trust the state to issue a valid set of credentials. He can check the CRL. He can either go into his mobile terminal or call dispatch and say, let me run this driver's license and see if it comes back as valid. If it does, then he can proceed either giving a warning or a ticket or, whatever he's going to do, but he checks the validity of that credential. Bob can check against the CRL to make sure that it is in fact valid. Assuming that it is, he will encrypt the session key he's used to communicate; he'll send that back. The bank is the only one that can decrypt. It will decrypt that communication, extract session keys, and they have a bulk encryption algorithm they can use to establish further communication over that TLS or SSL channel. It's encrypted, and it's secure.

CRLs

A CRL, or a client revocation list is published by the certificate authorities, and it's used to inform clients that certificates have been revoked or are no longer valid. Where a police officer pulls someone over and checks their license, they're going to check it either on their own mobile terminal, they'll run it against some type of state database, or they'll call into dispatch and say, hey, run this license for me, if that comes back as valid, well then you can go ahead and proceed. If it's been revoked, suspended, it's no longer valid and not in use. If a digital certificate is in fact on that CRL, it can exist in one of two states. We have revoked, which is irrevocable, or we have a hold or a temporary, which means it can be reversed. We have our digital certificate, if in fact it's been revoked, or irrevocable, that means it's done, it cannot be retrieved. Typically that's for a lost or compromised key, so a company can say, I think I've lost this key or I know for a fact it's been compromised, it will be revoked, pulled out of service, placed on that CRL as irrevocable, revoked. That way, no one else can use that certificate or try to initiate any fraudulent transaction. A hold is temporary, that can be reversed. With a hold, we can pull that back off again. Situations there, a client may think they lost their key or they think it may have been compromised, but then they later find out that it has not been, so they either find it or they have definitive proof that it has not been compromised. They can have that hold reversed and that digital certificate placed back into general use.

OCSP
OCSP, or an Online Certificate Status Protocol, and that's used to obtain revocation status of X.509 digital certificates. When we say X.509, we've talked about that previously, that is the format that digital certificates are issued in, it defines what information is contained within those certificates. It's an alternative to CRL, so the client revocation list. The benefits of using OCSP versus a CRL is the fact that OCSPs contain less information, so it puts less burden on the network and the client resources. If you have a very large

environment, then you're constantly doing this type of communication back and forth, checking these certificates, using OCSP will contain less information, still gives you what you need, you can tell if a certificate is valid or not, but it contains less information and will put less of a burden, network traffic, in other words, on that network. As an example, so Bob and Alice, they want to exchange communication. Alice wants to communicate with Bob, or Bob with Alice, vice versa. Well, when that happens, Alice will send her public key to Bob, he'll use that key to then exchange communication, he'll create the session key, send that off to Alice, she can decrypt, and then they can communicate over TLS or SSL. Well, what Bob can do in the meantime, however, is once he gets that public key from Alice, he can send an OCSP request to an OCSP responder, that's the terminology used for what these devices are. So that OCSP request goes out, the OCSP responder will check their database to see if that certificate is in fact on there. If it is, they'll respond back and say, hey, you may not want to talk to Alice, she's been compromised, or they'll respond back and say, nope, you're good to go, go ahead establish communication, at which point Bob uses Alice's public key, encrypts session keys and sends it off, and the same process happens as before, communication is then established over SSL and TLS, and they have a secure communication channel from thereafter.

CSR and PKCS Standards

Next we have is a CSR, or certificate signing request, and in this case, an applicant will apply to a certificate authority, or a CA, for a digital certificate. PKCS #10 is the most common type, and PKCS stands for public key cryptography standards, and here is the information that's contained in that request. We have a common name, the business name, department, city, state, and country, and then the email address. So some basic information about that entity that is, in fact, requesting that digital certificate. Just for your own information, the PKCS standards go through 1 through 15. The ones we've more or less focused on throughout this book would be number five, password-based encryption standards, and also PKCS #10, which is what we just talked about the certification request standard.

PKI

PKI stands for public key infrastructure, and it is the components that enable the usage of digital certificates, and that public key/private key cryptography or encryption, and that's going to include hardware, software, people, policies, and also procedures. Before we get too further along, I want to make sure you understand that when you visit a website, as we've talked about in our previous example, let's say that Bob wants to visit that financial institution. You might ask, well, where do these digital certificates come from? Well, they're built into our web browsers. In Firefox, if we go to Advanced Options, then go down to Options. Each web browser is slightly different, but they all contain roughly the same options. Under the Certificates section, it says requests, When a server requests my personal certificate, I can select one automatically or ask me every time. And then you see Query the OCSP responder. When Bob visits that bank, it's going to query the OCSP responder and say, hey, is this certificate that I'm being presented with, is this public key valid, is that certificate still valid, can I process it? And then we click on View Certificates, and this is all the certificate authorities, they have some pre-made or pre-canned certificates that are issued throughout all of our browsers. That allows us to have a built-in trust up to the root certificates, and there's a number of them. We see the

SHA-256 Fingerprint or the SHA1 Fingerprint, we know where it's issued from, the Common Name, the Organization, when it Begins, when it Expires. We can click on the Details, and then look at the Serial Number, or the Certificate, the Certification Algorithm, it's a SHA1 with an RSA Encryption. We can look at things like the Public Key, so this is the actual public key that's presented to someone that wants to communicate, and if they want to encrypt something, they can use this public key to then encrypt, which the recipient has the private key to decrypt. Getting back into the details of PKI, there are a number of components that make up a PKI environment, that public key infrastructure. The public key infrastructure is comprised of the certificate authority, or the CA. That issues and verifies digital certificates. Next, we have a registration authority, or an RA. That's going to verify the identity of users requesting information from the CA. Sometimes they're referred to as subordinate CAs. We also have a central directory, so that's a secure location in which to store and index keys, so that's going to be typically on an internal network. Then we have a certificate management system, so a method to manage valid certificates, publish CRLs. Then we have certificate policy, which defines who can request, issue, and use certificates, and of course what purpose can those certificates be used for? As you're studying for the exam, it's important that you understand what each of these components are and how they fit into the PKI environment.

Public Key
Public key is something that we should be familiar with at this point, but a public key is one part of a PKI, or a public key infrastructure, used to encrypt or to decrypt data. Remember, a public key can encrypt or decrypt just like a private key can encrypt or decrypt. It's a mathematically

linked key pair that has a corresponding private key. The public key is designed, as the name implies, to be made publicly available to anyone. If I want someone to be able to communicate with me in a secure fashion, I can give them my public key. They can then encrypt communication, a document, an email file, to me that only I can decrypt. Also, they can use that public key to encrypt session keys, so they can instantiate that communication, that TLS/SSL communication going forward. They'll send me those bulk encryption session keys, those symmetric keys. I can use my private key to decrypt, extract those session keys, and then communicate. Just to reiterate, the private key must be kept secret. If that gets compromised, then all bets are off, anything that you have that's been encrypted can be decrypted with that private key. It's very important that that be kept private.

Private Key
A private key is one part of that public key infrastructure, PKI, used to encrypt or decrypt. That's something to keep in mind that I want to say a few times just to make sure it sinks in. A public key can encrypt or decrypt, and a private key can encrypt or decrypt. However, they cannot do the same on an existing piece of data. If you encrypt with the public key, you'll decrypt with the private, or if you encrypt with the private, you'll decrypt with the public. It's a mathematically linked key pair that has a corresponding public key, in this instance, and the private key is, as the name implies, designed to be kept private. That should not be given to anyone.

Object Identifiers (OID)
Object identifiers, or OIDs are incorporated into a PKI, or a public key infrastructure and they're used to assign one or

more certificate policies to a given CA, or certificate authority. OIDs are built-in to Active Directory Certificate Services, or ADCS, as an example, can be randomly assigned for internal use only, can also be public or private. An organization can register a public OID to enable that organization's PKI to work with another organization's PKI, so if there is some interoperability that needs to happen there, you can register it publicly so that the OIDs and so that the individual components of that PKI, the certificate policies, can transfer or work between different organizations. If we look at this in a little more detail, an organization can register a public OID, it's a two-step process. One, you would register what's called a Private Enterprise Number, or a PEN. This PEN can be applied for at the address, pen.iana.org, and the following web address, and then once complete, a unique number will be assigned or issued that will be listed at this following web page, iana.org/assignments/enterprise-numbers. And within that there is a numerical prefix that is fixed, that's not changeable, that's 1.3.6.1.4.1, if you're familiar with SNMP and MIBS, it's similar. And then from there you would append whatever your organization's name, that PEN, that Private Enterprise Number, let's say in this example it's 56789, then your OID up to this point would be 1.3.6.1.4.1.56789, and then you would append an additional number or numerical addresses after that for each subcomponent. As it drills down through the organization, you would identify additional numbers, and there are things that you would create or sign internally for your use.

Types of Certificates
Let's go ahead and talk about the various types of certificates. There's a few that I want to cover. We have wildcards, SAN, code signing, self-signed, machine or

computer, email, user, root, domain validation, and extended validation. Each of these we'll cover in more detail. I just want to give you an idea of what they mean and the use cases or where they would be used in your environment. A wildcard is a digital certificate or a public key certificate that is used with multiple sub-domains of a domain. As an example, we may have *.Google.com as our main domain, that's the company domain, but we may have sub-domains within that. Well, rather than have individual SSL certificates for each of these, we can have a wildcard certificate that would allow us to secure all of the sub-domains with that same wildcard certificate. So, in other words, sales.Google.com or support.Google.com, they could all be secured with the same certificate. Next we have SAN, that's a Subject Alternate Name, not SAN as in a storage area network, but within a digital certificate or PKI infrastructure definitions it's Subject Alternate Name, and it's a certificate that allows multiple hostnames to be protected by a single certificate. Not sub-domains like a wild card, this is completely different names, completely different company names, up to 2000, in fact. If you're on a shared infrastructure and you have different hosts and different domain names, that single SAN, or Subject Alternate Name certificate can be used to secure all of those things. Next we have code signing. This is a type of digital certificate that's issued typically by a trusted CA, or certificate authority, and it's used to secure things like downloading code, macros, and objects. Many browsers won't allow code to run unless it is signed by a certificate from a trusted root, Verisign, Thawte, there are a number of them out there that are prebuilt into the browser, but they won't allow that code to run unless it's digitally signed by someone that it trusts. Next we have self signed. This is typically done to provide SSL functionality, or Secure Sockets Layer functionality in a temporary or a test and dev environment for servers that we're going to be temporarily using or in a very low secure environment. It would not be used for something in production, something public facing, but if we need that SSL functionality for testing, this works great. Or if it's in a very low, secure environment, that's internal use only, again, not an issue, just not for public use. And then we have machine or computer certificates. This is used to authenticate, a machine or a computer into an Active Directory environment, as an example. Just like we can verify a sender of a specific document in email, we can also verify, and depending upon how that PKI is used, the domain can verify the machine and also the machine can verify the domain to make sure that both are in fact valid and authenticated properly. Next, email, and that's a digital certificate used, to secure and authenticate email, Used for security, but also for authentication. Then we have a user, and a user certificate is very similar to a machine certificate, but it's used to authenticate users, not machines, but it's used to authenticate that user into that AD environment. In a very secure, or a PKI infrastructure, we're going to not only validate ourselves and we're going to log in with our own credentials, we're going to have our own certificates, we're going to authenticate to the network, but our machine is also going to authenticate to the network. We have two things that are authenticating before we can access resources on that network. And then a user certificate is similar in concept to a machine certificate. It's used to authenticate a user. Just like we talked about with a machine certificate, it's used to authenticate a user in this case into an AD environment. Next we have root, and a root certificate, it's a self-signed public key certificate, we're talking about PKI here, public key infrastructure, so that certificate identifies it as a root CA, or certificate authority.

Typically that's going to be an offline root that will generate certificates that are then put via USB or some removable media into our subordinate or our intermediary CAs. Domain validation is a server security certificate that provides the lowest level of validation available from a commercial enterprise. We can get them pretty cheap out on the Internet, and what happens is the company that's issuing that domain validation certificate will either automate it, or in some fashion contact the point of contact for that domain. When you register you put down this person is responsible for this domain, they'll verify that, quote unquote, wink-wink, and then issue that certificate. It's not very secure and is subject to spam and other types of misuse. Domain validation is a legitimate commercial certificate, but it offers the lowest level of security. Next, we have extended validation, and here it's increased security over domain validation certificates due to enhanced validation process. It's very similar as far as what you need to do to register for one, but the actual validation process is enhanced, "high assurance", meaning they have a human call in, validate that these people are who they say they are. Can it be misused? Of course, we can put in information that is bogus, and someone could validate that bogus information, so it doesn't 100% guarantee anything, but it does provide enhanced security over a simple domain validation.

Certificate Formats
A few certificate formats that we should be aware of. We have PEM, or P-E-M. This is the most common format that CAs issue, and they can have several extensions, .pem,.crt,.cer, and .key extensions. It's Base64 encoded, and it's an ASCII file. Next, we have DER, certificates. This is a binary form of the certificate instead of the ASCII PEM format. It can have extensions of either.der or.cer, and it's

very similar to PEM certificates except it's in binary instead of in ASCII. And then we have PFX. PFX certificates, typically encrypted, and it also typically will require a password to open. It can contain almost anything, certificates, certificate chains, or private keys, and it will have the extension of.pfx or p12,.p12. Next, we have something referred to as P7B. P7B certificates only contain certificates or certificate chains, No private keys. Also, Base64 encoded. P7Bs have the extension of.p7b, but it's also known as PKCS#7.

Online vs. Offline Certificate Authority (CA)
We need to make sure that we understand the difference between an online versus an offline certificate authority. An online certificate authority has a couple things. It's typically a subordinate CA, it's not going to be the root. It's going to be typically a subordinate CA, or certificate authority. It can, however, issue certificates. That's typically what it does. It issues certificates either to additional subordinates or further downstream subordinates, or to the actual users or the hosts that will ingest that certificate. Then, it also trusts the enterprise root CA, the enterprise root certificate authority. And then also enterprise CAs need to be joined to an Active Directory Directory Services, or an AD domain. Conversely, offline certificate root authorities, they're a trusted root CA. They're the tip of the iceberg. They are the top of the CA or the PKI hierarchy. And it's often referred to as a standalone root. so that's installed in offline mode. We don't attach the actual root CA to the network. We do that so that it can never be compromised. It's not connected to the network, and it is also not a member of that AD domain, the AD Directory Services domain. We install it in offline mode, we're going to generate that certificate, typically it's going to be put onto a USB drive or a CD or DVD, some

removable medium, we'll take that from that standalone root, and then we'll go over and sneakernet it to our subordinate CA. From there, we'll use that certificate to then issue certificates to either other subordinate CAs, or to hosts, or to things within the organization that apply or need that certificate. That way, if it's ever compromised, we can simply take that subordinate CA offline, get rid of it, and anything with it that's been issued from that subordinate CA is compromised, but the entire PKI infrastructure is not compromised. Conversely, if we had a compromise or a breach and the actual root of the entire PKI infrastructure has been compromised, then our entire PKI infrastructure, our entire security throughout the enterprise would be compromised. We purposely don't do that to avoid just that situation.

Stapling and Pinning
Another term I want you to be familiar with is something referred to as stapling. Stapling is also known as OCSP Stapling. It's formally known as TLS Certificate Status Request extension, and we've talked about TLS before and certificates in general before as well. What happens is the certificate bearer appends or staples timestamped OCSP responses to that initial TLS handshake. That gives an added layer of security, and it also removes the need for the client to contact the certificate authority, so it helps speed up the process. Next we have pinning. Pinning is the process of associating a host with their expected x.509 certificate, which is in effect, the public key, that digital certificate. So, more than one certificate or public key for a given host can be possible, and if so, then it's added to what's called a pin set. What we're doing is speeding up the process a bit, and we're also refining or narrowing what we expect that host to have.

Trust Models

When it comes to trust models, a couple things to be aware of. The first model is referred to as a hierarchical trust model, that's a single root CA that digitally signs all certificates. That's for small environments. We don't have a very distributed or a very large PKI infrastructure so that root, that single root CA could in fact sign all of the certificates, not recommended not in use in larger environments, but for smaller environments, you need to know that it exists. And the next model is referred to as a distributed trust model. In this model, we have multiple CAs with one master root CA, That route CA is installed on offline mode and what that does is it limits the risk if one of the CAs is, in fact, compromised before, and then it also distributes the load throughout the infrastructure. As an example, we have our root CA, that's going to be installed on offline mode, and will issue digital certificates, we're going to take that via USB or some removable media, so we'll take that from the offline root, and then use that to configure our intermediary CAs. Those intermediary CAs are the ones that will issue the certificates to clients. One other trust model I want you to be aware of is something referred to as the Web of Trust, or the WoT. That's going to be used in smaller environments or end user communication with no centralized certificate authority. So for the most part, if you're in a small to medium-sized business or anything larger or an enterprise, you're going to have some type of formalized PKI infrastructure, but in instances where there is no centralized CA and a Web of Trust can, in fact, be used. Commonly used with such things as PGP, which is pretty good privacy, is the public key private key encryption mechanism we use to encrypt files or emails, so it's commonly used when communication between two parties, they wish to communicate using what's called self-generated or self-signed encryption keys.

Key Escrow

A key escrow is a trusted third-party that's going to hold the keys needed to decrypt data, so to use in cases where keys are lost or some mandate, i. e. a court order or some situation that requires the decryption of data, it's also referred to as a fair crypto system., as you can imagine, there are some disagreements around the technical feasibility of having a trusted, third-party that can correctly manage access to keys or control collateral compromise if those keys are leaked. We all know that that never happens, I understand, but theoretically, if it did happen, how can we control that if a third-party manages all of our keys or perhaps they manage the keys for a number of different organizations, well, in doing so, we create some risk. There is definitely some historical precedent, it happens more often, cases where organizations are being breached, at record scale, hackers are becoming more and more sophisticated. The idea of having some trusted third-party hold all of our encryption keys, I'm not so sure uncomfortable with that. That's a business decision that you may have, there may be cases where you have to have that again, perhaps a court order or something where it needs to be kept so that law enforcement or whoever can get access to those keys if need be, but That's a case by case basis and something that you, as the security professional within your own organization would need to decide, work with your business units to come up with the best solution.

Certificate Chaining

With certificate chaining, we have something referred to as the path of trust, and that path of trust goes from a user certificate extends all the way up to the root certificate. As an example we have the root CA all the way down to the end certificate. That path of trust extends from that end certificate all the way up to the root CA, or the root certificate authority, and that allows us to ensure that everything is secure from the root down. Conversely, if the root is compromised, everything below that is potentially compromised, we can't trust anything that is valid and has not been tampered with. We made it to the end of the book. In this chapter, we talked about four main areas, we talked about PKI components, we talked about types of certificates, and then we covered certificate formats, and then lastly, concepts around certificates.

BOOK 2

CISSP:
CYBERSECURITY OPERATIONS
AND
INCIDENT RESPONSE

DIGITAL FORENSICS WITH EXPLOITATION FRAMEWORKS & VULNERABILITY SCANS

RICHIE MILLER

Introduction

IT Security jobs are on the rise! Small, medium or large size companies are always on the look out to get on board bright individuals to provide their services for Business as Usual (BAU) tasks or deploying new as well as on-going company projects. Most of these jobs requiring you to be on site but since 2020, companies are willing to negotiate with you if you want to work from home (WFH). Yet, to pass the Job interview, you must have experience. Still, if you think about it, all current IT security professionals at some point had no experience whatsoever. The question is; how did they get the job with no experience? Well, the answer is simpler then you think. All you have to do is convince the Hiring Manager that you are keen to learn and adopt new technologies and you have willingness to continuously research on the latest upcoming methods and techniques revolving around IT security. Here is where this book comes into the picture. Why? Well, if you want to become an IT Security professional, this book is for you! If you are studying for CompTIA Security+ or CISSP, this book will help you pass your exam. Passing security exams isn't easy. In fact, due to the raising security beaches around the World, both above mentioned exams are becoming more and more difficult to pass. Whether you want to become an Infrastructure Engineer, IT Security Analyst or any other Cybersecurity Professional, this book (as well as the other books in this series) will certainly help you get there! But, what knowledge are you going to gain from this book? Well, let me share with you briefly the agenda of this book. First, you are going to discover what are the most important steps for cyber security operations and incident response, specifically revolving around assessing organizational security. We'll also talk about network reconnaissance and discovery and the various things we can use to accomplish those tasks. Next, we are going to cover file manipulation and the tools we use to do that along with shell and scripting environments. We'll talk about packet capture and replay, data forensics with exploitation frameworks, password crackers, and data sanitization. After that, we'll be covering Appropriate Data Sources to Support an Incident, vulnerability scans and the output, SIEM and SIEM dashboards. We'll also talk about log files and how they can support an investigation or data analysis, trying to figure out what happened, where, when, why and how. Next, you will discover how to use syslog, rsyslog, syslog-ng, journal control and nxlog. We'll also talk about retention for email, audit logs, bandwidth monitors, metadata, and how it changes for different types of files. After that, you will learn how to use NetFlow, sFlow, protocol analyzers and outputs. Moving on, you will discover how to implement Mitigation Techniques to Secure an Environment, how to reconfigure endpoint security solutions, application whitelisting and blacklisting, along with quarantining. We'll also going to cover configuration changes, firewall rules, MDM, or mobile device management, and data loss prevention or DLP. Next you will learn about content filters, revoking and updating certificates, the concepts of isolation, containment, and segmentation and how those can help us secure the environment, along with secure orchestration, automation, and response, or SOAR systems, and runbooks and playbooks specifically. Next we will cover the Key Aspects of Digital Forensics, documentation and evidence gathering in general and why it's very important. We'll also going to talk about acquisition and what we should go after first and why. We'll also cover integrity and a few methods we can use to prove that the data we've collected has not been tampered with, along with preservation, ediscovery and what that means and how it applies to an investigation of data recovery, including the concept of nonrepudiation so the party in question can't deny ownership or a specific action. You are also going to learn about strategic intelligence and counterintelligence along with on-prem versus cloud and some of the challenges and nuances to where that data resides, some things around data sovereignty and applicable laws, depending upon where it's located in the country or in the world if we're doing global business. If you are ready to get on this journey, let's first cover vulnerability scans and the outputs, as well as what we can do with those outputs!

Chapter 1 Data Sources to Support an Incident

In this chapter, we'll be covering an Appropriate Data Sources to Support an Incident. We'll be talking about vulnerability scans and the output, what we do with those outputs. We'll talk about SIEM and SIEM dashboards. We'll talk about log files and how they can support an investigation or data analysis, trying to figure out what happened, where, when, why and how. We'll talk about syslog, rsyslog, and syslog-ng or next generation. We'll talk about the differences there. We'll also talk about something called journal control or journalctl, nxlog. We'll talk about retention for basic things like email, audit logs. Then we'll talk about bandwidth monitors, metadata, and how it changes for different types of files. We'll talk about NetFlow and sFlow, the differences between the two, and then a little bit about protocol analyzers and outputs. When we're talking about accessing all of these different types of data, interpreting assessment results, understanding what's going on, the amount of data that's being created is increasing exponentially, so the amount of sensors, telemetry data.

In this chapter, we'll be talking about Implementing Mitigation Techniques to Secure an Environment. We'll be talking about reconfiguring endpoint security solutions, talking about application whitelisting and blacklisting, how that can help us, along with quarantining. We'll talk about configuration changes, and that deals with firewall rules, MDM, or mobile device management, data loss prevention, or DLP. We'll talk about content filters and also revoking and updating certificates. We'll also talk about the concepts of isolation, containment, and segmentation and how those can help us secure the environment, along with secure orchestration, automation, and response, or SOAR systems, and runbooks and playbooks specifically.

In this chapter we'll be talking about Understanding the Key Aspects of Digital Forensics. We'll talk about documentation and evidence in general and why it's Very important to make sure things are documented properly. We'll talk about acquisition and some things around what we should go after first and why, some of the gotchas if we don't follow those procedures. We'll talk about integrity and a few methods we can use to prove that the data we've collected has not been tampered with. We'll talk about preservation along the same lines. We'll talk about ediscovery and what that means and how it applies to an investigation, along with data recovery, and then a similar concept of nonrepudiation so the party in question can't deny ownership or specific action. And then we'll talk about strategic intelligence and counterintelligence along with on-prem versus cloud and some of the challenges and nuances to where that data resides, some things around data sovereignty, applicable laws, depending upon where it's located in the country or in the world if we're doing global business.

Chapter 2 How to Assess Organizational Security

In this chapter, we'll be talking about operations and incident response specifically around assessing organizational security. We'll be talking about network reconnaissance and discovery and the various things we can use to accomplish those tasks. We'll be talking about file manipulation and the tools we use to do that along with shell and scripting environments. We'll talk about packet capture and replay. We'll also talk about data forensics along with exploitation frameworks, password crackers, and then wrap up with data sanitization. To start off, let's talk about traceroute or tracert. It's a network tool to test connectivity between the host and the target. What it does is allow us to see hops along the way. And when I say hop, meaning we're crossing a router. We're going from one network to another. It allows us to see the hops along the way and then the associated latency with each hop. As an example, when I do a traceroute, what I see is the hop count, and it will go from 1 to whatever number. Typically, it tops out at 30. And then it will show me the round-trip time or the RTT for those three attempts. All along the way, I will see an output that shows me those individual hops and the individual round-trip time or the latency for each of those hops. Whether you're troubleshooting network performance or you're just trying to determine what's in between you and your target, it can show you where things might be a bottleneck, where there may be some type of firewall rule, where things are not necessarily reachable. Just because you've see no response or an asterisk doesn't necessarily mean that there's an issue. It just means that that specific hop is not replying back. It can still pass that traffic through to the destination.

nslookup/dig

Next we have nslookup or the Linux equivalent called dig. It's a DNS troubleshooting tool for Windows or Linux and also for Mac operating systems. They can provide a wide range of information on DNS and associated troubleshooting. Nslookup can be used on Windows and Linux systems; whereas, dig is a Linux and Mac-only command. I can do a number of different things. Like I can say set type=mx, and I'm saying, give me DNS information, and I'm going to put in the domain name of Google. But I'm setting the type to mx, so give me only the mail exchanger records. It returns back when I'm using for DNS. And then it also provides a priority number of which ones that should try first. In this particular instance, it's hosted at google.com. Nslookup and dig can both provide a wealth of information. They can potentially do zone transfers. You can look at all of the DNS information if that specific domain allows those types of lookups. Then to put in the perspective of a forensic examination, these things come in handy when we're doing reconnaissance, trying to figure out where things are going, where they're coming from, perhaps a piece of malware we're trying to track back and get information on the systems that it's touching or reaching out to. All of these different tools, but they help to give us information when we're conducting our investigations or doing reconnaissance.

ipconfig/ifconfig

The next command line told you're probably familiar with is ipconfig or ifonfig. So on the Windows side, that would be ipconfig. On the Linux or Mac side, that would be ifconfig. If I type in ifconfig, you'll see the interfaces, like eth0. Some information about its IP address, its net mask or subnet mask, the broadcast IP address, also its TCP/IP version 6 address. Also, some information about the number of packets received, any errors, and then it's also showing the loopback address. These commands are great for getting your own information as far as IP address, whether it be IPv4 or IPv6. Also it can show you your configured DNS address and, on a Window system, perhaps your WINS Server, not much in use any more. But the point being it can show all the associated information with that specific interface. If you have multiple interfaces, you can bring up information about each.

nmap and nmap demo

Nmap is an open source network scanner and it can discover hosts, it can look at services, it can detect operating systems, vulnerabilities. It's very extensible through the use of the nmap scripting engine, or NSE, and some typical uses for nmap would be device auditing, whether it be host for firewall enumeration, and it can detect vulnerabilities in operating systems, network devices, applications, also, rogue machine detection to identify machines that should not be on a specific network or network inventory. It's a penetration testers tool and network troubleshooting tool that can be used by the good guys, and it's also used very much by the bad guys. Nmap is a very extensible, very powerful program, the full use of which is beyond the scope of the book, but let's just suffice it to say that is a very robust network scanning tool, host enumeration detecting flaws or vulnerabilities that we can then further penetration test, either with scripts that can add or increase the functionality or brute force techniques, or even using other tools that nmap can be a part of, we can use in conjunction with other things. As part of the toolbox that we would use for penetration testing and, of course, what hackers would also use for their malicious activities. We can do threat detections, we can incorporate scripts through the nmap scripting engine, I can target a specific host, or a subnet, or an entire network. With all of these switches and all of these parameters available to you, just understand that these types of tools should be used in a controlled environment. I would not recommend that you take this into your workplace and start scanning a production environment, that could lead to some bad juju. Your teammates or security folks in other areas perhaps, depending on how big your company is, could see that there are some port scans going on, it could raise some red flags, and then if by some chance it to take down production for some reason, causes congestion on our network, or something bad happens in any way, shape or form, you don't want to be responsible for that. These types of things, should be used in a controlled environment, and then as you develop your penetration testing skills, you can then start using it more in a production environment or in a pen testing engagement if, in fact, you know that's what you're doing at the moment, but just keep that in mind. Keep the usage of these tools to a minimum or in a sandbox environment, at least, until you have proper sign off from the powers that be so that if something does happen, everybody is on board, everyone knows what's happening.

Ping and Pathping
Let's take a look at a few command utilities for network troubleshooting, some things that you should keep in mind, definitely add to your tool bag if you're not already familiar. The first will be ping and pathping. These are two troubleshooting tools, command line tools, for both Windows and Linux., pathping is just for Windows. But ping is pretty much ubiquitous, and that's for Windows or Linux. And that's a network troubleshooting tool to test network connectivity by sending what's called ICMP packets to a host.

Pathping does something very similar, but it also combines the features of ping and traceroute. Next would be hping, and hping is a packet crafting tool that can be used to generate traffic, craft packets (spoofed IP addresses, ICMP floods). Then also Netstat. Netstat displays network statistics about TCP and UDP connections, various ports, routing tables, and also protocol statistics. If we look at ping or pathping, again, a tool to test network connectivity. And ping stands for packet internetwork groper, and it sends ICMP packets or internet control message protocol packets to a host to test connectivity. ICMP, internet control message protocol, and what it does is send an echo, and then it expects back a request. You can think of it as like a sonar, like a submarine that sends out a ping. It goes out and hits an object under the water, and it bounces back, and they can tell that that object is there. A very similar concept here.

hping
Hping, which is hping3 is a package generation tool that can craft packets, it can spoof packets, and configure any number of options as needed. We can do SYN attacks, we can flood the network, we can spoof IP addresses, so a lot of functionality here to test firewall collectivity, to test IDS or IPS systems, also for training with Wireshark to craft specific types of packets We can adjust source ports, destination ports, spoof IP addresses. We can simulate in a very small way a denial-of-service attack on a Linux host. I will be sending packets to another Windows host on my network. I have my Linux host, and then I have a Windows host. On the Linux machine if I issue the command hping3, which is going to invoke that hping program. I'm going to put hping3 -S, which is issuing a SYN packet. I give it the destination address, what port I want it to go over, port 135 in this case,

and then I'm going to flood the network. I'm telling it, send it as fast as possible.

If I go ahead and hit Enter, it's telling me it's going to go into flood mode. No replies are going to be shown because this is going so fast. If I flip back over to my Windows host, you see my Ethernet connection went from zero up to maxed out.

I'm receiving about 40MB per second, 40MB per second of throughput. This is just one machine sending to another. Imagine if we had 10 or 20 or 100 different machines all sending packets to a host on the network. Same thing with the CPU. We can see that CPU jumped up from nothing to about 38, 39, 40% of activity. That's one host attacking. If I had three or four of these, I could very quickly overrun that host machine. Just to go back in my Linux machine, if I cancel that out, Ctrl+C, I stop it, go back to Windows, you can see the activity drops, CPU drops, and then the Ethernet connectivity drops as well.

Each ping is a very powerful tool. It allows you to fire up Wireshark, look at different types of packets. You can craft packets in a number of ways and then, of course, use it for malicious purposes as well.

Netstat

The next one is netstat. And netstat is a command-line utility, and it displays, network statistics, hence the name netstat. TCP, UDP connections, also reports. We can even display the routing table and protocol statistics. Netstat is cross-platform. It's used to troubleshoot and provide network and host information. I can just type in from a command prompt netstat, and it will show me the active connections, the protocol, a local address, a foreign address, and then the state. Then, depending upon what flags you put in, it also gives me the process ID or the PID. That can be useful. You could look into a Task Manager on Windows and see what the process ID is and then associate that with the IP address it's accessing. netstat -a displays all connections and listening ports. If we add -b, that will display the executable involved in creating each connection or listening port. That may be helpful in troubleshooting what is making that connection if you're not sure. -f will display the fully qualified domain name or the FQDN, for that foreign address if it's possible or if it can determine that. It's not always available. But if it is, it will display that. And then netstat -r, will display the routing table. This is another tool added to the toolbox when we're doing network troubleshooting, connection troubleshooting.

netcat

The next one is an application called netcat. netcat is a network troubleshooting or a pen testing or a hacking tool, depending upon who's using it, that can read from and write to network connections, either TCP or UDP. And some common use cases would be port scanning, port redirection. It can be used as a port listener. It can even operate as a remote shell, serving web pages, or even transferring files. It's a very powerful program and can be used in conjunction with other tools like Metasploit. You could install this on a remote machine and then open up a listener on that remote machine and then run commands as if you were local on that machine. You could turn on Remote Desktop. You could do a lot of things that could have some malicious implications. A powerful tool, and like the majority of these types of tools, I recommend highly that you don't do it in a production environment unless you're looking for a new job. But seriously, make sure you do it in a controlled environment. A sandbox is best until you understand what the tools can do because they can kick off a lot of things behind the scenes or a lot of activity that you may or may not be aware of if you're not that well versed with the application. If it's in a production environment, it could certainly pop up on someone's radar. You don't want to draw unnecessary attention or take out an application or cause some type of production issue. Here's just a quick screenshot of netcat. It's included with Kali Linux. Not all distributions of Linux have it.

```
                                            kali@kali: ~
File  Edit  View  Search  Terminal  Tabs  Help

  kali@kali: ~                            ×    kali@kali: ~

root@kali:/home/kali# nc -h
[v1.10-46]
connect to somewhere:    nc [-options] hostname port[s] [ports] ...
listen for inbound:      nc -l -p port [-options] [hostname] [port]
options:
        -c shell commands    as '-e'; use /bin/sh to exec [dangerous!!]
        -e filename          program to exec after connect [dangerous!!]
        -b                   allow broadcasts
        -g gateway           source-routing hop point[s], up to 8
        -G num               source-routing pointer: 4, 8, 12, ...
        -h                   this cruft
        -i secs              delay interval for lines sent, ports scanned
        -k                   set keepalive option on socket
        -l                   listen mode, for inbound connects
        -n                   numeric-only IP addresses, no DNS
        -o file              hex dump of traffic
        -p port              local port number
        -r                   randomize local and remote ports
        -q secs              quit after EOF on stdin and delay of secs
        -s addr              local source address
        -T tos               set Type Of Service
        -t                   answer TELNET negotiation
        -u                   UDP mode
        -v                   verbose [use twice to be more verbose]
```

You may need to download and then install. With most of these applications, if you do just a -help or double dash and then the word help, you'll get the actual commands that are available to you. Some of them are very basic. Some of them are very complex. Then netcat, like most of these tools, has extensibility and can be used in conjunction with other applications, Metasploit being one of them. Just be careful with them, but definitely understand what they can do. For a deeper dive, I would definitely recommend some of the other books that go into these in a lot more detail. But for our purposes here, just understand what the application is. Its main use cases would be network troubleshooting, pen testing. Hacking, is one of those. But it's a great pen testing tool and allows us to operate in a listening mode or remote shell mode.

IP Scanners

An IP scanner, as the name implies, scans the network, a range of IP addresses. It can discover hosts. It can test for open ports, troubleshoot connectivity. Some of these things we've already talked about can be certainly identified as IP scanners. Then you can have scaled-down applications that just do the IP scanning part. They don't do a lot of the other enhancements, the remote shells, the remote scripting - all those types of things. Some just identify IP addresses, what ports are available. A few to be aware of, Solarwinds being one, PRTG, AngryIP Scanner, Free IP Scanner, and Nmap as we talked about previously. All of these things have IP scanning capabilities. Some are more full-featured than others. Some are free, some are paid applications. Everyone has their preference or their favorite. But just make sure you familiarize yourself with the functionality and be sure to add that capability to your toolbelt.

ARP

Another tool and concept to be aware of is arp, and that stands for address resolution protocol, originally developed in 1982. It's been around for a long time by RFC 826, and it resolves an IP address to a MAC address. A link-layer protocol, so it does not route. Arp stays within the local network. But an IP address is a layer 3, if you recall the OSI Model, to a MAC address, which is layer 2. There's also a thing called reverse ARP. That will derive an IP address from a MAC address. And then we talked previously about ARP spoofing. And that is where a malicious user can intercept and reply to ARP requests, also known as ARP cache poisoning so they can put malicious or fictitious information into the ARP cache and either block connectivity or have connectivity go to an improper host.

Route

The next command is route, and route is used to view and manipulate the IP routing table on either Windows or Linux machines. And when I say Linux, we can general refer to macOS as well. If I just do a route print, it will show me the routing table. And you can see the destination, the net mask, the gateway, the interface, and then the metric. We can also view the routing table if we do a netstat -r. So there are two ways to get to the same information.

Curl and Curl Demo

Next we have a pretty neat command, and that's called curl. And curl can transfer data to or from a server using one of various protocols. But the takeaway here is that it allows us to transfer files, to get web pages, to download things from the internet, as an example, without having to do it from a web page. Web pages are great. They're GUI. They're easy to deal with from a human's perspective. But if we want to script something, we can't script web activity very well. You can't script moving a mouse, clicking on a link. Within curl, you can do the same actions, but from a command line, and allow you to download a file, upload a file, transfer in some form or fashion using it programmatically via scripts. Let's do a quick demo and take a look at using curl to download a file via FTP. So here we are back at our Kali Linux terminal. If I type curl -h, then it gives me the options of what I can do.

I'll go out to a test website that allows me just to test download speeds, and I'll use the -o to give the same name as the one I'm downloading. In this case, speedtest.tele2.net, and we want to download just the sample 10MB file. By using the standard switches, it shows me the download. You can see we use curl to download the file via FTP.

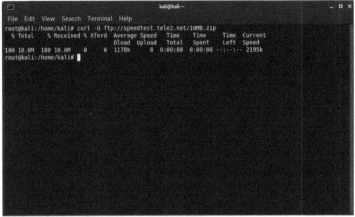

If I change that to a dash pound, you then see it changed the output from a standard download to I'm getting a progress bar. It will show me the progress of the file. And then once that's downloaded, it will finish.

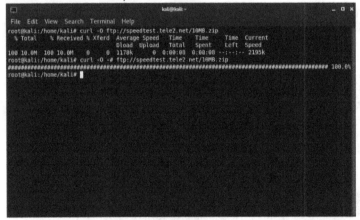

It allows us to do some things that we would typically do via an FTP program or accessing something via the web. We can do that programmatically and incorporate those things into our scripts.

The Harvester

The next one up is another penetration testing tool, and that's called the Harvester. The Harvester is a tool for gathering email accounts and subdomain names from public sources. A quick screenshot showing you the splash page when you fire up the application. I'm going to be running this from Kali Linux.

The Harvester has a number of different options. Two I just want to call your attention to. Number 1 is -d, and that is the domain name to search or the company name. And then -b would be your data source or where you want to look from. And you can pick one source or you can pick all of them. I have a number of things that I can search through, and you can see the list here. If you did a -b and then chose it would search through all of those different sources. Depending upon what of these that you're scanning, you may return a number of records or not much. It just depends on how much information is publicly accessible. But nevertheless, a great tool for information gathering as you work through your initial reconnaissance and pen testing activities. And it can also be used for malicious activities as well because any tool that can be used for good, it can also be used for malicious purposes as well.

Sn1per

The next one up is sn1per and it's another pen testing tool. This one is an automated penetration testing tool and it can operate in stealth mode, it can do a full scan, it can do port scans only, it can scan individual hosts or entire networks, much like some of these other tools that we've talked about, and it's also very extensible with scripting. It can use scripting via nmap or MetaSploit and others, along with creating reports, including screenshots of websites that it goes out and crawls. It also leverages several other testing and exploit tools, MetaSploit being one, nmap, Slack, Shodan, it integrates with these different tools, and it can also brute force all open services on a target system, so a pretty powerful tool, definitely one to take a look at, especially considering a lot of this can be automated, not a lot of heavy lifting. You point it at something, kickoff some commands, and then off it goes. Let's go ahead and take a quick look at installing Sn1per and then a basic scan. As you can see here from the GitHub page, there is a download location, What I would do is go to my Kali Linux terminal, put in that download location. If I jump into a terminal session and then I put in the git clone and then the HTTPS address, write the GitHub address of that Sn1per installation, from there, I would do a sudo command to get to an elevated prompt and then run a bash script that does the install of the Sn1per application, so bash install.sh and that would run me through the actual installation.

```
                                                      kali@kali:~/Sn1per                              _  □  ✕
File  Edit  View  Search  Terminal  Help
kali@kali:~/Sn1per$ sudo su
root@kali:/home/kali/Sn1per# bash install.sh



+ -- --=[ https://xerosecurity.com
+ -- --=[ Sn1per by @xer0dayz

[>] This script will install sn1per under /usr/share/sniper. Are you sure you want to continue? [Hit Ctrl+C to exi
t]
y
[*] Installing package dependencies...
Get:1 http://ftp.halifax.rwth-aachen.de/kali kali-rolling InRelease [30.5 kB]
Get:2 http://ftp.halifax.rwth-aachen.de/kali kali-rolling/main amd64 Packages [17.4 MB]
Get:3 http://ftp.halifax.rwth-aachen.de/kali kali-rolling/main amd64 Contents (deb) [38.8 MB]
38% [2 Packages store 0 B] [3 Contents-amd64 2,304 B/38.8 MB 0%]                        2,668 kB/s 15s
```

So on my machine, it's about a 7 to 8 minutes installation. On yours, it may be longer, maybe shorter, but rather than have you sit through everything, we'll zip through the installation real quick. Then once it completes, you'll see that it gives us the message saying all done. And then to run the application, you would type Sn1per from your terminal and then, you'll have to give it a target, and then if you have any options that you want it to run, you would put those in as well. As you can see here from the command prompt, if I type sniper -h, it gives me the help file and shows me all the different configuration commands that I can use with the application.

```
[*]                                                    kali@kali: ~
File  Edit  View  Search  Terminal  Help

+ -- --=[ https://xerosecurity.com
+ -- --=[ Sn1per v9.0 by @xer0dayz

[*] NORMAL MODE
sniper -t <TARGET>

[*] SPECIFY CUSTOM CONFIG FILE
sniper -c /full/path/to/sniper.conf -t <TARGET> -m <MODE> -w <WORKSPACE>

[*] NORMAL MODE + OSINT + RECON
sniper -t <TARGET> -o -re

[*] STEALTH MODE + OSINT + RECON
sniper -t <TARGET> -m stealth -o -re

[*] DISCOVER MODE
sniper -t <CIDR> -m discover -w <WORSPACE_ALIAS>

[*] SCAN ONLY SPECIFIC PORT
sniper -t <TARGET> -m port -p <portnum>

[*] FULLPORTONLY SCAN MODE
sniper -t <TARGET> -fp

[*] WEB MODE - PORT 80 + 443 ONLY!
sniper -t <TARGET> -m web

[*] HTTP WEB PORT MODE
sniper -t <TARGET> -m webporthttp -p <port>

[*] HTTPS WEB PORT MODE
sniper -t <TARGET> -m webporthttps -p <port>
```

I could run in normal mode just by saying sniper -t and then giving it a target, and then there is a number of other things, a lot of extensibility here. You could go into stealth mode, discover mode, you could run web only, Port 80, Port 443, but at a minimum, it goes in and scans the entire website, all the URLs, all the subdomains, and it puts all of those things into files you can later analyze or look at in more detail, it puts it into what's called a loot folder, and then from there, you can do additional vulnerability testing, penetration testing. A lot of information beyond the scope of this book here to dig into with any detail, but definitely be aware that it's a powerful program for pen testing. Based upon what options you choose when you initiate your scan, some of these things will be skipped, which it goes through a number of different things. It will numerate ports, it will do port scans, it will check the web application firewall if there is one, see if there is any vulnerabilities there, it goes through a number of different nmap scripts, and on and on. I'm just going to zip through this and you can just see there is a lot of information that it scans through, all of the subpages, and it puts all of these things into a file You can go back and analyze it at a later date so that you could go back and do further penetration testing. As you develop pen testing skills, this is a very powerful tool and something you'd want to use quite a bit for doing reconnaissance, but just to play around with, I'm saying, make sure you understand what you're doing before you point it into anything into production. But at the end, and this took about 20 minutes give or take, a scan will complete and then it saves all of those things into a workspace file that's on your machine that you could go back and there is probably 15 or 20 different folders and files that have all the information that was the outputs from these scans that you can then ingest into other applications or read through for further analysis.

Chapter 3 File Manipulation & Packet Captures

Scanless
Another tool that you should be aware of is one called scanless. And scanless is a port scanner that leverages online port scanning services to anonymize scanning a target system. You're not doing it from your own system. You're telling the application to go out and hit a number of websites and have port scans issued from those websites. You can see here, here are the ones that it can go out and target, so Hackertarget, Ipfingerprints, Spiderip, Standingtech. You can read through the rest. But you can initiate these scans from these web-based points of origin. You anonymize where it's coming from. They can't tell it's coming from a specific system. If I want to install scanless on my system, I did a quick Google search and found a link for scanless.

Download scanless:

scanless 1.0.4 can be checked out from it's GIT repository here.

Here it's saying 1.0.4., when I go over to Git's website, it's version 2.1.5 is the latest as of this time. It shows me the install, which is pip install scanless.

scanless	v2.1.5	last month
.gitignore	Update .gitignore	4 years ago
Dockerfile	Dockerfile added	2 years ago
README.md	v2.1.4, minor fix to web request func	2 months ago
UNLICENSE	initial commit	4 years ago
setup.py	v2.1.5	last month

From a terminal session, I'll go ahead and issue that command. It then downloads and installs scanless on my system.

```
File  Edit  View  Search  Terminal  Help
root@kali:/home/kali# pip install scanless
Collecting scanless
  Downloading scanless-2.1.5.tar.gz (216 kB)
                                   | 216 kB 2.4 MB/s
Requirement already satisfied: beautifulsoup4 in /usr/lib/python3/dist-packages (from scanless) (4.9.3)
Collecting crayons
  Downloading crayons-0.4.0-py2-none-any.whl (4.6 kB)
Requirement already satisfied: requests in /usr/lib/python3/dist-packages (from scanless) (2.25.1)
Requirement already satisfied: soupsieve>1.2 in /usr/lib/python3/dist-packages (from beautifulsoup4->scanless) (2.1)
Requirement already satisfied: colorama in /usr/lib/python3/dist-packages (from crayons->scanless) (0.4.4)
Building wheels for collected packages: scanless
  Building wheel for scanless (setup.py) ... done
  Created wheel for scanless: filename=scanless-2.1.5-py3-none-any.whl size=218506 sha256=53ca984c2a70971e7a78ef4a6d0039c0afcc13a7a381c75a07
  Stored in directory: /root/.cache/pip/wheels/31/5a/74/f50e9d4d132bfec8a48a6b221b89ea29a2ab9c5c8db1828cf6
Successfully built scanless
Installing collected packages: crayons, scanless
Successfully installed crayons-0.4.0 scanless-2.1.5
root@kali:/home/kali# scanless -h
usage: scanless [-h] [-v] [-t TARGET] [-s SCANNER] [-r] [-l] [-a] [-d]

scanless, an online port scan scraper.

optional arguments:
  -h, --help            show this help message and exit
  -v, --version         display the current version
  -t TARGET, --target TARGET
                        ip or domain to scan
  -s SCANNER, --scanner SCANNER
                        scanner to use (default: hackertarget)
  -r, --random          use a random scanner
  -l, --list            list scanners
  -a, --all             use all the scanners
  -d, --debug           debug mode (cli mode off & show network errors)
root@kali:/home/kali# s
```

It will upack it, install, and then I'm good to go. So from there, I can do a scanless -h as I talked about before. It gives me the arguments. I can see the current version. I can pick a target, with no additional switches. I can then run the same command again with a -a, which will give me all of the online scanners. And it will run through all of those. It might take a minute or two. And each of the online services might give me slightly different results. Some scan for more ports than others, so you don't get exactly the same results from each. But what it does do, is anonymize those scans.

DNSenum

The next one that I want to mention is one called DNSenum for enumerate. DNSenum is a command line tool, and I just have a screenshot here showing you the help file and some of the switches that you can use.

255

```
                                              kali@kali: ~
File  Edit  View  Search  Terminal  Help
kali@kali:~$ dnsenum -h
dnsenum VERSION:1.2.6
Usage: dnsenum [Options] <domain>
[Options]:
Note: If no -f tag supplied will default to /usr/share/dnsenum/dns.txt or
the dns.txt file in the same directory as dnsenum.pl
GENERAL OPTIONS:
  --dnsserver    <server>
                         Use this DNS server for A, NS and MX queries.
  --enum                 Shortcut option equivalent to --threads 5 -s 15 -w.
  -h, --help             Print this help message.
  --noreverse            Skip the reverse lookup operations.
  --nocolor              Disable ANSIColor output.
  --private              Show and save private ips at the end of the file domain_ips.txt.
  --subfile <file>       Write all valid subdomains to this file.
  -t, --timeout <value>  The tcp and udp timeout values in seconds (default: 10s).
  --threads <value>      The number of threads that will perform different queries.
  -v, --verbose          Be verbose: show all the progress and all the error messages.
GOOGLE SCRAPING OPTIONS:
  -p, --pages <value>    The number of google search pages to process when scraping names,
                         the default is 5 pages, the -s switch must be specified.
  -s, --scrap <value>    The maximum number of subdomains that will be scraped from Google (default 15).
BRUTE FORCE OPTIONS:
  -f, --file <file>      Read subdomains from this file to perform brute force. (Takes priority over default dns.txt)
```

If I go in and just scrape down through here, I can get a lot of information about a specific website, its zones and subzones. I can tell it where to scrape from, reverse lookup options or output options. If I just do a DNSenum -v for verbose and then I put in the website, it shows me the web servers, any name servers, mail exchangers. It can go out and, as the name implies, enumerate DNS entries and DNS information about a specific website.

Nessus and Cuckoo

Nessus is a commercial vulnerability scanner. There's three different versions. There's a professional version, a cloud version, and then a free version. The professional version you could install local or have it on your system.

256

A cloud version, as the name implies, runs in the cloud as a service. The free version will be good for very small environments or for educational use. That's limited to scanning 16 IP addresses. Very limited use, but still gives you a good opportunity to learn about the product. The nice thing about Nessus is it's a very mature product, and it has many built-in templates and scans for common threats, misconfigurations. Definitely one to familiarize yourself with if your organization is looking for a commercial vulnerability scanner. Next, let's talk about something called Cuckoo. Cuckoo is an automated malware analysis platform, and it runs in a sandboxed environment. You would want to run it in the virtualized environment with a sandbox set up so that you can download malware and let that malware execute in that sandbox to see what it does.

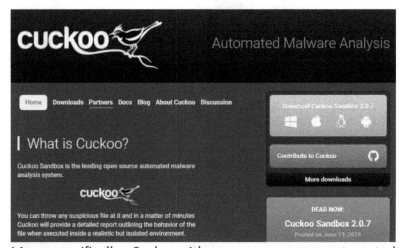

More specifically, Cuckoo, it's an open source automated malware analysis tool, and it's designed to be run in an isolated lab environment. It can analyze, trace, and document a piece of malware's actions. It can do tracing of API calls. It can analyze memory and network traffic. It's a great tool to have in a controlled environment. As an example, here we have a Cuckoo host machine. That's going to do our guest analysis management, traffic dumps, and reporting. That's going to be attached, to an isolated network, a virtual isolated network. It's important that we run this thing in a sandboxed environment so that when we do download malware and we run that malware, it doesn't have the potential to escape out onto our production environment. That would be very bad. That's what we call an RGE or a resume-generating event. Isolated network, and in this small example, we have three virtual machines. We have a Windows machine, a Linux machine, and an OSX machine, your virtual environment may be a lot larger, or you may have a different mix of hosts, but you get the idea. Then from there, you could have that host machine go out to the internet you can see if it is, in fact, pulling things down from some command and control server. Or you could have it point to a sinkhole so it goes here. And then you can download this from cuckoosandbox.org and try it out in your own environment.

File Manipulation
Next, I just want to talk about a few file manipulation commands that you can use from a command line. The first would be head. The head command would print the first x number of lines of a file, so the default would be 10. However, that's configurable. Tail is the opposite of that. That prints the last x number of lines of a file. The default is 10. We have the command cat, which would create, display, and also concatenate files or combine files together. And then we have grep. Grep searches plain-text data for lines that match a regular expression. It means globally search for a regular expression and then print matching lines. That's where the term grep comes from, but it's a very, very powerful tool. If you're not already familiar with grep and regular expressions, I definitely recommend you dig into that and learn all about that and add that skillset to your toolbox. From the command line, it's very, very powerful. Next, we have chmod or change permissions on files and folders. We can change permissions on files and folders, again from the command line. And then lastly, logger. Logger is going to create entries in a system log. It provides the shell command interface to the syslog system-log chapter. Back in my Kali Linux terminal, I have a text file here, just as an example, and, inside the file, just some random text. If I go into the terminal and issue a head command, and I can just drag this file in there.

```
 ┌──┐                          kali@kali: ~                           _ □ ✕

  File  Edit  View  Search  Terminal  Help
 kali@kali:~$ head '/home/kali/Desktop/ipsum.txt'
 This is the first line.
 Lorem ipsum dolor sit amet, consectetur adipiscing elit.
 Aliquam facilisis metus interdum leo bibendum, id mattis purus tristique.
 Aliquam bibendum consequat dolor at euismod.
 Integer nec enim et nulla cursus aliquet eu vel dolor.
 Etiam aliquam rhoncus lobortis.
 Vestibulum vulputate ullamcorper nibh, dignissim sodales arcu porta vitae.
 Sed maximus tellus purus, pellentesque porta tellus ultrices eget.

 Mauris finibus libero erat. Quisque ac pharetra massa. Duis dapibus tellus risus
 , ut sodales augue ultricies eu.Maecenas pulvinar faucibus ultricies. Nullam non
  enim bibendum sapien ultrices vehicula vel a nisi. Aliquam erat volutpat.Morbi
 elit ligula, dignissim mattis ultrices ut, porttitor quis lectus. Cras in augue
 eget ligula elementum tristique ullamcorper nec metus.
 kali@kali:~$ head -2 '/home/kali/Desktop/ipsum.txt'
 This is the first line.
 Lorem ipsum dolor sit amet, consectetur adipiscing elit.
 kali@kali:~$
```

That will give me the path directly to it. And I can just hit Enter. That's going to give me the first 10 lines of that file. If I want to just say the first one line or, say, first two lines, I could just hit a -2, and it would give me just the first two lines of that file. Conversely, if I type tail, same thing, and let's say do the last two lines of the file and drop that off, there's a space and then the very last line of the file. And if I open it up in the regular text editor, you can see the first few lines of the file and then, down at the bottom, the last line of the file. It makes it easy to work with very large files from the command line, getting to the beginnings or the ends of files. Same type of thing with the cat demand. If I just did a cat and then help, it gives me the flags that I can use. And if I just type in cat and then, let's say, for instance, a n for line number, again drop that file into the terminal window and hit Enter, it shows me then the same file, but it numbers every single line.

260

```
                                    kali@kali: ~                              _ □ ×
File  Edit  View  Search  Terminal  Help
Examptes:
  cat f - g  Output f's contents, then standard input, then g's contents.
  cat        Copy standard input to standard output.

GNU coreutils online help: <https://www.gnu.org/software/coreutils/>
Full documentation <https://www.gnu.org/software/coreutils/cat>
or available locally via: info '(coreutils) cat invocation'
kali@kali:~$ cat -n '/home/kali/Desktop/ipsum.txt'
     1  This is the first line.
     2  Lorem ipsum dolor sit amet, consectetur adipiscing elit.
     3  Aliquam facilisis metus interdum leo bibendum, id mattis purus tristique

     4  Aliquam bibendum consequat dolor at euismod.
     5  Integer nec enim et nulla cursus aliquet eu vel dolor.
     6  Etiam aliquam rhoncus lobortis.
     7  Vestibulum vulputate ullamcorper nibh, dignissim sodales arcu porta vita
e.
     8  Sed maximus tellus purus, pellentesque porta tellus ultrices eget.
     9
    10  Mauris finibus libero erat. Quisque ac pharetra massa. Duis dapibus tell
us risus, ut sodales augue ultricies eu.Maecenas pulvinar faucibus ultricies. Nu
llam non enim bibendum sapien ultrices vehicula vel a nisi. Aliquam erat volutpa
t.Morbi elit ligula, dignissim mattis ultrices ut, porttitor quis lectus. Cras i
n augue eget ligula elementum tristique ullamcorper nec metus.
```

This may or may not be useful for you depending upon what environment you like to work in. But definitely understand the uses of them, the flags associated with them, and how they can be used to in scripting or manipulating files from the command line.

Shell and Script Environments (SSH, PowerShell, Python and OpenSSL)

Just to cover some shell and scripting environments without digging too deeply, making you an expert in any one specific area, but some things you should be aware of for sure are SSH, or Secure Shell. It is a cryptographic network protocol for doing things securely over an insecure network or an unsecured network. We can do things like remote command line execution, remote logins. Next is PowerShell. PowerShell is a command line shell and associated scripting language. It was originally Windows-only, but has since been made open source, so its cross-platform. But without digging into the specifics, PowerShell has a multitude of commands and functions called cmdlets to access elements of the operating system, to do various functions. Next, we have Python, and Python is a cross-platform interpreted programming language. Meaning you need an interpreter with a focus on readability. It's widely regarded as one of the top three programming languages, Java and C or C# being some of the other ones. Then we have OpenSSL, which is a software library for applications that secure communications using an open-source implementation of SSL and TLS. With TLS 1.3 support added in September of 2018, TLS 1.0 has been deprecated, so make sure that's out of your environment if at all possible. But, TLS 1.3 is the current standard.

Packet Capture and TCPDump

As a security analyst, there's a lot of tools that we need in our toolbelt, a lot of various skills that we need to develop to secure our networks and our applications. When it comes to packet capture and replay, we have a security analyst that's attached to the network, and we have a few other hosts on the network. We have some database and some coding. There's other users on the network. Well, as a security analyst, there's a few different tools that you may use, one of which is tcpdump, which is a command line utility. Another might be Wireshark, which is a GUI implementation. Tcpdump gives you a similar capability as Wireshark, but it's a command line. And then the ability to replay traffic, tcpreplay, and that could be fed into IDS and IPS systems to ramp up traffic to keep it at scale just to give you a bit of an overview of where these things come into play. When we talk about tcpdump, it's a command line packet capture tool to capture and display packets in real time. It can be filtered by IP address, by port, by connection type or protocol. It's a very quick and dirty tool to be able to see what's going on in real time via command line, much like we do within Wireshark, but this is a command line utility. Next is

Wireshark. It's a graphical packet capture utility similar to tcpdump and can be used to troubleshoot network issues, to decrypt communications, assuming we have the proper certificates, and then also to eavesdrop on communications either for a legitimate purpose or an illegitimate purpose. Bad actors can use that maliciously. Then tcpreplay is a command line tool for editing and then replaying previously captured packets. It can be used for troubleshooting, for IDS and IPS systems, intrusion detection systems or intrusion prevention systems, for NetFlow systems. We want to be able to replay that traffic and analyze it in some form or fashion. This is very similar to what we would see in Wireshark. We're capturing packets. It just happens to be displaying in real time in my terminal session. Depending upon what types of tools you like to use, this could be another tool in your toolbelt. Some people prefer command prompt or command line or terminal session. Other folks prefer graphical user interfaces, like Wireshark.

Chapter 4 Forensics & Exploitation Frameworks

When it comes to forensics, there are a lot of nuances within the field. There are different specialties, different areas of expertise. But generally speaking, there are some tools that you should be aware of and some skill sets that you should develop if forensics is, in fact, an area that you want to dig into. Imagine that we have an investigator, and there are a few tools I just want to call your attention. We have the first one being dd, and that's a command line tool to copy and clone disks, partitions, and files. It can be used to erase disks. Some people refer to it as disk destroyer, but it's a very powerful tool, command line tool, built into Linux and allows you to copy, clone and partition files. Next, we have memdump. Memdump can dump either the physical or kernel memory to a file, and it can also be done over the network. You can connect to a machine remotely and do a memory dump to a file and get what's in that system's memory, either physical memory or kernel memory. Next, we have WinHex, and that's a hex editor for examining files, recovering files, searching for specific file types. That can dig into the code underneath of a file or contained within a file to help you look for specific patterns, hidden information, header-type mismatch. And then we have something called FTK Imager, and that stands for Forensic Toolkit, and it's used to acquire disk images and perform analysis for investigations, creating case files. Then we have Autopsy, another forensic toolkit for acquiring disk images and performing analysis and investigations. Two different ways, or two different programs to accomplish the same task. As an example, here we have a screenshot of Autopsy, this is a forensic tool for building cases for investigating systems, gathering evidence.

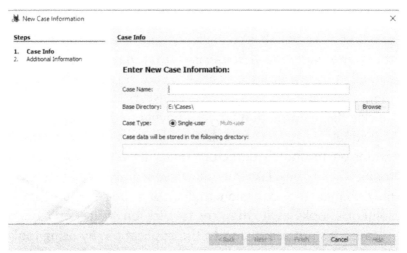

It allows us to create a case, we can name it, add additional information, we can put in the base directory of where we want to store that information. Then once we start the case, there are a number of things that can be automated as it searches through that system. We can do hash lookups.

So, if we're looking for illegal images or things we don't necessarily want to have to sift through one by one by one, we can have the application going in and hash all the files on that system and then compare those hashes to a database of

265

known hashes. In other words, if there's a bunch of files that are already known, like child exploitation files as an example, there are large hash databases that have already been compiled by law enforcement that you can subscribe to and then compare those hashes against that. You can very quickly find information without having to sift through each individual file. We can look for file type identification or extension mismatch detector. That's an old school way of trying to hide files. Like you may have a graphics file, but you may change the extension to.doc for a doc file, so that if someone looks at it, they try to click on it, it won't open because it's not associated to the application. By using tools like this, we can very quickly look at the file header and then match it to the file extension. And if those things don't match, it stands out like a sore thumb. It makes it even easier to find those types of files. These types of applications become very powerful. As it does all of these things, it does a lot of it automated. Some of it will be manual process, but some of it is just a matter of you setting things up in the beginning. And then it will go through and analyze that system, build the case file, put everything into proper files and folders, and then something that we've touched on before is the concept of hashing and making sure that hashes match to show that we have two identical files. Well, when we're talking about acquiring forensic images, it's the same process. We have an investigator that would use their forensic toolkit, one of the ones we just talked about, and they would connect it to a target system. They want to acquire an image from a suspect PC to analyze, to investigate. They would typically put a write blocker in between their laptop or their toolkit and the actual target system. That way, it would prevent their forensic toolkit from altering or writing to the target system in any way, shape, or form. It keeps everything pristine. The write blocker would then connect to the target system. Then the forensic toolkit would do its thing. We just saw the screenshot showing some of the capabilities. It would image that system and then write it out to a cloned system. We take all of the data off of the target system and make an immutable copy that's write protected. It may chunk it up into multiple pieces that can be copied out to a CD or a DVD so that it can be then imaged or analyzed over and over again. Then what we can do each time is take a hash of the target system and then a hash of the cloned system. That way, those things match. We know that they are identical, that nothing's changed. That way we can be sure that when we're working off of a cloned system, we're not introducing artifacts or changing data in any way, shape, or form. Those things, as you can imagine, are needed for court, preservation of evidence, chain of custody. All of these things apply when we're dealing with digital evidence, as well as physical evidence, and having a hash value that matches allows us to show when we present that report and say, here's all of the things that we found on that target system. The other side can't come back and say, oh, well, that's not my system. Things have been changed. You added things in there. Well, no, the hash values match. We initially took a hash of the system when we first acquired it, and it exactly matches the hash of our cloned system. Those things go a long way to help strengthen your case. It's a matter of following best practices when we're doing forensic-type work.

Exploitation Frameworks
Exploitation frameworks, and as the name implies, they are there to exploit weaknesses, exploit vulnerabilities in a specific host, or a network, or a system. They are tool sets that can be used offensively or defensively, and they're often

used by penetration testers, or pen testers, as well as hackers unfortunately. Popular exploitation frameworks, Metasploit is probably one of the most popular, and it's an open source and commercial, there are both versions available, you can download it for free, and then there's a paid version. It gives you a lot of amazing features and tool sets out of the box, hundreds of different exploits to test, and it's also widely used, by pen testers and also the hacking community. Next is CANVAS. These are just a small list, not an exhaustive one by any stretch and certainly not an endorsement of any one particular piece of software. But CANVAS was a development and pen testing platform originally, and then we have Core Impact, another one, which was designated as the first fully automated pen testing program that's typically used by enterprises and corporate environments primarily due to cost. There's also another one that's called RouterSploit, and as you might guess, that's specifically geared towards routers.

```
rsf (AutoPwn) > set target 192.168.1.254
[+] {'target': '192.168.1.254'}
rsf (AutoPwn) > show options

Target options:

    Name        Current settings        Description
    ----        ----------------        -----------
    target      192.168.1.254           Target address e.g. http://192.168.1.1
    port        80                      Target port

rsf (AutoPwn) > run
[*] Running module...
[-]   exploits/multi/misfortune_cookie is not vulnerable
[-]   exploits/dlink/dvg_n5402sp_path_traversal is not vulnerable
[-]   exploits/dlink/dwr_932_info_disclosure is not vulnerable
[-]   exploits/dlink/dir_300_320_615_auth_bypass is not vulnerable
[-]   exploits/dlink/dsl_2750b_info_disclosure is not vulnerable
[-]   exploits/dlink/dns_320l_327l_rce is not vulnerable
[-]   exploits/dlink/dir_645_password_disclosure is not vulnerable
[-]   exploits/dlink/dir_300_600_615_info_disclosure is not vulnerable
[-]   exploits/dlink/dir_300_600_rce is not vulnerable
[-]   exploits/cisco/ucs_manager_rce is not vulnerable
[-]   exploits/2wire/gateway_auth_bypass is not vulnerable
[-]   exploits/asus/infosvr_backdoor_rce is not vulnerable
[-]   exploits/asus/rt_n16_password_disclosure is not vulnerable
[+]   exploits/asmax/ar_1004g_password_disclosure is vulnerable
[-]   exploits/asmax/ar_804_gu_rce is not vulnerable
[-]   exploits/linksys/wap54gv3_rce is not vulnerable
[-]   exploits/linksys/1500_2500_rce is not vulnerable
[-]   exploits/fortinet/fortigate_os_backdoor is not vulnerable
[-]   exploits/technicolor/tc7200_password_disclosure is not vulnerable
```

As you can see here, it runs in very much the same fashion, you can put in a target, an IP address, and you can run a Metasploit-type command set, against this target IP address, and it will run different modules, it'll go through the list, and it will run all of these different types of exploits against that specific router, and it will see where there's a vulnerability or if any exist. And as you can see from the output here, that exploit does exist for a password disclosure, so it says is vulnerable. All the rest in this specific instance is not vulnerable, but it allows you to quickly go through a network and identify all the different routers within a specific subnet or the entire environment, and then run this test against all of those devices, and come back and report and say, hey, here's where we're vulnerable, we're locked down everywhere except, not sure if you knew this, but you're vulnerable here, here, and here. You can very quickly give a report back to management, executive management, or the company that's hiring you to come in if you're a penetration tester, and show them where those vulnerabilities do exist.

Chapter 5 Data Sanitization Tools

Next we have data sanitization tools, and wiping versus deleting, as you may or may not be aware, deleting a file doesn't do much in and of itself. If you delete a file, you're simply marking that file as being able to be overwritten, so the data is still there. There are tons of free tools and commercial tools that can recover that data very easily. If you need to make sure that data is gone and not recoverable, then we need to do something called wiping, Wiping is always going to be better than deleting. Sanitization tools overwrite the data x number of times to ensure that it's unrecoverable, and those number of passes, or that x number of times, is configurable. We'll also talk about SSD disk sanitization. That's going to be different. When we're talking about traditional hard disks, that's a magnetic media, so that's going to be a different method to sanitize than SSDs or the solid state or all-flash drives. With SSDs, each manufacturer typically has a secure erase tool, you'll need to either use that specific tool, or there are also some third-party tools that can work on SSDs as well, so as an example of SSD sanitization. Each manufacturer will have their own specific toolset that is geared toward that specific drive, Samsung, Intel, Corsair, SanDisk, they all make their own different tools. And then there's a third-party tool called Parted Magic, and that includes a sanitization or a secure erase tool as well. As an example, here we have SSD Secure Erase for Samsung drives.

Using the Samsung Magician toolset, we'll create a beautiful
drive, either USB or a CD or DVD, and we put that in the
machine, and we'll boot into this interface. From here, we
just say yes, we want to do a Secure Erase. It'll ask us again,
and then within a matter of seconds that drive is securely
erased. If we use Parted Magic as an example, it's going to
come up first and say, we want to do a secure erase, and it
can either be SSDs or it can be NVMe in this case.

It's going to do a drive-level erase, so Secure Erase issues drive-level command sets to that specific drive and tells it what to do. In this instance, we're going to do a Secure Erase of an NVMe drive. We're going to say, pick the drive from the list. There it is dev/nvme0n1.

It's a Samsung SSD 950 PRO. We're going to say yes, I want to go ahead and erase. From there, it literally takes 2 or 3 seconds, and then it's done. That quickly that drive is securely erased. And it can also generate a log output if you want to review the log settings or review the output, but very quick and much quicker than erasing a magnetic hard disk. When we're talking about data sanitization methods for hard drives, there are a few things or a few standards we should be aware of. There are a couple that I want to call your attention to, and there are others, but these are the main three that you should be familiar with. The first is the DoD 5220.22-M, that's a standard. This is from the Department of Defense, and it is a three-pass write, so it's going to overwrite that data three separate times. Pass 1 writes a zero and then verifies the write, Pass 2 writes a one and then verifies the write, and then Pass 3 writes a random character verifies that write. Once that's complete, that data is not recoverable. The next is RCMP, or the Royal Canadian Mounted Police, an outstanding cybersecurity division. They issue a three-pass write as well. The Communication Security Establishment of Canada, that's what the CSEC stands for. And what we're doing here is writing a one or zero in Pass 1, and then Pass 2 writes the complement of the previously written character, so if the first pass was zeros, then this pass would be a one and vice-versa. Then Pass 3 writes a random character and then verifies that write. Then lastly, something referred to as Secure Erase, and that's a one-pass. That writes a binary one or a zero, very fast, and that's only available for whole-disk sanitization. These other two methods I talked about, they can be used on individual files and folders as well. There are toolsets that you can run within the operating system that will allow you to use those techniques to erase individual files or folders, but with Secure Erase it works only on the whole disk. There are some other ones as well. There's the Peter Gutmann 35-pass, and that was developed back in the mid to late nineties, and back then, 35 passes was thought to be like the most extreme, and that was like super secure. We've found that over time that a subset of that is all you need to have data unrecoverable. It used to be DoD was a seven-pass overwrite, and that was like the most secure. It's going down to three. Same thing with RCMP. They went from a higher level down to three. Then Secure Erase is also acceptable by RCMP as well. That single-pass write has been found to be unrecoverable by pretty much every type of disk recovery software out there. In summary, we talked about network reconnaissance and discovery, along with file manipulation, various shell and script environments. We talked about packet capture and replay, some of the tools that we would use for that, whether they are command-line or GUI based. We also talked about forensics and some of the nuances of acquiring images, making sure that they match, holding up in court. Then we talked about exploitation frameworks, password crackers, data sanitization, and then some demos of various applications.

Chapter 6 How to Apply Policies, Processes and Procedures for Incident Response

In this chapter we'll be talking about applying policies, processes, and procedures for incident response. We'll be talking about incident response plans and process. We'll cover the various testing exercises that you may utilize in your environment. We'll also talk about the various attack frameworks, along with stakeholder management, communication plans, including disaster recovery and business continuity plans. We'll also talk about the continuity of operation planning, along with incident response teams, retention policies, and at the end, we'll put it all together and talk about responding to an incident. But who should read this chapter? Well, we have six main categories. We have computer security staff, people that are implementing this type of stuff day to day; we have computer security program managers, the ones that need to look at things at a little higher level and understand the big risk and also the financial impacts; tech support staff and managers, the folks that make IT run on a day-to-day basis; incident response teams, the ones that are responsible for coming out and handling things when an incident or a breach occurs; system and network administrators, again IT, in general; and then end users, both IT and non-IT. IT security is everyone's responsibility. It's not just for the IT security professional. Everybody is responsible or should be responsible for making sure IT security, information security, cybersecurity, make that a priority. Because, as we know, threats can come both internally and externally. They can come from hackers, organized crime, nation states, but they can also be done internally for things like espionage or to get back at a co-worker or a manager. Then when we look at the actual potential impacts, some things that you should be aware of, drives this home, and the real reasons why you should care, is the fact that companies, both large and small, are constant targets. It makes no difference the industry or the size of the company, not just high-value targets. Smaller victims can play a part in larger attacks. Meaning, you may think to yourself, well, we're a small company of 5, 10, 15 people. We don't have to worry about IT Security as much. Well, that's precisely why you should worry about IT security. The smaller companies that may not have their actual IT network defenses and perimeter defenses as tight and as rigid as some larger companies, they become easy targets. While the information that they possess may not be of a high-value nature to a potential hacker or nation state or what have you, what small company, or your small company, could play a part in a larger attack. You could become part of a botnet or some type of other larger organized or more organized scheme to attack a much larger company or a much larger victim. Don't think just because you're small, you may not play a part in a much bigger attack. Then also such things as loss of data, intellectual property, competitive advantage, or overall consumer confidence. These can all be downstream impacts and fallout from a breach. Then companies can also risk legal action if they're negligent and not properly protected. If there are things that you should be doing but for whatever reason you're not, and then a breach occurs and an incident occurs and consumer data is lost, or personally identifiable information, is leaked, that information, or that fallout could come back to haunt the company in the form of legal action lawsuits, or class action lawsuits. It's very important that we realize that IT security is everyone's responsibility. Everyone should be chipping in. If they see something, say something. Everyone should be playing their part to make sure that their small piece of this larger puzzle is as secure as possible.

Team Models

Let's now talk about the various team models that we should look at developing within our organization. So, we can have a central incident response team, and that means all of our team members are on site, they're in one central location, and they'll handle all incidents for that company wherever they may be. If we have a global presence, however, that may or may not be feasible. In that case, we would have a distributed incident response team, and that means we have incident response teams perhaps spread out through all of our different organization locations, geographically dispersed, either throughout a specific part of the world or potentially globally. And then we have a coordinating team, and a coordinating team would be centrally located. The coordinating team itself, they would coordinate the efforts of the other teams located throughout the various parts of either the country or throughout the world. No matter which of the last two we choose, whether it's distributed or coordinating, it's very important to understand that all of the different teams, whether they are reporting to a centralized coordinating team and they're advising them what to do, or they're distributed and they're each acting as their own entity, they all need to make sure that they adhere to the same sets of policies so a consistent application of that incident response plan and procedures, are in fact implemented and executed, no matter where that's taking place throughout any of the company's various locations.

Incident Response Process

When talking about the phases of incident response we've covered before, the six main phases, the preparation, detection, analysis, containment, eradication, recovery, and then documentation, or lessons learned. This process is a continuous cycle that's refined over time. None of these things are going to be static. It's a living document; it's a living process. Every time we have a breach or an incident, we're going to learn something from that, and we're going to refine our process. Those lessons learned, once you come to the end of that process, we go through preparation, detection, containment, eradication, we get to the end, the documentation and lessons learned, that helps us identify gaps and increase our preparedness for the next time. It would be nice to say there never will be a next time, but unfortunately, that's not the nature of breaches in today's environment. Most companies have hundreds, if not thousands, of breaches or attempted breaches per year. Some companies have thousands per day. It just depends upon the size of your company, the criticality of the information your company has, or the intellectual property or whatever data that's valuable to a hacker, whoever that hacker or hacking organization may be. Then additional resources are brought on line and into that response team's arsenal. It's not a static environment. It's dynamic, and so as we go through this process and we refine, refine, refine, lessons learned, we identify gaps, we close those gaps. We may need additional resources, additional team members with additional skill sets. Every company's going to be slightly different. Every company houses different information, has different potential targets for a hacker or a hacking organization. There is no one set document that will cover everything. There are certainly a guideline and a best practices, but as you go through this, you will identify specific things that are unique to your organization, and correct or add to that arsenal accordingly.

Preparation

When we're talking about preparation, we have a couple things. We need to make sure that we identify team members. It's very important that we identify what skills we need, how many team members we need. One person can't do all of this. It's too vast. There are too many things to do at once. In the middle of a breach, you're going to have multiple things going on at once, detection and analysis, alerting other people, alerting other teams, coordinating with media, coordinating with executive management, identifying the risk, shutting down ports, protocol, and so on. There's going to be a lot of things that may need to happen concurrently or in tandem in the middle of a breach, so it's too much for one person to handle, typically. We'll need to identify those team members. We'll need to identify and define roles and responsibilities. It should be clearly defined who does what and in what order, so in the middle of some type of crisis, we have a playbook or a run book we can go by and say, you do this, I'll do this, he's going to take care of that piece for us. Everybody works in concert and attacks the problem as a cohesive unit. It's very important to have that synergy. Then also develop defense-in-depth strategies. These things should be spelled out ahead of time. You shouldn't have just one lock on the door. There are many things that we can do, so that if a hacker breaches one method of defense, there's still another, perhaps two or three more that they have to get through before they can get into our network and into our systems, make it as difficult as possible. That also gives you time to become alerted, it gives you time to remediate before they penetrate all of the defenses and get at your critical systems.

Chapter 7 Detection and Analysis

In the detection and analysis phases, properly trained teams can assist and expedite all phases of the incident and response process. Having that team in place, properly trained, running smooth, that's going to help all phases of that process. A quick assessment can determine the level of impact and also help direct containment and mitigation efforts. That quick initial assessment; is this malware or is it not? Is this a virus? Is this a hacking attempt that came in through maybe a specific port or a protocol? Or they did some type of SQL injection, or they had a USB stick that was infected and brought into our system, or it was infected laptop. By identifying the source and the type of threat, the type of incident we're dealing with here can help quickly identify the level of impact. Is it going to be a nuisance or is it going to be a multimillion dollar event? Are we going to lose customer information? How quickly can we stem that bleeding? That helps direct containment and the mitigation efforts. Also, analysis of event files, log files, from things like intrusion detection systems, firewalls, routers, switches, directory servers. Anything on our network that can be audited or that creates log files that can be parsed and then correlated across different verticals, we can correlate timing from our routers and switches, our firewalls, IDS systems, access to directory servers, or perhaps pieces of critical infrastructure; if we're able to aggregate and then correlate those events across all those devices at one time, it allows us to quickly get a picture of what's happening, and how it's happening. All of those network systems should be brought into play. That helps us determine the true intent of that attack. So, is your company the clear target? In other words, are you the goal, or is someone just probing? They happened to come across one of your systems, and they're just probing just to see what's there. It's the old hacker mantra: Well why'd you climb that mountain? Well, because it was there. Sometimes people just want to probe and see what they can see. They don't have a specific goal, they're not trying to necessarily steal something or destroy something, and they just want to see if they can get in, more or less as a badge of honor, if you will. Alternatively, was your business the actual target, or are you a side door attack to some other company? And as I mentioned earlier, as far as things being a clear target or just probing, was this a true attack or just someone doing an initial network or resource mapping? They want to come in and probe our network and see how things are laid out. What are our routers and switches? Do we have a single namespace? Do we have different IP spaces for different areas, naming conventions? What type of systems do we have? Are we running Linux, Windows or virtualization. By coming in and doing that network mapping, they can get a good idea of what types of systems are on the network. By having that properly trained team, we can identify and say, is this breach? Are we in all hands on deck mode, and we having to go in and start bringing all of our resources to bear to try to confront this and contain it? Or, was this someone coming in initially? Do we catch them in the very beginning hopefully while they're still doing the network scan, trying to go in and see what there is of value. By being able to identify that, it allows us to quickly attack that in the proper fashion, assign resources correctly, and address that threat appropriately.

Stopping the Spread
When it comes to stopping the spread, we want to focus on a couple things. Containing a security incident is going to help mitigate loss. The quicker we can contain that spread or

that initial infection of that piece of malware or virus focusing on malware here, the quicker we can contain that, the quicker we can mitigate loss. After containment, then comes eradication. Eradication, it may consist of disabling compromised accounts, taking that machine out of service. Also, potentially wiping that machine and reinstalling from scratch. It all depends upon that part of the recovery process that deals with backups. If we can verify them as being valid backups, then we may be able to restore that system from that backed up piece of data, that backup tape. If it's not, however, then we may need to completely blow that system away or wipe that system or reimage that system. Also, check it for rootkits and because we want to make sure that that system is not compromised beyond what we initially thought. When it comes to eradication and recovery, we may need to disable affected accounts. We have to identify how that piece of malware was installed. What user account was used? Is it affecting admin accounts? Is our system set up or is our network set up to have admin accounts disabled by default? If there's a service account that it somehow is able to attach itself to and then spread throughout the network using that service account, we have to identify that quickly and disable that account so it can't spread. It just depends upon the nature of that piece of malware. Next, we have to identify what ports and protocols that piece of malware uses. And shut down those ports and protocols or at least monitor them very closely to make sure that malware is not spreading to other systems across that same transport mechanism, that same port or that same protocol. Next, recover from backup, will verify that the backup is, in fact, good. If it's not, then we need to do a fresh install. It's going to depend upon - the nature of that infection. And then something else that's equally as important, if not more important, and we have to do that very quickly, in tandem with the initial infection as we're going through our identification remediation steps, we need to coordinate with other sites and other locations within our company to make sure they're aware of the breach of the infection and so they can start monitoring their systems as well. That if a spread, in fact, does take place or tries to take place, they can mitigate that as quickly as possible. That goes back to what accounts are being used, what ports or protocols. That information should be shared with other sites and with other locations within the company.

Defining Goals and Expected Outcomes
When we're talking about defining goals and expected outcomes, a few things to keep in mind. First off, we need to periodically test the business continuity, cyber and also disaster recovery plans. We have to make sure and verify that the plans are valid, that they cover the required elements that we want to protect, that we're getting all the critical infrastructure, critical applications and all the critical business functions, and that the plan can be executed when the time comes. Doesn't do us much good to have a very grandiose plan, and we think it might work, but if it doesn't achieve the expected outcome or if it's not even an executable plan, it doesn't do us much good. Many companies have business continuity plans that they've written down, they sound great on paper, but they've never executed them, never tested them. It's important that we do that. Next, we want to make sure we have buy-in from senior management. We must have executive approval, and this should be disseminated, if possible, organization wide so that everyone is aware of what the plans are. We need to make sure that people who are involved with this process know that they're involved with the process and are able to complete and are competent in the roles that they're

assigned. Buy-in from executive management is critical in this regard, and then, if possible, it's going to depend on corporate culture, the size of the organization, but if possible, these plans should be disseminated company wide so that everyone is on the same page. Next, we should have post testing review. After we test our plans, we need to identify what's changed, if anything, because as we test our plan, we might identify, we didn't think of this, or, we thought we had this in place, but it's no longer valid, we can remove that. If anything's changed, we need to document, we need to correct any gaps, and then compare our goals and expected outcomes. We thought we were going to achieve A, B, and C; well we achieved A, B, and F, or we achieved none of it, depending upon the outcome of the exercise. Document, identify those gaps, correct the gaps, and then reiterate, go and test again at some point in time, make sure that it's a working document, it's a working plan that is executable when the time comes. Then also, an important distinction to understand is testing vs. exercises. We want to make sure we don't find ourselves in that situation. A test is a pass-fail scenario. An exercise is much harder to measure in that regard, because some elements of an exercise may be successful, some may not, so it's not an entirely pass-fail scenario. It's also good to put out to the organization, when you're conducting these exercises, make sure they understand it's just that, it's not a pass-fail. It takes some of the burden off the employees, and it also makes them not falsely report because no one wants to fail, so, you don't want them just going through and checking boxes just to check the boxes. If something fails, you want to know it fails realistically, so that you can correct. By letting someone know, we're letting the organization know, we're doing an exercise. This is not pass fail, you're not going to get fired, you're not going to have something drastic. It's going to be a learning experience, we expect some things to not work as planned, that's all part of the process, that's why we're testing. It's much better to find out than to think something worked because someone was afraid to say no or afraid to fail, they checked a box even if they didn't do the exercise or do that specific piece, and then find out when the incident happens where the catastrophe is in full swing, that the plan is not executable, so that's not the time to do that.

Chapter 8 Test Scenarios & Simulations

Testing needs to be realistic. Simply reporting back successful testing results is meaningless if the test is not realistic. Something to keep in mind is, we need to make sure that we test the plan. Don't plan the test. What do I mean by that? We need to make it as realistic as possible. In other words, don't let everyone know, hey, the test is coming. The catastrophe's about to arrive on our doorstep Let's go ahead and plan everything to the nth degree. Let's take everything into consideration, let's have all of our resources lined up, let's make sure we have everything in place because in reality, as we know, catastrophes don't announce themselves. They don't knock on the door and say, hey, I'm going to be here tomorrow at 6:00. Everybody get ready. If you want to test the reality and the validity of a test or an exercise, don't plan it to the degree. Throw in some variability. Make sure that you have some things that throw you off to see how the plan functions in a non-perfect world.

Walkthrough Tests
When we're talking about the various types of testing and exercises, we have five that I want to mention here. We have walk-through testing, or walk-through exercises, we have communications, communication exercises, simulations, we have a partial exercise, and then also a full exercise. Let's take a look at each of these in more detail. For a walk-through, that's a reading through the proposed plan. It's everyone gathering in a room together, or as close together as possible, whether it's over Skype, or some remote communication telepresence, you'll read through the proposed plan, and then you'll ask yourself some questions. Does the plan makes sense? it's a bit of a no

brainer, but depending upon who's reading, sometimes people are afraid to speak up, Everyone should be empowered to say, this doesn't make sense, or this isn't valid, or we're missing something here, go through that, that's the purpose of this exercise. Also does it follow a logical path? Are we doing things in the order that we would realistically expect them to either be restored, contained, mitigated. Also, is it understandable and easy to follow for those that must utilize that plan? If it's extremely complicated, full of legalese or ultra-technical jargon, that people reading that plan may or may not be understanding of or may not be privy to that information, it's important to make it understandable. In the middle of a crisis, the brain isn't as loose, it's tightened down, you're in a heightened sense of awareness, stress levels come up, and it becomes a little harder to focus, Making sure these things are easy to understand and easy to follow is critical. Then also revisions may occur numerous times throughout this process because it's not typically a one and done. As we go through this each and every time, it's understood that there's going to be gaps, there's going to be things that are missed, or things that need to be added, so a few revisions of this plan throughout this process or throughout this exercise is expected.

Communication Tests
Next we have communication tests, we want to make sure or ensure that all relevant personnel, all vendors, emergency responders are identified. We need to verify that we have accurate contact information, critical, it does not stay the same typically, and things can change over time, so a periodic review of this information will pay dividends if and when an actual incident occurs. Also identify backups, otherwise known as deputies, for each key position. We don't want to have just one person identified for each

specific key role, we need to make sure we have backups for them in case that person is out, unreachable, or they may be affected by the incident, or the catastrophe, or the event, and they can't reply or respond. We need to make sure we have a deputy in that case. Also identify gaps in response times and availability. As we go through this testing, understand are the people in place and is their response realistic? If we expect someone to be able to respond within 30 minutes, and it takes them 6 hours, well, that's not acceptable for this specific scenario. We need to either mitigate that risk, find another person, or adjust the plan to meet those real-world outcomes.

Simulation (Tabletop) Tests

Next, we have simulations. These are also known as tabletop exercises. The objective here is to be as real-world as possible without blowing up the building or having a tornado sweep through. But we want to make sure that we can make it as realistic as possible in a simulated scenario. To do that, we should inject some variability or randomness into the test before. Maybe not have everybody respond. That way, it mirrors what would happen if that specific person or group of people can't respond because the event is impacting them in some way. Also disasters typically don't announce themselves ahead of time. Injecting some type of variability into that test makes it a little bit more real-world and also shows you and the rest of the organization how you can adapt and overcome, still within the parameters of the plan. Because the goal is business continuity. We want to make sure that business can continue, business functions, business services. By doing this, injecting some variability, we ensure an even greater chance of success.

Partial Exercise

Partial exercises are somewhat intrusive so it's going to require people from various areas throughout the organization. Depending upon the size of that company, you may all be located in one location, you may be spread out within a state, throughout the country, or even globally. There may be some disruption as all of these folks are gathered together. You're going to have to coordinate logistically how to make that happen. Some actions will need to be taken that may disrupt normal operations. That's just the nature of the beast. When possible, do these types of exercises when it's least disruptive to the business, after hours, on the weekends. It just depends upon your business and when your busy times are. The goal here is to prepare for disaster recovery up almost to the point of failing over, but not failing over completely, because that would be a full exercise. But we want to take it halfway or three quarters of the way, gaining a much better understanding of how the operation and how the plan functions, but not a full-blown exercise.

Full Exercise

Full exercises are most disruptive to the business. It's a complete testing of the business continuity and disaster recovery plans. It's going soup-to-nuts, from beginning to end, so a complete failover of systems to ensure continuity, again, a continuity of the business, business services. Then, it should be performed, like we talked about with partial exercises, at times that are least intrusive to the company's operations. It could be after hours, over night, weekends, or it may be certain times of the year, maybe there's a slow period. Coordinate that so it's least disruptive, and then you'll ensure the highest chance of participation and buy in, especially from senior management.

Overall Cost and Complexity of Testing

When we're talking about the overall cost and complexity of testing, understand that each one of these different types have a different dollar amount, amount of time, complexity, associated with them. Starting off, we have a walkthrough exercise. Pretty much free, it's just people in a room reading through the exercises, understanding where the gaps are. Not a lot of dollar value, or time. As far as the five different types we're talking about, this is the least cost and the least complex. Next, we have the communications test. We're going to have to test some of our systems, we're going to have to get people engaged from various parts of the business. A little bit more time, a little more complexity; and then we have simulations, partial exercises, and then full exercises. A full exercise is a complete failover, logistically getting everyone together, staging areas, command center, incident response. It's a lot more to put together, takes a lot more preparation, and it's a lot more complex.

Plan Review and Maintenance

When we're talking about maintaining our business continuity plans, it's very important to review and maintain those plans periodically. Plans should be updated as changes occur, if possible. The size of the organization may dictate that. Well we want to make sure we update these things as often as necessary to make sure the information in the plans are accurate. Business processes, key personnel, vendors and suppliers; all should be updated as things change, because they will change over time. Also, verify contact information. Again, very important, we need to make sure that when we have to go out and call someone, the number doesn't ring back and say, that number's been disconnected, or that's a totally different company because the vendor has changed or has been acquired. It's important that we verify that contact information periodically, update as necessary. Also, site access plans. Have site access plans changed? Have you acquired new buildings? Have you gotten rid of certain facilities. These things need to be up to date as well, and that includes maps, drawings, schematics. All of these things should be included in our business continuity planning, our business impact analysis, disaster recovery documents; and what that does is it demonstrates a continued due diligence. That's critical to insurers, maybe partners you may be working with, interested parties or stakeholders; all of these things show that you have plans in place to recover from a disaster, continue business. You're much more likely to get insurance, to have third-party folks and vendors work with you. Some insurance companies, some vendors, look for that and require these types of documents to do business with you. It depends upon, again, your industry, but it's a great approach to have this and have it continually updated so that you can show, hey, we take this seriously; it's company wide, we have executive buy-in, and we update our documents periodically, it's not a one and done.

Review Process Outcomes
Next, we want to make sure we do a lessons learned. We want to review that process outcome. That's going to ensure the highest probability of success, our implementation and also our recovery efforts. We need to review and constantly refine over time. That shows continued competency. That's very important for our vendors, insurers, third parties, key stakeholders. Also, it will prepare the organization for either internal or external audits that you may or may not be interested in preparing for certification. Maybe ISO 27001 for cybersecurity or 22301 for business continuity. But, if in fact that is a goal or a requirement for your organization or your industry, having this continued refinement and the

reviewing of your processes and your plans will help auditing and also help prepare for those certifications.

Intelligence Lifecycle

When it comes to the intelligence lifecycle, we have the six phases: direction, collection, processing, analysis, dissemination, and feedback. You can look at that as more or less of a loop. It starts off with an evaluation of the environment, understanding what the goals are, the roadmap to get there, and throughout that process, there's a feedback loop. We'll do it at the end, but it can also be done at each stage to make sure the process is functioning as intended, and we're getting the results that we're looking for.

Chapter 9 Threat Intelligence Lifecycle

To put that into a different format, we start off with our objectives and our key questions. That's fed from several things, internal sources, technical sources, and, of course, human sources. Some of it may be automated, some of it may be through manual intervention, talking with other analysts as well, seeing what's happening in their space or in their part of the world. All of these things, again, are fed with threat intelligence. That's comprised of the threat intelligence itself and the various security tools, the SIEM tools, and then also analysts, and that will go back and forth. Those two things feed each other, comprised from these different sources, and making sure we're starting off with understanding what it is we're trying to accomplish, what are our goals and key objectives. All of that then turns around and feeds the actual teams that will go out and utilize that information to defend the network. Incident response teams, it could be security operations, it could be a vulnerability management team, risk analysis team, perhaps maybe a fraud management team, and then, of course, security leadership. We talked about the different teams and why that's important and why they need that information, starting off with defending the actual network, the folks that are on the front lines making sure that these threats are mitigated as much as possible or remediated as quickly as possible, security operations, vulnerability, management, patching, all the way up to security leadership so that they have proper data to make informed decisions of where to invest time, resources, money, infrastructure and so on.

Cyberthreat Intelligence Frameworks

Cyber threat intelligence frameworks, a definition would be: it's a structure for thinking how attackers operate, the methods involved, and where in the overall attack lifecycle that event is occurring. More specifically, that cyber threat intelligence framework allows us to be very prescriptive in how we attack a specific situation. It focuses attention on the proper areas to ensure follow up to make sure eradication and mitigation of future threats. It also provides a common language to communicate internally and also externally, regarding threat details, interrelations between events, and correlations with external data sources. It's a framework that allows us to plug in and understand where something is occurring in the process, focus our resources within that small area rather than trying to take the shotgun approach, allows us to be much more laser-focused on the specific area that needs our attention. That way, we don't waste time, waste effort, and resources working on areas that don't necessarily matter or perhaps aren't necessarily relevant.

Cyber Kill Chain

The first one I want to call your attention to is something referred to as the Cyber Kill Chain. This was developed by Lockheed Martin in 2011, and it's based upon the military concept of the kill chain. We have seven distinct areas, and it allows us to understand where in the process a specific attack is occurring, whether it's in reconnaissance, weaponization or delivery, but if we understand where in the process that specific attack is, we can focus our resources and our mitigation efforts, and if they have a proper framework, we can understand what actions need to be taken in that area, We can quickly respond. First off, reconnaissance, the adversary is probing for weakness, so such things as harvesting login credentials, or info that can be used for a phishing attack. Next is weaponization, that is creating the deliverable, the payload, using an exploit as a backdoor typically. Delivery is the process of sending that payload to the victim, it could be a malicious email, it could be a thumb drive left, on a desk or on the floor, someone picks it up and says, what's this, next thing mission accomplished, it's been delivered. Then we have exploits, and an exploit is the act of executing the code on the remote system. Installation is the actual installing of malware on that target asset, and it brings us to command and control, or C Squared, or C&C, that creates a channel or persistence where the attacker can control the system remotely. At that point, they have control of perhaps one system, perhaps a number of systems. Then actions, so that's carrying out the intended goal, whether it's encrypting data, destroying data, exfiltrating data. If we can understand where in the process a specific action is, we know how to focus our efforts to quickly shut that thing down. If we can interrupt the chain, the kill chain, if we break that chain just like you break a link in a real life chain, then the chain breaks apart. You can stop it from progressing.

Diamond Model
The diamond model is a complementary model to the cyberthreat kill chain. This was developed by the Center for Cyber Intelligence Analysis and Threat Research. It was designed to track attack groups over time rather than individual attacks. The diamond model states for every intrusion event there exists an adversary that takes a step toward an intended goal by using a capability over infrastructure against a victim to produce a result. What we

see is we have this diamond model set up, and you can see we have an adversary, and that can be certain pieces of metadata that we need to understand about that adversary, their persona, an IP address, network assets, the capabilities that they have, malware, exploits, stolen certificates. We're going to use those capabilities over infrastructure, network assets, devices, domain names to launch some type of an attack on a victim. we need to understand the persona like who that person is, what type of group, what type of industry, role, the persona of that victim, the IP address, network assets. Once we have all these things understood, we can create a persona or an avatar or some type of profile of that person, allow us to understand quickly the types of the remediations that can be put in place to shut those things down. Some of the meta-features that we would also capture to make sure we have data about that specific event in a specific threat group, timestamps, the attack phase, which complements the cyber kill chain, the attack result, the direction, methodology, and resources. Going deep into the diamond model is beyond the scope of this introductory portion, but just understand that these frameworks exist to allow our threat analysis teams to quickly identify where to focus resources and also pass that information on to the defenders that go out and defend against, mitigate or remediate.

MITRE Attack Framework

MITRE is a not-for-profit organization, and they manage federal funding for research projects across multiple agencies. They're responsible for a number of things, some of which you may already be familiar with. For instance, the Common Vulnerabilities and Exposures database, the CVE database. If you've ever done patching, you see the different

CVEs that come out and say the CVE and some number attached to it, here's the exposure, here's the vulnerability, here's how you remediate. Also the Common Weaknesses Enumeration or the CWE database. The MITRE ATT&CK framework has a few complementary things that I'd like to call your attention to as well, one of which is the Trusted Automation Exchange of Intelligence Information or TAXII. What this is a transport protocol that allows sharing of threat intelligence information over HTTPS using common APIs and then also Structured Threat Information eXpression or STIX. This is a standardized format for presenting threat intelligence information. It allows different disparate systems to communicate using a common language and exchange information, all with the common goal of eradicating threats as quickly as possible. Just you're aware, the MITRE ATT&CK, the actual name of the framework, stands for adversarial tactics, techniques, and common knowledge. We touched on it again briefly before, but just to dig in a little bit deeper, it is comprised of tactical categories. There's 314 tactics spread across 12 different categories. We have initialize access, execution, persistence, privilege escalation, defense evasion, credential access, discovery, lateral movement, collection, command and control, exfiltration, and then impact. If we understand where something is happening in the cyber kill chain, as an example, and we're able to identify through our threat intelligence analysis what type of threat group is executing or attempting to execute the specific attack, we can use something like the MITRE ATT&CK framework to understand, that specific group uses these x number of tactics, 3, 5, 10, whatever the number might be.

We can quickly focus our attention. We can start enriching that data, pass it on to our defenders so they can go out and do their job of either trying to mitigate or remediate that threat as quickly as possible.

Key Points to Remember

Disaster recovery efforts should be formally started and stopped. People need to know when to start and stop that formal recovery effort. That way they can focus on bringing up secondary systems, recovering full service. If everyone still was under the operating guidelines that it is a recovery effort, they're only going to be focusing on the primary systems. They're not going to be looking at secondary tertiary systems. Once the recovery efforts have stopped, then they can get back to the business of bringing up those other systems as well, and restoring full functionality to the business. Next, tracking systems should also be defined and put in place. Ensure people are accounted for, especially if we have some type of disaster where we have injuries or potentially fatalities. Families notified if applicable, emergency services alerted if required; all of these things should be documented People know how to act, know the steps they're supposed to follow. Then, each tower has a specific area of focus. Executives should address the news media, customers, key stakeholders, as an example. Security will protect corporate assets, our IT admins would bring up key systems, making sure that our data is intact. HR would protect human capital, make sure that those people are accounted for, families notified, hospitals, clinics notified. Then lastly, several call lists should be maintained, and this will go throughout each plan. These things are common to every plan that we develop. That way we can enable quick notification to various groups. We may have an executive call list, then a functional staff, our key people that need to come in away to bring our systems back up and running: managers, supervisors, and maybe a call list for everybody, like a company wide call list. That way we have multiple communication lists that can be triggered or called into action depending upon what needs to be done. We can have different folks focusing on different lists and have them work in tandem. That way, everybody's working in concert to try to get things back up and running as quickly as possible.

Types of Plans
When we're talking about types of plans, there are four categories that we should be aware of. There's incident management, there's business continuity, there's disaster recovery, and then business resumption, business resumption may or could be interchangeable with business continuity, but understand, generally speaking, these are the four categories that your planning will fall into. Plans could be separate and they could be distinct. They don't necessarily have to be one large document, however they

certainly could be. It depends upon the size of your company or your organization, how cohesive the planning is, is it tower by tower or do you have a blanket organizational-wide policy. It just depends upon the individual corporation or the individual company.

Chapter 10 Disaster Recovery & Business Continuity

Disaster recovery plans are similar in scope to business continuity, but it's focused more on information technology. Tasks, action lists, order of recovery. Some of the same things we talked about before, emergency contact information for key personnel, interested parties. Also documentation and references to incident management or command center location because, as we know, information technology, or IT, doesn't necessarily, and quite often does not, sit where corporate sits. It may be in a remote data center, it may be some other location. The things that may be readily apparent to the business, like incident management or command center location, may not necessarily be readily apparent to IT folks. It has to be documented, and we have a standardized way of going through these things. Also, activities associated with people, process, and technology. But again, remember, this is for IT-related activities, not necessarily the initial incident management or initial business recovery efforts

Business Continuity Plan
Business continuity plans deal with the resumption and recovery of business operations once the initial disruption is contained. The incident management plan will deal with the immediate. And then once the bleeding is stemmed, we can move on to business continuity efforts, recovery efforts. How to begin recovery is a key element of the plan, again all of these things will be documented, location of key personnel and key resources, disaster recovery locations or alternate work locations, staging areas. Also, needed resources, whether it be supplies, logistics, interested parties, stakeholders. Also, standardized data collection and

reporting templates, forms, portals. How will people start to do their work, do they need to go to a specific location or a portal or fill out a form if they need supplies, how do they request assistance?

Business Resumption Plan

Business resumption plans can be the same or part of the business continuity plan. It doesn't have to be, it can be a separate document, but keep in mind these things could be one and the same. It defines who owns the resumption process because, keep in mind, it may be different than the people who are responsible for incident management or disaster recovery. It may be a separate team. We may have business folks coming in and spinning and owning the business resumption process, processes for determining the replacement of staff, if necessary, perhaps even buildings, depending on how bad the incident was, infrastructure, things could be damaged, compute network storage, power, heating, cooling, HBAC, our heating, ventilation, air conditioning units, also services. It just depends upon the nature of the incident and the scope of damage.

Incident Management Plan

When it comes to an incident management plan, it's going to deal with the initial response to an incident, so that means tasks, and the actions, and the priorities that which things should be addressed. What do I need to do specifically immediately after an incident happens? How do I triage that event? Emergency contact details of key personnel and interested parties, or stakeholders, activities required as it relates to people, process, and technology. This is limited in scope to the things we need to do immediately, not necessarily long term. This is incident management. We need to contain the existing incident, and then we can move on to recovery efforts. Also contact guidelines, internal contacts, media, emergency responders, that's going to include documentation, maps, charts, maybe third-party response details, site access info, especially if we have geo-dispersed locations, and we need to understand how to get into specific locations, what's the best way to get in, get out. Then insurance contact and claim procedures, which is always high on everyone's list of favorite things to do, but dealing with insurance companies, especially if it's a major incident, is particularly helpful if you start documenting from the beginning, so you don't leave anything out or it doesn't get misconstrued.

Data Retention

When it comes to data retention, there's a number of reasons why data may need to be retained, or not be retained, there's various reasons for either side of this coin. It could be for compliance, it could be for eDiscovery, for data mining, to understand customer history, or to improve the customer experience. However, there also may be implications for keeping data too long. Some companies don't want to store data after a certain period of time, just to get rid of data that's no longer necessary, to prune their data to save on storage costs. The longer the data's retained, those costs and storage requirements, they increase, because things start to accumulate over time. Proper data governance helps with this, and when we're talking about data retention, there are a number of options, there's a number of ways to skin the cat, so to speak. Replicating offsite is one option, whether that be a remote data center or a cloud provider, so that can protect against disaster, a smoking hole incident where the entire data center goes out, cyber incidents, ransomware attacks, breaches. If we're replicating to another location, that can help guard against those types of incidents. As an example, we have a user, and she is accessing using some data, using an application. Well that data is stored in her primary location, her primary data center. There may be primary storage that that network or that system is attached to, and that's fine. She's pulling data off of that primary storage, but, we need to make sure that that's protected. Typically, that storage will be offloaded to a backup device, or backup arrays, so that is off of primary storage, it's on backups, but, it's still sitting in the primary data center. That solves for the problem of if the array were to go out, but it doesn't solve against the problem of what if the data center goes away, we have some type of disaster. We have a couple options. From there, we could backup to a cloud provider. That could be AWS, it could be Google, and it could be Azure. There are a number of options. There are a lot of other providers as well, those are the big three, and then there's hot storage, things that have a higher degree of performance, it's not going to be as good as onsite performance, but it's still there. Or if it's long-term storage, you could even push it down to a lower level of storage within that cloud provider. As an example, AWS has a service called Glacier, which is a very cheap and deep storage, but it's not very responsive, but, it's there for long-term retention. Alternatively, we could replicate to a remote data center. It's something that we own, and in doing so, we maintain that geographic dispersal. If something were to go wrong, a power outage or some type of disaster at our primary data center, we have that data replicated offsite somewhere. A third option might be to have those backups stored on tape, and have those tapes physically transported to a storage facility. The more modern ways, however, will be to replicate either to a cloud or a remote data center.

Putting It All Together

Proper procedures, documentation, and of course, practice, - all of these things together heightens the degree of success when responding to incidents. Because unfortunately, it's not a matter of if something happens, it's more likely a matter of when. It just becomes more and more frequently, unfortunately, more or less as the cost of doing business almost. There are a number of teams that would be involved when dealing with an incident. We have executive management. We have business leadership and the various lines of business. There will be leadership from various areas, not just one group. Typically, it's going to be a number of groups from different types of businesses or lines of business, depending upon the nature of the breach, what applications and services it affects. Then we have IT operations and infrastructure, they're the folks that will be responsible for getting all these things back up and running, and then we have security operations, who will be heavily involved in analyzing and making sure that these things are covered going forward. We have engineering, which may need to change the way that things are done, depending upon, The nature of the breach, the application, maybe there's a hole or something that needs to be patched; and then DevOps, potentially, depending upon the nature of the breach. Do you have to change something in your CI/CD pipeline? All of those types of things. Each of these groups, as you may imagine, have sub components. If we dig into security operations as an example, here we have our CISO sitting at the head of the organizational chart, but there's a number of groups under them: risk management, identity management, security operators, security architecture; and each of those have separate subgroups. Your organization may not necessarily be this large or it may be bigger, it just depends, but there are detection, prevention, incident handling, and even within incident handling, we have forensics and incident management, and incident response teams. Again, if it's a large organization, you may have all of these or more, if it's a very small group, you may have one person wearing all of these hats, it just depends. Digging in just a bit further, we can see we have, under detection we might have security event triage, and security analysts, and then hunt operations and intelligence, threat intelligence analysis, and then we might have security administrators and security engineering. I'm just trying to give you an idea that there's a number of people that may be involved when handling a breach. No need to necessarily understand each of these down to the nth degree, just understand that it's not necessarily just a one person operation unless you're a very, very small company. There's a lot of coordination that takes place when an incident occurs.

Example Process
Let's say unfortunately the inevitable has happened, and a Coffee shop has a breach. So once that happens, a number of things need to take place. Initially we'll have the alert, and that could be from an automated alert from one of our seen systems or some type of monitoring system. We have IOCs, or indicators of compromise, that are observed. It could be an outage that's reported, it could be customer-reported degradation of apps or services, so on. There's some reason why we're alerted to that breach. From there, we're going to have to jump into action and analyze what's taking place. That consists of a number of things, again identifying the issue, understanding what is taking place, take corrective actions as quickly as possible, that's feasible, without going overboard. We need to engage proper teams very quickly to make sure they're aware, they're spinning themselves up,

and we begin communications. From there, the communications take place, and that goes amongst a number of groups. It goes through management, it goes through business partners, peer groups, potentially customers, the media, it could even be law enforcement, and of course vendors. Depending upon the nature of the breach, we may need to bring vendors in very quickly to help us recover or to harden the systems, potentially even bring in additional equipment depending on how big and how widespread that breach is. All of these things are happening in parallel, so this is not necessarily a serial timeline, it's not one after the other, a number of these things will start to spin up in parallel, and you'll have to have someone that sits at the head of that in your command center and coordinates all of these efforts? We've talked about all of these things before, but just understand that there are a number of things that take place at the same time when we're dealing with these types of breaches. So from there, we have to recover and then harden those systems, so that may be rebuilding those systems, restoring from backup, in some form or fashion, we need to recover those systems, validate that those systems are in fact functional, and again that's going to be spinning up a bridge, having all the different app teams involved, having those guys and girls all on the phone saying yes, we're back up online, or yes, I can perform action A, B, and C, so the application is recovered. And then from there, we would take preventative corrections, and then monitor to make sure that things are working, that the corrections work. We want to make sure we don't just bring the system back and leave it in exact same state it was before. We need to make sure that we take preventive action, harden that system, if possible, to make sure if that same type of attack were to occur again, we're protected against that attack. And then we need to make sure that we document and do an AIR, or after incident review, or a peer incident review, or whatever it may be called in your specific organization, but you should do that after the fact, you can review what you've done, lessons learned? Lessons learned, the steps that were taken, also communicate with executives, so they have a level of comfort around the incident, understanding that we have a handle on things, and then and after-incident review, so that we can understand across all the different teams that are involved, what happened, how we can respond better, or perhaps quicker the next time. And then in reality, we want to make sure that we audit the environment. Audit for similar gaps in other systems, and ensure that those corrective actions or corrective measures that we took on that one system or that one application are applied consistently throughout the environment? We want to make sure that we're patching all of our systems that are similar, maybe the same operating system, or the same code level, depending upon what the actual gap was, where the vulnerability was, we need to make sure that we're patching against that across the environment. And then lastly, develop new MOPs, or methods of procedures, so that way we have a documented way of moving forward, ensuring that those best practices are applied when new systems are built and brought into the environment. In this chapter, we talked about a number of things including incident response plans and process, we talked about various testing exercises, walk throughs, tabletops, simulations. We talked about the various attack frameworks, the MITRE framework, Diamond Model. We talked about stakeholder management and also communication plans, disaster recovery, and business continuity plans, along with continuity of operation planning, and then various incident response teams, retention policies, data of retention, and then responding to an incident, putting it all together and understanding all of the various teams that need to be spun up, how things happen in parallel, not necessarily a serial process, and how we get things back up online, communicate properly to all the teams involved, and restore our systems, patching and documenting, making sure that doesn't happen again in the future.

Chapter 11 How to Implement Data Sources to Support an Investigation

In this chapter, we'll be covering Understanding Appropriate Data Sources to Support an Incident. We'll be talking about vulnerability scans and the output, what we do with those outputs. We'll talk about SIEM and SIEM dashboards. We'll talk about log files and how they can support an investigation or data analysis, trying to figure out what happened, where, when, why and how. We'll talk about syslog, rsyslog, and syslog-ng or next generation. We'll talk about the differences there. We'll also talk about something called journal control or journalctl, nxlog. We'll talk about retention for basic things like email, audit logs. Then we'll talk about bandwidth monitors, metadata, and how it changes for different types of files. We'll talk about NetFlow and sFlow, the differences between the two, and then a little bit about protocol analyzers and outputs. When we're talking about accessing all of these different types of data, interpreting assessment results, understanding what's going on, the amount of data that's being created is increasing exponentially, so the amount of sensors, telemetry data. Security tools, analyzers, packet sniffers, all of these things, they generate a massive amount of data. Part of the job is to filter through all of that data and to find out what's relevant, to filter through the noise. Relevance is different for each environment, so it's not going to be a one size fits all. Something that may be normal in one environment could be abnormal in another and vice versa. It's important to understand what is normal for your specific environment. Also, understand what is the goal of the tool or what is the goal of the assessment? What are we looking to gather when we're sifting through all of this data. Then automate where possible. Automation is going to be key here because we want to be able to trigger an alert when a real issue occurs and then filter through all the noise. Filtering through the noise boils down to establishing a security baseline. That's going to help us understand what's normal. This will apply to no matter what the environment is, whether we're doing packet sniffers or a SIEM dashboard or any type of telemetry data. Once we understand what is normal, then we can very quickly or at least more quickly understand what's abnormal. This enables an analyst to quickly see anomalies and deviations from normal. If you understand what's normal, if you see a spike that's not normal, we see a spike in the middle of the night or a spike on a specific port or a spike on a specific type of application that's not normally doing that, then that can alert us to some type of abnormal activity, potentially an indicator of compromise. There are tools that can automate data collection and simplify that task, and we'll talk about a few of those in just a moment. But, we want to alert when a threshold is reached X amount of times within a certain interval. Rather than every single time a threshold is breached, that's going to create a ton of noise because things can spike constantly. If it's an intermittent spike or a one-off, we don't necessarily want to be notified of that. If we have something down the road that becomes a problem, we can go back historically and look for the one-offs and maybe see a trend over time. But every single time something hits a threshold, we don't want to necessarily be alerted by that. By creating these baselines and then setting thresholds or triggers, if X amount of triggers within a certain time interval, that will help us to filter through the noise. One of those tools that can help us is something referred to as a vulnerability scanner, and a vulnerability scanner can determine where there are gaps in defenses. There are a lot of them out there. They all have similar functionality, but some of the more well-known ones are OpenVAS or GVM, Nessus, Retina, Nmap, SAINT. There are a number of other ones as well. I'm not necessarily recommending or endorsing one over the other. Just understand that generally speaking, vulnerability scanners give us a lot of information about our environment. They allow us to scan the environment for vulnerabilities, for gaps in our defenses, if you will. As an example, GVM is a vulnerability scanner that does a number of different things. It gives us a number of vulnerabilities, but it allows us to scan our environment, scan all the different devices within our environment, and then show what gaps exist, if any, on those different pieces of equipment, those different nodes in our environment, whether it's a Linux server, Windows server, some type of endpoint. So from there, once the vulnerability is discovered, we can drill down, see all about that vulnerability, see what the potential severity is, and then potential remediations. It allows us to stack rank what's in the environment and then remediate appropriately.

SIEM

SIEM is the security information and event management system. What this does is do a bit of data aggregation and correlation, doing automated alerting and triggers, time synchronization, event deduplication, and then logs that are in a WORM format or write once, read many. A SIEM platform, is a security tool that allows us to aggregate data from a number of different sources, and it correlates that data to make it easy to identify when things happen. We can look at things from a number of different parameters, whether it be CPU utilization, network utilization. Let's take a look at this in a little more detail. Here we have one called Metricbeat from Elastic, and it's being displayed in Kibana.

This is a dashboard, and it shows us a number of different things. Memory usage, number of processes, disk usage metrics, and this is for a specific host. But then it also show us the I/O on that specific host, the network traffic, and this can be used to look at individual hosts on a network. It can be used to look at switches and routers, to look at network flow. It gives us a lot of insight into the network, and then we can drill down, and you can see we're looking at the same time slices across all of these different metrics. It allows us to correlate that data and make sure we're understanding what's happening from a global perspective. And if we drill down a bit, we see that we have CPU usage, also system load.

We can see a spike here around 15:15 or 3:15 in the afternoon, and we can see there's a spike. If we click on that, highlight that area and drill down, we can look in the logs for that specific event and see in more detail what's happening. We can search for specific parameters, we can look at anomalies in the network, or we can browse through to see if anything stands out. If we look at this in more detail, we have a graphical representation of a SIEM correlation dashboard. We have application, network, storage, firewall, and compute, and we have a time scale. We can see that is traffic. There's activity on various metrics within this correlated dashboard. Well let's say, for instance, we see this, and then all of a sudden the next day or, let's say, the time slices that we see here represented are the next 12 hours as an example. But we see this generic data. Nothing necessarily stands out. For this example, this could be considered a baseline, and nothing stands out. However, if we then see a spike pop up, and we see a lot of increased traffic, a lot of increased activity, disk I/O, firewall utilization, we can then drill down on each of those specific metrics and see what, in fact, is happening. These could be indicators of compromise. We could see that they could potentially be doing some type of data exfiltration or some type of Smurf attack or amplification attack, some type of breach into the network or least trying to do some type of denial-of-service or distributed denial-of-service attack. These types of things, this correlation engine, allows us to correlate across a number of different metrics and see the trending and then see the aggregate total because if we're looking at just one of these metrics, it may or may not stand out as an anomaly. But if we're looking at it across the board, and we can see well normally it looks like this. But today, for some reason or a couple hours later, it should look like this, but it's jumped up. Those things stand out immediately as red flags. It allows us to go and drill in deeper to see what's going on.

Log Files

Next we have log files, and log files can be a rich source of information. Or they could be ridiculously boring and put you to sleep. It just depends upon how you use the log files, what types of tools you have to parse through them, what automation you may have in place. But, it is a very rich source of information and can be used for many purposes, including audits for discovering IOCs or indicators of compromise. It can be used for forensic investigations, general alerting. There's a number of different types of log files, all of which have various nuances, but we have log files for network traffic, for system utilization, application logs, security logs, web, DNS, authentication logs, log ons, log offs, dump files. We could have VoIP and call manager logs, session initiation protocol or SIP traffic logs. All of these things can prove very valuable when we need to investigate some type of breach or some type of incident. I will say that when you do log, you have to be very careful not to log too much because if you generate just too much noise, then it becomes pretty much just that, noise. By the same token, if you log too little or if you audit too little, then you have a false sense of security thinking that you're capturing the information that you need. But then when something happens, you either don't have that information readily available, or you don't have it in which case, then you start to get calls from VPs and executive management and say, I need that information and you're like oops, well, I don't have it. That, as you could imagine, is a lonely place to be and not somewhere that we want to be. We want to make sure that we proactively adjust and identify what we need to log, that we store it property, that we audit and retain that information long enough so that it retains its value, but not indefinitely so that it becomes, again, just noise or things that we're never going to look at and it just takes up space, which, everything reverts back to things cost money. Storage costs money. Getting back to the previous example, we may see a spike in traffic. We might see a spike of activity, and it's correlated across our network. Not necessarily just on a specific host. It could also be on the network, the firewall. Well, using our logs and analysis tools, we can dig in, pull in event IDs, log files that are stored on the server, in this case a DNS server, and we can see there are a number of hits for two different ports.

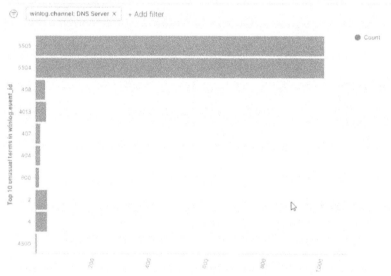

That is an anomaly that's not necessarily normal for that environment. That would be potentially an indicator of compromise and would require further investigation. In this case, it's quite possible that someone's trying to do some type of data exfiltration through our DNS channels or some other type of malicious activity. All of these tools allow us to continually drill in. If we double-click down even further, we can see that in this specific instance, the DNS server encountered a domain name packet exceeding the maximum length in the packet. And it shows the event ID, it shows the IP address. All of these things can be used to identify indicators of compromise. It's not normal, it's not something that we see every day, and it's an anomaly. In this case, someone is trying to breach the network, and it would require again further examination. In the real world when something like this happens, depending upon the size of your organization, you may or may not be doing this yourself. You may be a junior analyst, and you would pass this on further up the chain for further investigation. You might have a network security team. You might have the server admins themselves, the DNS administrators. They may jump in and start trying to identify where that traffic is coming from. You'll have server admins, you might have virtualization admins, the network folks, firewall folks, and, of course, security personnel. You might spin up a war room and have everyone sit around the table and everyone looking at the same thing at the same time. They may all be together trying to understand what in fact is happening. Log files become critical in that case. Everyone can look at the data historically, and you can look back a day, a week, a month, depending upon how long you retain that data, and understand what is normal and what's not normal. Is this something that happens once a week? Is this something that happens once a month? Or is this the first time it's ever happened? By getting a bit of a historical view of events, it helps to identify how serious something may or may not be. It could be just someone probing, just seeing if they can get what they can get, and just doing some general reconnaissance. Or, it could be a targeted attack, which would warrant much more of a response.

Log Management, Syslog, Rsyslog, and Syslog-ng

When it comes to log management, log management can help reduce complexity, it can help reduce cost', and increase speed on ingestion for downstream consumers. What do I mean by that? Well, data quality, normalizing, parsing, and filtering out the noise, the uninteresting traffic, that's a big time saver. It gives us information that is usable, actionable. It also helps with cost reduction. We can optimize our SIEM, we can reduce storage, and also ingestion costs because depending upon the platform that we choose, it can be costly to just bring in data from various sources. If we can parse that further upstream, get rid of the things that aren't necessarily interesting, then we're only paying for what we're consuming or ingesting. And then also security, we can encrypt data both in motion and also at rest. As an example, here we have a number of things that are producing log files, firewalls, applications, it can be compute network logs, storage logs. All of those things can then be put into a syslog server, a relay or a server, in this case syslog-ng, and then forward it on to whatever applications we want to use or have be the consumer of those specific log feeds, and it could be Splunk, it could be ELK, Kafka, it could be Hadoop, databases, so on, and so on. There are a number of things we can feed those different log files to. syslog-ng, as an example, allows us to do that. If we wanted to install syslog-ng into our system, as an example, here we have a Kali Linux session open, and from a terminal, I can just do a sudo apt-get install, and then choose syslog-ng, and a from there it's going to ask me do I want to do this, and of course the answer is yes. Then it's going to pull down the files, takes a few moments, it'll read through the database, then it'll install the various sub files, and within a matter of, say, a minute or so, we're done.

When it comes to syslog,syslog-ng, and also something called rsyslog, a few things that I just want to make sure that you're aware of. Syslog was developed in 1980, so it's been quite a while, but it's a tried and true mechanism. It was developed initially as part of the send mail implementation for collecting system logs. It was UDP only, User Datagram Protocol, which is a connectionless delivery system, so there's no guaranteed delivery, and it operated on port 514. Years later in 1998, syslog-ng comes out. That extended the functionality of syslog by adding TCP, or Transmission Control Protocol, which is a connection-oriented delivery mechanism, content-based filtering, database logging features, and also TLS encryption. Then roughly about 6 years later, as a competitor to syslog-ng, rsyslog came out, and that extended syslog functionality even further by adding buffered operation support. If connectivity was lost, it could still buffer on the client until connectivity was re-established. That buffered operation support and then also RELP, or RELP, protocol, which is Reliable Event Logging Protocol, so that made for a much more robust delivery system. It was guaranteed, or at least we knew when messages weren't delivered, so it could retry again. These types of things are used by like the financial industry, things that cannot tolerate dropped messages. Just understand that there are a few different variations of syslogging, whether it's syslog, syslog-ng, or rsyslog, all have the same basic features; however, with each iteration, new features are added.

Journalctl

Next, let's talk about a tool called journalctl, and what journalctl is is a Linux command to view systemd, kernel, and also journal logs, and allows us to parse through those things, configure the output. We can search through all entries, we can look for entries by keyword, by type, by date, and then also output to a file, or also to a JSON format. It gives us a lot of options when parsing through system logs. To use the command, we can open up a terminal, and type sudo journalctl, and we'll want to use sudo in this case, so that we get all the messages, including kernel messages. And if we didn't do sudo, we wouldn't get all of the messages displayed to us.

So from there, sudo journalctl, and from there, we can parse through all of the entries in the log, and there a number of options that we can use to show just kernel messages, just messages since last boot, by a certain date or time, so on and so on. Let's take a look at this in action and get a little more detail here. So from a terminal, again, I will run journalctl, and that gives me all of the current information. If you do sudo journalctl, and then as new entries are added, that log file gets updated in real time. I'll open up another window, and just do a quick check on my GVM setup that we installed previously. As that happens, you'll notice, as I'm running commands, and I'll pull it off-screen for just a moment, but as I run commands, you'll see the log files get updated. Since I'm following the journal, anytime anything happens, any entries get put in, it gets updated in real time. I can also turn around and say journalctl -n, and give it a number for 10, Just 10 entries, and then put in the output and make it json-pretty. It formats that output, rather than the line-by-line that we just saw, and it formats it, quote/unquote pretty, giving it the proper coding, the proper indentation. just scratching the surface of what journalctl can do, but it gives us a lot of flexibility in parsing our logs, searching for specific events, formatting the output.

```
^C
kali@kali:~$ sudo journalctl -n 10 -o json-pretty
```

And, as usual within Linux, if there's something that you're not sure of, or you need to know a command, we can always do what pretty much every guy doesn't want to do, and that is read the manual. But, journalctl, journal c-t-l, --help, will give us all the commands that are available.

```
kali@kali: ~                                                    _ □ ×
File  Actions  Edit  View  Help
journalctl [OPTIONS ... ] [MATCHES ... ]

Query the journal.

Options:
      --system              Show the system journal
      --user                Show the user journal for the current user
  -M  --machine=CONTAINER   Operate on local container
  -S  --since=DATE          Show entries not older than the specified date
  -U  --until=DATE          Show entries not newer than the specified date
  -c  --cursor=CURSOR       Show entries starting at the specified cursor
      --after-cursor=CURSOR Show entries after the specified cursor
      --show-cursor         Print the cursor after all the entries
      --cursor-file=FILE    Show entries after cursor in FILE and update FILE
  -b  --boot[=ID]           Show current boot or the specified boot
      --list-boots          Show terse information about recorded boots
  -k  --dmesg               Show kernel message log from the current boot
  -u  --unit=UNIT           Show logs from the specified unit
      --user-unit=UNIT      Show logs from the specified user unit
  -t  --identifier=STRING   Show entries with the specified syslog identifier
  -p  --priority=RANGE      Show entries with the specified priority
      --facility=FACILITY ... Show entries with the specified facilities
  -g  --grep=PATTERN        Show entries with MESSAGE matching PATTERN
      --case-sensitive[=BOOL] Force case sensitive or insensitive matching
  -e  --pager-end           Immediately jump to the end in the pager
  -f  --follow              Follow the journal
  -n  --lines[=INTEGER]     Number of journal entries to show
      --no-tail             Show all lines, even in follow mode
  -r  --reverse             Show the newest entries first
  -o  --output=STRING       Change journal output mode (short, short-precise,
lines 1-30
```

You can see, we can do things like -b. That will give us the current boot or specified boots. We could put a --boot -1 to show us just the kernel messages from the last boot. We can

320

look at things like priority range, or we can grep for a specific pattern. That way we can show messages that only match a specific thing that we may be looking for. We also, -f, or follow, and that will follow the journal. It will show the most recent entries, and then anything new that gets added as we go. we just scroll down, we can keep seeing there are many, many options here available to us. We can do merge, we can output to a file, we can show the disk usage, the total disk usage for all of the journal files. We can vacuum the journal, reduce the size and delete older entries. We can flush the journal from any point in time, and so on. I encourage you to go against your intuition and read the manual on these things, because a lot of times, there's some useful information in here that you wouldn't necessarily know unless you dig in under the covers just a bit. Poke through this when you have an opportunity, and familiarize yourself with the options available.

NXLOG

One other log and aggregation platform that I want you to be familiar with is something called NXLog. This is a multi-OS log aggregation and collection platform. It can collect and aggregate from Windows, from Linux, Mac, even Solaris. And we can also aggregate, filter, and enrich that data and then integrate with other SIEM software. I'm not going to dig into too, too much there, but just be aware that it is a multi-platform collection and aggregation tool and also integrates with SIEM software. It pulls all those different files together, all those log files from different operating systems, collects it, aggregate that data, and then passes it on to SIEM software or some other platform for further usage and consumption.

Chapter 12 Retention Auditing, Compliance & Metadata

We have all of this auditing information, What do we do with it? Retention policies should be defined and may be mandated by certain compliance regulations. When it comes to auditing, we need to determine what is most valuable when auditing that information. If we audit too much, if we collect too much, then it becomes noise, and it becomes limited in value because we just have so much stuff, it's too hard to sift through. That's where taking some time to clearly define what we want to audit and why and then how long are we going to retain that data for. That way we balance between the amount of data that we collect and the amount of time that we're collecting it for. It probably doesn't do us much good to go back 8 years, 10 years for something for a log on or log off. But yet, 2 or 3 days is probably too short. Maybe 2 weeks, a month, a month and a half? It just depends upon your environment. It depends upon what you're auditing for. But you definitely want to make sure that you clearly define it, and it's going to be a group effort here. You might have security folks, you might have administrators collectively understanding what it is we're logging for and how long we're going to keep it. Then we talk about compliance. There are certain things, certain regulatory bodies or local laws that may require data be retained for a certain period of time. That will vary by location. There is no or wrong answer across the board. Make sure you check with your local municipality, local, state, federal, or whatever country may be residing in, make sure that those things are in compliance and that you're retaining that information for the required period of time if applicable. Then for investigations, good data is critical to investigations on incidents, breaches. It could be criminal activity, it just could be malicious activity, or it just could be an anomaly that you need to investigate. Logs, audit data, file metadata, all of these things are very critical when we're trying to determine what happened, who did what, where, when, why, and how. Preservation of evidence is critical. Chain of custody is critical. Not Much just for an internal investigation, but chain of custody becomes crucial if those things ever need to go to court for prosecution.

Bandwidth Monitors

What a bandwidth monitor does, as the name implies, it's going to monitor network traffic and overall bandwidth. It can identify anomalies if we have some type of spike on the network or something that's not normal. We can identify IOCs or indicators of compromise potentially. It doesn't necessarily mean that all IOCs will come through this type of monitoring tool, but it certainly can be a help in that regard. Such things as data exfiltration, we can see things that aren't necessarily normal and identify those trends and those one-offs or the spikes. Then unusual traffic in general, the type, the source, the destination, or perhaps the application. All of these different things can appear once we understand what's normal. If we have a baseline and we establish what is normal, then it's very easy or at least I should say easier for us to identify what is not normal. We can see just a normal amount of traffic, whether it be network, storage, compute. All of a sudden, we see a spike, and then we can go hey, wait a minute. What's going on here? And it gives us an opportunity to then drill down and look in deeper to see what's going on. That's where log files come into play. That's where our aggregation and collection things come into play, our SIEM software. All of these things work in tandem to help us identify IOCs. We'll talk about NetFlow and sFlow here in just a moment, which can also function as bandwidth monitors and help us understand the flows between the different nodes and endpoints on our network.

Metadata

Metadata is data about data. It's data that provides information about other data. That means different things in different context. For email, as an example, an email header can show things like the sender info, the date and time, the IP addresses that it came from or the hops that it went through as it gets from point A to point B, the intermediary hosts. All of this metadata can become important when we're trying to understand where things are coming from. If we're getting a lot of spam, perhaps malicious activity, malware, that metadata around that email can become very, very valuable for investigations. How about for mobile devices? Details about phone calls or messages, perhaps location or GPS information, all of these things can divulge information about a caller, even medical information, associations. When it comes to the web, we can use metadata to optimize for web sites, but it can also be used in a not-so-nice way. It can be used to identify visitors. We can fingerprint their browsers, look at certain things within the screen resolution and the fonts that are installed. All of the different graphical back-end pieces that don't necessarily or aren't necessarily visible to the end user can be used to fingerprint that browser and identify that person. If they visit again using that browser, even if it's from a different IP address, you could identify that person based upon those web browser metadata characteristics. Metadata can be good in a lot of instances. It can be not so good like for advertisers, and spammers. Then it can also be used maliciously to identify things or give away information that we don't necessarily want to become public knowledge or have visible to other users. Then we're talking about file metadata. So file attributes can identify, the owner of that file or the author, the date and time it was created or modified, the word count, even GPS coordinates if it's a photograph and, the type of device used, the type of camera, the f-stop, the aperture, all of these things can be pulled from the metadata on specific types of files. But this EXIF information, the GPS coordinates, it's important to understand that as you upload pictures to social media or send from one person to another, if you don't remove that information, it's quite possible that that actual metadata information gets passed along with that file as well. So keep those things in mind and understand that if you don't want this information to become public knowledge or at least associated with that specific file, then remove those properties whenever possible.

Netflow, sFlow, and IPFIX

NetFlow is a way of monitoring our network, and it takes it a step further, than just looking at typical network monitoring, as it will group the communication between two hosts on a network into flows? It's not just simple packet capturing. It's grouping that into flows to give you a more holistic view of traffic on your network. We have a few things in place here. We have a router, which is typically where you're going to have NetFlow enabled. That's going to be a NetFlow exporter, and that's going to be connecting to various networks, whether it be the internet, remote sites, a LAN, a WAN. Then we're going to be connecting to a NetFlow connector, and we'll have an administrator console where you can see a graphical representation, an application that will take the NetFlow data that's exported from the NetFlow exporter and display it graphically. We also have flow storage that's connected to the NetFlow connector. So, we have NetFlow packets of flow from the router to the collector, and then we also have the administrator that will query the collector. One's feeding data into the collector, one's accessing or querying data from the collector. The collector and the storage itself are collectively known as the NetFlow cache. As we enable NetFlow on the various devices in our network, one thing just to keep in mind is that each device should have its own separate port number. We can have multiple devices in the network reporting into or sending data to a NetFlow collector. Just make sure that each one has its own port number so that the NetFlow collector can differentiate between. Otherwise, the collector won't know what's what, and it would just group everything together and give you bad data or a bad view of what's happening on the network. Some data that is collected by a NetFlow collector would be the source and destination IP address, the IP protocol field value, source and destination port numbers, also counters, whether it be packets or bytes, timestamps, the start time and end time, and then also where observed, the interface and the direction, whether it's ingress or egress and whether it's unidirectional or bidirectional. And just for your own knowledge, there's two main flavors of NetFlow. We have version 5 and version 9, with version 9 being the newer one. And the other implementations that we'll talk about, sFlow and IPFIX, are based off of NetFlow version 9 as well. There's a similar implementation called sFlow, and we'll talk about some of the differences here. With NetFlow, its Cisco proprietary, meaning it only works or functions on Cisco gear, and more granular collection of IP traffic to create flows. It does it packet by packet. We can get very granular. It only collects IP traffic, however, and we'll notice the differentiation here in just a moment. It's a more detailed collection, but it's also more CPU and resource intensive. Then, if we want to display that data graphically, we'll need a third-party collector such as SolarWinds, PRTG. And it's comprised of two components, the exporter and then the cache or the analyzer. As far as sFlow is concerned, that was introduced by HP in 1991, years after NetFlow came out. It samples packets and counters to create flows similarly to what NetFlow does. But the distinction here being that it's samples, so it doesn't do it packet by packet by packet. By sampling, we're getting more of a trend, but it's also less resource intensive. It potentially scales better. It also can collect traffic from OSI layers 2 through 7. It's not just IP traffic. It doesn't provide as detailed packet-level information as

NetFlow, but it samples the data, and that's configurable, how often it samples, so that it has the ability to scale. All devices need to be sFlow compatible, so that's something to keep in mind. Then also, two components, an agent and a collector. There are some similarities between the two. Then we've evolved into a new standard called IPFIX, and that stands for Internet Protocol Flow Information Export. That is a collector export protocol, and it's based on NetFlow version 9. All of the features that you would see in NetFlow, however, it's not Cisco proprietary. It's nonproprietary. It also does packet count, byte count, type of service, flow direction, and routing domain. A lot of good information there. That allows you to monitor your network, see what types of services are running, what are the top sites, the top domains, who's the top talkers? It allows you to go in and get very granular with the network and understand what's going on. If you have lags or if you have applications that are performing poorly, these are, of course, good reasons to use NetFlow or IPFIX. It can be used for network monitoring, for measurement. It can be used for threat detection, and then also, some service providers will use it for accounting and billing purposes as well. All three are great tools. They need to be implemented on the devices in the network, and then all the devices that you're monitoring need to be compatible. You configure the exporters of the agents to report to a collector, and then you can go with an analyzer or a dashboard, and then get all the information that we talked about before about how your network is functioning.

Detecting an Amplification Attack (ICMP echo)
We've talked about Smurf attacks, and we've talked about amplification attacks. What I wanted to talk about real briefly here is how we could use NetFlow or sFlow to help thwart a Smurf attack, or an amplification attack. If you recall, with a Smurf attack, otherwise known as an amplification attack, a hacker would send a directed broadcast with the victim's IP

spoofed to a network segment, to the broadcast IP address on a network segment so that everybody on that network would get that request, but instead of replying back to the attacker they would reply back to the victim and flood that person's machine or that server or whatever the intended victim is. So here we have all of the different computers attached to the network. Once that spoofed ICMP echo is sent they all reply back to the victim's computer again, a victim's PC, desktop, laptop, or a server, depending upon what the target is, that can potentially overrun the host system, the amplification attack, if you have enough hosts on that network. Because, again, it could be dozens, it could be hundreds, or it could be thousands of computers all replying back to that specific victim. Using NetFlow or sFlow, or another network monitoring solution for that matter, but since we're talking about NetFlow and sFlow it makes sense to cover that here. What we could do is use NetFlow or, again, sFlow to identify ICMP echo requests or these pings, these Smurf attacks or these amplification attacks to detect that network attack. We could identify the victim using traffic monitoring to identify top destinations for ICMP echo responses. We could identify that within the tool. From there we could use NetFlow or sFlow to filter for the top subnets sourcing ICMP echo responses. We could then identify the port used for ICMP echo response to enter the site or to enter our network by using, again, NetFlow or sFlow to show top router and switch ports, receiving ICMP echo requests and packets destined for that specific victim, and then we can create an ACL filter on the router or the switch port to block ICMP traffic from the source subnet. Just a quick example of how we might use this tool. Automate to some degree, create filters and triggers so if these things happen we can be alerted, and either automate that process and automate that response or at least become aware of it, and then manually investigate and intervene as necessary.

Protocol Analyzer Output

Let's now talk about protocol analyzers and a little bit about what they do. A protocol analyzer is a packet inspection tool, and there are ones out there like Wireshark, which is probably one of most popular ones. It's an open source packet analyzation or packet analyzer tool. Retina, Nessus, Nmap can also be used to map protocols and see what protocols are available, what ports are open. And it can be used to troubleshoot network issues. It could be used to detect or inspect indicators of compromise and even decrypt SSL transmission if you import the certificates into Wireshark and use those to decrypt the traffic that you're capturing. Just to give you an idea though of what it can and can't do, here are some common use cases, and the one that I will draw your attention to is where it says spy on other network users. You can collect sensitive information, such as login details, users cookies depending upon the content and the encryption methods that they may use. A lot of it is done for legitimate purposes. But protocol analyzers can also be used to sniff traffic and gather information on other users. It can be used for good and used for bad. Not intending to make you a Wireshark professional at this point, but I just want to introduce you to the tool. Understand that protocol analyzers can give you a lot of deep, deep information about communication on your network. You can go in and examine packets. You can look at the actual flow of information. You can follow it back and forth. And it gives you a great amount of detail from a security professional's perspective, but also for network analyzation. Network professionals look at it for troubleshooting applications, for troubleshooting network performance, seeing where things might get held up. Maybe packets are dropped quite a bit. I would definitely recommend digging in when you have an opportunity and familiarizing yourself with Wireshark and the other protocol analyzer tools that are available. In this chapter, we covered vulnerability scan output. We talked about

SIEM dashboards along with log files, such as syslog, rsyslog, and syslog-ng, how we can use those things to centralize our logging capabilities and then feed those in to other systems. We talked about journal control and some of the flags and some of the commands that can make that a useful tool for us along with an NXLog and then also retention of various types of things, like email and different types of data, and then the different types of compliance or regulations that may mandate that we retain certain types of data for certain periods of time. We also talked about bandwidth monitors and then metadata for various file types and how that can certainly divulge more information than we initially knew about. Then we talked about some network monitoring or optimization tools, such as NetFlow and sFlow, and then wrapped up with a brief look at protocol analyzers and protocol analyzer output.

Chapter 13 How to Implement Mitigation Techniques to Secure an Environment

In this chapter, we'll be talking about Implementing Mitigation Techniques to Secure an Environment. We'll be talking about reconfiguring endpoint security solutions, talking about application whitelisting and blacklisting, how that can help us, along with quarantining. We'll talk about configuration changes, and that deals with firewall rules, MDM, or mobile device management, data loss prevention, or DLP. We'll talk about content filters and also revoking and updating certificates. We'll also talk about the concepts of isolation, containment, and segmentation and how those can help us secure the environment, along with secure orchestration, automation, and response, or SOAR systems, and runbooks and playbooks specifically. When it comes to application whitelisting, that's going to be a list of applications that are allowed to run on a host. All other applications are blocked from running. That makes catching everything much easier. You don't have to know every single thing that could potentially run and explicitly deny that? In a whitelist, you say I have 10 applications that my users can run, Word, Excel, maybe a chat application, web browser of course, and a few other things. That's the 5 or 10 things you can do. That's all you can access. Everything else is blocked. Conversely, you can say blacklisting of an application, you can say, you know what, you can run everything except for these 5 or 10. All other applications are allowed to run. The downside being, if you have enough privileges you can go in and simply rename an executable that was previously blacklisted. As an example, you don't want someone to run regedit so they can't modify the registry. Well, if they have command prompt access or they can -click on regedit, they can browse to it, click on it, and rename it. They can rename that application and then simply run it at that point because it's checking against that file name. Depending upon how you're set up and what types of controls you have in place, it's important to check through these things all the way through, take the mindset of an end user, look at all the ways they can get around the controls you put in place, and make sure the things you have implemented function the way you intend them to.

Quarantine

One method that we can use to make sure that applications don't run, that we don't want malicious applications, malicious scripts, or hosts that perhaps aren't patched or don't meet our specifications before they enter the network, we can do something called quarantine. A quarantine is a proactive blocking of access or the ability to run or execute applications. Hosts that don't meet certain criteria, perhaps they don't have a certain code level, firmware level, patch level, applications or processes that are flagged as suspicious or malicious, we can keep them from accessing the network. Depending upon how our infrastructure is set up, we can identify those machines when they first enter the network and then cordon them off into a DMZ, or a demilitarized zone or a screened subnet, at that point we can make sure that they get patched or updated or somehow remediated to meet our specifications, and then allow them onto the network. Another way of doing that is having applications, whether it be antimalware or antivirus, block applications before they're able to do anything. Popular antimalware applications like Malwarebytes or Windows Defender or Sophos, there's a lot of them out there, McAfee, etc. They can block suspicious activity and they can quarantine downloads, applications before they're allowed to run. Then when we're talking about whitelisting applications, we can also have an allow list. You can see here we can specify certain applications that are allowed to run so that way if the antimalware software blocks that for some reason, we can add it in into a whitelist, so that way the next time we run it, the antimalware software won't block that application. These things are potentially malicious, they're going to be malware, ransomware, cryptojacking software, they would automatically be quarantined because the antimalware software would identify this, whether it be through a signature or some type of heuristics. We can then choose to either keep them quarantined and not allow them to run, or you can check the specific ones that you want to run and it will bring it back to life, and allow you to run that application. Typically not recommended, but if you know for a fact that something is safe, you can go ahead and check it off and then allow it to run.

Firewalls
A firewall is designed to isolate one network from another. It can be hardware or it can be software based. It can be either. It can be a standalone device, or it can be an integrated device, integrated into some other equipment, in other words, routers or switches. Whether you're a small office or a home office, you may have a small Netgear, or a Linksys, or even a Cisco router that combines a lot of functionality together. It can have a firewall. It can do NAT or network address translation, and, of course, routing functionality, as well, perhaps even switching. It just depends on the size of the network, how specific you want to get. There are different devices that can perform very specific functions, or there are integrated devices that can perform a lot of different functions together. If we have a diagram of outside users outside of the firewall, and you see

the firewall denoted by a brick wall. And, incidentally, the term firewall historically came from buildings that were built very close to one another, and in order to prevent fire from jumping from one building to another when they were very close together, think like row homes, for instance, they would build brick walls in between these different buildings to prevent that fire from jumping from one to the other. That brick wall would act as a firewall, to prevent fire from jumping from one building to the other. The same concept is carried, and that's why you typically see a firewall being illustrated as a brick wall. Firewalls are typically used to block or limit outside traffic from entering a network. Whether it's corporate, medium-sized office, small office, or a home office, they all serve pretty much the same types of functions. However, firewalls can also be placed internally, inside of a network, to segment one area from another. For instance, you may have a large corporate environment that has different areas that you don't necessarily want them to communicate, or they shouldn't communicate from one to the other very easily. You can punch holes in the firewall to allow traffic, but generally speaking, these things are cordoned off from one another. For instance, if you have a PCI secure zone, like, say you have a very large enterprise that has some typical day-to-day workers, and you may have an R&D department, you may have an accounting department, a finance department. PCI secure means it contains credit card information and some type of personally identifiable information, you want to have that information cordoned off from the rest of the network. The finance folks don't necessarily talk to the R&D, or maybe the graphics department, just to prevent internal browsing of those resources. A firewall can be put into place between those segments on your internal network as well. It's important to understand, hardware versus software, firewalls can either be hardware or software based. They can be standalone devices or integrated into other devices, like routers and switches. Even if it is a hardware-based solution, it's still going to contain software. You can't just run it on hardware by itself. There has to be some software running behind the scenes. You can drop it onto a server and have that server function providing firewall functionality, or it can be a separate standalone piece of hardware. However, that hardware is still going to contain software or firmware. What are some types of firewalls? Well, we have packet filtering firewalls, and packet filtering firewalls allow or block traffic based upon a specific port, HTTP traffic, as an example, web traffic. That typically comes in over port 80. FTP, or File Transfer Protocol, that's generated on port 21. You can configure the firewall to allow web traffic but don't allow FTP traffic, or allow DNS but don't allow NetBIOS, or time lookups, or whatever the case might be. You can break it down by port by port by port and get very specific, get very granular. Doing it based just on port, there's not a lot of intelligence there. It just simply looks at the port, and then it will either allow or block the traffic at that point. Next, we have proxy firewalls. A proxy firewall's going to be dual-homed, which means is going to have two network interfaces, typically one on each network, or on separate networks. That's going to segment internal users from the outside world, and it can mask the IP address using something called NAT, or network address translation. That gives an added layer of security because the outside world won't know who's communicating. All they'll see is the address of the proxy firewall. The proxy can also cache requests to improve perceived speed. If you have multiple users, as an example, that are accessing the same website while the first person to access that website or that URL will go out and pull it down from the web or from whatever resource it's getting it from. Subsequent requests, as long as that information is still sitting in the cache on that proxy server, so the next user goes out to that same web resource. Instead of going out to the web, or out to whatever resource they're getting it from, they'll get it directly from the proxy server, from the cache. It gives the perception that things are faster and that your network is all of a sudden more responsive. The next type of firewall is something referred to as a stateful packet inspection firewall, or SPI. An SPI firewall examines the packets and keeps the packet table of every communication channel. In other words, it has more intelligence than a simple packet filtering firewall, and it does a deeper dive. It examines what's inside. SPI tracks the entire conversation, so it gives you an increased level of security because it only allows packets from known active connections. If someone's trying to spoof or jump in the middle of a connection or a conversation, an SPI firewall understands that, and they say, wait a minute, I don't know who this is from. I haven't seen this before. This is in the middle of a conversation. There's no initiation. There's no back and forth to establish that connection. This just came out of here, so I'm going to drop that. It drops the packet. It gives you that added layer of security. It's better than simple packet filtering, which only looks at the current packet. However, it's possible to attack by overloading that state table. As we go through all of these different types of routers and switches and pretty much any type of infrastructure or equipment in our network, just understand that nothing is foolproof. There's always going to be a way, and there's always going to be hackers that are trying to somehow penetrate that device, crash it, get elevated privileges. Nothing's foolproof. That's why we're all employed. When it comes to configuring our firewall, we have a couple options. We have firewalls that are built in to our operating systems like we have here in Windows 10. There are other firewalls that are standalone devices, there are ones that are software based, hardware based, like we've talked about before. They all operate in the same fashion. They all allow you to go in and either allow or deny, implicitly deny, explicitly deny, or allow, applications, ports, users, IP addresses. Let's take a look at this. On my Windows 10 Desktop here, I have Windows Firewall open, and this is the Advanced Security? If you go into Windows Firewall Advanced Security, you'll see a number of rules for Inbound Rules and also Outbound Rules, some Connection Security Rules, some Monitoring Rules, and you can monitor in real time, but for this demo, we're going to look at Inbound Rules, specifically around Remote Desktop.

We want to enable Remote Desktop for this workstation. Conversely, if it was already enabled, and we think that might be a threat, we can disable that? Block that. So for here, if I double-click on any one of these, then I have a number of options. I can go in and look at the rule, the description, I can enable that rule, and if I hit Apply, you'll see the checkbox next to that rule. Programs and Services, there are some specific things around that application, Remote Computers. I can say, allow connections from these computers, or skip this rule for these computers. You can think of it as an application whitelist or a blacklist. Same thing for protocols and ports. I can go in and say remote ports, local ports. some of these things, depending upon what it is you're configuring, you may have to change port numbers within the registry, there might be some additional configuration that's needed, but the general gist is here. The Scope, I can say Local IP addresses, allow these IP addresses, or only these specific ones.

Same thing for Remote IP addresses. I can say Any IP address, or only allow these IP addresses. We're white-listing. Same thing for Advanced. I can say, which profile does this apply to? Is it Domain, is it Public or Private?

Then as far as Local Principals and Remote Users. I can say Local, only allow connections from these users, or skip this for these users?

Again, white-listing and black-listing for Local users; same thing for remote. That's one way of doing it. I can go in manually, and you can also start from scratch and just say new rule, and create everything from scratch. If you have a specific application that might be brand new and you want to allow a certain port or a certain IP address, you can do that as well, or you can also configure some of these rules just by turning on, or turning off specific services. If I go and click on my Start button, and go up to System, then I'll see, at the bottom, Remote Desktop. This is one way to get to it. There's always more than one way to get to pretty much anything within Windows, but in this instance, I'm down at Remote Desktop.

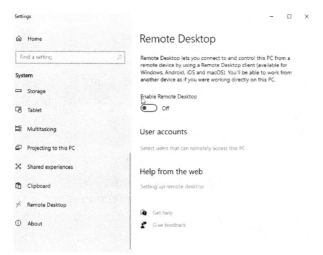

If I open that up and just turn on Enable Remote Desktop, it asks me, do you want to do this? I'm going to confirm, Yes. And if I close that, and Refresh, and I go back down to my Remote Desktop, you'll see those three rules have been enabled.

Remote Desktop - Shadow (TCP-In)	Remote Desktop	All	Yes	Allow	No
Remote Desktop - User Mode (TCP-In)	Remote Desktop	All	Yes	Allow	No
Remote Desktop - User Mode (UDP-In)	Remote Desktop	All	Yes	Allow	No

The same thing I just did before manually, I did automatically just by enabling Remote Desktop. If I go back up, go to System, down to Remote Desktop, and turn that off, I'm going to again, confirm I want to Disable Remote Desktop. Refresh, go back down again, and we see those three things are turned off. Just an example of how to configure a firewall rule, whether I want to allow or deny, based on port, based on IP address, it could be based on user, or it could be based upon application. There's more than one way to do that. You can do it manually, as we did here within the actual Management Console, or I can do it automatically, just by turning on or turning off certain features within the operating system.

Chapter 14 Mobile Device Management

Mobile devices provide users with the flexibility, and they can access work from anywhere, access documents, pretty much anywhere on the planet, and they can conduct business as easily as they could if they're sitting in the office. But with any enterprise technology, security must be at the forefront. It's crucial that these things get vetted and thought through, and designed, and architected upfront with security in mind. We can't allow functions within the business to pick a solution, drop it on our lap. And then say, Hey, make this work. It happens, but if at all possible, we need to insert ourselves into the process far enough in advance so that's not the issue. Such things as insecure access to websites. If we don't make sure we have mobile device management in place, and we don't have some way of controlling what people use their corporate assets for, then they can access insecure websites, download malware, download viruses, data leakage. We have the insecure axis to websites, we have insecure Wi-Fi connectivity. If they're sitting in a coffee shop somewhere and they're accessing our corporate network, if we don't allow them VPN access or give them some secure method to do that, well, everything they type in, everything they browse on with that mobile device could be potentially sniffed from that device, and then company secrets, company proprietary information walks out the door. The other thing is lost or stolen devices housing corporate data. If someone sits at a coffee shop, we'll use that example, they lay their phone down on the table, they get up to go to the bathroom, they go up to pay for their drink or food or something, they turn around and the phone's gone. Well, if that device is not encrypted, there's a high probability that someone can pull that information off the phone very easily. Could be company secrets could be proprietary information, or if you don't have any way of locating that phone or remotely wiping it, there's no way for us to even tell where it is or if it's being used. There are a few things that should be put in place, and we'll talk about those more in detail in just a moment. But then again, geolocation services, if that phone gets lost or stolen, we should be able to figure out where it is. If that phone gets turned back on again and checks into the network, cellular network or Wi-Fi network, it should be able to phone home, and we should able to ping that device and see where it is; and then missing upgrades and security patches. If we don't have any mobile device management in place, we can't limit what they see, we can't make sure they secure their connections. We can't prevent it from being lost or stolen and having that data gone, we can't locate it on a map, and then we can't even make sure that the users install upgrades and security patches. mobile device management is critical on a number of levels to make sure that people are doing what they're supposed to be doing; unauthorized downloads, applications, games, and so on. With iOS devices, iPhones, it's a little easier because everything that goes through the app store meets certain criteria, so there's not as many rogue applications or things like viruses and Trojans, and back doors. On Android devices, their app store is a little more open. The platform is more open, so there's a greater opportunity to have applications or games that may be compromised, that may contain malware and viruses. With mobile device management, MDM software is what enables a company to secure that users BYO device, bring your own device, without compromising their personal information. Some MDM software can partition that phone, that "corporate asset" so that there is a partition that houses company data, and then the rest of it is the user's personal device. here's a couple of companies that can do that, I'm not recommending one over the other, I'm just giving you a couple examples: Good Messaging, Airwatch, and Mobile Iron are three very popular MDM companies that provide software that can allow you to do just that. Someone can bring their own phone, they install this MDM software, creates a separate partition, or it can create a separate partition on that phone, so that way the user can access company assets, company resources, but yet the company is not going to interfere or co mingle with their personal data. They can use it pretty much as a dual device. However previously, if the device gets lost or stolen, the company can at least wipe the corporate partition. They can make sure that any company data, any company secrets, so on can be wiped. They can remotely wipe the entire phone, they can geolocate it, they can require passwords, require patches, and security fixes are upgraded or downloaded and applied in a timely fashion. It gives much more control over that phone, and you can do it in such a way that it doesn't completely hamstring the user and turn that device into only a corporate device, they can use it as a dual purpose asset.

Using MDM to Locate and Secure and Lost Device
Now that we're clear on what MDM software is, the capabilities, let's talk about using this to secure a device, securing a lost device. But we have Alice, and Alice loses her phone, which has very important personal information, as well as corporate data. If Alice is anything like me when I lose my phone, I'm not very happy about it, and I panic quite a bit. Immediately, Alice turns around and calls her good friend, Bob, who happens to be the mobile device management admin. Bob goes ahead and logs into his MDM console, brings up his tracking software, and is able to locate her phone. He's able to remotely access that phone via the

MDM console over the internet. The phone's connected. It's turned on. He's able to access it. It's not somewhere they can readily get to the phone, so they make the decision to remotely wipe the phone. They issue a wipe command. It goes back to its default factory state. There's nothing on there. On the off chance that somebody comes by, let's say, Harry the hacker, and grabs that phone, there is no corporate data, there is no personal data. And that phone can be replaced, and the data is secure.

Chapter 15 DLP, Content Filters & URL Filters

Let's just set the stage here for a moment, and all of the things that we're talking about, we need to make sure that we can implement those things in the event of an incident. Let's just say, for argument's sake, that there's an incident that's happened at the company. It's been discovered that there have been several breach attempts over the last 4 to 6 weeks targeting financial systems, web servers, and potentially customer data. Malware has been discovered on numerous systems, several which have been found trying to connect to C2 or command and control servers, to download additional malicious software. Data exfiltration attempts have also been made using several techniques over common ports, and then reconnaissance-type activity has been observed, and it's currently unclear if corporate web servers have been compromised. Keeping that type of incident in mind, which is not an uncommon scenario, lots of companies have exactly those types of things happen, if not more, and a lot of times those things go undetected for months and months. The average breach is about 18 months, give or take, before it's detected. These things can happen in the background for quite a while. Some additional mitigation techniques that we can use, one will be data loss prevention, or DLP software. DLP software can mitigate data exfiltration, which is what we mentioned in the previous scenario. That data exfiltration can be blocked or that activity can be blocked by DLP software, anything that we deem suspicious. That can be blocked from many sources, whether it be web, email, removable devices, USB drives, as well as suspicious activity such as file access or suspicious user actions. Next, we have content filtering and URL filtering. Content filters and URL filters, we've talked about those before, but they can block access. We can cut that link so that the hosts cannot reach out to those command and control servers. That malicious site that they would typically connect to can download additional software, that link is broken. Whether it's downloading additional software, connecting to botnets, participating in distributed denial-of-service-attacks, all of those types of things can be stopped if we can do content filtering and URL filtering at our own location. Then even further up the food chain, those things can be stopped at the root and the top-level domain servers. Then it's possible to stop that activity at a much larger scale. Then also within our organization, we can update or revoke certificates. Expired or compromised certificates can allow attackers to falsify their identity, they can create trusted applications, steal data. We need to make sure that we revoke certificates, we publish it to a CRL, and those things are updated constantly. We need to make sure we update our browsers, patch when appropriate, as soon as possible, and also patch all the systems very, very quickly. It's also a matter of user training to make sure that users know not to click on expired certificates. If they get a warning that says, that certificate is expired, don't assume that it's just because, well, it was valid yesterday. It's expired today. Someone in IT probably just forgot to renew the certificate, so I'll just go ahead and click on it anyway. Make sure they understand it's all part of cybersecurity training and the culture of security, but make sure they understand that those things are not to be trusted. Trust no one. If you get an expired certificate warning, then take it to heart. Don't click on it. Don't engage in that activity.

Segregation, Segmentation and Isolation
Next, let's talk about segregation, segmentation, and isolation. We have a few security or segmentation models I

want to call to your attention. First, is physical. We can physically separate or segment nodes or hosts on a network. We can also do that logically with something called VLAN, or virtual LANs, virtual local area networks. We can also do it with virtualization. It's an isolation model or a segmentation model. Then we also have air gapped, meaning there is no connectivity to the internet or to the network at large. Well, with physical or logical, we have devices that are all on the same segment, the same Ethernet segment, or the same LAN, the same local area network, and in this example, you can assume that they're all connected to the same switch. That is a physical connectivity to the network. Well, we can also logically separate those networks. We can take that same layout, but we can use something called virtual LANs, or virtual local area networks, and group them accordingly. We could have a VLAN10, we could have a VLAN20, and a VLAN30. And what that does is separate those devices out. And what it does is create separate broadcast domains, separate security domains, and it reduces the chatter. Let's look at another example. Now we have a multi-floor building. We have wiring on each floor that goes back to a home run, and it goes down between floors. We have devices on the first floor and a switch, we have devices on the second floor and a switch, and then devices on the third floor and a switch. In this example, and it's not the only way to wire, not the only way to do it, but in this example we have each floor going to a wiring closet. In that wiring closet is a switch, and then the switches are connected via home runs. Vertical up and down wiring goes between floors, so they're all physically located in different locations. Well, we can also group those together, just like we did in the previous example. They don't have to be sitting next to each other. We can group them, again, logically, VLAN10, VLAN20, and then VLAN30. In other words, if we had groups of computers that may be on different floors. Let's say we have finance people that sit on all three floors or HR, or our graphics department, whatever the case might be, we can group them within our switches. We make sure that all the switches have the same VLAN associations, and that way they're grouped logically together. These VLANs can group hosts that are in different locations, into logical groupings. That creates smaller collision domains and reduces chatter. As an example, if you have a very large cafeteria, everyone's talking, it's very hard to understand because everyone's talking. Everyone's clashing into each other. They're colliding, their conversations. If I took all of those people in that cafeteria and separated them out into, say, five different rooms or, in this example, three different rooms, well, I have one third of the amount of people in each room, so the chatter's going to be less, so the collisions are less, so it helps increase efficiency. Then also it can be used to create security boundaries to segment traffic so that one host doesn't necessarily see broadcasts and doesn't see traffic designated for hosts in another VLAN.

Virtualization

Virtualization is the method of segmenting or isolating. We can keep a host in a sandboxed and isolated environment, meaning it's separate from the host that it's sitting on. It can also allow for snapshots. We can quickly revert changes, we can use virtualization to isolate our segment. We can do all of our testing. We can test changes we can even test viruses or malware to see what it does without affecting the rest of the network and without affecting the host that it sits on. It also separates the guests from the host, the guest from the hypervisor. If we have Hyper-V or VMware, or KVM, or VirtualBox, whatever our virtualization technology is, this allows us to keep those individual guests separate from the host. Other devices can be virtualized as well. We can virtualize other infrastructure, such as routers, switches, load balancers, firewalls. But the nice part is those things can be instantiated or spun up on demand. As a load increases, we could spin up additional load balancers or, if we have applications that need specific firewalls, instead of having to go through the normal change process and buying the equipment, and racking and stacking, and all the things that are associated with physical infrastructure, we can do it virtually very quickly, spin that device up, use it while we need it, and then we can tear it down just as quickly.

Air Gaps

An air gap is a method of isolating a computer or a network from the internet or from other external networks, or other networks aside from the one you're on. It doesn't necessarily have to be just from the internet. It could be from other networks within your company. If you have a very highly secure environment that you need to make sure that there's no chance of malware or viruses being introduced, then you would set up an air-gapped network. As with anything, there is no 100% guarantee, as we've seen in the past, with things like Stuxnet and some other very highly visible and highly cited instances where malware has jumped into air-gapped environments, nothing is 100% certain. But anyway, it's used for critical infrastructure, SCADA systems, as an example, and I refer back to Stuxnet, where the SCADA systems were still compromised, highly secure classified networks. There are some advanced techniques, however, to jump air-gapped networks. That's been demonstrated. Emanations, there's a technology, and it's been completely demonstrated, where they can view the emanations coming off of a computer, whether it is the sound of the hard drive whirring, or even the heat being generated by the hard drive spinning up. If you're close enough to that device, you can pick those things up from the device and discern what's going on. You can read data from that device, pretty scary stuff, pretty advanced stuff. It's not something the average hacker I can do. But just understand that an air gap is a very good way of isolating the network, but it's not 100% foolproof. In fact, the US government and other agencies around the world have specific guidelines to create additional security. The US uses something referred to as TEMPEST, which protects that room, has to be certain thickness of walls and has to have additional coating and protections, Faraday cages, and things that just prevent emanations and monitoring from nearby locations. Emanations, FM frequencies, even some hard drives that have a small LED light on the front that shows activity of that drive. You don't see that too much anymore, but it is possible that if you have a line of sight visibility to that light going on and off as the hard drive writes, you could read, almost like Morse code, what's going on with that hard drive and read data from that device.

Securing the Environment using Isolation, Containment and Segmentation

Now getting back to our previous example, and we're talking about this incident that occurred and how we want to secure the environment, we can use these three technologies and techniques to secure the environment. We need to make sure that we air gap a network. If we have automation in place to create an air-gapped network, great. If not, and it's a manual procedure or we need to shut down ports, then, so be it. But if we're able to air gap that network, we can keep attackers out or keep compromised systems from spreading. There should be plans in place, and we'll talk about runbooks and playbooks here in just a moment, but there should be some things in place defined so that if and when an incident happens, we have the ability to isolate when possible or where possible, especially as I mentioned around our most critical environment or most critical assets. Next, containment. Virtualization can separate hosts from guests and also guests from each other. We can also use that technology to revert to an earlier snapshot. If we find that we're compromised, we can revert that machine back. We can clone systems as necessary, spin up additional systems or additional resources. We can also use that cloning technology to clone a system, take it offline, and then forensically investigate that system or do whatever investigations are necessary to help us track down what happened, where, when, why, how. Then also, segmentation. We can use VLAN technologies I talked about before to create separate subnets, separate logical subnets within our environment that help to mitigate the risk from ransomware, malware. By creating those logical separations, we can break the connections between the two. We can isolate or contain, if necessary, if we have VLANs set up or we can also very closely watch or tighten down our firewalls, tighten down our routers, and we only allow certain types of traffic through. We can allow critical things to allow business to operate, but not necessarily everything through. We can ratchet that down or turn it up as necessary. All of these technologies can help us secure an environment in the event of a breach and also proactively if we suspect something may be happening.

SOAR and Runbooks/Playbooks

Next, we have something referred to as SOAR, and that stands for Security Orchestration, Automation and Response. What this does is complement your SIEM software. They do have some overlapping capabilities, but it complements SIEM software versus replacing it. It's going to allow us to aggregate all of the tools within a SOC, or security operations center, and then provides automated playbooks. We can script a lot of these actions together, not just within our SIEM software, but it may also kick off ticket creation, case management. It also has integration with third-party products. There's numerous things that it can integrate with, and then it automates, it orchestrates and automates that response. The SIEM software will collect all this data, it'll generate alerts, it'll do all of its things. It can bring in other sources to help enrich that data, and then it can help kick off investigations, open cases, open tickets, take remediation steps. It provides a full toolbox of capabilities. Imagine if we have a SOAR platform that sits in the middle. We're going to have different things on the left here. Events are coming in, our SIEM software, our endpoint detection, endpoint detection and response software is all going to be generating information and data. All of that stuff can then be fed into the SOAR platform, which can then do other things like ticketing, IT ticketing, change control, and it can also integrate with other controls, alerting, whitelisting applications or whitelisting protocols, and then also are third-party tools. You can think of it as the glue that holds a number of different applications and capabilities together and allows them to talk and integrate with each other, orchestrating and automating that interconnectivity. Getting back to the earlier incident, we've experienced some incident, and we need to have these different tools and technologies to help us secure the environment. We can leverage the SOAR platform to help us with orchestration and automation, the whole point of the platform. But these things are all predicated on us having very clearly-defined runbooks and playbooks so that we understand what needs to happen, in what order it needs to happen, who needs to be alerted. Let's take a look at this in a little more detail. These runbooks and playbooks, and this is just an example, this is not an exhaustive list, but some things that need to be defined and then put into the SOAR platform where possible to help us automate some of these actions. What tickets are to be created? What changes need to be implemented and also in what order? Depending upon the size of the environment, you may have a very complicated or a very wide-reaching change management system. A lot of different systems that are integrated, some things feed other things. You might be a 24/7 organization. You might have a lot of public-facing customers. You might be mandated by certain regulations and compliance mechanisms. All of these things have to be carefully vetted and also orchestrated so that they happen as quickly as possible, but without creating additional disruption to the business. What tickets need to be created? What changes have to be implemented? And in what order is critical. Also, what teams need to be engaged? What management teams need to be alerted and when? Also, what additional resources should be added? Whether that be monitoring resources. Do we need to spin a site up? Do we already have a site? Are we in the cloud and we need to spin up additional resources? Also callouts; do we have additional resources, vendors, third-party labor that needs to be engaged, also vendor engagements? Most of these systems are provided by some type of vendor, we should engage them as well to get their subject matter experts on task as quickly as possible. And then some additional items that should be defined, network changes. Are we going to look at isolation or containment or segmentation? Some of these things can be automated. Are we going to be taking clones or reverting from snapshots? Again, failing over to a remote site or up to the cloud. Do we have a dark IP space that's air gapped that we can move things over into or we may have been synchronizing with? Our most critical systems may have been synchronizing in the background and then logically air gapped. Well, do we need to spin up that dark IP site and revert to a last-known good configuration, or a last-known good set of data? Then from an investigation standpoint, spinning up investigations, who do we contact? What types of things do we preserve? Do we need forensics in place? Is there a preservation of evidence or a chain of custody that needs to be maintained? All of these things should be defined ahead of time. We don't want to be flushing these things out in the middle of a breach or in the middle of an incident. The more planning we have in place ahead of time, the more documentation that we have, and that everyone knows what the roles and responsibilities are, and then the runbooks and playbooks can then run that much more efficiently. We can automate where possible. The SOAR platform, this orchestration and automation is a big piece of this puzzle. It's the glue that holds all of these things together. The more planning we do ahead of time, the more successful the outcome. In this chapter, we talked about reconfiguring endpoint security solutions like application whitelisting and blacklisting. We talked about quarantining, whether it be applications or processes or downloads and. We talked about configuration changes like firewall rules, MDM, wiping devices remotely, DLP. We talked about content filters and also revoking or updating certificates. We also talked about isolation, containment, and segmentation and how that can help us secure the environment. Then we talked about SOAR, which is Secure Orchestration, Automation and Response, along with runbooks and playbooks and how those things will help us be successful in the event of an incident.

Chapter 16 Key Aspects of Digital Forensics

In this chapter we'll be talking about Understanding the Key Aspects of Digital Forensics. We'll talk about documentation and evidence in general and why it's Very important to make sure things are documented properly. We'll talk about acquisition and some things around what we should go after first and why, some of the gotchas if we don't follow those procedures. We'll talk about integrity and a few methods we can use to prove that the data we've collected has not been tampered with. We'll talk about preservation along the same lines. We'll talk about ediscovery and what that means and how it applies to an investigation, along with data recovery, and then a similar concept of nonrepudiation so the party in question can't deny ownership or specific action. And then we'll talk about strategic intelligence and counterintelligence along with on-prem versus cloud and some of the challenges and nuances to where that data resides, some things around data sovereignty, applicable laws, depending upon where it's located in the country or in the world if we're doing global business. But what is computer forensics? Well, it is the analysis of digital data in a very simple term. A forensics-level investigation would be something a lot more sophisticated and typically a lot deeper than simply just logging into someone's computer and reading through their internet cache or their internet history. The mere fact that we log in to someone's computer and try to check those things, we tamper with that data. It renders the investigative process, or the probative value, it renders it more or less useless. We have to make sure that we do it when we do investigations in a very controlled, predetermined fashion so that we don't either knowingly or unknowingly tamper with or contaminate the evidence that we're trying to preserve.

It's an analysis of digital data, and that can be computers, it can be smartphones, USB drives, it can be the internet activity taking place, text messages between two people or groups, game consoles, and more. Everything that's connected to the internet, even the Internet of Things, whether it's a refrigerator or, all of those things generate information. They generate data that can be used to either put someone at the scene of a crime or at least help to corroborate a chain of events. Who uses computer forensics? But, anyone who has a need to gather and retain digital evidence. Anyone, whether it's a small mom and pop shop and they may hire a third party to come in and do that, a criminal or computer forensics investigation, or it can be a very large company, a corporate enterprise, a Fortune 500 or a Fortune 150 global organization, they may have an entire team of forensic investigators that they can either dispatch anywhere around the world or they can work remotely anywhere in the world. A small business investigating an internal data breach, a large corporation investigating a hacking attempt or data theft, so anyone from small to the very large has a need for computer forensics. Also, law enforcement investigating a crime. It doesn't necessarily have to be an internal group or department within a company, law enforcement oftentimes will do some type of computer forensic examination, and that's becoming more and more prevalent as time goes on. 10 - 15 years ago it was relatively unheard of to have each department have a specific computer forensics lab or a computer forensics division. Nowadays, pretty much every department has either one or two, or maybe an entire department devoted to computer crime investigation and computer forensics. Additionally, we have private detectives, investigating spouses and insurance fraud.

Order of Volatility

Computer evidence is stored in a number of locations. It can be stored on a magnetic disk, it can be stored in a flash, it can be stored in RAM. Some locations are very temporary. RAM, or random-access memory, is one of those. Everything that your computer does, when it interacts, the CPU, or the brains of your computer or your smartphone or your game console or whatever it is, all of those things have a CPU of some sort. That CPU cannot communicate directly with the data on disk or the data on a flash drive or what have you. It has to pull that data into RAM. That's the intermediary, or the staging area. That is the place where the CPU talks to when it needs to do something of a process. The information in RAM is fresh, it goes in and out very quickly. There's only a finite amount of RAM, and things that come into RAM, if it's already full then it will cache out or swap out or page out, depending upon the operating system that you're using. It'll take that data out of RAM and place it on the disk. Well, that RAM can go away very quickly if the computer is turned off or if it loses power. That's one thing we have to be aware of. Some locations are longer term, Even after deletion that information or that data remains. Magnetic hard disks are a good example of that. If you delete a file from a disk, in other words you just simply highlight it and then click Delete, that file is not deleted. What it is is it takes off the master file table, or again, or it depends upon the operating system how that functions, but there's some table of contents, that has all the pointers to where those files are located. When you delete a file you simply remove that marker. You ultimately say, hey this file is capable or able to be over written. This location of data is no longer needed. It takes the pointer away, so it makes it look like the file is no longer there, but the data itself remains until it's overwritten. This pertains to hard disks. Flash drives are a little bit different. But for magnetic hard disk, if you delete something it doesn't go away. Some locations, are long term, but once deleted they quickly become irretrievable. This specifically refers to SSD or flash drives. With magnetic disks we can place our 1s and 0s, or our bits on the disk. And if we erase that or we mark it for deletion those bits remain. With an SSD, you can't overwrite information in an SSD. If I have information there and I mark that file for deletion I can't simply just overwrite it because it can only have two states, on or off, it's a flash drive. I need to erase that and set it back to 0s so that it can then be over written. When that happens I'll mark the file for deletion, and then very quickly behind the scenes there's a trim process or a garbage cleanup function that takes place and it will then clear that data out. Once you delete it off an SSD, sometimes within minutes, sometimes within half an hour or an hour, depending upon the type of flash drive and what functionality it has, that data will be deleted and it's irretrievable. From a forensics perspective, where that data is stored has some type of bearing on how quickly you need to access it and the order in which you should access it. With the order of volatility, data should be gathered based on the life expectancy of that data. The CPU, cache, and register content, okay the things that are closest to the CPU that need to be there, or need to have power there for it to exist and continue to exist, that is the top of the priority list. We want to try to capture that information first because that information, most often than not or more often than not, will have the most probative value. But it's also the easiest to disappear. If we turn the computer off that information is gone. Next, we have the routing tables, ARP cache, process table, kernel statistics, again, all things that are very volatile. Memory, RAM, all of these things, temporary file space, swap space, data on hard disk, remotely logged data, data contained on archival media. It goes from the things that are very ephemeral, where if we power that computer off it goes away. Those things need to be captured, if at all possible, first. There are tools we can hook up to a computer, we can attach either locally or remotely that allow us to capture that data without contaminating it. Then we can do the same thing with routing table, ARP cache, and memory. The remaining things, temporary file systems, swap space, we can capture that because it's written to disk and the data on the hard disk. We can do that in a slightly more methodical, deterministic fashion. With the data in that volatile space, memory and RAM, that's a little more difficult to capture, but it also provides, a lot of times, the most value because it shows us exactly what was happening just within a few moments ago.

Chapter 17 Chain of Custody & Legal Hold

There's something that can be critical to an investigation, and it can also sink an investigation. Even if it's the best, most meticulously conducted investigation on the planet, if it fails during the chain of custody, if and when it ever has to go to court, that could sink the investigation. When collecting evidence, maintaining that chain of custody is crucial. We want to make sure that we have no gaps in the chain of custody because why? Well, because that can destroy a case. If in other words, if there's a gap and we collect all of our evidence, we do all of our due diligence, we get our search warrant, we go in and we take possession of equipment, we document, and do all the things that we're supposed to do, but then we bring that back to our headquarters or to our office, and we don't document where that evidence goes, whose hands it changes along the way, where it's stored, and so on, it's very easy for a defense attorney, at that point, to interject and say, well, wait a minute. How do we know this wasn't tampered with during the process? How do we know that this wasn't swapped out or something wasn't manipulated or tainted in some fashion? There's hours, there's days, there's weeks where no one had eyes on this specific equipment. How do we know this is even my client's computer or hard drive? You don't want to have that discrepancy come into the investigative process. Evidence can become contaminated, if we don't have it accounted for each and every step of the way. It also introduces reasonable doubt. The defense attorney can turn the tables on an investigation. It's important to lock this thing down tightly and do not leave any room or any chance for error. When we're dealing with custody logs, it should accompany each piece of evidence. Everything that we secure, everything that we take away from a scene, should have a chain of custody tag attached to it, an evidence tag, depending on how your specific department or organization works. That chain of custody tag should have who acquired it, who received it or who it was received from, the date, and the time. That should account for everything, including when it's logged into an evidence locker, when it's removed from an evidence locker, so, there is no gaps in time. Every time the evidence is logged in or out of evidence or an evidence locker or some type of containment facility or changes hands in any form, that should be documented, the date, the time, the location, the person checking it in, checking it out, and then seals and/or tags on evidence bags. If an evidence bag needs to be opened, then it should be written on there why that seal is broken and when a new seal is applied, and, of course, initialed. That way everything is accounted for from the moment it is acquired to the moment it's no longer needed.

Legal Hold

Legal holds is data that has been identified as material to an investigation. It's copied or moved to an immutable location. Immutable means it can't be altered in any way. That way it's write protected, so that way it helps us maintain a continuity of evidence. there are different applications out there that will do a lot of this for us, so all actions, access, anything that's done to that data, if anyone accesses it, moves it, uses it in any type of searches, all those things will be logged. There are a number of applications and application suites or tool sets that will do all of that for us and automate a lot of this process. Something else to keep in mind is the fact that it's not subject to typical retention policies, so it may in fact be held indefinitely. Your organization may have, say, a 30-day, or a 3-month, or even a 3-year data retention policy, or 5 or 7 years, depending upon the type of data. Well, legal hold data will be held indefinitely until that specific case is over, and in some instances, that data may be held indefinitely. Some companies may keep that data in an immutable location on a higher class of storage or a higher tier of storage while the case is active, and then archive that off to something else, whether it be DVD or some write-once media, or it might move to tape backup or some type of archive location, so that way it can be held indefinitely but then recalled, if need be, whether it's part of its own case, or it may be part of some other case.

Chapter 18 First Responder Best Practices

The first responder can be on scene, or you can image your computer remotely over a network, again, depending upon the role that you play, whether you're law enforcement or an internal corporate investigator, whether you work for a state or a local, or the federal government. Each of these different tiers, have different capabilities. Once you're there, you need to photograph the computer, photograph the scene. It's critical to get a good understanding of how things are, again, if you're local to that scene, if you're not doing it remotely. If you're on scene, photograph the computer and the scene. That way, you know exactly from beginning how things are laid out, how things are connected. Then if the computer is off, do not turn it on. The simple act of you turning on a computer and booting it up changes thousands of files, changes the timestamps, the last access, last modified on a number of files, hundreds of thousands of files, just simply booting the operating system. That can have a negative effect on your investigation. It can wipe out some things that could be extremely valuable down the road. It's off, don't turn it on. Then if it's on, don't turn it off, at least not yet. We want to photograph the scene, make sure we have everything in place. Then, if you have the proper tools, again, you can connect to that computer, whether it's USB, whether it's some other type of method, and you can image, you can write block the computer, and then image it without contaminating anything. You can capture the information that's in RAM, that's in all the volatile areas that we talked about in addition to imaging the actual disk itself. That way you can get an exact duplicate of the data that's on that computer and the state that it's in when you come across it. You want to turn off if you have the tools available to do that type of imaging. Then, depending upon your role, whether it's IT security or whether you're law enforcement, will dictate whether you can or can't put your hands on someone, if you're law enforcement and you're doing the search warrant, you want to make sure you separate that person from the device. Because if they have the chance to get to the computer, start erasing files, turning it off, or doing something to manipulate the device. In some instances, there have been cases where people have their computers hooked up to explosives, they have degaussing coils, so if they flick a switch they can turn around and wipe their hard drive instantly. Some extreme cases, but depending upon your role, you want to separate the person and the computer, image it on site. That's not always possible, but these types of things are best practices that allow you to get with the least chance of contamination the data that you need in a format that will stand up and hold up in a court of law, if it ever has to go through an investigative process and it ends up in court. I don't want to get off on a tangent too, too much, but, again, you'll separate the person, then you'll collect live data. You want to start with the RAM image. You want to get all that data that you can off the computer in its live, volatile format so that you can look at and parse through what that person was doing at that exact point in time. Because if they just had a chat conversation with someone, or if they were just logging into a website, doing some type of hack or a breach, the things that they typed most recently in that conversation, the data that's passed through the computer will be stored in RAM. That gives you a high-value target. Then you want to collect a local image of the hard disk using forensics tools, and there are many tools out there, so this is not an endorsement of any one product. But there are tools like dd, Helix3, EnCase, F-Response. There's a number of tool. AccessData is another. There are a lot of ones out there that can give you a forensic bit-by-bit copy of a hard drive without writing to that drive at all. Takes an exact copy, bit-level copy, creates a hash against that copy, so it does a hash on the original, does a hash on the copy, and those hashes will match up. It gives you the ability to say definitively, yes, that's exactly the same data as what was retrieved or what existed on the suspect computer. Once that's finished, then you can unplug in the power cord from the back of the computer or remove the battery. The power cord is the best way to go, or removing the battery. There have been instances where the power button has been wired to a degaussing coil or some type of explosive, in some cases. If you flick that power button, you have the potential to not get the desired result. So removing the power cord, removing the battery if it's a laptop, is the best option. That way it shuts it down ungracefully, doesn't write to the swap file, any of those things. It just shuts it off at the point in time that it was. Then once we're done, we want to diagram and label all cords, document all devices themselves, model numbers, serial numbers. That part of an investigation is very time consuming. It's certainly not the most glorified part of the investigation, but it is critical because all of those things need to be documented properly, so they can be reconstructed, if necessary, or at least very accurately describe the scene as you found it.

Capture a System Image
A system image can be captured locally or remotely using special software or devices. There are applications that can do it via software, but there are also other applications or devices that can do it through a hardware connectivity. It will write-block the computer or the device in question, and when I say write-block, you're not able to write to that disk

at much like read-only, but better. That way, even if it's read-only, there are still some things that could be accessed just by the nature of you interacting with the file system. When you write-block the computer, you literally turn off its ability to write at all. That way you can image that disk, you can create a forensic image, a bit-level, bit-by-bit image of that disk, even the slack spaces on the drive, is then copied to a duplicate. When you're done, you would run a hash, and if the hashes match up, you know it is an exact duplicate of the suspect device or the suspect file, folder, disk. There are live USB or CD/DVDs, whatever your media of choice is, and when I say live, what I mean is that these are ISO images that are on the USB or a CD or a DVD. That computer will boot up, but it boots up completely off of the USB drive or the CD. Nothing is written on the hard disk, and there are a number of devices out there. Kali Linux is one but there are literally dozens of different distributions and programs from encase, access data, and there's lots of them out there that can give you these live, bootable images that can give you forensic capabilities on a target PC, laptop, etc. Something else to keep in mind when talking about capturing a system image is to make multiple copies of the imaged data. The reason for that is that we want to make sure we have a copy that we're working off of, never the original data. We don't want to work on the original image or the original PC or laptop, simply because, that will contaminate the data. We make multiple copies; that way, we can work off of a copy if something goes wrong, or we need to in some way destroy it or go through some type of destructive analysis, we can always go back and start with a new or a fresh image to copy the next time we have to do something again. That way, we're always working off of a copy that we can verify via that hashing algorithm. We can verify it is an exact duplicate of the original. We never want to use the actual target hard drive, simply because it contaminates the data. Forensic software will log and timestamp every action that we take during the investigation. That way, we can build what's called a case folder to aid in the documentation and the reporting, because if we're simply trying to determine what happened, if it's a breach, if it's someone that's trying to hack into our system, we may never have any desire to take this to court, or we know it's not going to go anywhere from a legal standpoint, but we want to understand what happened, how we can harden our defenses. In that case, it's not as important. But if we're talking about a criminal case where we think, or there has the potential for that case to go to court at some point in time, it is crucial that we maintain proper evidentiary procedures, and making sure we maintain chain of custody. But having that documentation again is critical, because it's very important if it ever goes to court, we want to make sure that we can recall that testimony and make sure that we can understand, very systematically what we did, and it may be six months, a year, two years down the road before that goes to court. If we're not aware of what we did, we don't have a photographic memory, that documentation is going to be extremely important.

Chapter 19 Network Traffic and Logs

The next thing that you want to look at, or a potential for digital evidence would be network traffic and logs. If you think about it, every single thing that's attached, whether it be a local network, a small office, home office network or a SOHO, SMB, small- to medium-sized business, or a corporate enterprise, again, a Fortune 500 or Fortune 150, every single device that's connected in any fashion generates logs, generates traffic. Network traffic, including IP addresses, the data that sent, the actual websites we're browsing or the photos that we're accessing, the data that we're either copying or saving, the protocols that we use, all can be used to investigate a crime or a hacking event. An IP address, for example, can be used to locate the source and the destination of an event. It can help us to narrow down where a suspect is located. It could be on our internal network. We could be in a corporate environment trying to identify who a suspect is, who's accessing files. It doesn't necessarily mean that we know exactly who that person is because, again, someone could be sitting at that person's computer. Same thing if we're investigating a crime from a law enforcement perspective as well. Just because we have someone's IP address doesn't necessarily mean we know exactly who that person is. That gives us an idea, that gives us a start, but that only begins the actual investigative process. Once we have the IP address we can narrow it down, we can potentially see where they're coming from, what, perhaps, hops they're taking to get from where they're located to their destination. They may be trying to hide where they're located, we can backtrack and see if that leads us to the end, or to the suspect, rather. Sometimes it will go to a dead end, if they're smart enough and they jump through enough hoops. It doesn't necessarily always mean we have a person of interest. It can help place the suspect behind the keyboard, but, that's just a piece of the puzzle. We have to have more than just that. Then logs themselves are generated by a variety of devices. If you think about desktops and laptops, there's lots of logs within the actual computers themselves as to what they're doing, when they're doing it, the registry on a PC, there's configuration files on Macs and Linux devices, lots of log files that are generated and saved, typically for troubleshooting. But it also identifies when files were accessed, when system parameters and variables were changed, when people logged on, or when they logged off. All of these things can help us to build a case. Routers, switches, and firewalls on our corporate network, or even if it's in a home and we're trying to identify what's taken place from my location to a corporate location. In other words, someone's outside of our corporate network and trying to come in. Routers, switches, and firewalls, both within our own environment and potentially within a suspect environment, can all create log files, syslog files on routers, switches, the firewalls themselves. All of these things should be gathered and then correlated. Once we have all this information, we then need some way of either feeding it into a big data analysis type of tool, something like Splunk or some type of other big data analysis tool so we can correlate all of these different pieces of information, log files from here, switch files from here, configuration files from here, and put them all together. Then we can correlate the times and get an idea of what's going on. Smartphones, gaming consoles, some other things that people typically don't think of, but, they all generate logs. Smartphones have diagnostic information. We can tell when it was used, what was installed. Gaming consoles, whether it be an Xbox or a PS3 or PS4, all of these things get

IP addresses that they connect to the internet. They generate log files and generate data. Everything, if you take it and put it into a combined case folder, can lead to a pretty precise picture of what happened and when.

Capturing Video

Video can be a crucial component to documenting an investigation. It can be taken of ourselves or of yourself as you're in your investigation, You can wear a camera to record your movements or you can simply just video the scene itself you have a good picture of how things were laid out, where they are, record what's on the screen, the position, the location of various components, and so on. Also, video can be from a surveillance camera, whether it be on site or perhaps outside of a business or a specific data center or a location. Do we have evidentiary value or do we have evidence from video cameras inside of our data center about an office or a remote site, the entrance or an exit of a building. Video can be something that we take or it can be taken from an outside, third-party source that we can then use to help build our case. Video can be used in a number of different fashions.

Record Time Offset

When I talk about recording the time offset you might say, well why is that important? Who cares? Well, it's extremely important when we're trying to corroborate and correlate all these different log files that we have. There's something referred to as UTC. That stands for Coordinated Universal Time. It stands for Coordinated Universal Time. It's the mean solar time at the Earth's prime meridian. 0 degrees longitude located near Greenwich, England. The time zones from around the world are expressed as positive or negative offsets from the UTC. Why that's important? Well, we may have people, whether they're suspects or even within our own corporation or our own corporate networks, that are global. Or they may be at least within different time zones. If we don't have the proper offset and we're not sure that everything is in sync then it's going to be very hard to try to build a case based on time. We could have multiple breaches within a corporate network, that take place across multiple time zones. It could be globally. If we're not able to correlate exactly what happened when it's going to be very difficult for us to then match up, Person A, our suspect, was at their location here and they hit our PC or our network here. Well if the times are completely offset and they're not accurate it's going to be much more difficult for us to lineup than if we can see that on the suspect computer at exactly 15:15 it did this, and here it is 15:15 on our systems as well and here's where the breach occurred. It's going to be much more difficult if everything is out of whack to try to correlate that. It's just, it's important for us to make sure that within our own systems that we have control over that we have all of our systems in sync pointing to a network time server. Okay? They can either be internal or it can be external. We can point our devices, routers, switches, PCs, we can point them to an external time source so that way everything is in sync. Typically in most environments, whether it's, a Linux environment or an Active Directory environment, more than likely you'll have the Active Directory server or, some component within your Active Directory environment, point to a time server. They will coordinate time and push out the proper time for all the computers within that environment. However, your switches and everything else, routers, they need to be in sync as well. That way it's very easy to corroborate and correlate time.

Taking Hashes

When we're talking about hashes, a hash can be an MD5, SHA1, SHA256 or SHA512, it's a mathematical algorithm that's applied to a file folder or an entire disk that verifies the integrity of the evidence. The hash is taken prior to imaging. If we arrive on scene and we take possession of a suspect computer, we have a device we can either connect externally or we boot up using some type of write-blocking software, we're going to connect to that target PC locally or remotely. We will then run a hash against that target hard disk, typically it's going to be the entire hard disk. We'll run a hash against it. It will come back when it's finished and spit out a number, a long string of characters and numbers telling us this is a unique fingerprint for that specific drive. When we're done, we'll then take an image of that hard disk and we'll run that same hashing algorithm against the copy. If both of those numbers come back the same, we know beyond a shadow of a doubt that they are absolutely identical. If one letter, as an example, if we were to hash an entire dictionary or an entire encyclopedia or the entire Library of Congress, whatever it is you want to focus on, if you took a hash of that entire body of work, let's just say a dictionary, well, if we changed one letter in that dictionary from a lowercase to an uppercase, the hash would be completely different. In other words, if we were to make the analogy to a computer, if we went to a computer and just simply turned it on, accessed some files, logged in, things are going to change, timestamps, file access, whether we're read, write, modify, anything that we do at that point to that computer changes something. When that happens, it would then change the hash, and if those hashes are different between our target and our copy, well, then it's no longer valid, and in a court of law that would be thrown out.

Chapter 20 Screenshots & Witnesses

A screenshot of what is on a suspect's computer, on their screen at that moment in time, gives us an idea or a good indication of what they were doing, what they were working on, perhaps before they had a chance to destroy evidence. especially if we don't have the opportunity for the tools to take a proper image and grab what was in RAM and volatile memory, if we don't have the ability to capture that information, then our second best option is to take screenshots., again, we don't want to interact with the actual computer itself. If we have no other choice than yes, something is better than nothing; however, remember back to what I said if we have to go to a court of law and it depends upon the type of investigation, but we don't want to tamper with the original suspect PC if we can help it, but if you can't then taking screenshots can help. An alternative would be, either video or to take pictures and physically take a picture of what's on the screen at that point in time. Depending on what's on the screen, it may outweigh the risk, losing that information.

Witnesses
Something else that we want to not overlook for sure are witnesses. Witnesses and witness accounts can be crucial to an investigation, and more often than not, a witness can help or kick off an investigation. A lot of times crimes, attempted crimes, breaches have been solved by tips from witnesses from the general public. Don't overlook the fact that there are always a second set of eyes, that can be crucial to your investigation. When taking statements from a witness, always try to ascertain the general who, what, where, why, and how, but also the date and time, what else

was going on at that point in time, who else was there, because you may be able to have follow up witnesses. Maybe that person that you initially talked to didn't see everything or they weren't there long enough, but if they can also say who else was in the room or who else was in the general area and you're able to contact those people, you maybe able to get additional information as well. Also, what other equipment was present, because that may give you more things that you want to search, especially if you're going to prepare a search warrant and you want to make sure you include everything in your search warrant, but you don't want to be overly broad because as you take things before a judge, if it's overly broad, a lot of times they will shoot that down and make you go back and rework that search warrant you're wasting valuable time depending upon the nature of the crime. If you can pinpoint it, narrow it down, and get it the first time, then that's going to expedite your ability to get that warrant and go and get that evidence and then, you want to make sure you capture the who, what, where, when, why, and how. But if you capture all of these things and you touch all of these points when you're doing your interview, you're going to capture the majority of information that you need.

Chapter 21 Preservation of Evidence

As an example, let's say we have our target system. We have a couple of options. We could attach to it with a laptop and we could use software where I protect that computer. We could also use a USB or bootable disk we could boot into that system and boot to that live CD instead of allowing the system itself to boot. Because if you recall, the actual act of booting that system changes hundreds, potentially thousands of system files, access times, dates, so it tampers with that evidence. We want to use something, some device to write-protect that target system so that it's not tampered with. Alternatively, we could use some type of hardware or software device to connect, a USB token or a specific, or an actual device specifically built for forensic purposes that allows us to attach to that machine via USB or some other connection, and write-protect that system, and from there we would take a bit-level copy and we would create, in essence, a cloned image. Typically we'd take that bit-level copy, that entire computer, and copy it to an image file. That image file is then what we would work from. We would then take our forensics workstation, and we would work from that cloned image, we would not work on the actual target system. We can use a hashing algorithm to hash the original system and then hash our cloned working copy or copies and make sure they are identical. That way we can prove that nothing's been tampered with or have been added or changed in any way. But we always want to work off of an image. That way the original target system is preserved.

Recovery
When it comes to recovery from a forensics' perspective, data can be recovered forensically if it hasn't been

overwritten. That's it at the end of the day. If the data has not been overwritten, it can be recovered using forensics tools. If it's been wiped, in other words it's been overwritten by multiple passes, that's going to make it very difficult, if not impossible, to have that data recoverable. If it's an SSD, if those NANDs have been reset, there are some tools, both from the SSD manufacturers and also some Linux tools from third-party tools that allow us to reset those SSDs so you can wipe that entire drive in a matter of seconds. If that, in fact, happens, recovery of that data is very, very difficult, if not impossible. Additionally, the media itself needs to be intact. If someone were to take a drill and drill through those hard drives or drill through the SSDs or otherwise break them apart, degauss them if it's a magnetic media, something where it physically destroys that disk, it's going to be very difficult, again if not impossible, to recover the data. Depending upon what it is, the nature of the investigation, and who's doing the recovery, impossible is a relative term. There are some Three Letter Agencies that have access to tools and toolsets that the average person and the average company does not have. Impossible is not necessarily a finite term, but for all intents and purposes for the average company, for the average person doing forensics recovery, if the media is physically damaged, broken apart, drilled through, scratched beyond repair, that data is going to be unrecoverable.

Strategic Intelligence / Counterintelligence Gathering
Whether we're talking about strategic intelligence or counterintelligence, it's done to allow the person or the company commissioning those actions to make real-time, actionable decisions. The actions are going to be proactive based on real-time data. We're not looking at historicals, we're not looking at trends, this is real-time data, it's very

fluid, it's real-time analytics, active logging activities that will typically have clearly defined rules of engagement and allow us to make very quick decisions based upon real-time data. Next, it relies on human interaction, as well as automated methods. Human reconnaissance or boots on the ground, as well as active logging and automated toolsets to gather that intelligence. We're not looking at logs and looking back historically, we're not looking in the rear view mirror, and we're looking at real time and looking forward to make these actionable decisions on how to act proactively. Then it can also be either defensive, which is our intelligence gathering, or offensive, which is counterintelligence. Intelligence information can be used to defend a company's or a country's interests or they can be offensive, and that's done to neutralize an adversary or an adversary's intelligence gathering capabilities. The mandate of most counterintelligence agencies are to go out and actively pursue, actively neutralize, or try to neutralize, an adversary's intelligence gathering capabilities. We're trying to thwart their ability to perform espionage, exfiltrate data from us.

Chapter 22 Data Integrity

Data integrity is part of the CIA triad, confidentiality, integrity, and availability, but with regard to digital forensics, just a few things to clarify. With data integrity, we have a couple of ways to provide data integrity, one of which is hashing. And as we know, hashing is a mathematical algorithm that maps data of an arbitrary size. It can be a variable, it could be short, it could be long, to a hashed value of a fixed size. It's pretty much deterministic. Every time we do a hash of a specific piece of information, we're always going to get the same result. It's a one-way function that's infeasible to reverse or inverse. There are a few different hashing algorithms, MD5, various flavors of SHA, SHA-1, SHA-256. So from a forensics perspective, you can hash the files on a drive and get a specific value. Then when you're done, when you've done your investigations or if you have a copy of that data, you can run that hash algorithm again. If those two hashes match, that means that the data has not been altered in any way. Next will be checksums. It's very similar in functionality to hashes as far as what the end result is, and it's used to verify the integrity of data, but not the authenticity. We can run checksums against a piece of data, and we do this with error-correcting code, with RAM, we do it with checksums when we're sending packets on a network, and we can do the same thing here. A checksum would allow us, so to test before and after, and if those checkssums match, then we know the data has not been tampered with. We can't necessarily prove the authenticity, but we can prove that the data itself is the same. Then we have the concept of providence, which is the metadata that documents the inputs, the changes, to data and provides a historical record of the data and also its origins. In essence, it allows us to track who created the data, any changes to that data throughout its lifespan. It's a way for us to verify the integrity of data and to get a bit of a historical view on what has happened to that data since its origin.

Non-repudiation

Next we have nonrepudiation, and nonrepudiation is an accountability concept. It is an inability to refute an action or an ownership. It says the person that we think has done this or owns this or has interacted with this, they can't reasonably say no, it wasn't me. Cryptographic nonrepudiation we can think of as digital signatures. That provides the inability to refute something. If a person, as an example, has a public key/private key and then they sign something with that certificate, then that proves that they are who they are. Of course unless someone steals their certificate, then of course all bets are off. But as long as that secret is kept safe, that PKI certificate is kept safe, then that would prove that that person is who they say they are. We can also have network nonrepudiation, and center around the generation of enough data of activity so that it can't be refuted, so the action itself cannot be refuted.

On-prem vs. Cloud Challenges and to Audit

Let's talk about some of the on-prem versus cloud challenges. We have three things to cover. We have the -to-audit clauses, we have regulatory and jurisdictional issues, and then data breach notification laws. Auditors will typically routinely access on-prem data centers to perform audits as needed. It can be regulatory or compliance mandates. It can be investigations of breaches. It can be contractual, annual, or biannual audits. You could have customers and your customers need some type of certification or understanding that you are providing security controls and that you're doing things effectively, best practices. If that's the case, you want your customers to be able to have documentation and proof that these things exist. But having things in the cloud can pose unique challenges to auditing, because cloud providers typically don't allow auditors in, just because of their sheer size. Cloud providers typically have thousands or potentially tens of thousands of clients or tenants, and if those tenants were routinely allowing auditors or having auditors come in to audit their infrastructure, it would get very unruly, very quickly, and the cloud provider wouldn't be able to get anything done, like business-as-usual, day-to-day work, because they'd have auditors in there, inspecting things 24/7, 365. There are ways around that, though, and you can still prove that you are, in fact, following best practices and having your security controls in place. Let's say, for instance, we have a data center or a cloud provider, a co-location facility, and in there, we have a number of tenants who have IaaS and SaaS, infrastructure as a service, software as a service, virtualization equipment. Well, we need to be able to provide a way to have those things audited and show definitively that we're following best practices, our security controls are in place. There are two organizations that I just want to call to your attention. One is SSAE 18, and that stands for the Statement on Standards for Attestation Engagements, number 18, and then internationally, we have ISAE 3402, that provides similar guidance. Those certification bodies have three different types of reporting. We have SOC 1, SOC 2, and SOC 3, and SOC stands for Service Organization Control, or SOC reports? There are three different types: SOC 1, 2, and 3. SOC 1 deals with financial reporting controls, SOC 2 deals with security controls, and then SOC 3 is publicly accessible. What these do is they ensure that data centers, channel partners, and vendors, utilize the same security controls as the data center or hosting provider? And all of these things are in place. Then there are two different types. Within SOC 1 and SOC 2, there are two different types, which we'll talk about here. Type 1 is an attestation of controls at a service organization, at a specific point in time. An auditor will give their opinion and say, they have these controls in place, but they don't verify or validate their effectiveness; they don't test them. It's a point in time. Type 2 reports is an attestation of controls at a service organization over a minimum six-month period, so it's a much more involved type of report, but they go through and not just validate that the controls were there, but they test them, and make sure that they're workable, they're effective, and they do what they say they're going to do. Two types of reports; 1 is easier to get or get certified against; Type 2 is more comprehensive, as you may guess, but once you're certified, your clients, customers have a strong understanding of what controls are in place and that they're effective. Then the SOC 3 type of report, those types of reports have the basic information, but the details, the under-the-hood type of things, are stripped away, and that's made publicly accessible, so that anyone can look and see what controls are there or what types of controls are there, but not the details, not the inner workings.

Chapter 23 Jurisdictional Issues & Data Breach Notification Laws

As a business, once you start to put things into the cloud you run into some potential issues, not necessarily every time, but some things to definitely think about. Data sovereignty and accessing that data, who owns or maintains or has jurisdiction over that data, can vary from country to country. Some countries are stricter, they have stricter laws, while others are less restrictive. It just depends upon where that data is stored. That can impact the ability to access the data, to audit data. So, data sovereignty, that states that the legal restrictions of any jurisdiction where data is collected, stored, or processed can apply. Depending upon where your information is stored, what region, what part of the world, different jurisdictional laws can apply. It's important that you know that. As an example, let's say we have a global business. We're doing business all over the world. We have customers all over the world. We may have a data center in one part of the world, maybe another data center somewhere else, and then another data center somewhere else. If we're a cloud provider or we're using a cloud provider, it's important to understand that cloud providers typically will have data centers all over the world. They do that purposely, so they can disperse that infrastructure globally, provide for geo redundancy and failover. Data can potentially be copied, stored, or processed anywhere globally. SoData is often copied between data centers in different regions. ? They might stay within a specific country, but it's copied within regions to make sure you have that redundancy, high availability. But it could potentially be copied somewhere else. ? Be sure to know where your data's stored. If it's copied between regions or between geo dispersed regions outside or into other countries, make sure you're aware of the applicable laws that may be in play. Also, if you have customers in other countries then data might be stored local to that region. An investigation or a breach or some type of audit could be impacted by that specific country's data privacy laws, data sovereignty laws.

Data Breach Notification Laws
They were first enacted in 2002, roughly almost 20 years ago. All 50 states have data breach notification laws, although it took probably 15-18 years to get all 50 states on board. But individuals and companies affected by a data breach must notify their customers. That's the general gist of the laws. Then they must also take specific steps to remediate any deficiencies. If a breach occurs and we identify why that happened, the companies must make sure that they're doing the proper steps to remediate and get rid of those issues, fill those gaps and make sure it doesn't happen again. Something also worth noting is that there's no federal data breach notification law currently. There are certain regulatory mandates that have certain industries disclose breaches, but not across the board of federal notification law. There are also data breach notification laws in other countries, so it's not just a US thing. Australia, China, the EU, Japan, New Zealand, etc., they are examples of other countries that have similar data breach notification laws. Then there are certain regulations that can affect customers or companies globally like GDPR, California's CCPA, there are a number of other ones in other countries as well. But just understand that just because you reside in a specific location, if you do business globally or if you utilize a cloud provider you may potentially be subject to other countries' laws, data sovereignty laws, or to privacy, to notification laws. It's very important that you understand all the

nuances, and then wherever that data resides, if it's processed, collected, stored, there are applicable laws that may impact how you do business, depending upon where it's located. In this chapter we talked about documentation and evidence, the acquisition of that evidence, how to collect it, the order of volatility, where you should start collecting data first. We talked about the integrity of data and how we need to ensure that it hasn't been tampered with, and we can prove that. We talked about preservation and e-discovery, along with data recovery, non-repudiation, being able to certify or attest that something is what they say it is or some action was performed as we suspect it was performed. We talked about strategic intelligence and counterintelligence and then some nuances and challenges on-prem versus the cloud when it comes to storage of data, data acquisition, data sovereignty.

BOOK 3

CISSP
CYBERSECURITY GOVERNANCE
AND RISK MANAGEMENT

POLICY CONCEPTS & DEPLOYMENT
WITHIN
ORGANIZATIONAL SECURITY

RICHIE MILLER

Introduction

IT Security jobs are on the rise! Small, medium or large size companies are always on the look out to get on board bright individuals to provide their services for Business as Usual (BAU) tasks or deploying new as well as on-going company projects. Most of these jobs requiring you to be on site but since 2020, companies are willing to negotiate with you if you want to work from home (WFH). Yet, to pass the Job interview, you must have experience. Still, if you think about it, all current IT security professionals at some point had no experience whatsoever. The question is; how did they get the job with no experience? Well, the answer is simpler then you think. All you have to do is convince the Hiring Manager that you are keen to learn and adopt new technologies and you have willingness to continuously research on the latest upcoming methods and techniques revolving around IT security. Here is where this book comes into the picture. Why? Well, if you want to become an IT Security professional, this book is for you! If you are studying for CompTIA Security+ or CISSP, this book will help you pass your exam. Passing security exams isn't easy. In fact, due to the raising security beaches around the World, both above mentioned exams are becoming more and more difficult to pass. Whether you want to become an Infrastructure Engineer, IT Security Analyst or any other Cybersecurity Professional, this book (as well as the other books in this series) will certainly help you get there! But, what knowledge are you going to gain from this book? Well, let me share with you briefly the agenda of this book. First, you are going to comparing and contrasting various types of controls, including managerial, operational and technical, and physical controls. We'll also talk about deterrent, preventative, detective, corrective and recovery, and then compensating controls, the methods and procedures, along with the logical and physical ways that we can restrict access and deter the bad guys from trying to get into our systems. Next we will cover applicable regulations, standards, or frameworks that impact the security organization. We'll also talk about key frameworks, benchmarks and secure configuration guides. After that, you are going to discover how to implement policies within organizational security, as well as personnel and the associated issues with managing, maintaining, and keeping things secure. We'll also cover diversity of training techniques, along with third-party risk management, data classification, governance, and retention, and then we'll talk about various credential policies along with organizational policies. Next, we'll review the risk management process and concepts such as the risk types, risk management strategies, risk analysis, along with disasters, and business impact analysis. Moving on, you will learn about privacy and sensitive data concepts and considerations as well as organizational consequences of privacy breaches, notification of breaches, and the various types of data and how they're classified. We'll also cover privacy enhancing technologies, roles and responsibilities, information lifecycle, impact assessment, terms of agreement and privacy notices. If you are ready to get on this journey, let's first comparing and contrasting various types of controls!

Chapter 1 Threat Types & Access Control

In this chapter specifically we'll be talking about comparing and contrasting various types of controls. We'll be talking about the various categories, including managerial, operational and technical, and then physical. Managerial, operational or technical, and then physical control types, we'll be talking about deterrent, preventative, detective, corrective and recovery, and then compensating controls, the methods and procedures, along with the logical and physical ways that we can restrict access and then deter folks from trying to get into our systems. The goal of this chapter is threefold. Number 1, I want to make sure that you understand the threat types and understand that not all threats are created equal. No one control type can deter or prevent everything. We need to have multiple arrows in the quiver or tools in our toolbox, but the point being, make sure you have enough tools available to take care of threats from various types, various groups. Next, realize that different groups have different motivations. What motivates one hacker or one group may be completely different than another, which is why multiple control types are needed. Things that may deter one group may not deter another. Even a technical control that may deter or prevent one group may or may not prevent another, depending upon their skill level, their motivation, how resilient they are, the amount of resources or money. Thirdly, I want to make sure I reinforce the importance of defense in depth. one size does not fit. Multiple layers of defense are required to properly deter and prevent breaches. We won't have multiple locks on the door. It doesn't do us much good to have this super strong door, this thick, impenetrable door and then have a window on the side of the house wide open. We have to make sure we have multiple layers of defense at all access points so that a properly motivated attacker doesn't bypass one control and go in through one that's may be less complicated or less restrictive.

Threat Types

As far as threat types go, we have script kiddies, which are not necessarily that sophisticated, but they can cause some damage. We have hacktivists, which a lot of times are maybe politically or motivated by a specific cause. We have organized crime, which everyone knows more or less what organized crime does. They're motivated a lot of times by financial gain or some type of power. We have nation states and advanced persistent threats, or APTs, and they're motivated quite often by power, control, espionage, country secrets, proprietary information as far as technology is concerned. Then we have insiders, and they may be motivated by money or to get back at a specific person or a boss or management or the company in general. They might be motivated by some type of revenge. Then we have competitors. They're looking for espionage, looking for competitive advantage, some type of proprietary information that might give them an edge over you or other competitors. All of these different types of attacks and all these different types of threats require different levels and different types of deterrents and control types.

Types of Access Control (Managerial, Operational, and Physical)

To make sure that you understand the various types of access control, let's go over a few of those. We have managerial, otherwise known as administrative, and these are the policies, the standards, the processes, various procedures, guidelines, risk management policies, account management policies, and various regulatory controls that mandate certain things be put in place and also things that we can do or we can administer, or manage, to make sure access is restricted in some form or fashion. Next are operational controls, otherwise known as technical controls, and these things revolve around endpoint protection, antivirus software or anti-malware software, anti-ransomware, various methods of encryption, whether at rest or in transit, access control in its various forms, intrusion prevention systems and intrusion detection systems, along with firewalls. Then we have physical, as the name implies. That would be locks, fences, mantraps, CCTV, guards, and things that are physically put in place to deter or prevent access to a system, to a building, a datacenter

Deterrent
When it comes to the actual control types, a deterrent is a system or signage that's designed to discourage people from doing something, so accessing a network as an example, entering a restricted area. It could be to keep them from accessing some type of information, or it could be to prevent them from getting hurt or injured, so it could be for their own safety as well. Then it can also alert those people, those trespassers, to the potential of additional controls, cameras, or guards.

Preventive
Preventive controls are something that's designed to keep someone from doing something. Some of these control types overlap, and a specific type of control can fall into multiple categories. As an example, guards, fencing, locks on doors windows or cabinets. We're preventing someone from accessing an area. We're preventing them from doing something. Whether it's a physical control or administrative

control or technical, they could all be preventive, so there is an overlap on some of these.

Detective

Detective controls are controls that detect activity and initiate some type of action. It could be an event manager or some type of intrusion detection system or prevention system. It could sound an alarm. It could send an alert, whether it's to management, administrators, police. It can also record the activity for later analysis. It doesn't prevent the access, but it can assist in analyzing and investigating. It doesn't keep anyone from doing something, but it can send alerts, and it can also record for later analysis or investigation.

Corrective / Recovery and Compensating

Corrective and recovery go hand in hand. Depending upon where you read about them, these might be two separate categories, or they may be one, so I'm just going to include them both here. It's a type of control used to get a system back to normal, so that could be restoring from a backup, it could be updating antivirus or antimalware software, it could be installing patches or fixes or firmware updates. This is something that we would want to do as an administrator or as a security professional or some type of IT staff member. We're going to be doing something to help get a system back online. We're going to correct some deficiency, or we will recover from some type of crisis. On the recovery side, a disaster recovery site is an example, or in HA, or high availability site, is another example. Also we have system and data backups. We're going to recover or restore from those backups to get our systems back up online. Compensating controls are controls that provide an alternate or an alternative solution to a countermeasure that's either too difficult or potentially impossible or just too expensive to implement. As an example, we might choose to install a gate or a swipe card system instead of paying for guards 24/7. We may decide that updating all of our operating systems is too expensive, too time consuming, to technically challenging, We're going to just application whitelist. We're going to create lists of only the applications that can run in hopes of covering some type of maybe operating system deficiency, as an example. We can substitute one control for another in hopes of achieving the same result. In this chapter we talked about several categories of controls, such as managerial, operational, and technical, and then physical controls. Then we talked about the various control types, including deterrent, preventative, detective, corrective and recovery, and then compensating. In essence, the various ways we can protect our systems, our files, folders, data from unauthorized access.

Chapter 2 Applicable Regulations, Standards, & Frameworks

In this chapter, we'll be talking about applicable regulations, standards, or frameworks that impact the security organization. We'll be talking about regulations, standards, and legislation. We'll talk about key frameworks and then benchmarks and secure configuration guides. The challenge is the global nature of the internet can cause communication and expectations of privacy to vary widely throughout different parts of the world. Behavior that is totally acceptable in one part of the world can be a capital offense in another. The nuances of these laws and these regulations, especially if you travel globally, are very important to keep up on and make sure that you're familiar with. When we're talking about doing business in a global economy, a few things you need to keep in mind. The United States used to traditionally set the tone for data privacy laws. Up until recently, the last 5, 10 years or so, the US more less led that initiative. However, other countries have stepped out and taken the lead, specifically countries throughout the European Union. More restrictive regulations aimed at consumer privacy and protection, so a lot more geared towards privacy of the consumer. The whole data protection laws and regulations that are coming out both in the UK or the European Union and also the US and other parts of the world are again geared towards protecting that consumer information or that customer data. The onus is being placed on the organizations or the companies to make sure that that data is protected. Companies must comply with the laws of each country in which they do business. This is where it can get a bit cumbersome because the laws will change or vary from region to region. They may be very restrictive in one area and not so restrictive in the other. But as you can imagine, the best bet will be to comply with the most restrictive policies. That way you ensure that you're covering all bases. Let's take a look at some of the privacy compliance challenges. Data security requirements come from all angles. Data privacy laws, cybersecurity regulations, trade secret law, customer-specific contracts, consumer protection statutes, all of which can vary depending upon jurisdiction or location. These things can potentially overlap depending upon where you do business or, in some cases, may be slightly contradictory. It's important to thoroughly understand all the regulations in the areas in which you do business. Deletion of data is another big one. Understanding what data a company has in its possession, where it resides, and how long to retain that data is a major challenge. As companies grow, and we have terabytes upon petabytes, potentially exabytes of data, and that data is accumulated over a large period of time, user files, application files, data files, logging that grows and grows and grows. We have separate environments within our infrastructure. We have production. We have testing, dev, QA. And you may have multiple copies of that data. As things grow, data grows. A lot of times in a lot of situations, we don't understand, at least at a macro level, what all that data is because, there are copies of copies in many instances. We may delete the primary copy of that data, but there's like 5 or 6 or 10 other copies in lower environments or in test and dev, QA environments that exist that we may not necessarily be fully aware of. Data governments is a big one. Also, documentation, keeping up with requirements, especially with global companies. It's becoming increasingly complex. Requirements between various countries and even between states, local, federal, etc., they can sometimes overlap or even become slightly contradictory if you don't understand the nuances of those specific regulations. Some other ones to keep in mind, ethics and compliance. Collection of massive amounts of data from an ever-increasing number of sources, that can create, as you can imagine, privacy and also security challenges. Big data aggregation and analysis can create PII or personally identifiable information from disparate sources. What does that mean? Well, it means then we have pieces of information that by themselves don't necessarily identify someone. But when I start doing data aggregation, data analytics specifically, I can start pulling all these different pieces together and build a profile of someone that is very accurate. Those individual pieces of information become very telling of who a person is when looked at the whole body of information. Also, inadequate data management, defining who owns the data. Who's the data owner, or the governor. This also includes data lifecycle, how we delete, how he manage, how long that data is processed, analyzed, and secure. This entire conundrum becomes more and more complex. Then also we have insecure infrastructure. Data environments are often designed for speed or for scale, but not necessarily for security. In many instances, security is a bit of an afterthought as we know. It's not necessarily designed with that in mind from the beginning. A lot of companies with their dev and engineering departments, they view security as no as a service and that's changing luckily, the perception at least is changing. Security is an extremely important part of the entire ecosystem, and it has to be thought from day 1. It can't be an afterthought. It can't be a bolt on. The insecure infrastructure is creating major challenges because we have to go back and try to retrofit a lot of these environments. IoT devices or the Internet of Things devices, posing a major challenge because these things, again, are a lot of times consumer devices not necessarily designed with enterprise-type security in mind. When you bring those devices into an enterprise, you start to crack fissures in the security infrastructure, and you're fragmenting the security posture.

GDPR and Key Terminology

Next, one of the ones that gets a lot of attentionadays is GDPR, or the general data protection regulation. It's a privacy and security law that originated in the European Union in May of 2018. It imposes obligations onto organizations anywhere. This has reached beyond just the EU, Long as they target or collect data related to people in the EU. Just because you're located in the United States or maybe somewhere outside of the European Union, it doesn't necessarily mean you are not impacted by GDPR. What type of data does the GDPR cover? Well, it provides individuals, which are known as data subjects, more control over how organizations process or control the processing of their data, such things as names, locations, patient data and health records, email addresses, photos, essentially any data that could be used to identify a living person. Let's look at some GDPR key terminology. When it comes to personal data, let's say we have Mary here. Anything that could identify her, such as names, ID numbers, dates of birth, email addresses, online identifiers, photographs, religious beliefs, location data, and a number of other things, anything that can be used to uniquely identify her is covered under GDPR. So keep those things in mind when you're collecting data from customers. Do you have a legitimate use to know all of these things? As an example, are you collecting someone's date of birth, but you never have any need for that data? You're not going to wish them happy birthday. You're not going to send them a birthday card. It's not used for loyalty purposes or anything. Well, that might be ruled then as an unnecessary piece of information and you could be subject to regulation under the GDPR. It has to be specific. The Use has to be relevant, it has to have a purpose for being collected and also maintained.

GDPR Key Terms and Data Processing Principles
Processing is any operation, whether automated or a manual process, that is performed on personal data. A data processor is responsible for the processing of personal data on behalf of what's known as a data controller. A data controller is the person or the thing that determines the purpose and the means by which personal data is processed. as far as GDPR is concerned, there are six data processing principles. When we're collecting all this personal information, we need to make sure that they fall under these data processing principles. There needs to be lawfulness, fairness, and transparency. We have to have a lawful or a legal reason to gather that information. Purpose limitation, a specified use and explicit use and specified limit of time. Data minimization. We're only collecting what is necessary. If we're collecting someone's date of birth and we have no need for that data, then why are we collecting it? If we can't demonstrate and document why we need that data, then we could be subject to those regulations. Also accurate and, where possible, kept up to date. If we're gathering someone's information, they have the to update their own information. They have to have access to it and see what we're keeping on them. But also it needs to be kept up to date if it all possible. Also, storage limitation. Keep only as long as necessary. If we're keeping data for an indefinite period of time, we could be liable to GDPR regulations. If we only need that data for 6 months, then only keep it for 6 months and delete afterwards. Most importantly, we have to document and be able to show that that data is being

deleted. We just can't say it. We have to have processes in place and documentation in place to show that. Then integrity and confidentiality. Just like we have for any security tenant, the triad confidentiality, integrity, and availability, well, same thing here. We need to make sure that the data is kept secure. We have to demonstrate via documentation and the systems we have in place that we're making a best effort to keep that data secure. If we fail any of these six tenets, these six data processing principles, then that company can be held liable under certain parts of the GDPR.

Six Legal Grounds for Processing Personal Data
We have six legal grounds for processing personal data. We have to make sure we have that person's consent, it has to be explicit, and they have to be able to opt out just as easily as they opted in. There also has to be a legitimate interest. We need to be able to demonstrate and document that we have a legitimate interest to that data. Is there some contractual obligation that we process that data? Then a legal obligation, are we legally bound to either gather and process that data? Public authority and this one goes without saying. a lot of the things of the GDPR, public authorities aren't necessarily bound by those same underlying principles. Then vital interest is a matter of life and death. Whenever a company processes a customer's or a user's data, it has to fall under one of these six legal grounds as to why they're processing that data, consent, legitimate interest or some type of contract, a legal obligation, you're a public authority, or it's a vital interest, a matter of life and death. If you can demonstrate, and, This all has to be demonstrated and documented, it can be subject to audit of course, if one of those six things are being addressed, and typically it's going to be the top three that

you'll see consent, legitimate interest, or some type of contractual obligation, most companies will utilize those three as one of their legal grounds for processing, then you've met, at least on the surface, the grounds for GDPR processing of data.

GDPR Compliance and Penalties

But what happens if GDPR compliance is not met? Well, the GDPR provides for significant fines for non-compliance. There are two tiers of fines depending upon the type of infraction. Let's take a look at these. GDPR penalties, there's two tiers. A less severe infringement can go up to €10 million or 2% of the firm's worldwide annual revenue, whichever is higher. Not whichever is lower, whichever is higher in this instance. The second, more serious or more egregious infringements, can result in fines of up to €20 million or 4% of the firm's worldwide annual revenue, whichever is higher. It can be, very significant.

Compliance Frameworks

What is compliance? It is the adherence to a set of rules pertaining to people, process, and technology as it relates to policies, standards, regulations, laws. Let's look at some examples of compliance frameworks. We have HIPPA, the Health Insurance Portability Accountability Act. We have the GLBA, the Gramm-Leach-Bliley Act. And the other is PCI-DSS, the Payment Card Industry Data Security Standard. These are all very structured, very detailed compliance frameworks. A single business can, in fact, fall under the purview of multiple different types of regulations, depending upon where they do business with in the world. There are two different types of security compliance drivers. There's legislative mandates, things that must be done, and they're external to the organization, and then good business practices. That's what we should do or what should be done, and they're typically internal to the organization. Let's look at how these two things interact. We have external requirements, and we have internal requirements. External might be legislation like GDPR as an example or various laws or policies throughout, different parts of the world. Those things are all going to have external forces or external pressure on the company, and that's going to drive some of the internal requirements to make sure that they're complying with external requirements. We have enterprise security management. We have an overarching mandate or an overarching guideline. That's going to drive our enterprise security compliance requirements, such as policies, standards, procedures, and guidelines. Those things then have a direct impact on internal operations, security operations and other operations. They fall under that larger umbrella. The enterprise security compliance requirements also drive external operations as well and how we deal with partners, how we deal with vendors, how we deal with contractors, customers. All of these things are done to make sure the business operates in a good fashion or in an ethical fashion. We're driving revenue. But then it also makes sure that we are in compliance with external factors that could, if not followed properly, have a very negative impact on our business, a risk as great if not greater than any type of security breach, depending upon the severity of the non-compliance. If it's an egregious event that keeps taking place over and over the fines could be so great that it could put a company on a business. It's very important to take these things seriously and to devote the proper resources to make sure that they are adhered to properly.

NIST and the Cyber-security Framework (CSF)

NIST stands for the National Institute of Standards and Technology. And what they do is come up with frameworks for a number of different things, all different types of things related to IT in IT security, how things are deployed, best practices. And this specific one refers to a presidential executive order, and that's executive order 13636, that was designed or relegated to improving critical infrastructure cybersecurity. It's an important one for you to become familiar with. You can download this and read through this at your leisure. But a lot of companies, it's not just applied to a specific type of IT company, companies in all different types of industries that have any type of cyber security needs are adopting this framework as the basis of their own internal policies. It's a framework that was originally created in February of 2014, it was revised in January of 2017, and it consists of three parts. It's beyond the scope of this book to dig deeply into each of those three parts, but I want you to be aware of what they are. We have the framework core, we have the framework profile, and then also the framework implementation tiers.

PCI-DSS

PCI standing for payment card industry data security standard, hence the DSS. That protects, cardholder data. The IT impact, various levels of controls depending upon how a company interacts with credit card data. The more they interact with that data, there's different levels of controls that may apply. It gets deeper and more complex. Self-assessments, on-site audits, and also quarterly network scans are typically required to make sure you're in PCI compliance. Depending upon the size of the company and the things that you deal with, the level of transaction, you may have on-site auditors from PCI, on site to do these types of things, on-site audits, quarterly network scans, to make sure that cardholder data is not being exposed, is not being compromised, or doesn't have the potential to be compromised. We need to make sure we have the security controls in place. Organization types, merchants, banks, credit card processors, and others, anybody that deals with PCI-related data or credit card information. If you deal in one of those industries. PCI is probably familiar to you as well.

Enterprise Security Framework (ESF)
Next up, let's talk about enterprise security frameworks, what it is. An enterprise security framework, or an ESF, is a guide that we can use to create all of the documentation, the reporting within our organization. There are a number of free and existing guides already out there, we don't have to start from square one. Use existing guides where possible as a starting point. A great example comes from the National Institute of Standards and Technology, or NIST. They have a publication SP 800-53 that is a great guide to act as a starting point. It's recommended security controls for federal information systems and organizations, but it doesn't apply just to federal organizations. It's the standard enterprise security framework that's used by organizations of all types, all sizes, not necessarily just federal organizations. Another good one is ISO 27001/27002, also COBIT, which stands for control objectives for information and related technology. There are a number of guides out there that gives us structured documentation around planning, assessments, and also monitoring. These guides are very comprehensive, and in some cases, they may not be comprehensive enough. It depends upon your organization, but at least it gives you a good starting point.

NIST SP 800-53 and ISO 27001

The NIST publication SP 800-53 is comprised of a number of categories, a number of families, and each of those families have a number of subsets or controls. There are 18 different categories or IDs, access control, awareness training, audit and accountability. Each of these are broken down into subsets that have definitions and parameters around each of these subsets, each of these individual controls, that you can then used to formulate your own enterprise security frameworks within your own organization. Let's take, for instance, we take one of these IDs or one of these families. If we break it down a little bit further, we can see security assessment and authorization or configuration management. Each of those has subsets. As an example, security assessment and authorization policies and procedures or security assessments or how about information security connections. If you further drill down, each of those has a number of processes and procedures that need to be followed or should be followed. This is a guideline. It's not a hard fast rule. But these are guidelines of best practices that should be followed to make sure that your organization is secure. And what this does is it allows you to provide due diligence and say, hey, we've done the research. We're following best practices. We have a guide in place that shows every aspect of our business, every aspect of our information security controls, our security posture, and here's what we're doing to address any issues that may come up. Another good example is ISO 27001. It has similarly a number of different controls, a number of different IDs, or, in this case, references and then a number of controls within each. Information security policies, organization of information security, human resources security. And then each of these, you'll see in parentheses is the number of controls that apply to that category. Again, a slightly different approach, but the same net effect. It gives us a guideline that we can use to formulate our own framework for our organization. If we drill down as an example into, let's say, A.9, Access Control, it has 14 separate controls within that group. If we take a look at that under Access Control, these are all the different things, and each of these has additional parameters and additional guides and best practices under each of these topics that we can use to follow and draft our own documentation, our own policies, how we monitor things. And then, depending upon your organization and how you want to formulate your own plan, you may map one to the other. You may have NIST controls, or you may have the ISO 27001 controls, but you may have a plan, or you may be following compliance guidelines by some external regulation that says you need to map to one or the other. Well you can show by saying, hey, under the category of least privilege, AC-6, under NIST, this is what I'm following. But it also maps to ISO 27001 under A.9.1.2, 9.2.3, and so on and so on. You can show that you have controls in place that will put you in compliance with various regulations.

Cloud Security Alliance (CSA)
The Cloud Security Alliance or the CSA have defined a number of categories for Security as a Service offerings. I just want to list these out you have an idea of what types of services or the breadth of services that these Security as a Service providers can offer to customer organizations. So business continuity, disaster recovery, continuous monitoring, data lost prevention, email security and encryption, identity and access management. Also, intrusion management, network security, security assessment, the SIEM service that we talked about, vulnerability scanning, and web security. That's pretty much everything or at least a

very large part of the security services that a company would want to have in house. If you're a small company or a mid-sized company and you don't have the expertise and the personnel to handle all of these things, Security as a Service would definitely be a viable option to take a look at.

SSAE 18, SOC 1, 2, and 3

To mention risk assessment frameworks without getting into the weeds too, too much, I want to make sure that we're aware of SSAE 18, which stands for Statement on Standards for Attestation Engagements., it's an accounting framework, and that governs the way that organizations report on their various compliance controls. Our own environment, if we're SSAE 18-certified, we understand that all of our security controls are in place. Or if we're dealing with a hosting or a cloud provider, if they are certified, then we know that their controls are up to snuff and also the vendors that they deal with. Let's take a look at that in a little more detail. When talking about geolocation or hybrid cloud security, as an example, let's say, for instance, we're not going to stand up our own data center, so we want to stand up our infrastructure, our applications, web servers, and also customer-facing applications. We want to instantiate those things at someone else's data center, so a colocation facility. Since we're a security-minded organization, we want to make sure that the people we deal with, the colocation facility, we want to look for that SSAE 18 certification. We're talking about Infrastructure as a Service, Software as a Service, and also their virtual infrastructure. It also applies to bare metal, but in this instance, we're talking about as a service type of applications. All of those things, we're looking for that certification. That certification has three main components. We've got SOC 1, and that deals with compliance on financial reporting controls. Then we have

SOC 2, certification, and that deals with actual security controls themselves. That's what we're most interested in, making sure that the facility is as secure as possible. And then there's SOC 3, which is like SOC 2 certification, but it leaves out the specifics, the specific systems. That way, that information can be publicly accessible without giving too much information about the actual systems and the underpinnings behind the scenes, of how things are run. It allows someone who's evaluating a hosting provider or a managed service provider. It can look and say, they're certified, they have SOC 3 certification, but it doesn't give the nuts and bolts as to what applications and what systems are running behind the scenes. And what this also does is ensures the data center's channel partners and vendors also, very important, the channel partners and the vendors also utilize the same security controls as the data center and the hosting provider because, as you may or may not know, a lot of times they will subcontract out certain work, whether it's working in the data center. There may be contractors that are doing the racking and stacking, the cabling. It could be power and cooling, the HVAC folks. All of those different subcontractors and vendors and also the vendors from the actual hardware, whether it's network, compute, or storage, when those vendors come in, it makes sure that they are also certified to the same level that the data center is certified, and it gives you the added layer of confidence that you're dealing with a secure facility.

Chapter 3 Benchmarks & Secure Configuration Guides

Next we have benchmarks and secure configuration guides. Some things that I want you to think about are web servers, or public facing servers, operating systems, application servers, and then network infrastructure devices. All of these things I talked about just a moment ago, are ways that we can either keep people out, or if we don't lock them down enough, they are ways that they can get in. Web servers are public facing, that's one of the biggest targets because it's publicly accessible. People can bang against those types of servers all day long, and if we don't have safeguards in place and we don't become aware that people are doing that, they can spend a lot of time brute forcing their way into those servers, and from there it's off to the races if they're able to elevate privileges, execute some remote code, crash the system, or gain, administrative or root level privileges come in, pivot, go through our network. We don't want to allow that to happen. Same thing with operating systems. We want to lock it down as much as possible. We want to make sure that we disable services we don't need. We want to make sure we harden the services that are there to limit that attack surface or reduce that attack surface as much as possible. Application servers, again, are very critical as well. Applications need to be constantly updated, just like we update the servers themselves with operating system updates, security patches, firmware updates, BIOS updates, HBA or NIC drivers. The applications themselves also experience issues, vulnerabilities, so the applications have to be patched and kept up to date, just like everything else. And then network infrastructure devices, our routers, switches. All these things need to be patched, updated as much as possible. We need to make sure we establish a routine a lifecycle management, a patch management process, whether that's weekly, monthly, quarterly. But then also a process in place for out-of-band updates. If something comes out as a critical or zero-day, you need to make sure we have processes in place to alert everyone and then also to push those changes out as quickly as possible.

Systems Hardening

Some concepts that apply to all of the things, systems hardening, disabling or uninstalling unnecessary services. Make sure we use secure protocols. Don't use Telnet, use SSH. Use FTP Secure instead of FTP. Use HTTPS when possible instead of just HTTP. Encrypting when possible, using secure protocols when possible. We also want to make sure we use least permissive or least privilege principles. Don't give people more access or more so than they need. If all they need to be able to do is read something, don't give them the ability to maybe modify or delete. The more we give them, the more chances they have to exploit those extra privileges. Least permissive/least privilege. Also, set up monitoring and alerting. Things that are not monitored are not payed attention to that just increases our risk. Disable the things we don't need, and the things that are left, make sure you monitor, you set triggers with thresholds, whether it's through machine learning and you learn over time what's normal or what might be an anomaly, or you just set up thresholds and triggers. If it hits a certain percentage, a certain number of failures in a period of time, there needs to be some type of alerting set up. Logging and alerting, logging so we can go back and identify trends, and then alerting so that we can become aware away when these security breaches or potential breaches are in fact incurred. Also, you have to establish baselines. If we don't have a baseline, we don't have a way to determine what's normal and what's abnormal. If all we know is the server is running at 85%, or we have 500 failed login attempts a day, or we have whatever the case might be, if we don't know that well, 500's normal, every single day it's the same way, we have thousands of people in the environment, yep, 500 people a day mistype their password or they fail a login, we might think that's ridiculously high and spend a lot of resources trying to dig in when it's not necessary, or we may think it's low, and we may think we have thousands a day, and we only have maybe a dozen, but on this specific day there's 500, well, if that doesn't raise a flag with us and we don't start investigating, that could have been someone either attempting or getting into our system and breaching our defenses, and we did nothing about it. Having baselines in place allow us to very quickly determine, it raises the red flags when something is not. Then also periodically audit. It's important that we periodically go through and establish new baselines, update when appropriate, what's the new normal, and also audit all of our different systems to make sure we're not missing anything or to make sure people are not trying to cover their tracks. Because if we had insider threats, people inside the company, they can, do their dirty work, and then if we don't monitor closely and periodically audit, well, then they can come in and cover their tracks very effectively, making it much more difficult for us to try to track anything down.

Vendor and Control Diversity
With vendor diversity, we want to utilize more than one vendor. We reduce impacts of vulnerabilities, upgrades, and patching potentially. If we have only one provider of all of our switches or all of our servers or all of our network cards, if we only have one of them, we're locked in. If we have a breach or a vulnerability, that vulnerability is potentially

everywhere. If we have multiple vendors, well, yes, you have multiple vendors to deal with, but you also limit the impact of a specific vulnerability because maybe only a third or a quarter of your environment may be impacted. Some other things that are the intangibles from an IT security perspective, things that the IT security professional may or may not think about, is also vendor diversity gives you some leverage when dealing with those vendors. You get better pricing. You might get better attention from that vendor, so they're updating their systems more often because they want to earn your business. They don't just think that they're the only game in town. If they realize they're competing with other vendors for your business, they're going to be a lot more attentive typically. There's some intangibles there as well. Also control diversity. More gates for a hacker to get through. The more locks on the door, the harder it is for them to accomplish their task. A lot of times they're going to say, well you know what? I'm going to spend my time on something that's a little bit easier of a target. So control diversity, again, for the same reason we talked about vendor diversity, control diversity gives us the best of breed in a number of areas as well, not the least of which is additional protection against vulnerabilities. In this chapter we covered regulations, standards, and legislation. We talked about several key frameworks that you should be familiar with, and then benchmarks and secure configuration guides to make sure our systems are as secure as possible and some of the ways that we can either automate or templatize that process.

Chapter 4 How to Implement Policies for Organizational Security

In this chapter, we'll be talking about Implementing Policies within Organizational Security. We'll be talking about personnel and the associated issues with managing, maintaining, and keeping things secure. We'll talk about diversity of training techniques, along with third-party risk management, data classification, governance, and retention, and then we'll talk about various credential policies along with organizational policies. Let's first talk about the importance of policies in reducing risk. Policies provide standards for use and behavior, such things as a privacy policy and acceptable use policy. It could be security policies, or it could be things like mandatory vacations, job rotations, separation of duty, or things like the concept of least privilege. Guidelines provide advice on how to proceed. They're not necessarily hard-fast rules. They could be rules within an organization, but typically they're just guidelines on how to proceed.

Job Rotation
When we talk about job rotation, what it does is keep one person from becoming so ingrained in a specific role that they can easily hide their tracks. That helps to mitigate against things like embezzlement, fraud, espionage, data, exfiltration? So one person doesn't sit in a job Long and just think or assume they're going to be there forever so they can go ahead and do whatever they want. They know they're going to be rotated out every so often. That keeps them from doing things that may or may not be on the up and up because they realize they're going to be out of that position before too long. Then also, when folks are moved or rotated

from one job to the next, be aware of job creep or responsibility creep. That's where people retain s and privileges as they move from one role to another? Over time, people have the potential to accumulate things they no longer need. So by having things set up via group policy or some type of automated method so when they change roles or change jobs they're pulled out of one group, those s go away automatically, and then when they're added into a new group, they have new sets of s provisioned. Even if for the most part they're the same s, it's a good idea to remove them from one group and then put them into a new one. That way there's no guessing involved, and there's a much smaller chance for things getting missed. Then provide least privileges, making sure they only have enough to do their current job. These things prevent things like snooping, inadvertent access, accidental deletion of files or folders, and that could be potentially hundreds or thousands or even millions of files and folders. If someone were to accidentally delete or rename a root folder, all of the things underneath could potentially disappear, depending upon if that's a share or a group folder. So having just the amount of privileges that someone needs goes a long way to help prevent these types of things.

Mandatory Vacations
When it comes to mandatory vacations, some of the reasons behind requiring that is it keeps personnel away from company assets for a period of time? That enables anomalies to be discovered much, much more easily because things like fraud or theft or even collusion, when we have a fresh set of eyes, we can see things that may otherwise be overlooked or potentially hidden. When someone else comes in and then sees how that person previous was doing things, they can uncover potentially unscrupulous activities, things that are

against company policy, or potentially down illegal? So having mandatory vacations helps uncover some of these potential pitfalls.

Separation of Duties

This is a security practice that doesn't allow one person to control all facets of a transaction, checks and balances you can think of it as. Writing checks versus cashing checks, approvals for expenditures, bookkeeping and accounting? We don't want people who write the checks to be able to also cash the checks. There's no oversight at that point? We need to make sure that things are able to be audited and not easily hidden or covered up. Another way of putting it is it keeps one person from wearing too many hats.

Least Privilege

Next, we have the concept of least privilege. This is providing a user with the least amount of privileges they need to do their work. Providing just enough that it helps mitigate the risk, installing applications that they shouldn't, malware, spyware, viruses. Keeps them from accidentally accessing stuff they shouldn't be accessing or deleting a renaming files and folders that they shouldn't. It also helps mitigate configuration drift issues in that it prevents users from installing or updating drivers. Firmware, patches? Those types of things typically should not be done by the user themselves. It should be pushed out by IT administration, or IT security, or whatever centralized group would be responsible for provisioning.

Clean Desk Policies

If you think about it, it can go a long way to reducing data theft? It can discourage prying eyes, and it also may be compliant with various regulations? Enforcing that policy, you should have that documented in writing, part of their onboarding or new hire presentation or new hire packet, and then also do random checks. Making sure they don't have excess clutter all over the place. They don't have usernames, passwords, confidential information, account numbers written on sticky notes or written on pieces of paper that can be easily observed by others. And then also, when they leave their workspace, make sure those things are locked up in a secure drawer or some type of secure location. A little bit of common sense, just making sure that confidential information or things that should not be seen by others are not lying around on the desk. So keeping a desk nice and orderly and clean goes a long way. When you leave, you just clean your desk for the night, put things that should be secured in a secure location.

Background Checks, NDAs, and Role-based Awareness Training

A few additional personnel management concepts would be background checks. Ensure employees are appropriate to work in a specific environment, adhere to company policies. Some organizations, some companies require background checks, others do not. But background checks go a long way in helping to make sure that the people that you hire either have the credentials that they say they do or have the ability or the permissions, the clearance to work in a specific area. Depending upon the nature of your environment, if it's classified or highly secretive information, background checks very well may be in order. Next we have nondisclosure agreements, or NDAs. It's an agreement, usually at the time of hire that employees will review and sign and agree not to disclose company secrets, proprietary information. An NDA may also be given by third parties or vendors that you deal with so they can review new information, things that may not necessarily be publicly available yet, like road map items or new technologies, so that you have an opportunity to try them out or at least plan for them. They may have you sign an NDA at the time of the meeting or the presentation, or you may have in NDA on file with that company or with that vendor that covers any of those types of presentations. Next is role-based awareness training. These are simulated situations to ensure that employees know how to respond appropriately in a specific scenario or specific situation. It could be failover testing for applications, like in a DR, disaster recovery, or business continuity setting, application testing. It could also be things like even an active shooter situation for things where the building may be compromised or breached. It could be phishing campaigns. IT security may put out some scam emails or phishing emails to make sure employees know how to recognize them and then report them to the proper location. Role-based training periodically is a great idea to help reinforce concepts and to make sure that people are adhering to company policies and procedures.

Chapter 5 Monitoring & Balancing

Let's talk about monitoring in general and why a company can do that, why they should, and perhaps why they shouldn't. Use cases for monitoring. Number 1 would be to boost productivity. That may or may not be true depending upon your company, but boosting productivity. You can track time spent on social media, on web surfing, non-related work activities. Number 1, the company can be aware of what's happening. Number 2, the employee knows if they're monitored, and if those activities are looked at, they will typically do less of that with the hope being spend more time on actual work. Next, deter or detect criminal activity. Detect intrusions or breaches, criminal activities such as threats and harassment or illegal behaviors. employees doing things they shouldn't be doing, whether it's out illegal or if they're harassing other employees or using it for non company-related activity that may come back to the company and cause ill will or cause harm. And it can also be used to track employees location. In this case, we would ensure that remote workers are adhering to company policies, working at their prescribed locations, traveling safely. We have the opportunity or the ability to monitor where they're at so that if they say they're going to be a location A, we can look at our GPS tracking software and say, yep, they're at that location, they're at that job site. If they're traveling to or from a specific job site, especially if they're in a company vehicle, then you can potentially track the speed that they're going, the direction they're going, making sure they're taking main roads versus back roads or tolls. It's also possible to geofence locations so that if they leave a specific area, you get notified. Or if they enter a specific area, you're notified. Then, lastly, to protect IP or intellectual property, you want to ensure that proprietary company, employee, or customer data is secure and not being removed from the company. We can monitor things like data exfiltration. You can monitor ingress and egress, firewalls, DLP or data loss prevention systems, intrusion detection and prevention systems. All of these things can work together in tandem to make sure that your intellectual property is protected. A company, again, has the opportunity or the ability, not necessarily saying it's or wrong, it's going to depend upon your location, your part of the world that you live in, and, of course, the company that you work for, but they have the ability to monitor an employee. That would typically be monitoring desktop activity or laptop activity, what they do on that specific piece of equipment, because, again, it's company owned, the company has the to see what data is on that device and how it's being used. It could also be email - typically it will be work related email, but depending upon your location and your jurisdiction, a company may also be able to access personal email. If you're using a corporate device to access personal email, then they may have actual rights to see that personal email. So keep those things in mind. Then it goes without saying, a smartphone, especially if its company issued, all of the transactions on that smartphone could be monitored by the company. Even if it's a BYO device, depending upon the MDM software, the mobile device management software on that smartphone, they may be able to view or should be able to view content on that phone that is corporate or company related, not necessarily personal information. That's the nice part about some of the MDM software, it can partition a smartphone between a corporate side and a personal side so that it can be wiped or remotely access only the corporate data. And then activity logs. Coming and going logging on, logging off, entering a building, exiting a building. GPS activity on cars, locations, speed, all that good stuff. All of these things can potentially be monitored, not saying that they are or that it's. Again, it's going to be jurisdictionally based and also, to some extent, based on industry.

Balancing What's Reasonable

All of that comes down to balancing what's reasonable. A defined privacy and acceptable use policy goes a long way. We need to make sure that the employee knows from the beginning what is acceptable and what's not. And they also understand what can be monitored and what not, and they sign off on them. Then we're balancing that with an employee expectation of privacy, like what is reasonable for an employee to expect is private versus public or versus corporate viewed, and making sure everyone is on the same page. Then, making sure we have BYO devices and remote employees covered as well so they understand if it's a BYO device, if you're accessing corporate resources, then the corporation or the company has access or should have access to that data. If it's personal data, then maybe not. But, again, depending upon the MDM software that's installed, the company may have the ability to see only the corporate-related information, be able to wipe that device remotely.

New Tools Are Constantly Developed

It's important to understand, however, that new tools are constantly being developed, and we can monitor things like login time, logout time, overall productivity, social media postings, again not saying it's or wrong, but the ability is there, emails, full content of emails, keywords so you can check to see if specific things are being talked about or mentioned in emails, also live stream of users desktops.

Depending upon the company that you work for and the software they have installed on desktops, it is possible with the tools to bring up a user's desktop and see what they're doing in real time, livestream what that user is doing, and then remotely lock screens, or covertly install or uninstall agents to do additional features and functionality, additional monitoring, security-related things. Then also display messages on users desktops so that you can get the word out about specific security initiatives, or company initiatives, or just general company branding.

Monitoring Social Media

When it comes to monitoring social media, it's worth noting that 26 states currently in the U.S. have passed laws barring employers from forcing employees to provide access to social media accounts. But it is worth noting that over half the states in the U.S. have in fact passed laws barring employers from that, and then 16 states have barred academic institutions from forcing students to provide access, refusing to admit or otherwise disciplining for social media posting. It gets back to that balancing act between what is public or what is personal versus company related. As far as social media is concerned, the law is starting to lean more to the side of the user.

Employee Protections

That leads us into our next topic, and that is employee protections. The Fourth Amendment protects against unlawful search and seizure here in the US. It applies to the public sector, which is government and law enforcement, but it does not apply to the private sector. That's a key distinction that people may or may not necessarily be aware of. Companies are free to monitor employees. That can be work-related or personal, email, communications while at work. You're at the office, and you're using the company network, using the company Wi-Fi, resources, potentially laptop or desktop, mobile phone. All of those things are, in fact, company assets, so they have the right to monitor those assets to make sure they're being used appropriately.

Onboarding / Offboarding

Processes should be defined for both onboarding and offboarding, so that users should have a clear understanding of what's acceptable, what's allowed, and what is expected. This should be in writing. It should be presented during that onboarding process, and then they should sign some documentation stating that they've read it and understand. Additionally, companies should ensure they take possession of all company assets when an employee leaves. That way, secrets or data or confidential info, doesn't walk out the door. They should also conduct what's called an exit interview, so they understand why the employee is leaving, was there a gripe, was there some grievance? In other words, what was the reason for them leaving the company? The company can address those issues if valid, and improve their overall process and procedure.

Culture and Creating a Culture of Security

Culture is the set of shared attitudes, values, goals, and practices that characterizes an institution or an organization. When talking about creating culture, where do you start? Well, first and foremost, focus on the weakest links. Individuals are the weak link in that they have access to the business' systems, computers, networks. Make sure we understand where we focus on our people. Part of that is bringing in diversity, disparate groups to share experiences. This enables executives, managers, and also individual contributors to all share and learn from one another's experiences and understand each other's needs because not everybody is going to look at things the same way. They're not going to experience things the same way. If all we do is surround ourselves with people that are just like us, then we develop a bit of an echo chamber, and we never change. We're never able to grow and develop other ideas, other opinions. By having that diversity of thought, you bring in expertise, you bring in opinions, viewpoints from different directions. By having all these differing views, it benefits the collective. It makes everything better. Then also, ensure that training is timely, relevant, and interactive. Engaging training that is applicable to a person's job or function is much more likely to be interesting, memorable, and actionable than some cookie-cutter presentation that deals perhaps with an industry they're not even in or with a highlight reel from 30 years ago with technology that doesn't even exist anymore. Make sure that the training is relevant. It applies to that specific industry. And if it can be customized specifically to that company, that's even better.

Chapter 6 Awareness & Skills Training

Setting the stage as far as understanding what is appropriate, what types of training, what types of skills need to be developed. You can put this on a map and say, here where we are today, and here's where we want to get to in the future. You can plot your current level of awareness. And then after meeting with senior management and getting an understanding of what their expectations are, you can say, here's our desired level of awareness. In between there is the gap. That's the gap analysis. That allows you to list out and create a skills matrix, of what's necessary. What skills, resources, and infrastructure may be needed to make these things happen, and then devise a training plan to achieve those awareness goals. Everyone's on the same page. We understand where we are today, where we want to be tomorrow, the skills and resources and infrastructure that's needed to make that happen. And then once the plan is in place and we set in motion, we understand it's an iterative process, it's continuous improvement. This can also span suppliers, vendors, stakeholders, and, of course, key customers. Everyone's on the same page, and they all have the ability to contribute to the overall success.

Awareness Training
When it comes to delivering this training, the awareness training, we need to understand who the intended audience is. Are they individual groups, or is it company-wide? Are they internal only or suppliers and also key customers? Then talk about the methods of delivery. That could be posters spread throughout the company, it could be company swag with a mission statement, it could be on the company intranet, via newsletters. All of these things should reinforce

that common message so that the target audience sees that message over and over again. Then make sure we have clearly defined expected outcomes. What is success? It's very hard to understand if you're successful if you have no idea what success means. Having these things clearly defined goes a long way to understanding when you've hit the mark.

Skills Training

When it comes to skills training, we have goals and objective. We need expected outcomes and success criteria. We need to make sure we define those things we understand what is success. We also want to make sure that we adhere to company standards. Also, a big part of creating and delivering quality training and making sure that we're covering all the bases is proper funding. Executive buy-in and participation is also key. Next, when we're talking about the specific skills, we need to make sure that we define the intended audience. Different training based on different groups, so not necessarily a one size fits all. There may be instances where training fits across the board, but make sure it's as individualized as possible. Then identify gaps in skills and create training to level up employees to make sure that they have the skills they need to do their jobs. Also, it's beneficial to create varying methods of delivery, whether it's classroom, online, study groups, or it could be CVTs. Then lastly, we have metrics and KPIs. We have to make sure that we measure the effectiveness. That also makes future funding requests much easier because you can go ahead and show the actual benefits and results of the training that you've delivered. This also has the byproduct of continuing awareness, and it builds upon itself. There should also be a continuing effort, whether that be monthly, quarterly, or yearly, it's going to depend upon your organization and your needs, but it should be an ongoing effort. Then gamify things where possible, contests or games to help measure participation and also make things competitive. People tend to perform better when there's some type of competition involved.

Funding and Executive Buy-in
How is the awareness and skills training funded? It could be department funded. It could be cybersecurity or business continuity budgets. It could also be company-wide if it's a much bigger endeavor. Then when it comes to presenting our idea and making sure we have executive buy-in, do we create the training internally, or do we contract third-party training materials? Measurements of effectiveness are critical to long-term success, especially when we're reporting back to executives and key stakeholders. They want to make sure that the funding they provided is effective and they're getting some type of return on investment. Then, lastly, create mechanisms for feedback and for constant improvement, a feedback loop, as much of real-time feedback as possible, but then make sure that feedback is acted upon. It doesn't necessarily do a lot of good to gather all this information, all this feedback, and then do nothing with it. Take the information that's given and then tweak the training. Next time around, make it a little bit better. Constantly improve, continuous improvement.

Continuous Improvement
You need to identify needs, design the training, deliver the training, do assessments, and evaluate. That's a continuous loop. The goal is long-term awareness, increased readiness, and continuous improvement. We're not training just to train people, we want to have specific skills developed to help improve the security posture of our organization, developing methods to obtain feedback, metrics, and KPIs to

measure effectiveness. Then refine that over time and act on the feedback, fix what doesn't work, and strive to constantly improve. It's a never-ending process, it's not a one-and-done, it's an iterative, ongoing process.

Chapter 7 Technology & Vendor Diversity

When it comes to diversity, technologies, vendors, cryptographic keys even, security controls, all of these things will benefit from diversity. The more diversity that you have, you typically get best of breed, you get differing opinions, different ways of looking at things, different ways to solve problems, and then with security controls, you're not as reliant on any one specific technology or vendor. As far as technology diversity is concerned, utilizing more than one type of technology to accomplish a given task. The thought being that it would safeguard against a bug or a vulnerability being able to take down an entire system. If you have more than one technology in play, if one is affected by a bug or a specific vulnerability, it doesn't necessarily affect the rest. It also provides a method of failback or failover in the event of an incident.

Vendor Diversity
Next when it comes to vendor diversity, vendor diversity helps safeguard against supply chain attacks, also vendor lock-in, more financial leverage. If you have all of your eggs in one basket, with one vendor, than they potentially have more financial leverage over you and could be less willing to negotiate on price. And there is a real business risk of having all systems, data, technology, and knowledge in the hands of a single vendor. It's not necessarily a bad thing. If the vendor's good and they represent more than one company and you're getting diversity of thought, that's not necessarily a bad thing. But generally speaking, vendor diversity in and of itself helps safeguard against those things.

Service-level Agreement (SLA)

SLA or a service level agreement is a legal document that you need to be put in place before you engage the services or interact with third parties. That way you clearly identify a number of things. It identifies and defines things like uptime, reliability, and response times and then also penalties for non performance and spells out things like vicarious liability if, in fact, the folks that you do business with subcontract some of their work out as well. That liability may pass down to their contractors as well.

Memorandum of Understanding (MOU) and Master Services Agreement (MSA)

An MOU, or a memorandum of understanding is a letter of intent, it's not a formalized contract, and it specifies mutually accepted expectations between two or more people, typically not legally binding and more flexible than contracts. Then also, certain legal remedies like liquidated damages, vicarious liability may not be available. Just something to keep in mind, though, regardless of how cautious the authors might be, MOUs pose risks. In a business environment, these informal agreements lack the formality and the standardizations of a contract that would protect both parties during a project. As a result, legal remedies might be nonexistent in the event of a nonperformance issue or a lack of adherence to the MOU. While these things may be good or good enough to get the ball rolling, I would recommend contracts and SLAs in place wherever possible. Next, we have something referred to as a master services agreement, or an MSA. This is a contract reached between two parties in which the parties agree to most of the terms that will govern future transactions and future agreements. We're trying to expedite future transactions. Most of the terms are negotiated ahead of time, and then that way only terms specific to the transaction at hand need to be negotiated. Everything that's pretty common across the board can just be referenced in the MSA. That way, every time you have a new engagement with your vendors and suppliers, instead of having to renegotiate pricing and margins and all that good stuff, and performance penalties and SLAs and all the things that may be pretty much standard across the board, you can negotiate those things out ahead of time. Then for each new engagement, only the things that are specific to that engagement need to be negotiated. Everything else can just have a pointer or a reference to the MSA.

Business Partner Agreement (BPA)
Next is the BPA, or a business partner agreement. This defines the roles on each side of a manufacturer and reseller relationship, also, the decision making process and the management style, how capital is to be distributed, salary, distributions. All the things between business partners that should be spelled out so there's no confusion. There's no, I want this and I want that, but we never talked about it. There's some type of confusion. No, all of those things should be spelled out and defined ahead of time via a BPA. That way, that confusion gets taken out of the equation.

EOL / EOS
EOL and EOS, stands for End of life and end of service. Maintaining documentation of contracts and service dates, it's critical here, so it helps with budgeting and with long term planning. We have to understand when our equipment hits the floor and when it's going to leave the floor, so that way we can budget properly and that way, we're also not at risk. Because if we don't plan those things, then we're going to invariably get hit with some type of funding surprise, we're going to have extended maintenance fees at the end of our contract. In other words, let's say we bought 500 desktops and at the end of a 5-year period, if we're not prepared to buy brand new, typically the vendor will extend maintenance, but at an uplift or an up charge, so it's going to be more than it would be if we bought

new. But if you don't have the capital to buy new, all we have is opex, not capex, we have to extend maintenance, that could be a surprise, that could be a hit to our budget and create a shortfall that we're not necessarily prepared for. Also, there is some increased risk as the vendors gain leverage because they understand that, hey, we need to refresh our equipment or we're at risk of things failing or if the equipment is not just end of life, but end of service. We can't even get service on it anymore, and they realize we have to upgrade, well, they're are a lot less likely to negotiate because they realize they don't have to. By maintaining end of life and end of service documentation, proper planning, all these things help reduce that risk to help reduce budgetary surprises and also helps reduce headaches for you down the road when management comes knocking and saying, you have that LRP for me, that long-range plan, I need to understand what's our budget looks like for next year and you don't have that, well, that's not a necessarily good place to be, so always make sure you have documentation, it's kept up to date, and you understand when things hit the floor and when things were set to leave the floor.

Data Retention

All of this boils down to data retention, so the continued storage of an organization's data for compliance or for business reasons. Data retention policies are created often as a collaboration between legal, IT, and business owners. You may have a company-wide policy that says you're going to maintain data for X amount of months or years, or it may vary depending upon the type of data or by department. But generally speaking, creating a data retention policy and adhering to that policy can reduce an organization's storage costs by purging old data or by moving that data to lower tiers of storage.

User Account

User accounts are unique and used for each person accessing a resource. That should be common knowledge, but just to make sure. A unique identifier is assigned to each account. As an example, in a Windows environment, every user account gets what's called a security ID, or a SID. The computer systems identify the user by the SID. The user account name is a human readable one that we can remember, but the SID is what's used to identify that user. Every user should have their own account, and as we've talked about before with the concept of least privilege, the users should have the least amount of privileges required to do their work.

Shared, Generic, Guest, and Service Accounts
We have shared and generic accounts and credentials. Each user should have their own non-administrative account. Shared accounts are too difficult to troubleshoot or audit in the event of a breach, so, we should avoid them whenever possible. Do not share accounts between people, because if you think about it, if you have 10 or 15 or 100 people using the same account, how can you possibly know who logged in, who logged out, who accessed the file? You might be able to see the username, but you don't know who that user belongs to, who that username references. Make sure everyone has their own account. That way, you can lock individual people out if necessary, or if you do have to go back and audit, you can tell who accessed the file and when. Next is guest accounts. Guest accounts should be used very sparingly, so kiosks and other public access locations are fine, typically, but the OS should be reimaged frequently and locked down or hardened as much as possible. The takeaway here is guest accounts for the most part are a no-no. We should not use them. Again, it's very much the same as a shared or generic account because we don't know who's using the account. Using them in a very specific situation or scenario is but generally speaking, disable them whenever possible. Next, we have service accounts. A service account

should be used only for services, as the name implies, but not for users, and unique for each service. Troubleshooting, audits, and revoking permissions when necessary are much easier if we have clearly defined service accounts. The service account name references what service it's using, and then we maintain individual ones as much as possible. That way, auditing becomes much easier. Otherwise it can turn into a nightmare.

Privileged Accounts

Privileged accounts should be used sparingly, only to perform admin-level functions. Even administrators should have a regular user account that they use typically throughout the day. If they need to do something on an administrative level, then they can invoke that privileged account when necessary to perform specific tasks. But, otherwise, generally speaking, use that non-admin account. That helps with the spread of malware, worms, all types of ransomware, because typically those types of malicious programs will operate in the context of the user that's logged in. If you're logged in as an admin, and you have the ability to do pretty much anything, well, then does that piece of malware. If you're logged in as a regular user who doesn't have a lot of privileges and you download or accidentally download a piece of malware or ransomware or what have you, there's a lot less chance that an actual piece of malicious software can do as much harm.

Chapter 8 Change Management & Asset Management

The ultimate purpose of change management is to reduce risk, it's also an administrative and a technical control. What we're doing is coordinating changes throughout the environment. We also need to ensure that procedures are followed, such things as established change or maintenance windows and also documented methods of procedures, or MOPs. Then, if something were to go wrong during a maintenance as an example, if we have a properly documented MOP, or an M-O-P, then they should have backout instructions as well, so that if something goes south halfway through the maintenance, we know how to back out of that and get back to a last known good state. Along those same lines, change management should have approval, an approval chain to document understanding and compliance. Has the change been tested? Is there a rollback or backout procedure documented, that should be included in the MOP. Has it been peer reviewed or is it just the person implementing the change? If it all possible, it should be peer reviewed so that code can be looked at, a second set of eyes can catch mistakes, reducing risk wherever possible. Then lastly, have affected users been notified? It's very important that users understand what's happening, if their servers need to be rebooted, if their service is going to go down for a period of time. All of these things should be communicated way ahead of time so that they have ample opportunity to reduce risk on their side and then also have someone available to validate changes, validate success once the maintenance is complete. Then lastly, when it comes to documentation, we need to make sure we document the work to be performed, any downstream systems that might be affected, servers, storage, network, applications. Also make sure we notify everyone involved or everyone that needs to be notified when that change begins and then notify when the changes end. And then if we have a maintenance call or a maintenance bridge setup, the teams that need to jump on and verify and then validate their applications and make sure that everything is back up and running before that maintenance window comes to a close.

Asset Management

It's very important from a compliance standpoint we understand how many of any one thing we have in the environment. As an example, if we have 5,000 servers, but we only bought 3,000 licenses or we have 500 instances of an application, but we only bought 2 copies, when it comes time to do a true up, that company comes in and asks to audit our environment. If we're not compliant, there could be a big, hefty fine associated with that or we have to quickly come up with the money to pay for the licenses and make things whole or remove those things out of the environment, which could create even more work and more effort. So it's important that asset management is properly maintained. Same thing when it comes to patching and updates. We need to have a clear understanding of how much of any one thing we have in the environment, whether it's Windows servers, Linux servers, IoT devices. All of these things need to be documented and understood in some type of asset management software so that we can quickly, at a glance, understand where we're deficient from a patching level of perspective, from an updates perspective. All of these things help to mitigate risk in the environment. It's hard to monitor what you don't know about. Asset management is a critical, critical component to a successful and secure system and an overall secure environment. In this chapter, we talked about personnel and the various things that we need to have in place to make sure our personnel is managed and administered properly. Also, we talked about the diversity of training techniques, third-party risk management, data classification, governance and retention, along with credential policies, and organizational policies, change management, asset management.

Chapter 9 Risk Management Process and Concepts

In this chapter, we'll review the risk management process and concepts. We have a few main areas. We have risk types, risk management strategies. We'll talk about risk analysis, along with disasters, and then business impact analysis. When it comes to risk and managing risk, I want to make sure that you and I are on the same page, and that we understand what are the various types of risk and where do they come from. You can generally categorize risk in one of six categories. There are some others, but these are the main ones. We talk about external risk. That's things that are external to the company, things you don't necessarily have control over. That could be man-made disasters, that can be a terrorist attack, it could be a bomb, it could be a plane running into the building, it can be a multitude of things that are not within your direct control, they're outside or external to the company. Next, there's internal risk, and that can be inside the company, whether it be hardware or software faults. It could be faulty equipment, it could be a power outage, or it could be insider threats. It can be hackers or internal bad actors. It doesn't necessarily have to be hardware related or power related, it could be personnel related. Then we have legacy systems, and by legacy, we mean old. A legacy system is something that's aging out of its useful life. For instance, if you have a 3-year or a 5-year lifecycle on equipment, and perhaps it's 6, 7, or 8 years that that piece of equipment or piece of infrastructure has been on the floor, well there is risk being injected into the environment because you're at a greater risk of things failing, components failing, hard drives, internal components, motherboards. Additionally, not just referring to the hardware components, but the actual systems themselves, if they've been around for a long time, if a legacy platform, as an example, has been around for 5, 10, 15, 20 years and has not been updated, it might be a homegrown application or something that was developed in-house, well that person may not even work for the company anymore. By having those things in play and not having a good way to support them, that introduces risk into the environment. Next, we have multi-party, and as you might guess, if you have multiple parties or multiple folks, multiple vendors or multiple applications that are responsible for something, then you have multiple people that can point fingers back and forth, it takes a while to figure out whose responsible for what, and that again can add additional risk into the environment, especially if folks are not on the same page, or if you're the middle of a crisis and you need support and then you get a bunch of finger pointing, that certainly adds additional risk and frustration into the environment. Next, we have IP theft, and, intellectual property is big business. That's one of the things that potentially differentiates one company from another, provides competitive advantage. IP theft, or theft of that intellectual property or that critical data, can be very problematic to a company. It can be their lifeblood, and if it's stolen and given to someone else, that could have huge impacts and huge ramifications to the bottom line, to reputation, to a company's overall viability,. That's a big risk. And then we have software compliance and licensing. As we get further into the chapter and talk about asset management, if we don't keep track of what we have in the environment, especially if we're in a big environment and we have software compliance and licensing issues, that could end up introducing a big risk to the company. For instance, if you have 10,000 copies of a piece of software, but you're only licensed for, say, 5000, or 500, even worse, when it comes time to true up, and that can potentially happen and does happen quite often where software vendors will ask to come in and audit a company's environment to make sure they're in compliance, so if you're not in compliance, that could be a hefty bill that you either have to pay, negotiate down, or remove that software from the environment, all of which introduce their own version of risk into the company or into the environment. As you might guess, it's very important that we focus on each of these different areas to make sure that we're keeping the environment as clean as possible and as secure as possible, but also de-risking as much as possible.

Managing Risk

There are multiple ways, of managing a risk. We can do one of several things. We can accept certain levels of risk. We understand it's never going to be 0, we'll reach some type of posture and say, we're going to accept this level or this threshold. We can also transfer risk and say, we're not going to accept that. We don't want to necessarily take the burden of trying to constantly mitigate that ourselves. We'll transfer that, let's say, to a third party. We can also implement controls to reduce risk as much as possible. Then in some instances, we can avoid it altogether. Every company is different, and as such, each has a different tolerance for risk. That's what this boils down to is, what is your risk tolerance?

Risk Management Defined

Risk management can be defined as the identification, the assessment, and the prioritization of risk, along with the mitigation and the monitoring of those risks. As an example, when dealing with computer hardware and software, risk management is also known as information assurance, or you may see the abbreviation IA. And that will depend upon the company's risk tolerance, your risk tolerance, and that can vary by industry, a government versus a tech startup, as an example. Also, the value of the data that you're protecting. If it's something that's maybe ephemeral, it's not going to last very long, or it's not a high value piece of data or dataset, well then you're not going to do a lot to protect that necessarily. If it's something that's extremely valuable, critical to your business, then you're going to invest time, resources to make sure that that data is protected. Then, lastly, the ability to recover that data. If it's something that can be easily regenerated, well then the risk of it going away is not so high. Maybe the risk of it being stolen is great, but if it's capable of being recovered or regenerated quickly, then the controls in place to allow that regeneration to take place don't necessarily need to be as complex or perhaps as costly.

Risk Management Concepts
When we talk about risk management, there's several concepts I want you to be aware of, and that is the concept of risk transference. If we transfer risk to a third party as an example, we may insure our datacenter or insure some part of our business so that if disaster strikes, well, insurance will protect us. And all of these things tie into compliance because a lot of these different things are components of being compliant with various regulations. If you're wondering where these things tie together, all of these things go hand in hand. We have to make sure we're doing things in an ethical way. We have to make sure we're during our business in a standardized fashion across our footprint, whether we're in the US or the UK or anywhere abroad. And then we have to make sure that everyone is acting under the same guidelines. And then next we have risk acceptance. What's the cost of removing the risk versus dealing with the issue if and when it occurs? And that's what we talked about

before. That's going to vary upon the type of data, how quickly it can be regenerated, recovered. Is a business critical, or is it business necessary, or is it just something that's nice to have, or perhaps even scratch data. And then risk mitigation and deterrence. What level of reduction is acceptable? We talked about that risk posture. What controls can be put in place to effectively minimize that risk? And then we also have something referred to as risk avoidance. She's very upset and wants to avoid that risk at all costs. Many organizations will simply opt to not do something, deciding that the risk is too high. An example might be deciding not to patch a certain piece of infrastructure. And you might say, well, why wouldn't we do that? Well, in some companies, in some environments there is infrastructure that's been there for Long, it's been up and running, and it's working, so it's like if it's not broken, don't fix it. If it's a critical patch, well, that's a different story. But if it's just a patch and just because its patch Tuesday and it's that time, well, we may not want to take that piece of infrastructure down because we're not sure if it's going to come back up again. In certain cases, it may be better to not do something. How about migrating to a new platform? If the risks of migration are too great, there's a potential for downtime, and it's an application that needs to remain up at all costs, well, that risk might be too great at this point in time, We're going to avoid that risk altogether. Also perhaps launching a new site or a new service. If we're not ready, if we don't have the infrastructure, if we're afraid we're going to launch it and then it immediately crashes because we're going to get too much traffic, and then that will hurt our brand or our reputation, well, then that might be a risk that's worth avoiding at the moment. Regroup and then come back with a different plan. It all depends upon the situation, but risk avoidance is in fact, a mitigation strategy that you can add into your overall processes.

Strategic Options

Some strategic options we can look at it, we have something we need to understand how we're going to address this issue. There's a risk that we've encountered, if we start it left to, we can go should we avoid or terminate, share or transfer, reduce or modify, or accept or tolerate? Let's expand this out a bit. If we avoid or terminate, if we say no, well, then the next thing is, do we share or transfer, if we say no, do we reduce or modify it. If we avoid or terminate and we say yes, well, then let's cease activities that create the risk. If we can do that, then it drops down into, is it acceptable? Is that an acceptable level of risk? And if it is yes, then say that residual risk will be monitored and we'll just accept it and just keep an eyeball on it. If we go over to share and transfer, again, if we decide that's the book that we want to go, we can say, let's move that over to a third-party and allow them to manage that risk. And same thing, is it acceptable? If so, yes, then we'll just simply monitor and go forward, and you get the idea. Same thing with reduce or modify and accept or tolerate. Each has its own yes or no fork, and we can make subsequent decisions based upon which way we choose. All of these things lead themselves, when we're talking about actual security, when we're talking about compliance. The thing that we're driving towards or the things that were driving toward are the three core principles of IT security at the end of the day, and that is confidentiality, integrity, and availability, otherwise known as the CIA Triad. This is the basic fundamental purpose of implementing security within our system. We want to make sure that our data is confidential, that it's available, and that the integrity is there, so it's not tampered with. If we can do those three things well, then we're going to be in compliance probably 99% of the time, because if in fact those things are done properly, and there's no breaches, there's no inappropriate access, there's no data unavailability, the bulk of most compliance mandates will be met.

Chapter 10 Risk Register, Risk Matrix, and Heat Map

The first thing I want to cover, we have what's referred to as a risk register or a risk matrix or sometimes referred to as a heat map. You may hear it referred to as any one of these things. They're all the same concept. What we have here is a matrix, and it's showing us that we can rate a specific risk from likelihood of occurring on the left with a vertical axis, you'll see the likelihood of that thing happening. It's Rare, Unlikely, Possible, Likely or Almost Certain.

		Consequences – Maximum Reasonable Consequence				
		Insignificant	Minor	Moderate	Major	Catastrophic
Likelihood Rating	Almost Certain	Medium	Medium	High	Extreme	Extreme
	Likely	Low	Medium	Medium	High	Extreme
	Possible	Low	Low	Medium	High	High
	Unlikely	Low	Low	Low	Medium	High
	Rare	Low	Low	Low	Low	Medium

And then on the horizontal axis, we have consequences. What's the maximum reasonable consequence? It's either Insignificant all the way over to Catastrophic. As an example, if we have a specific risk, and we can take any risk that we want, and we can say, well, it has a rare chance of happening, but a Catastrophic if it did happen, well, then that risk will be rated as a Medium. We can see where they intersect on that axis. Conversely, let's say we have a likelihood rating of Unlikely, but catastrophic if it happened. Well, that would give us a rating of High. You get the idea here. If it's almost Certain, and it's Catastrophic if it happens, then that would be Extreme. That takes us from one end of the spectrum to the other.

Risk Control Self-assessment (RCSA)

Next, we have a risk control self-assessment, or RCSA. This is a process by which management and staff of all levels collectively identify and evaluate risks and associated controls. So, everyone that's involved with a specific process, a business process, line of business, they would all get together from individual contributors up through management, and they make sure that they identify and prioritize business objectives, assess and manage high-risk areas of business process, self-evaluate the adequacy of the controls that are in place. This is a time to be brutally honest. We want to be very self-aware and very honest about what works and what doesn't work. If we have gaps, we need to identify these gaps because one of the points of this entire process is to inject risk assessment and risk awareness into business processes. When we develop our business processes, we have that risk awareness in the back of our mind, and we understand where we need to mitigate and, hopefully, de-risk the environment as much as possible. Moving on, we also want to make sure we develop risk treatment action plans. We have to not necessarily just identify the risk, but how are we going to either transfer, mitigate, or somehow get that risk out of the environment? And then ensure reporting consistency across all levels of the organization. It's important that everyone is reporting the same language, the same metrics so that we can gauge what's effective and what's not effective. As an example, the RCSA workflow may go something like this. We select our participants, who is going to be in this process, who is going to collaborate? We're all going to get together and discuss all of these things. We want to make sure we get a cross-section of everyone involved. We need to identify the risks. This is a collective process. Everyone together identifies the risks. Assign risk against business objectives. We say, which is most important? What aligns with our business objectives and what doesn't? Then we identify controls to mitigate those risks. We assess those controls. And then actions if those controls fail or they lapse. What are we going to do if something doesn't work, in other words? And then we continue to monitor that and then report the results. And then, finally, take corrective action. This is a looping process, that we continuously look for risks. We continually look for ways to get those risks out of the environment and make things as smooth as possible because, again, unplanned downtime, outages, failures, just having to redo work over and over again, unplanned work, all of these things add to our cycle time. They add to our ineffectiveness, and that's the opposite of what we want to do. We want to increase effectiveness. We want to make our processes more effective but also more secure.

Risk Awareness (Inherent, Residual, Control, and Risk Appetite)
That brings us to risk awareness. Understanding what types of risks exist in the environment, that's part of that risk assessment we just talked about, but just understanding what the different types are. We have inherent risk, which are things that are, as the name implies, inherent in the process, inherent in what we do. It might be a dangerous process. It might be a very complicated process. There are some things that just inherently have some risk to them that we may end up having no choice but to just accept or transfer maybe to an insurance company or something else. We reduce that risk as much as possible. But it may not be feasible to remove it completely. And then we have residual risk, and that's risk that's carried over from some other process. If we're going through all of our steps to derisk that environment, and there's still some left over, and that carries forward into other processes, that could be

445

considered a residual risk., just understanding how to control risk. What controls can we put in place? Are they technical controls? Administrative controls? Can we do it via people, process or technology? What are the different ways that we can control risk? These are all things that factor into risk awareness. And then risk appetite, what is our actual appetite or our tolerance level for risk? Are we very adverse? Are we okay with some certain levels of risk? Are we going to just accept certain pieces of it and have it be residual risk that will carry forward? Or are we very risk adverse, and we're willing to spend whatever it takes to get that specific risk out of the environment? All of these things need to be known and understood so that we can formulate plans accordingly.

Chapter 11 Regulatory Examples

Let's go and take a look at a few examples of regulations that may affect your ability to do business, depending upon what region you do business in, where your company resides, where your customers reside. Starting off, the Gramm-Leach-Bliley Act, the GLBA, and we'll cover each of these in more detail in just a few. Also, the Health Insurance Portability and Accountability Act, otherwise known as HIPAA, Health Information Technology for Economic and Clinical Health, otherwise known as the HITECH Act. Also, Sarbanes-Oxley Act, otherwise known as SOX. And then one of the newer ones that have been getting a lot of press lately is General Data Protection Regulation, or GDPR. And then a bit of a US version of that regulation, the California Consumer Privacy Act, or CCPA.

Gramm-Leach-Bliley Act (GLBA)
To start off, the Gramm-Leach-Bliley Act, GLBA, also known as the Financial Modernization Act of 1999, and what this does is specify that financial institutions must secure any and all personally identifiable information, or PII, so tax agents, mortgage brokers, banks, credit unions. And then there are a few sub-bullets, within that regulation that provides additional regulations, as an example, the Safeguards Rule. This stipulates that financial institutions must implement security initiatives to protect confidential information. The Financial Privacy Rule, this stipulates that financial institutions must provide a privacy notice to the customer both when the relationship is established, and on an annual basis. You may notice that you'll get pop-ups or information from your banks and your financial institutions once a year saying, we've updated our privacy rules, or here is a

reiteration of our privacy notices, just You're aware. And then we have pretexting protection. This prohibits access to personal private information without proper authority. What this is supposed to help with is things like social engineering, where a hacker or bad actor would call into a company, pretend to be someone in the know or someone that has a legitimate interest for information, and ask probing questions to try to get information out of the unsuspecting victim. This type of regulation helps put some guard rails around that, some training, and also just awareness around the fact that these types of things need to be protected and they need to be protected at scale throughout the entire company.

HIPAA
Next we have the Health Insurance Portability and Accountability Act, otherwise known as HIPPA. This is also known as the Kennedy-Kassebaum Act, implemented in 1996, and the one that we are concerned with, or probably most applicable, is Title II: Preventing Health Care Fraud and Abuse; Administrative Simplification; Medical Liability Reform. What this has is two main sections. We have the Privacy Rule, which defines patient medical records or protected health care information, PHI, and then also the Security Rule. The Security Rule defines security measures required to protect electronic protected health information, or EPHI. Without digging too much into any one of these specific regulations, because, quite frankly, each one of these would be probably a couple day book in and of themselves to fully understand, in most cases very complex, but the thing you need to understand is, if you're dealing with these types of situations and you're doing business and you're maintaining health records or financial information, or you're dealing with business outside of the country, it

behooves you to dig in and start understanding the nuances of all of these different regulations and how they apply. There are rigid sentencing guidelines, up to criminal prosecution can result for violating HIPPA rules. Very important that these things are followed to the letter.

HITECH Act

Next, we have the HITECH Act. The HITECH Act is the health information technology for economic and clinical Health act. It became law in 2009, and in 2013, provided updates to HIPAA based upon the HITECH Act, so that included additional reporting requirements around significant harm and also removed the requirement that there needed to be actual proof that harm was done. At this point, it's just possible to prove that harm could have been done and that would satisfy the requirement. Before this, you had to prove that harm was done. As long as it's reasonable to believe that harm could have been done, the regulation provides for penalties. Additionally, it also added business associates of parties handling medical information or medical data are included. Not just the primary business, but business associates are covered under this HITECH Act as well. And then the length of time that PHI, protected health information, is protected was shortened from forever, which is, as we know, quite a long time, down to 50 years, which for the most part is the majority of a human life or at least a human adult life. A few HITECH considerations, Wilful neglect can result in significant penalties and we're talking up to $250,000 with repeat or uncorrected violations extending up to $1.5 million, Not an insignificant amount of penalties for non-compliance. Very important that these things are followed as much as possible. Also, penalties can extend, to business associates. As a covered entity, you must get assurance from any business associate that you do business with or whom you share EHR or EPHI that they will protect that data. If not, you can be held liable, HITECH Act considerations, very important to understand the nuances of all of this. And then also, breach notification, patients must be notified of any unsecured breach. If 500 or more patients are impacted, health and human services must also be notified. The media must be notified. So breach notifications are not optional, it's a mandatory thing that must occur if patients are, in fact, impacted.

Sarbanes-Oxley Act (SOX)
Next let's talk about the Sarbanes-Oxley Act, or SOX. The actual title of the regulation is the Public Company Accounting Reform and Investor Protection Act of 2002. Sarbanes-Oxley, the names of the people that presented or introduced the legislation created primarily to protect investors and improve the accuracy and the reliability of corporate disclosures around security laws, so on. The CEO and the CFO are both required to certify financial reports. It provides for greater accountability, and holds them accountable for inadequately protecting IT systems responsible for financial reporting. After such corporate meltdowns and debacles such as the Enron fiasco of years ago, Sarbanes-Oxley was designed to prevent those types of things from being able to happen again. If you're involved in these types of corporations or companies or organizations that are around finance, investing, securities, people that are responsible for that specific part of your organization I'm sure are very familiar already with the Sarbanes-Oxley Act, but if you are not in that scope specifically but within that company, I still would recommend that you familiarize yourself dig into the nuances of these acts, and that should go enterprise-wide or company-wide, everyone is driving the same objectives, and also making sure that the accounting is

done properly. When the books are messed with and accounting is not accurate, there's a huge potential for investor loss, so this type of legislation is designed to help prevent that. When it comes to SOX compliance, what are the main areas that the regulation is looking to cover? Well, first off, maintain data integrity and confidentiality. In other words, keep the data safe and secure, remember, SOX compliance, the CEO and the CFO need to sign off that these controls are in fact in place; that they're there, they're documented, they're demonstrable, we can show that they exist and they are protecting the data, keeping it safe and secure. These deals with financial systems, access to files, access control lists, auditing who can access what. Also, track any attempted security breaches, and also, what are the actual resolutions. What happened, and what did we do to prevent it or mitigate that risk going forward. Next, maintain event logs and make available for independent audit. That's one of the key takeaways. This is not one of those things where you just have a checklist and you're checking the boxes, you put it into a folder and put it on the shelf. These things need to be able to be audited every so often, and they will in fact be audited every so often, and if those controls are not in place and they're not demonstrated that they are working and functional, then you can be found not in compliance document that compliance and be able to show the prior 90 days. Since we don't know when the audits are coming, what does that mean? Well, that means we need a running log of the previous 90 days pretty much at any point in time. The moral of the story, friends, is keep the systems functioning, make sure they work, make sure they're documented and also demonstrable, make sure logging is in place, we track any attempted breaches, we know who's trying to access what files and when, who they are, and if they try and fail, that's logged as well. All of these things have to be in place and be able to be shown at a moment's notice when those auditors come knocking on the door.

GDPR
Next, one of the ones that gets a lot of attention days is the GDPR or the general data protection regulation. It's a privacy and security law that originated in the European Union in May of 2018. It imposes obligations onto organizations anywhere, so this has reached beyond just the EU, Long as they target or collect data related to people in the EU. Just because you're located in the United States or maybe somewhere outside of the European Union doesn't necessarily mean you are not impacted by GDPR. What type of data does the GDPR cover? Well, it provides individuals, which are known as data subjects, more control over how organizations process or control the processing of their data, such things as names, locations, patient data and health records, email addresses, photos, essentially any data that could be used to identify a living person.

Chapter 12 Qualitative and Quantitative Analysis

A qualitative analysis is an assessment that assigns a numerical value to the probability of a risk and the impact it can have on a system or network. The point to take away here is that no monetary value is assigned for our assets or the possible losses when we're talking about qualitative analysis. As an example, we would assess a risk of not installing; let's say, for instance, an antivirus application on our end user systems. We would range that or give it a range from, let's say, 1 to 100, and that range is arbitrary. We can assign it whatever number scale we want. For this example, let's just go 1 to 100. The probability of risk of an infection at some point, if it's an outwardly-facing system, again, if people have access to the internet, the probability of risk is, let's just say, 99. The amount of impact, we'll rank that at an 80. Again, arbitrary because there's a 20% chance that our systems would still be functional even if we caught a virus or a piece of malware. So, we may be able to still do some work, but it's going to be significantly slowed down. Our ability to get things done is going to be impeded. We'll give it a ranking of 80. If you multiply that 99 times 80, that gives us a ranking of 7920 or 7,920 out of a possible 10,000. Because if we took our 1 to 100, both of those categories would have a maximum value of 100. If we took 100 times 100, that would give us 10,000. That's where we get the 7,920 out of 10,000. That's on the high end. It's in the top, the top quarter or the top 25% of risk. That's, relatively speaking, it's a high risk. The flip side of that is a quantitative analysis. Quantitative, it signs an exact monetary value to assets and then attempts to give expected yearly loss in dollars for any given risk. What that does is allows us to prioritize based upon the financial losses to be incurred versus the cost of protecting. As an example, and it's comes down to a business decision, but if we said, we have 10 systems, and it's going to cost us, let's just, hypothetically speaking, cost a $1,000,000 to put antivirus on those 10 systems., it's not going to cost that much, but just for this example. It costs us a $1,000,000 to protect them, and the systems themselves only they cost $1000 or $1500 a piece. They only do very minimum amount of work. And if they all were compromised and went down, it would cost us maybe 30 or $40,000 in damages. Well, it's not worth spending a $1,000,000 to protect $30,000. So, in that instance, we could say the financial loss is not as great as the cost of protecting.

Risk Calculation
The risk calculation is the process of identifying the likelihood of a threat, the impact from the threat, and then how quickly our systems can become operational again. The likelihood is, as the name implies, how likely is that threat? Is the vulnerability likely to be exploited? The other thing is the ALE, and that's the Annual Loss Expectancy, and, how much do I expect to lose throughout the year if I combine my Single Loss Expectancy and my Annualized Rate of Occurrence? That's the total amount that I expect to lose throughout the year. There's an algorithm or a formula that's applied to get to that value. The impact is as the name implies, it's the impact of having that threat exploited. Is it downtime, is it complete loss of data, is it loss of customer confidence, it just depends upon what the asset is. The Single Loss Expectancy, or the SLE, is how much will that single loss if that threat is exploited, how much will I expect to lose on that single occurrence? Then the Annualized Rate of Occurrence is how often do I expect that to be successfully exploited throughout the year. Just understand

that these things are combined to give us a formula on how much we can expect to lose throughout the year.

Likelihood of Threat

The likelihood of the threat is the possibility of the threat initiation. It can be ranked qualitatively or quantitatively. Just because a vulnerability exists doesn't mean that it can necessarily be exploited. If it's an internal system that can't be reached from the outside world, then some type of external facing threat, we don't necessarily need to be concerned with, we may or may not want to take the time and effort to patch that. I just want to make sure you're aware that understanding the risk enables proper prioritization. Everything cannot be the highest priority, and everything, can't be the lowest priority, We have to rank our likelihoods and our threats so that we can remediate those things appropriately.

Impact of Threat

The next thing is the impact of the threat. If the threat is successfully initiated, then what's the impact? Could it be systems are slow and unresponsive or completely offline? Does it mean data loss? Does it mean destruction of systems or data, customer confidence, downstream effects? Downstream effects meaning if one system goes offline, does that then affect five other applications or five other systems? And it does it have dependencies that can create a much bigger outage than just the threat itself? All of these things have to be planned, and that's why it's very important to do planned maintenance versus unplanned outages.

Loss Calculation Terms (ALE, SLE, and ARO)

Some loss calculation terms that we use to calculate some of these things, are the annual loss expectancy, or the ALE, the monetary measure of how much loss you can expect in one year. The single loss expectancy, or the SLE, is the monetary measure of how much you can expect to lose at any one time, so single loss. That's calculated by the value of the asset by the exposure factor, AV times EF. Then we have the annualized rate of occurrence, or the ARO. That again, gets back to the likelihood, and that's usually determined with historical value of an event occurring within a year. We're going to go back and look, what's the realistic number? How many times did we get hit with this last year, for the last 2 years, the last 5 years. You look at some type of historical trending You get an idea of what's the likelihood I'm going to be hit with this specific, either vulnerabilities going to be exploited or I'm going to have some type of threat. Then when you do that, you times the SLE times the ARO of the single loss expectancy times the annualized rate of occurrence and that's going to give you your annual loss expectancy. As an example, let's say we have an ecommerce company that generates $100,000 in sales per hour from their website. The probability of the server failing during the year is 30%. If it's a highly functioning ecommerce site, it's not going to have a single server, but it's going to have a server cluster, load balancing. The probability of that server failing during the year is 30%. The failure would generate 4 hours of downtime and $6000 in components to repair. We may have to put in new hard drives, maybe a new motherboard, a new power supply. It's going to cost us 4 hours of downtime plus $6000 in components. The SLE, the single loss event, or expectancy is $406,000, $100,000 per hour because we're going to be down for 4 hours, plus the $6000 in repair for the parts. So our ARO is determined to be 30% because we said the probability of the server failing during the year is 30% so that's our ARO. If we then calculate the ALE, or the annual loss expectancy, it's going to be

$121,800. That's how much we can expect to lose each year, or this year, we can expect to lose $121,000 because we have our $406,000, which is the single loss expectancy, times the actual annualized rate of occurrence, What's the likelihood of that happening?

Threat Assessment (Disaster)
There are three main categories. First off we have the environment or natural threats. These are threats that can come from natural disasters such as a hurricane, an earthquake, a fire, flood, and so on. These things there are impossible to predict, but you can look historically to see how many times has each of these or any of these happened to that environment, to that building. If you're in an area that floods once or twice a year, then you need to put more prioritization on those types of threats. If your datacenter or your environment's out in the middle of the desert, as an example, you probably are not going to be flooding all that often, but you may have other natural disasters such as fire, earthquake. Next will be manmade. These are intentional attacks, such as breaches, viruses, malware, spam, and the distributed denial-of-service attacks. We can look historically and say, how many times have I been breached in the past? How many attempted breaches do I have per day or per week or per month? There is no way to predict necessarily what may happen in the future, but it can give you a rough indication of how much that specific environment gets targeted. You can also look at an industry standard and say, I'm in the healthcare industry, or I'm in the construction industry. You can look at the industry as a whole and get some approximation of how often that specific industry is targeted as well. Then next we have internal versus external. Internal would be internal to the company or inside an organization. External will be from the outside, hackers.,

depending upon which study you read, most threats are coming from internal, or that's the biggest threat, because these folks have the most intimate knowledge of your environment, where things are located, naming conventions, infrastructure, what operating systems are run, what applications are run, and so on. It's important to understand that just because our perimeter defenses might be shored up very tightly, we may have very good defenses against the outside world, if we don't also check and audit and monitor our inside environment as well, we put ourselves at risk.

Additional Risk Calculation Terms (MTBF, MTTF, and MTTR)
When it comes to risk and risk calculation, what exactly is that? Well, risk calculation is the process of identifying the likelihood of a threat, the impact from the threat, and then how quickly systems can be operational. There's three terms I want you to be familiar with, and that's MTBF, or the mean time between failures, the MTTF, the mean time to failure, and then also MTTR, the mean time to recovery. Let's take a look at each of these individually. When we're talking about the MTBF, or the mean time between failures, that is the statistical average a device or a component lasts between failures, and that's referring to things that are repairable. If things are not repairable or they're so insignificant we just rip them out and put in a brand-new one, then this doesn't apply. But for things that can be repaired, what's the average a device or component lasts between those failures? Then we have the MTTF, the mean time to failure. That is the average of how long a component lasts. That refers to things that will be replaced rather than repaired. We want to get ahead of that and replace those things before they fail. That's always our goal here, is to understand when we can proactively get in and have planned downtime, as opposed to unplanned downtime. Then the MTTR is the

mean time to repair, so the statistical average of how long it takes to repair that failed component.

As far as BIA, or business impact analysis is concerned, there's some key terminology. We're talking about maximum tolerable downtime, or MTD. That is how long can something be down before it has a significant impact to the business? That ties into our mean time to repair and the mean time between failures, also the RTO and RPO. All of these things combine so if we know the maximum amount of time that we're allowed or we should be able to be down before we start seeing a significant impact, then we can work backwards from there and adjust our policies accordingly. The mean time to repair, or MTTR, is the mean time that it's going to take to repair a specific piece of equipment. If something fails, and it's going to take us 6 hours or 6 days or 6 weeks to repair that, and our maximum tolerable downtime is only an hour or 2, well, then, we're going to have some issues if that were to go down. That stresses the importance of having planned downtime and planned outages we can make sure we periodically and preventatively take these things offline We can fix them, repair them, replace them without having an impact to our business. Next, we have mean time between failures, or MTBF, and that is a calculation of how long a specific piece of equipment will be in service before it fails. That allows us to calculate should we take this thing offline during a planned outage or a planned maintenance versus unplanned? Planned is always better than unplanned. Having an idea of what the MTBF for specific components within our infrastructure is, whether it's disk drives, storage arrays, computer servers, desktops, laptops, switches, routers, the individual components themselves, the line cards, the supervisors, all these things have their own individual MTBF metrics. By knowing what those things are, we can plan accordingly. Then, next, is our recovery time objective, or our RTO. How long does it take us to bring that specific piece of infrastructure or that specific piece of data back online? Next is the recovery point objective. How far back do we want to go? This revolves around data protection and backups. But we could do a recovery time objective. It might take us a half an hour to get that data back, as an example. But a recovery point objective is we want to recover up to an hour or if it's 5 minutes, that's going to have an impact on our RTO as well. What you can take away from that is the RPO and RTO, the recovery time objective and the recovery point objective, as those things slide closer to zero, the expense is going to go up. But, again, it depends upon the industry. If we're making millions of dollars a second per transaction, as an example, then it's going to be worth spending that money to have a very short RPO and RTO. Conversely, if it's something that doesn't have a large impact on our environment, maybe some archival data or just some log statistics and, well, then our RPO and RTO can slide way to the left. It could be hours. It could be days. We don't have to spend as much money to get that information back as quickly as possible. Next, we have work recovery time, or our WRT. It might be best if you look at this in a chart format just to see how all of these different terms tie together. Here we have a situation where we have some type of disaster, when disaster strikes. We have our RPO, RTO, our work recovery time, and then something else referred to as our maximum tolerable downtime, or MTD.

At 3 a.m., business as usual, cooking along just like we do every other day. Well, at 7 a.m., some type of outage occurs. Well, our RPO gives us a 4-hour window. We have a 4-hour recovery point objective. We would have the actual outage occur at 7. We're going to go back 4 hours. That might be the first earliest backup. That's the earliest that we can recover information based upon the RPO in this specific example. These things are fluid. Our RPOs and RTOs could change depending upon the parameters and the acceptable limits that we set as a business. In this example, 4 hours. So outage occurs at 7 a.m. Our RPO is 4 hours. We're going to go back and recover up to 3 a.m. Well, from 7 a.m. until 12 p.m., that's our recovery time objective. That means that's how long it will take for us to get that information back either off tape, VTL data domain, Avamar, or some type of backup device, some type of backup appliance is going to bring us back to 12 noon. From 12 p.m. to 6 p.m., that's our WRT, or our work recovery time, that's the amount of time it's going to take us to bring all the various teams in, have them validate their applications, make sure the log files and databases are intact, all of the things that we need to have in place before we're live in production. The maximum tolerable downtime is from 7 a.m. until 6 p.m. That's an 11-hour window. The work recovery time is the MTD minus the RTO. That work recovery time is how long we have to validate before we exceed our maximum tolerable downtime. If our MTD was, for instance, say, 7 hours, well, if our RTO is 5 hours, it takes us from 7 a.m. to noon to bring that information back, well, then we only have 2 hours for our work recovery time. We only have 2 hours to validate and get back online, get back in production before we exceed that maximum tolerable downtime. WRT is the difference between the RTO and the MTD.

Mission Essential Functions
Let's talk about mission essential functions. What we are talking about here are operations that are core to the success of the business. It's imperative that we, as IT professionals and security professionals, understand which ones are absolutely critical, essential to the functioning of the business. Revenue generating applications, billing applications. Every environment's going to be different. Every business will be different. Some will have two or three core applications. Some may have dozens or more. But as a security professional, it's critical that we understand what those systems are, how they interoperate with other systems, and make sure we secure them as much as possible. Not just the application itself, but understand what applications feed these applications and also what other applications these core ones feed into. We have to make sure we secure all of those systems appropriately because if there's a chain of applications and one breaks down, well, then that has a cascading effect. All of the other systems, all of the other systems go offline as well. If it takes 5 minutes or 5 hours or 5 days to get that one system back up in that chain, and it feeds information to subsequent systems, the entire system has the possibility of being down as well. To that effect, are those systems backed up or protected? Are the highly available? In other words, if one system goes down, can we bring up another one, or can we fail over to another one instantly or quasi-instantly. And are they redundant? Are all the sub-components within these

different systems redundant? Do we have multiples so that if one goes down, we're still up and running? And then disaster recovery or BCP. Do we have disaster recovery in place so that if we have a "smoking hole" scenario, where our data center or our supply closet or whatever the situation might be, where we're housing our data and our infrastructure, if that goes away, do we have another place that we can bring those systems back up? Is there business continuity planning, or BCP, in effect? And disaster recovery and high availability, these are all components of a larger BCP plan, a business continuity plan. All of these things should be taken into account and audited, making sure they're documented, stack ranked by order of importance, and then remediated appropriately.

Chapter 13 Identification of Critical Systems

Next we're talking about the identification of critical systems. A full audit of the environment can turn up application dependencies that you may or may not know exist. How does data flow through the network? Don't just assume that an application is in a vacuum in and of itself, it's its own tower. Most applications and most systems will either feed data into something else or get data from some other system. There's going to be a flow of data through the network. When a customer visits a website, as an example, and they put information in some web portal, that gets stored in a database in some multi-tier application, it goes through a number of different systems, and may go to order a processing and customer attention and analytics platform and data lakes and so on. All of these things apply or supply data to and from our critical systems, quote-unquote. I can guarantee you that when something goes offline that you didn't necessarily deem important and you didn't even know all the different systems that it feeds, well, it's going to have downstream impacts and you'll very quickly understand the interdependencies at that point. You might ask yourself, well, how does that happen? I mean, I know everything in my environment. Well, that might be true. For small environments or midsize environments that might be very true. But as things grow over time, they grow organically, things come up as skunkworks projects or little side-of-desk or side-of-table projects that eventually grow. Sometimes when things are not funded, but all of a sudden, hey, that's pretty cool when everyone starts using it, and it never gets properly architected, properly backed up, and as it grows and grows and grows, it morphs into a critical system. Here you end up having something that the business relies on that's not fault tolerant, redundant, backed up. A full audit of your environment periodically will prevent those types of things from happening. And is each system or application in that chain that we spoke about, do they all have the same level of availability and redundancy? Because again, we can't say that a system is a tier 1 or class 1 or whatever classification system you use within your organization, you can't say it is a top-tier application just because the application itself is top-tier infrastructure. If all the things that it feeds or the power grid that it sits on, or all of the different interdependencies are not also class 1 or tier 1 your classification is, then that application or that system is not at that level either. Because if something breaks down and it's critical to feeding that application or that system, well then that system's going to go offline, just as easily as the downstream or the weak link in that chain goes offline. A full audit of the environment is critical, understanding what these systems are and how they all interrelate.

Single Point of Failure (SPOF)
Having two of something doesn't necessarily mean that it's redundant. The fact of the matter is just because we have two of a certain component, a server, or whatever, it doesn't mean we have redundancy, or it doesn't mean it's still not a single point of failure. As an example, a dual-port HBA, or a host bus adapter, connects a server to a Fibre Channel network or to a Fibre Channel storage array. Well, if we have a single HBA in that server, it's a dual-port HBA, and we have two ports coming out, one to each fabric, we have dual fabrics, we have a server, and we think we have two paths of storage, well, we may say to ourselves or think, everything is covered. We're redundant. We have two of each. But the reality is, as you can guess, is no because it's a single HBA. There may be two ports coming out of it, but if that HBA

were to fail, you'd have lost connectivity to both fabrics. You're much better off to have two single-port HBAs. That way, in case one of those ports goes down, the other is still functioning. Same thing with two servers connecting to the same line card on a switch. We may have two servers clustered together. But if they're both connected to the same line card in a switch, well, if that line card goes down, both servers are down at the same time, so that becomes a single point of failure. You see where I'm going with this. We have to break these things down and look at the individual components and make sure that there is no single point of failure in any of those sub-components as well. Power and cooling, making sure we're not on the same power grids, all of the servers. If power goes down on one side, it doesn't take down the other. Multiple server paths to storage, we could have some type of multipathing software in place, whether it's PowerPath or MPIO or some native multipathing. But if the configuration files are not set correctly, well, there's a good chance we may not be using multipath. We still may have only one path to storage. It just depends upon your environment, what equipment you have in there. But I encourage you to go through an audit and make sure that you identify and understand what your applications and your systems are made of and that the components then to that level are, in fact, redundant. We do this by fully auditing and documenting the environment for potential risk. Then we rank in order of importance and, remediation. That way we know where we need to focus our resources for first because typically with any IT department or any business in general, there's only a certain amount of resources. So by prioritizing, you know where to put those resources first.

Chapter 14 Order of Restoration

Let's talk about the order of restoration. We have to get our information back online. What do we need to do? Well, a few things. We need an understanding of that application's full stack. Define what network, what storage, and what compute components make up that application or service. That sounds like a no-brainer, but as these applications grow, or if it's a very large environment, you may or may not necessarily know all the things, all the interrelations, all the interconnections, all the teams that are involved, what applications feed into it, what applications that specific application feeds out to. A full understanding of everything that's required to bring this application either down or back up is critical. Next, what teams need to be involved? Typically, more than one team manages the various components of that application or that service. The assumption is going to be that we're going to do this in a very controlled fashion. There's going to be some type of bridge set up. You have all the teams connecting. They're all dialed in. They're all either in a board room or they're going to dialed in remotely. They're all going to be aware of what's happening, and things will be brought down and then brought back up again or vice versa in a very programmatic fashion. That way there's consistency with data, there's no corruption, and also we have everyone on site if something were to go wrong, and they can quickly jump in and help get things back online. And then, ensuring backups can be recovered and restored. This is also a bit of a no-brainer, but not necessarily that something is done all the time. Test backups and restores prior to bringing that application up or down. Test backups and restorations of the application or the service before a crisis occurs, that's the critical component here, before the crisis to ensure that that required data is available.

Phased Approach
We need to have a phased approach when we're talking about tackling some of the issues that we have at hand. We have to identify what's critical and then do things in a very systematic approach. We can't do everything at once. We can't boil the ocean. We need to identify what is most critical, and that deals with infrastructure, with applications, with people and skills, all of these things, understanding what fits in with our grand vision, what's in alignment with business objectives, business outcomes. Then out of these things, infrastructure, application, people, skills, what's most critical? What do we have to tackle up front? Let's make those things a top priority. Again, ensuring alignment with business objectives, and then also revisit these periodically to make sure they're still valid because, guess what? If it's a brand-new business, we simply don't know what we don't know. There's no necessarily tried-and-true proven roadmap. Maybe there is to a certain extent but not typically across the board. There are always going to be variables. There are always going to be bumps in the road. By re-evaluating and understanding that this is a fluid document, a fluid process that's going to change over time, it allows us to pivot our objectives or, as we achieve objectives one, two, and three, we can add some additional ones to that list so that we have a rolling list of objectives or tasks that we want to accomplish as we drive towards getting this business up and running and making it as secure as possible.

Identifying Most Critical Systems First
We need to identify what services and what products that we're providing. As a brand new business, what is it that we

468

want to bring to market, provide to our customers? Provide that list and rank them by criticality. Revenue generating, business critical functions. Next, identify what is required to provide those services or products to customers. That can be our computers, our servers, networking. We decide whether we're doing on-prem or cloud. How about digital or physical? Are we going to be doing things completely in the digital realm? Do we have physical products and services? Do we need physical infrastructure? All of these things have to be stack ranked in criticality we can understand where we need to focus our resources first. Next, define how to secure that infrastructure and that data that encompasses that service or those services, or those products. Firewalls, encryption, multi-factor authentication, understanding what in-house expertise, what we need to outsource. A lot of things to consider. There are a lot of things that can revolve around starting up a business. A lot of times we think of only the product or the service and not all of the underlying nuts and bolts on how to make that thing a reality. It's important for us to understand how to rank these things so we can drive most efficiently. Next, identify and document any compliance or regulatory requirements. This is critical depending upon the industry that you're in. So, healthcare, finance, are going to be much more regulated, have a lot more compliance and data governance issues, data governance is very, very important and can be the actual undoing of a business if it's not done and managed properly. It varies by industry, but some examples could be the California Consumer Privacy Act, it could be GDPR, it could be HIPPA, SOX. There are a number of different compliance frameworks, regulatory frameworks that may apply to you in your specific industry. Then lastly, rinse and repeat for the remaining applications and processes. go through that list for revenue generating and back-office functions, and then also document any gaps that exist because you may or may not want to necessarily address that specific thing here and, but by documenting it at least allows you to table that effort for the moment and then come back to it when you have time and resources available.

Risk Assessment

We need to make sure that we are identifying potential risks that are most harmful throughout the entire business, not just one area. What is the most harmful, and then what do we need to do to mitigate against that specific risk. The risk assessments are useful, but understand, they may not account for everything. It's very difficult to understand every tiny piece of a business from top to bottom. Understand that you potentially, may miss some things. That's why testing, that's why going through this process is so critical, because as things are missed, it's a living document, we're going to go through an iterative process, and we're going to measure those risks over, and over, and over again. We'll take a first pass, we'll get everyone together from Legal, Accounting, HR, Finance, IT., all these people together, and we'll flesh it out, and we'll figure out does this work, does that work, if this happens, what are you going to do, if this happens, what are you going to do? And everyone chimes in, and then you'll go through an iterative process and you'll understand over time what works, what doesn't, and what needs to be adjusted, so it goes back and forth.

Chapter 15 Continuity of Operations

That all revolves around something called the continuity of operations. All areas of the business are connected. That's just a fact of business. Every area of the business relies on IT in some capacity. If you're in HR, Finance, Accounting, Marketing, you name it, every area relies on IT whether it's for your PCs, your smart phones, telecommunication systems, and it all revolves around that central hub. So have an understanding of that and the reach of IT itself has throughout the entire business helps you to understand what areas will be most heavily impacted, a mitigation plan, and we can understand where we need to focus resources, and then rate them and go from an order of priority going forward. Continuity planning centers around what alternatives exist to keep the business running in the event of that disaster. We have fault tolerant systems, we have redundant systems. Well, what if they fail? What if we can't get those things to come back online? That's where continuity planning comes into play. We need to have alternates or a plan B.

IT Contingency Planning
We want to put things into play or into place so that we can mitigate risk. We can either have redundancy or fault tolerance and just skip over that blip in the network if you will. But there are going to be times, for whatever reason, that we can't do that. If that disaster strikes and that uninterrupted continuity is not an option, then we have to have a contingency plan or a plan B. Procedures for relocating operations to a new location is an example. Minimizing disruption and downtime is, always our main mandate. But just for your own information, the federal

government has some guidelines, as they do, NIST. There is a special publication, SP 800-34 that outlines the methods and gives guidance for providing alternative methods for infrastructure, for telecommunications, and for mainframe systems. I definitely recommend that you review this publication. It's great information. It covers all the main areas that you need to be concerned with. And it gives you some guidance from high level all the way down to some granular step-by-step instructions on how to protect these things and how to set up your own policies and procedures within your company. The discovery process can identify gaps and potential remediation steps. That's going to be a process in and of itself that can help us mitigate risks, and we can identify, Oh, we don't have enough resources here, or we didn't realize the impact of this specific area on the rest of the business. We saw them sitting there in the corner. We never knew what they did. But we understand, wow, they have a huge impact on every area of the business. You might find these things out through your process. In doing that, you identify the gaps. You can add additional resources. You may need to buy new equipment or additional pieces of infrastructure, maybe to have duplicates if you're going to have a hot site, adding resources, and increasing resiliency. And then on top of that, you may identify gaps in training. Will all the necessary personnel be available to relocate? What happens if you have 500 employees locally, your disaster site is, let's say, 2000 miles away or 1000 miles away, and all those 500 people cannot or will not or, for whatever reason, can't relocate from one location to the other. Are there people available in the new location that you can bring on board relatively quickly? How long will it take to train those people? Does the new location have available personnel at all? You might be in an area where there aren't 500 people that you could bring on at a moment's notice. All of these things need to be taken into account when we're doing our BCP and our business impact analysis and our contingency planning so that we have the bases covered. That's the name of the game is we want to make sure we have as little disruption to the business as possible in the event of some type of downtime. In this chapter, we talked about risk types. We talked about risk management strategies along with risk analysis, different types of disasters, and then business impact analysis, and how all of these things collectively allow us to become more aware of risk, how to integrate risk awareness into our processes and planning, and then, of course, also devise ways to remove risk or de-risk our environment as much as possible.

Chapter 16 Privacy and Sensitive Data Concepts

In this chapter, we'll be talking about privacy and sensitive data concepts and considerations. We'll be talking about organizational consequences of privacy breaches, notification of breaches, the various types of data and how they're classified. We'll talk about privacy enhancing technologies, also roles and responsibilities, information lifecycle, an impact assessment, and then terms of agreement and privacy notices. So let's talk about some company obligations to protect security, again, getting back to whether it's the US laws, UK laws, or elsewhere in the world, a lot of countries are adopting similar regulations. Physical security goes without saying, we need to make sure that we're providing adequate protections against physical break-ins, people crossing into the barriers of our workplaces doing physical harm, but then also breaking into our data centers and accessing data inappropriately or without authorization, then computer and network security, making sure we're putting things in place so that our computers, our networks are secure, we have policies in place like password complexity issues, two-factor authentication, if possible, different types of encryption, encryption at rest or in transit. And then also network infrastructure security to make sure that our routers, switches, and the perimeter devices that may be accessible from the outside, anything that's public facing or internally facing, assuming someone more to breach our perimeter and get physical access to the building. Is our network infrastructure secure? Do we have such things in place so they can't just plug into a network jack and gain immediate access to our network and then proper training of employees. This is an ongoing thing, it's not a one and done.

We must periodically make sure that our employees are all on the same page, they all understand that security is everyone's job. They also understand what's expected of them, what's an acceptable use, and what's, of course, unacceptable, and then also understand to the extent that they're potentially monitored so that they have a proper expectation, or perhaps depending upon the location, no expectation of privacy. If they're using corporate resources, laptops, phones, well, then they should be properly trained to understand that anything on those devices could potentially be accessed by the company at any time. That lack of expectation of privacy will go a long way to making sure that they're using those corporate resources for corporate purposes.

Potential Damages from Mishandled Data
If we don't have things properly set up and we don't have the systems in place to make sure that we're protecting our data, what can possibly go wrong? We could have loss of intellectual property Proprietary information, data or programs could be stolen, used by competitors, or in one form or fashion, bring damage to the company. Intellectual property as we know can be a key differentiator, it can be a competitive advantage, so if that goes away, if that goes out the door, then that potential competitive advantage may go out the door with it, so it's very important that the company does, in fact, safeguard this data. Next, we can have loss of revenue, financial loss due to disruption of business, loss of, the competitive advantage. These things can happen very, very quickly up until the point where it could force the company out of business, depending upon how great the loss is. Next, we have loss of brand and reputation. That could be loss of consumer confidence, investor confidence, employee trust. It takes a long time to develop trust, to

develop a brand, and develop a company, a persona that people want to do business with and interact with. It takes a long time to build that. It takes a very short amount of time to lose it if things aren't secured properly, if there is a customer breach and sensitive information is leaked out into the public, or proprietary information is gone and competitors can potentially do what you do, maybe even better, so those things have to be secured as much as possible.

Chapter 17 Incident Notification and Escalation

Next is incident notification and escalation. We need to make sure that we quickly assess and triage as appropriate. Triage means we handle the most important things first, just like an ER nurse or an ER doctor would do in the emergency room. You have a bunch of patients coming in; they're going to quickly assess the damage and treat the most critical patients first. We need to do the same thing when we have a breach or an incident in our IT environment. We have to handle the most serious things first. Depending upon the nature of the attack, different groups may need to be notified, and those things will hopefully become apparent as we're doing our quick assessment. We're handling the most critical things first and notifying the appropriate groups. Some of those might be security teams. That might be your own security team, or there may be other teams within the environment, within the company, that should be notified. We could also talk about executive management. Again, depending upon how serious it is, the CEO, CTO, CIO, or the CISO, they all may need to be notified. Also, human resources, public information officers or public affairs, all of these groups may need to be contacted so the damage can be handled as quickly as possible. Also we have a legal team. If it's PII or something that may have customer impact or proprietary or sensitive information, legal teams may need to be notified so they can start working on damage control as quickly as possible as well. Then we also have social media teams. We live in the age of social media. When things happen, almost instantly, it's known around the world, and if it's something bad, we want to make sure we get ahead of that. If you don't have a social media team in place, you may want to consider having one on staff or on retainer full time. First and foremost, when good things happen, let's not focus on the bad things for a minute, but when good things happen, you should be putting that out there on your social media platforms. Every social media outlet available, you should be pushing that information out so that everyone knows about the good work that you do. But by the same token, those teams should be in place and ready to activate when bad things happen. They need to be able to get in front of that so that the company image, reputation, customer satisfaction can be managed and damage control can be done as quickly as possible.

Notifying Outside Agencies

When it comes to notifying outside agencies, we're talking about law enforcement, and that could be local, state, or federal, U.S. government agencies if we're talking about a breach in some type of government agency, they may need to contact US CERT, which is the United States Computer Emergency Readiness Team. If it's a critical infrastructure or a government entity, then more than likely US CERT should be notified. Their website is www.us-cert.gov. You can check them out for more information. Then when it comes to the communication itself, if we rely solely on email as our form of communication, well, what happens if your internal email system is the one that's compromised? You're dead in the water at that point. We need to make sure we establish out-of-band communication methods. We need to understand the location of our war rooms where we can all congregate, have all the different teams that are involved all meet in a central location. If email is our only place or Skype or some type of Webex, or if we all rely on technology, and that main technology is the one that's impacted, then how do we communicate? How do we coordinate our efforts? We need the location of these war rooms we can all meet in person, face to face, everyone working on the issue in real time. Management can get updates very quickly that way. It ensures everyone is on the same page. A centralized location, also for information dissemination. It could be done electronically. It could be done via some network operation center where things are done over a phone line or a landline. There also needs to be a centralized location for information dissemination, both internally and externally, whether that's voicemail, website, social media.

Chapter 18 Data Classification

Next, let's talk about data sensitivity, labeling, and handling, or data classifications. When we classify data, it's important that we do it properly so the data can be secured properly. We make sure only certain people have access to it, and then also it's disposed of properly in the proper fashion as well when it comes time to get rid or purge that data. We have a couple different types or a couple different classifications. Confidential is material that is meant for internal use only, and it could cause damage to the organization if disclosed. This is the stuff that we don't want getting out to the public. Private is compartmental data that must be kept private for various reasons. It could be regulatory compliance. It could be HR data. Its things that should be within specific departments or compartments within an organization. It's not just for anybody within the organization. And then we have public and that's the least sensitive data type, and that can be used for various purposes. Marketing, just general release to the public, website data. Then we have proprietary data, and proprietary is data that should be disclosed on a limited basis, as it contains information that could diminish a company's competitive advantage, technical specs on a specific piece of equipment or infrastructure, some type of patent they're working on or what have you, something that gives that company an edge. That proprietary information, if it were to get out, a competitor got a hold of it, it could diminish that company's advantage. Next, we have such things as PII, or personally identifiable information. PII is any data that could be used to distinguish or trace an individual's identity. And an interesting point to take away is that PII is not a single set of data. Non-PII or non-personally identifiable information could become PII when additional information is combined and used to identify an individual. Things that are not necessarily in and of themselves, PII, but if they're coupled together and we have three or four different pieces, we start to paint a picture. Collectively, once they're all aggregated together, that could, in fact, become PII. It's not just a rigid set of data. It's a fluid line in the sand that you have to keep your eye on if you're managing or dealing with PII in your workplace. Next, we have protected health information, or PHI. PHI is protected health information, and that's defined as part of HIPAA regulations, and it's a subset of health information that could be linked to a specific individual. That includes any information about health status or provision of healthcare or payment for health care, anything that's collected by a covered entity or a business associate of a covered entity and can be linked to a specific individual. You see the recurring theme here, things that can be deanonymized or refer back and traced back to a specific individual. Anything around their health status or care they've been given or payments for health care, any business that collects that type of information or other businesses, third-parties that work with health care providers there in that loop, and they potentially have access to that information, they should be wary of PHI regulations as well.

Chapter 19 Privacy-enhancing Technologies

Let's now talk about some privacy enhancing technologies. One is data minimization. What this boils down to is only keeping what is necessary. When you collect data, anything that's not pertinent to what you need to market or use to identify someone or process an order or any of those things, that data should then be removed, deleted, destroyed. Next is data masking. Data masking we've talked about before, and that's replacing one piece of data with another. Next are tokenization, which we've talked about previously as well, and then anonymization, and then pseudo-anonymization. Let's dig in for just a moment. And data masking where we can mask data by removing or masking things that are used to identify someone. While using data masking techniques, we can replace that with asterisks or some type of wildcard. That way we still retain the essence of the data, but the sensitive information has been removed or masked. That way someone viewing that data does not get access to that critical or that sensitive information. Next is tokenization. But tokenization is replacing sensitive data with a non-sensitive equivalent. The token can be a single use, a multiple use, it could be cryptographic or non-cryptographic, and it also could be reversible or irreversible. It just depends upon the use case and the technology being implemented. High-value tokens, or HVTs, can be used to replace things like primary account numbers on credit card transactions, they can be bound to specific devices. Then we have low-value tokens. They can serve similar functions, but need the underlying tokenization system to match it back to the actual primary account number. Two systems that do the same type of thing.

Anonymization and Pseudo-anonymization

These entire things boil down to anonymizing data, Protecting private or sensitive information by erasing or encrypting identifiers that can connect an individual to stored data. We have anonymization and then also pseudo-anonymization. Anonymization we've talked about, data masking, it could be tokenization, all of those things are ways to anonymize data. And then pseudo-anonymization, that's a data management technique where it will deidentify data. We're taking off identifiers and replacing them with fake identifiers or pseudonyms. So, we could take a person's name and replace it with something else or any other identifier for that matter. We could replace it with something else. What it does is it preserves the statistical accuracy and the data integrity. It allows that data to be used for training, for development, for testing, for analytics, while still protecting data privacy.

Chapter 20 Data Owners & Responsibilities

Data is not typically owned by individuals. We want to give ownership to the enterprise itself. Data is owned by the company or by the enterprise or the organization. Owners are assigned for management, compliance, and accountability. Within your organization, you'll typically have a data owner, a data steward. But it's done for accountability and also for management. When it comes time for compliance, we need to know who owns that data, who's responsible for maintaining it.

Data Controller and Processor
Processing is any operation, whether automated or a manual process, that is performed on personal data. A data processor is responsible for the processing of personal data on behalf of what's known as a data controller. The data controller is the person or the thing that determines the purpose and the means by which personal data is processed.

Data Steward / Custodian
A data steward and a custodian, sometimes those terms are used interchangeably, although they do have some distinctions depending upon the role or the size of the organization, but a data steward or custodian is responsible for maintaining data quality. They incorporate processes, policies, guidelines. They're going to define the terms and the metadata that they will steward. We're talking about databases; we're talking about business analytics. There's going to be terminology. There are going to be classifications within the data. We have tons of data coming into an organizational, a lot of unstructured data, a lot of database type data. Well, the fields themselves and the types of data

and the metadata need to be defined ahead of time. They need to be a strict set of guidelines as to what type of data can be used, where it can be brought in, how it's classified. That way, that data can be managed. It can be mined and analytics run against it. That ensures that the data is relevant and also fit for use. That means it's data that can become actionable. It doesn't do us much good to take in tons and tons of data, terabytes or petabytes of data, if we can't do anything with it. It just becomes a waste of space at that point. By proper data management by a steward or a custodian, it ensures that the data coming in can then be analyzed properly, can be mined, can be categorized so that it's actionable and of value to the business.

Privacy Officer

Next, we have a privacy officer, and a privacy officer oversees all the ongoing activities related to the development, the implementation, and the maintenance of an organization's privacy policies. Everything you can think about regarding PII and PHI and sensitive data and the different types of data classifications, all of those things fall under the auspices of a privacy officer or a chief privacy officer. Depending on the size of the company, it may be a single person, or it may be an entire team. They also may wear multiple roles working with legal, compliance.

Chapter 21 Information Lifecycle

Next, let's talk about the information lifecycle. So, what we're talking about here is how we collect and what we do with the data once we have it. The lifecycle itself, depending upon where you read you may see some additional steps, there may be some other ones thrown in there, but generally speaking we have the steps that I have outlined here. We have collection, and then we have access, usage, storage, the transfer, and then deletion or destruction. Going through that we're going to collect data some way, somehow, whether it be a form, whether we collect data behind the scenes when someone visits a website, take some action. Somehow or other we're getting data. And then we should define how we access that data and then how we use the data. All of these things should have a defined process and rules around them. And that's part of our transparency policy, our privacy policy. Our terms of agreement we'll talk about in just a moment as well. That way we're making sure that it's kept secure. Confidential information remains confidential. Do we interact with third parties or share that information with other folks? And then once it's no longer needed, how do we get rid of it? The deletion or destruction. All of those things should be spelled out and then the process adhered to. And then on top of all of that, we need to have data protection in place to make sure that that data is safeguarded from prying eyes, from data breaches. What that does is maintain compliance with various regulations, as an example GDPR. It also ensures that data is collected properly, used, and stored in accordance to policy, our defined policies, and destroyed once no longer needed. It also helps us build consumer trust, the overall brand and reputation. So by letting users know what we're doing, how we're doing it, and what goes on behind the scenes, what we're doing with that data, it just increases the level of trust, and it ensures that they understand that the data is being protected, or we're doing everything we can to protect that data. And lastly, the point of all that is to help guard against breaches, unauthorized access. As a security professional, one of our tenants is CIA, the confidentiality, integrity, and availability of data. All of these things go a long way to making sure that that stays intact.

Privacy Impact Assessment
This is used to identify and manage privacy risks arising from new projects, new systems, processes, or even business relationships. When these things spin up, we're starting something new, whether it is internal, whether it is technology based or process based, maybe starting to partner with another company or another vendor, all of those things should require that we do a privacy impact assessment. It's a self-directed assessment to make sure things are secured properly and that we're baking that privacy into the process, or it's not a bolt-on after the fact. The privacy impact assessment achieves three main goals. It's going to ensure compliance with applicable legal and regulatory laws. It also identifies and evaluates risks of privacy breaches or other incidents. We'll go through our various systems, our relationships, technologies, applications and identify what risks exist. And then we'll stack rank them to make sure that we understand what are the ramifications if one of those breaches were to be, in fact, successfully executed so that we can then plan and direct resources appropriately. And then, identify appropriate privacy controls to mitigate those unacceptable risks. We talked about risk before, so there are some things that you probably would be willing to accept, and it is what it is.

486

We're not going to spend the money to necessarily mitigate those things, but there are certain risks that are unacceptable. We then need to identify, how are we going to de-risk that environment? How are we going to take those risks out of the equation? And that boils down to time, money, resources, people, process, and technology. We need to direct resources in some fashion or maybe all three of those things to implement a control or a piece of technology or software to mitigate that risk. We need to stack rank in order of importance so that we would focus our resources on the most important things first and then work our way down from there.

Terms of Agreement and Privacy Notice
Two additional terms that I want to make sure you're familiar with. First one is terms of agreement. This ensures that the specific terms of a relationship are spelled out, discussed, and agreed upon prior to beginning that relationship. A lot of times it's one of those things where you go to a website and it'll flash up a little end user license agreement or terms of agreement, the things that no one ever reads. Well, in there typically will be what type of data is collected, how it's used. All of those things are there to protect both the company and also to inform the user. And then next is a privacy notice. That's one of those things you may have gotten in the mail before, email, saying, hey, we've just changed our terms, here's a link to our new privacy policy. And it's one of those things where you probably don't read, most people don't, but I would encourage you to go through it and look at that next time you see one, because it's there for a reason, and it provides easy access to information for users, customers on how data is collected, what it's used for, how it's stored, and if it will be shared with other folks, third parties. The privacy notice is

important, and it should be accessible from websites, from places that you visit and places you do business with, so that you understand how your data is being collected and being used. In this chapter, we talked about organizational consequences of privacy breaches; we talked about notifications of breaches; along with various data types; also privacy enhancing technologies, various roles and responsibilities around data privacy; along with the information lifecycle; an impact assessment; terms of agreement; and then lastly, a privacy notice. That wraps up this book. We made it to the end. I'm so happy that you took this journey with me. Best of luck with your training and certification endeavours, and thank you very much for completing this book.

Conclusion

Congratulations on completing this book! I am sure you have plenty on your belt, but please don't forget to leave an honest review. Furthermore, if you think this information was helpful to you, please share anyone who you think would be interested of IT as well.

About Richie Miller

Richie Miller has always loved teaching people Technology. He graduated with a degree in radio production with a minor in theatre in order to be a better communicator. While teaching at the Miami Radio and Television Broadcasting Academy, Richie was able to do voiceover work at a technical training company specializing in live online classes in Microsoft, Cisco, and CompTia technologies. Over the years, he became one of the top virtual instructors at several training companies, while also speaking at many tech and training conferences. Richie specializes in Project Management and ITIL these days, while also doing his best to be a good husband and father.

www.ingramcontent.com/pod-product-compliance
Lightning Source LLC
Chambersburg PA
CBHW071231050326
40690CB00011B/2063